**Mario Eras**mo is Pr~~ofessor~~ Univer~~sity~~ of Georgia.
He is the au~~thor of several books on the cultural history of Ita~~ly and
the legacy of Classical Antiquity including *Reading Death in Ancient
Rome* (2008) and *Death: Antiquity and Its Legacy* (I.B.Tauris, 2012),
with extensive experience teaching and leading tours throughout
Italy, France and the UK.

# STROLLING THROUGH ROME

## THE DEFINITIVE WALKING GUIDE TO THE ETERNAL CITY

MARIO ERASMO

I.B. TAURIS

LONDON · NEW YORK

MIX
Paper from
responsible sources
FSC® C007584

First published in 2015 by
I.B.Tauris & Co. Ltd
London • New York
www.ibtauris.com

ISBN:   978 1 78076 351 4
eISBN:  978 0 85773 889 9

A full CIP record for this book is available from the British Library
A full CIP record is available from the Library of Congress

Library of Congress Catalog Card Number: available

Printed and bound in Sweden by ScandBook AB

# CONTENTS

# LIST OF ILLUSTRATIONS

Images are photographed and supplied by the author with the exception of the *Aurora* by Guercino, which is supplied and reproduced by the kind permission of HSH Prince Nicolò Boncompagni Ludovisi and HSH Princess Rita Boncompagni Ludovisi.

All maps © OpenStreetMap Contributors. Data is available under the Open Database Licence.

# Acknowledgements

I am honoured by the kind and generous assistance of HSH Prince Nicolò Boncompagni Ludovisi and HSH Princess Rita Boncompagni Ludovisi. I am also grateful to Filippo Amisano, T. Corey Brennan, Danielle Carrabino, Penelope Davies, Dora Erasmo, Josh Koons, Christopher P. Robinson and Tim Smalley for research assistance and support. I owe special thanks to Tatiana Wilde and the editorial staff at I.B. Tauris.

# ACKNOWLEDGEMENTS

# PREFACE

Unlock the secrets of the Eternal City through step-by-step walking tours of the historic areas of this beguiling city, from evocative ancient ruins, solemn early Christian and Jewish sites, winding medieval streets, Renaissance palaces and theatrical Baroque architecture in the heart of the vibrant modern city. Itineraries include parks with sweeping vistas and quiet places to enjoy a romantic stroll or *al fresco* lunch. Go under the city to explore earlier layers: the sources for Rome's perennial rebirth.

Rome's most recent Imperial past under Fascism restored the antiquities of the city for ideological purposes. That Rome, modern yet rooted in its ancient past, is what still greets visitors today. Ironically, what survives from antiquity survives despite its connection to Imperial Rome as Christian Rome erased its pagan precursor and reused its materials for the construction of its own identity. Monuments once destroyed for building materials are now valued as memorials of Rome's glorious past. *Roma sparita* ('Rome disappeared') is gone but it asserts its presence in the urban fabric of the city and in the popular imagination. There is no place like Rome.

Tours are sequential but they may also be taken in any order. The walking distance of tours and times will vary depending on the number of sites visited. Many itineraries include options to visit additional sites requiring a longer stroll or transportation by ATAC, Rome's integrated public transportation system (bus, metro and regional train). Just when you feel you have seen too many chapels or paintings, think of them as ancient Roman tombs whose inscriptions call out to passers-by to take note of the deceased's identity: 'Yes, you have seen this theme before, but have you seen my version?'

Stroll on …

# INTRODUCTION

## The Eternal City

The Eternal City, enticing yet aloof, has staged more events from the annals of history than any other city. The idiom 'When in Rome do as the Romans do' speaks to the historical power of its sense of self enforced by the censorial brows of the *conoscenti*. Rome loves a winner and since antiquity the streets have witnessed their triumphs and the humiliation of history's losers. Strolling the streets of Rome is to participate in the theatre of history as spectator and actor.

Ancient Romans traced their ancestry back to the mythological **Aeneas**, the son of the goddess Venus and the Trojan Anchises. After the Fall of Troy he settles in Italy and establishes the royal line through his son Ascanius (also called Iulus from whom the family of Julius Caesar claimed descent) that leads to **Romulus** and **Remus**, the children of the god Mars and Vestal Virgin Rhea Silvia (or Ilia). After vying with his brother, Romulus founds Rome on 21 April 753 BCE. He is deified as the god Quirinus and not until Julius Caesar would another historic figure be deified. The **Archaic** period of the **Kings** under whom the village of the **Seven Hills** is transformed into a city ends with their expulsion and the founding of the **Roman Republic** in 509 BCE. Against the backdrop of Periclean Athens in mid-5th century BCE, Rome continues to grow and the next century witnessed the highs of defeating their **Etruscan** rivals to the north in 396 BCE and the lows of being captured by the **Celts** in 391 BCE. After Philip of Macedon and Alexander the Great took control of the eastern Mediterranean, Rome fought a series of wars in central Italy and against the **Carthaginians** in North Africa that culminated in the defeat of **Hannibal** (202 BCE). Rome controlled the Mediterranean from Spain to North Africa and finally Greece in 146 BCE but it was still governed by the Republican political offices of consuls and tribunes whose powers were checked by censors and aristocratic factions in the Senate.

In the 1st century BCE, the generals **Sulla**, **Marius** and **Pompey the Great** exploited Rome's weaknesses in a series of **Civil Wars** causing the breakdown of the Republic bemoaned by the orator **Cicero** that culminates with the dictatorship of **Julius Caesar**. After Caesar's assassination on the Ides of March in 44 BCE, his great nephew and adopted heir Octavian, the future emperor **Augustus**, vies with **Mark Antony** for sole political control. Following his victory over Antony and **Cleopatra** at the **Battle of Actium** in 31 BCE, Augustus establishes a principate that is a veneer for monarchy. Rome's first emperor, as the son of the deified Julius Caesar, emulates his mythological ancestor Aeneas in refounding the legendary Golden Age based on peace, the **Pax Romana**. Augustus founds the first dynasty of **Imperial Rome**, the **Julio-Claudian** (Augustus, Tiberius, Gaius Caligula, Claudius and Nero). As **Christians** form their first communities in Rome in areas of older **Jewish** communities visited by **St Peter** and **St Paul**, pagan worship continues and eastern cults such as the **Cult of Mithras** are popular empire-wide including the city of Rome.

After a succession of emperors in 69 CE, **Vespasian** founds the **Flavian** dynasty, through his sons **Titus** and **Domitian**, that monumentalised the city with the **Colosseum** and Imperial palace on the Palatine Hill, the site of **St Sebastian**'s martyrdom. In the 2nd century CE, Nerva and the **Antonines** ushered in the era of the **Five Good Emperors** who adopted their successors (Nerva, Trajan, Hadrian, Antoninus Pius and Marcus Aurelius) that ended with the accession of Marcus Aurelius' son Commodus. The instability of the **Severan** dynasty (Septimius Severus, Caracalla, Geta, Macrinus, Elagabulus, Alexander Severus) in the 3rd century causes anxiety witnessed by the Emperor Aurelian's construction of the **Aurelianic Walls** that expanded the boundaries of the **Republican Walls** from the 6th to 4th century BCE (also known as the Servian Walls) to withstand Barbarian incursions. After **Constantine**'s victory over his co-ruler **Maxentius** at the **Battle of the Milvian Bridge** in 312 CE, the **Edict of Milan** (313 CE) gave legal protections to Christians and he founds Christian basilicas on Imperial property at the edges of the city. He called the **Council of Nicaea** in 325 from which came the Nicene Creed. Constantine moved the capital to **Constantinople** (Byzantium) and the Empire was ruled by **Byzantine** emperors in the east. Figurehead emperors control Rome following the Sack of the **Visigoths** (410) and **Vandals** (455) and the power of the popes grows under **Pope Leo the Great** (440–461) and **Pope Gregory the Great** (590–604).

The population of Rome in the **Middle Ages**, greatly reduced since antiquity, was centred in the **Borgo** and the bend of the **Tiber** when water supplied by aqueducts was cut by **Ostrogoths** in the 6th century. The transformation of the city into the Christian *caput mundi* included the Pantheon as S. Maria ad Martyres, the first temple consecrated as a church in Rome (609 CE). The **Norman** invasion of Rome under **Robert Guiscard** (1084) devastated the city that was rebuilt with newly decorated churches in the 12th century continuing into the 13th century with **Pietro Cavallini**'s realism replacing Byzantine aesthetics. The First **Jubilee** in 1300 attracted the Florentines **Dante** and **Giotto** to Rome. Power over civic control of the city by the popes was briefly won by **Cola di Rienzo** and expressed through the revival of the ancient SPQR (*Senatus Populusque Romanus*) by the city's Senate. The *rioni*, or regions, were controlled by powerful families often living in ancient ruins converted into fortresses. The end to the **Great Schism** brought the return of the popes from Avignon, through the efforts of **St Catherine of Siena,** who took up residence in the Vatican. The visits of **Brunelleschi** and **Donatello** (1402–1404) rekindled interest in antiquity and inspired the birth of the Renaissance in Florence.

**Renaissance** Rome began under Pope Martin V Colonna (1417–1431) but flowered under **Pope Sixtus IV della Rovere**, who founded the nucleus of the **Capitoline Museums** (1471), and his nephew **Pope Julius II della Rovere**, whose rebuilding of St Peter's Basilica included architects **Bramante**, **Michelangelo**, **Raphael** and **Baldassarre Peruzzi**, who reframed the aesthetics of the Classical past. **Martin Luther** witnessed the transformation of the medieval St Peter's and the vast expenditures of the popes met through the selling of indulgences that fuelled his dissatisfaction with the Church. The flowering of the Renaissance and **Humanism** under **Pope Leo X de' Medici** ended with the reigns of his successors Pope Hadrian VI and his cousin **Pope Clement VII de' Medici** under whom occurred the pivotal events of the **Sack of Rome in 1527** by **Charles V, the Holy Roman Emperor** (Charles I of Spain), and his refusal to annul **King Henry VIII**'s marriage to **Catherine of Aragon**, the aunt of Charles V. **Pope Paul III Farnese**'s revival of Renaissance Rome relied on Michelangelo.

Following the **Council of Trent** (1545–1563), the **Counter-Reformation** fuelled the exuberance of the **Baroque** transformation of the city that challenged the restraint of Renaissance classicism in art and architecture. Popes and religious orders such as the **Jesuits** promoted the construction of lavish churches to advertise the Church's vigour. Urban renewal continued under **Pope Sixtus V**, who erected **obelisks** as pilgrim guides and urban ornament, and under **Pope Paul V Borghese**, who commissioned **Carlo Maderno** to complete St Peter's Basilica. Important church and private commissions went to the leading painters including **Guercino**, **Guido Reni**, **Caravaggio**, **Annibale Carracci**, **Domenichino** and **Pietro da Cortona**. The so-called Baroque Popes **Urban VIII Barberini**, **Innocent X Pamphilj** and **Alexander VII Chigi** commissioned **Gian Lorenzo Bernini** and **Francesco Borromini** and others to transform the city into a spectacular showpiece. The taste for Flemish and French landscapes often with Classical references reflects the influence of **Claude Lorrain** and other foreign artists residing in Rome at this time.

**Giuseppe Valadier**'s **Neoclassical** designs for Piazza del Popolo set the stage for visitors on the **Grand Tour** drawn to the monuments of ancient Rome and the splendours of the Baroque city. Neoclassicism inspired sculptor **Antonio Canova** and fuelled the collection of antiquities and the growth of archaeology and art history. Famous visitors included **Johann Wolfgang von Goethe** and the Romantic poets **Percy Bysshe Shelley** and **John Keats** who are buried in the **Protestant Cemetery**. The portrait painters **Pompeo Batoni** and **Angelica Kauffmann** immortalised visitors amidst Romanticised antiquities.

**Giuseppe Garibaldi** was a pivotal figure in the **Risorgimento** battles fought in Rome and Italy that led to **Italian Unification**. When papal forces were defeated at the Porta Pia on **20 September 1870**, Rome became the capital city of a unified Italy for the first time since antiquity under the monarchy of **Vittorio Emanuele II.** The 'Roman Question' of the number and extent of papal territories in Rome was not settled until 1929 with the pacts of the **Lateran Treaty**. The rapid growth of **Modern** Rome destroyed medieval areas and the surrounding countryside but construction turned the city into an archaeological site that uncovered ancient art and monuments. The **Stazione Termini** became the new gateway to Rome, with **Piazza della Repubblica** commemorating Italian Unification and the founding of the Italian Republic. **Fascism** under **Benito Mussolini** evoked Rome's Imperial past through the restoration of ancient monuments and construction of **EUR (Esposizione Universale di Roma)** for the cancelled **1942 World's Fair**. The **Liberation of Rome** in World War II ended the Nazi occupation of the city and the persecution of Jews in the **Ghetto**. Post-World War II Rome became synonymous with **Federico Fellini**'s *La Dolce Vita* and the **1960 Olympic Games** held in the **Foro Italico** formerly dedicated to Mussolini. The **Ara Pacis Museum** (2006) recontextualises ancient Rome for the new millennium but as Rome's history bears witness, its modernity is tied to its recent and ancient past.

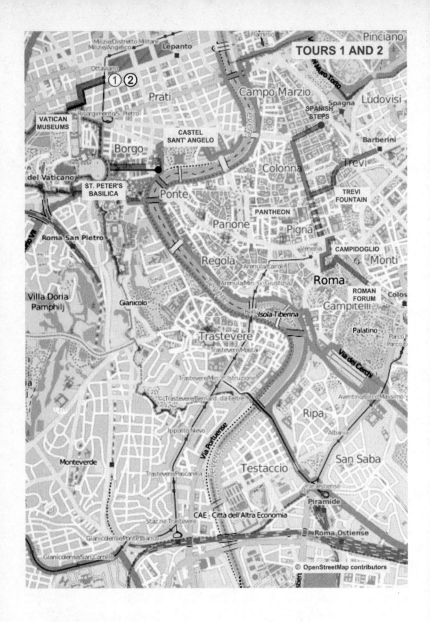

Sites: Stazione Termini; Vatican Museums; St Peter's Basilica; Piazza Venezia; Piazza del Campidoglio; Capitoline Museums; Roman Forum to the Colosseum; Trevi Fountain; Spanish Steps.
Distance: 4.75km.

Tour 1

# ROME IN A DAY

This fast-paced itinerary takes you to the Vatican Museums and St Peter's Basilica, Piazza del Campidoglio and Capitoline Museums, the Roman Forum and Colosseum, the Trevi Fountain and the Spanish Steps and passes several prominent landmarks along the way. The tour begins at Stazione Termini for transportation to the Vatican but you may begin the tour at any of the locations. An ATAC day pass is essential to get around the city by bus and metro. There are several options throughout the tour to personalise the itinerary.

## *Vatican Museums*

From Stazione Termini, take Metro line A in the direction of Battistini to the Ottaviano/S. Pietro stop. Exit the station by Viale Giulio Cesare and walk straight ahead on Viale Giulio Cesare for two blocks to Via Leone IV. Turn left for the queue to the Vatican Museum entrance along the Leonine Walls that begins on Viale Vaticano to your right (.45km). See Tour 2 for a full description of the Vatican Museums. Designated routes take you through the various collections including the **Sistine Chapel**. The Sistine Chapel has two exits. The right-side exit is for groups (except on Wednesdays) and leads directly to St Peter's Basilica, by-passing the security check-point in St Peter's Square. The left-side exit is for non-group visitors and continues through the various museums to the main exit on Viale Vaticano. Turn right upon exiting to walk along the wall on Via di Porta Angelica until you reach the Colonnade and the security check-point to St Peter's Basilica.

## St Peter's Basilica

See Tour 2 for a full description of St Peter's Square and Basilica with Michelangelo's *Pietà*, Gian Lorenzo Bernini's baldacchino under Michelangelo's dome, the Vatican Grottoes, and papal tombs by Bernini and Antonio Canova. From the basilica, walk to the obelisk in the centre of the square. Walk out of the square onto Via della Conciliazione straight ahead and follow to the intersection at the end of the street (looking left when crossing the side streets for views of the **Vatican Corridor**). Piazza Pia is located beside **Castel Sant'Angelo** (Tour 3). The stop for the No. 40 bus is to your left.

Take the bus to the Piazza Venezia stop on Via Cesare Battisti alongside Palazzo delle Assicurazione Generali di Venezia. Walk to the front of the palazzo facing **Piazza Venezia** (Tour 7) and continue across the front to reach the **National Monument to Vittorio Emanuele II**. The Campidoglio is to the right of the Monument but it is not yet in view. Walk along the front of the Monument and follow the sidewalk to Piazza del Campidoglio beyond the steep staircase leading up to S. Maria in Aracoeli. Walk up the stepped terraces of the **Cordonata** designed by Michelangelo to climb the Capitoline Hill to Piazza del Campidoglio.

## Piazza del Campidoglio

Piazza del Campidoglio (Tour 5) was designed by Michelangelo who also redesigned the medieval facades of Palazzo Senatorio (centre) and Palazzo dei Conservatori (to your right) and added Palazzo Nuovo (to your left) that now house the collections of the **Capitoline Museums** including the *Capitoline She-Wolf*, colossal portraits of Constantine the Great, the *Capitoline Venus* and the *Dying Gaul*. The **Equestrian statue of Marcus Aurelius** is a copy of the original now in the Capitoline Museums. For a sweeping view of the Roman Forum, facing Palazzo Senatorio, walk around the right-hand side to the **Roman Forum Overlook**. From here, there is a good view of the Arch of Septimius Severus (to your left), the Arch of Titus and the Colosseum in the distance beyond. To your right is the Palatine Hill.

From here, continue to the Roman Forum and Colosseum, or if the view from the overlook is sufficient, proceed from here to the

Trevi Fountain and the Spanish Steps by returning to Piazza Venezia and walking up the Via del Corso (with a view of Piazza del Popolo at the end). Follow signs to the **Pantheon** and **Piazza Navona** (on the left side) or to the **Trevi** Fountain (on the right side) and the **Spanish Steps**.

## Roman Forum

To continue to the Roman Forum and to the Colosseum from Piazza del Campidoglio, take Via di S. Pietro in Carcere to the left of Palazzo Senatorio to the staircase next to the overlook of the Roman Forum that descends along the church of S. Giuseppe dei Falegnami (the ancient **Mamertine Prison**). At the bottom of the stairs, walk across the front of the church and follow the ancient Clivus Argentarius up and around the Forum of Julius Caesar. Turn right on Via dei Fori Imperiali and continue to the Ticket Office entrance to your right next to the church of S. Lorenzo in Miranda. On the other side of the street to your left as you walk to the entrance are the Imperial Fora (Tour 6). Currently, the admission ticket covers entrance into the Forum, the Palatine Hill and the Colosseum. Purchasing an individual entrance ticket at the entrance to the Forum means avoiding the long lines at the entrance to the Colosseum. See Tour 6 for a detailed tour of the Roman Forum (1.5km) and exit options to the Colosseum (.41km). If you would like to stroll amidst the ruins of Domitian's palace on the Palatine Hill then add 1.75km to your stroll.

## Colosseum

If you purchased a ticket at the entrance to the Forum, bypass the lines and go directly to the entrance turnstiles inside the Colosseum. Walk up a level for the exhibition area and for a view of the interior. See Tour 6 for details on the Colosseum's history and architecture.

To proceed to the Trevi Fountain, exit the Colosseum and walk around to the entrance on Via dei Fori Imperiali. Cross the street to enter the Colosseo Metro station. Take Metro line B to Termini train station and transfer onto Metro line A to Piazza Barberini. Exit into Piazza Barberini with **Bernini's Triton Fountain** in the centre. With the fountain behind you, walk west a few blocks downhill on Via del Tritone to the curving Via della Stamperia in Largo del Tritone on the left side of the street and follow to the Fountain (.50km).

## Trevi Fountain

The famous Trevi Fountain begun in 1732 by Nicola Salvi attracts crowds day and night for an opportunity to throw a coin into the fountain to ensure a return trip to Rome. The central figure of Oceanus who presides over the hippocamps is by Pietro Bracci (1759–1762). See Tour 8 for more detailed information and for other sites in the area. To continue to the Spanish Steps, when facing the Fountain, Via del Corso is on your left so take either Via delle Muratte or Via dei Crociferi that turns into Via dei Sabini. Turn right on Via del Corso and walk past the **Column of Marcus Aurelius** to your left with **Piazza del Popolo** ahead at the end of Via del Corso to the fashionable **Via Condotti** (officially called Via dei Condotti) and turn right to reach the Spanish Steps (.94km).

## Spanish Steps

The monumental staircase (1723–1726) by Francesco de Sanctis that connects Piazza di Spagna with Piazza della Trinità di Monti is a popular destination to sit and view the crowds around the **Fontana della Barcaccia** (1627–1629). See Tour 10 for more detailed information and for other sites in the area including the Keats-Shelly Memorial House, the church of Sant'Andrea delle Fratte, the Parco del Pincio and Villa Borghese. The Piazza di Spagna Metro line A station is only steps away.

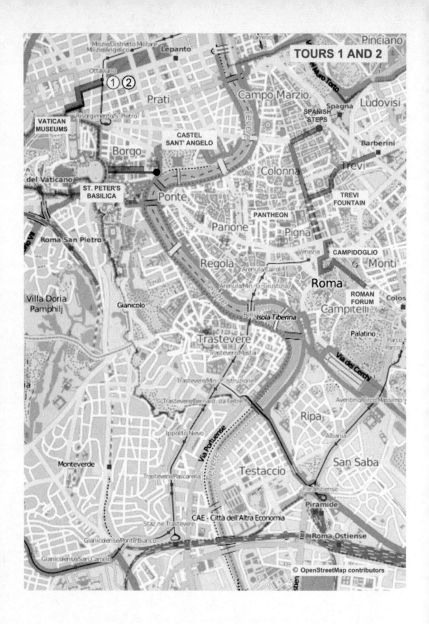

Sites: Vatican Museums; the Borgo; the Vatican Corridor; St Peter's Square; St Peter's Basilica; Via della Conciliazione; Palazzo dei Penitenzieri; Palazzo Giraud-Torlonia; S. Maria in Traspontina, Vatican Corridor.
Distance: 3.75km (Vatican Museums/St Peter's Basilica 3.0km + St Peter's Square to Castel Sant'Angelo .75km).

# THE VATICAN

The Vatican is a city within a city and a state within a state. It is the spiritual and artistic destination of pilgrims and tourists drawn by the relics and history of popes and palace intrigue that played out against the artistic backdrop created by towering figures in the history of art including Bramante, Michelangelo, Raphael and Bernini. The Renaissance and Baroque architecture of St Peter's Basilica lend a timeless and majestic air to the sacred space that attracts millions of visitors each year. The Vatican Museums include artistic masterpieces of ancient sculpture and the frescoes of Michelangelo in the Sistine Chapel and Raphael's frescoes in the Raphael Rooms. A stroll around the Borgo to Castel Sant'Angelo highlights sites associated with the Renaissance and the Sack of Rome in 1527. Almost 400 years later, the 20th-century demolition and reconstruction of the area once again altered its medieval appearance for the construction of Via della Conciliazione, named for the Lateran Treaty (1929) that settled the 'Roman Question'.

## Vatican Museums

The entrance to the museums is located on Viale Vaticano (Tour 1). From the **Atrium of the Four Gates** (Atrio dei Quattro Cancelli), the Vatican marks route options throughout the collections. Off the atrium, the terrace (Cortile della Pinacoteca) overlooking the Vatican Gardens contains the base of the **Column of Antoninus Pius** found near Piazza di Montecitorio in 1703. The various museum collections span centuries and are spread out in numerous buildings. The nucleus is the collection of antiquities displayed by Pope Julius II della Rovere (1505–

1513) that was later expanded under Pope Clement XIV (1769–1774) and Pope Pius VI (1775–1779) to form the Museo Pio-Clementino, and Pope Pius VII (1800–1823) who founded the Museo Chiaramonti. Pope Gregory XVI (1831–1846) founded the Museo Gregoriano Etrusco (1837) and the Museo Gregoriano Egiziano (1839), with other popes expanding the collections of the museums to recent times. Papal apartments such as the Borgia and Raphael Rooms and the Sistine Chapel form important parts of the Vatican Museums.

The **Egyptian Museum** (Museo Gregoriano Egiziano) features Egyptian sculpture from Egypt and sculpture imitating Egyptian sculpture (Egyptianising) from the Roman Empire, including the Serapeum at Hadrian's Villa at Tivoli and the Iseum (Temple of Isis) in the Campus Martius of Rome, but also pieces from ancient Mesopotamia and Syria.

The **Courtyard of the Pine cone** (Cortile della Pigna) refers to the ancient bronze pine cone that was originally part of a fountain found near the Pantheon that gives the district Pigna its name. Canon Benedict, in his 12th-century guidebook *Mirabilia Urbis Romae* (*The Marvels of the City of Rome*), claimed (erroneously) that it once topped the oculus of the Pantheon. The peacocks are copies of originals from the Mausoleum of Hadrian (Tour 3) that are now displayed in the Braccio Nuovo (below). The peacocks were part of the *Fountain of Paradise* commissioned by Pope Symmachus (498–514) for the atrium of the Old St Peter's.

The **Belvedere Courtyard** (Cortile del Belvedere) was built by Donato **Bramante** (1444–1514) in 1506 to connect Palazzo del Belvedere to the Vatican Palace. The long sides (now broken up in the centre with the Braccio Nuovo) ended with an exedra to disguise the difference in height between the Vatican Palace and the Palazzetto Belvedere. The Cortile design was immensely influential in the development of courtyard designs in the Renaissance. Pope Leo X de' Medici (1513–1521) displayed here his elephant 'Hanno', a coronation gift from King Manuel I of Portugal. The epitaph written by the pope for Hanno's burial in the Cortile (1516) was satirised by Pietro Aretino in a pamphlet, 'Hanno's Last Will and Testament'. The niche of the upper terrace was completed by Pirro Ligorio (1562–1565) for Pope Pius IV de' Medici (1559–1565), a distant relative of the Medici. Ligorio, best known for designing the water fountain garden at the Villa d'Este in Tivoli, added the third storey and the half-dome to Bramante's exedra design. This is the first half-dome since antiquity. In the centre is a sculpture of two spheres by Arnaldo Pomodoro added in 1990.

The interior of the **Chiaramonti Museum** (Museo Chiaramonti) was designed by Bramante, but the collection of about 1,000 ancient sculptures was arranged by Antonio Canova in 59 sections for Pope Pius VII Chiaramonti. Among the Republican and Imperial era portraits, funerary altars, sarcophagi and dedicatory sculpture line the corridor. At the end of the corridor is the **Galleria Lapidaria** (by appointment only) that was founded by Pope Clement XIV and includes over 5,000 funerary inscriptions, pagan and Christian, that were discovered at necropolis and catacomb sites in Rome.

The **New Wing** (Braccio Nuovo) was designed in the Neoclassical style by Raffaele Stern (1817–1822) for Pope Pius VII to house more Roman antiquities especially Roman copies of Greek originals, such as the *Giustiniani Athena* discovered in Rome in the 17th century. The *Augustus of Prima Porta* is named for the villa north of Rome that belonged to his wife Livia where it was discovered in 1863. The portrait was modelled after the famous Greek statue *Doryphorus* by Polyclitus (Polykleitos) in 440 BCE, copies of which are in this collection. The idealised features that suggest immortality became the standard portrait type of Rome's first emperor following his victory over Antony and Cleopatra at the Battle of Actium in 31 BCE. The cupid figure formed part of his political propaganda and alludes to his descent from the Goddess Venus after his adoption by his great uncle Julius Caesar. Opposite, the statue of the Emperor *Domitian* from the successor Flavian dynasty shares stylistic elements but presents the emperor in a more authoritative manner in keeping with his adopted titles of *Dominus et Deus* ('Lord and God'). The *Nile* sculpture of the reclining river god is a Roman copy of a 1st-century BCE Hellenistic statue that was found in the Iseum (Temple of Isis) in the Campus Martius (Tour 8). Opposite are Imperial-era stone funerary markers found near the Mausoleum of Augustus (Tour 9) and the original bronze peacocks from the Mausoleum of Hadrian.

The **Pio-Clementino Museum** (Museo Pio-Clementino) that begins above the short flight of steps from the Chiaramonti Museum consists of the older collection of ancient Greek and Roman sculpture in Palazzo del Belvedere. The *Sarcophagus of Lucius Cornelius Scipio Barbatus* (consul in 298 BCE) bears the earliest surviving Latin inscription found in the Tomb of the Scipios on the Via Appia Antica. The **Cabinet of**

**the Apoxyomenos** is named for a Roman copy of Lysippus' statue of an athlete that was found in Trastevere in 1844 (Tour 4). The **Bramante Staircase** designed by Bramante with varied architectural orders as it ascends to the floor above is accessible from a glass door.

Pope Julius II della Rovere commissioned Bramante to design the **Octagonal Courtyard of the Belvedere** (Cortile Ottagonale del Belvedere), connected to Palazzo del Belvedere, to house the collection of ancient sculpture that would become the nucleus of the collection. It was known simply as the Cortile delle Statue del Belvedere. The architect Michelangelo Simonetti gave the courtyard its present octagonal shape for Pope Pius VI in 1775. The courtyard, filled with famous sculptures in each *gabinetto* (corner niche), funerary altars, sarcophagi, friezes and cinerary urns, was an essential stop on the Grand Tour.

*Laocoön* in Classical mythology was a Trojan priest who warned the Trojans not to accept the Trojan Horse as a gift from the Greeks. The sculpture group was found during the excavations of the Golden House of Nero (Domus Aurea) in 1506 and was added to the Vatican collection by Pope Julius II with restorations by Michelangelo. The statue was taken to Paris by Napoleon and displayed in the Louvre but it was repatriated here after Napoleon's fall. Other discoveries at the excavation of the house gave rise to the term *grottesche*, 'grotesques' from 'grotto', to describe the cave-like excavated rooms with fantastic mythological figures, masks and landscape frescoes that decorated Nero's Golden House and became immensely popular in the Renaissance.

The *Apollo Belvedere* is a 2nd-century CE Roman copy (dating to the reign of Hadrian) of a Greek bronze original of the 4th century BCE perhaps by the sculptor Leochares. Apollo stands holding his bow (now missing) in an elegant chiastic or contrapposto pose. Julius II owned the statue before becoming pope and moved it here in 1511. At the same time he brought the so-called *Venus Felix* in the niche between the *Hermes* and *Perseus* that is a Roman copy of Praxiteles' *Cnidian Aphrodite*. The Apollo was celebrated as one of the finest ancient sculptures by the art historian and archaeologist Johann Joachim Winckelmann, but was later criticised by John Ruskin. It was also taken to Paris by Napoleon. Across the courtyard, the *Perseus* sculpted by Antonio Canova (1801) is modelled after the *Apollo Belvedere*. Canova also sculpted the boxers *Creugas* and *Damoxenes*. The *Hermes* is a Roman copy of Praxiteles'

*Hermes Psychopompos* that is the title given to the Messenger god in his role as escort of souls to the Underworld.

The Pio-Clementino collection of Classical Antiquities continues beyond the courtyard. The **Hall of the Animals** (Sala degli Animali) displays ancient and modern pieces made for Pope Pius VI by Francesco Antonio Franzoni. From here is access to more ancient sculpture in the **Gallery of Statues**, the **Gallery of Busts** and the **Mask Room**.

The octagonal **Hall of the Muses** (Sala delle Muse) is named for the statues of the Muses and Apollo found near Tivoli that date to the 2nd century CE (the heads are not original). The *Belvedere Torso* in the centre is signed by the 1st-century BCE Athenian sculptor Apollonius, the son of Nestor, who lived in Rome and influenced the heroic nudes and figures of Michelangelo in the Sistine Chapel. The identity of the seated figure is uncertain, but it likely depicts the Greek hero Ajax contemplating suicide. The statue was found in the Campo de' Fiori area and first attested in the collection of Cardinal Prospero Colonna from the 1430s. It was in Palazzo Colonna (Tour 7) during the Sack of Rome in 1527 and sometime after this in the 16th century was procured for the collection of the Vatican Museums, likely by Pope Paul III Farnese who had confiscated the Colonna collection for their alliance with Charles V.

The **Circular Hall** (Sala Rotonda) forms the corresponding end point of the vestibule that begins with the Hall of the Muses, both designed in the Neoclassical style by Michelangelo Simonetti (*c.*1782) who used the Pantheon as inspiration. Alternating colossal statues and portrait busts are arranged around the monumental porphyry basin found in Nero's Golden House including *Antinous as Bacchus*, restored by Bertel Thorvaldsen in the early 19th century; the bust of the *Emperor Hadrian* found in his Mausoleum (Tour 3); and the gilded bronze statue of *Hercules Righetti* found in Palazzo Pio Righetti (Tour 7). The ancient pavement mosaic was found in the Roman Baths in Otricoli, Umbria.

Simonetti also designed the Neoclassical **Hall of the Greek Cross** (Sala a Croce Greca) for the two monumental porphyry sarcophagi. The sarcophagus (right) belonged to Constantine's daughter Constantia (St Constance or Santa Costanza), and was moved here (1791) from her mausoleum on Via Nomentana, now the church S. Costanza (Tour 11). The decorative motif of the grape harvest, employing putti and pastoral scenes of grape vines, peacocks and a ram, symbolise Christian rebirth. The sarcophagus (left) belonged to Constantine's mother, St Helena. The military motif may signal that the sarcophagus was intended for her son Constantine. The sarcophagus was reused by Pope Anastasius IV (1153–1154), survived the fire of 1308 and was restored in 1509.

The **Etruscan Museum** (Museo Gregorio Etrusco) offers one of the world's best collections of Etruscan artifacts, housed in the Palazzetto of Pope Innocent VIII (1484–1492) and in the adjoining building that dates to the reign of Pope Pius IV de' Medici, decorated with Mannerist frescoes by Federico Barocci and Federico Zuccari (1563) and by Santi di Tito and Pomarancio (Niccolò Circignani) in 1564. The vast collection displayed in 22 rooms dates from the 9th to the 1st century BCE and come from Etruscan tombs from areas in southern Etruria and northern Lazio (ancient Latium) that once formed part of the Papal States.

Beyond the **Hall of the Chariot** (Sala della Biga), with Roman sculpture including the namesake *biga* from the 1st century CE (heavily restored in 1788) and a Roman copy of Myron's *Discobolus* found near Hadrian's Villa at Tivoli, begins the long march to the Sistine Chapel. The **Gallery of the Candelabra** (Galleria dei Candelabri) was originally built as an open-air loggia in 1761 that was enclosed at the end of the 18th century. Lining the corridor are Roman copies of Greek sculpture from the Classical and Hellenistic periods, funerary art and dedicatory altars. The **Gallery of Tapestries** (Galleria degli Arazzi) consists of a series of tapestries that depict the *Life of Christ* made in Brussels from Raphael's designs under Pope Clement VII de' Medici. The tapestries formerly hung in the Sistine Chapel in 1531 but were moved here in 1838. Other tapestries on display include a series depicting the *Life of Pope Urban VIII Barberini*, a series of 15th-century tapestries depicting the *Creed*, and a 16th-century Flemish tapestry that depicts the *Assassination of Julius Caesar*.

The **Gallery of Maps** (Galleria delle Carte Geografiche) is comprised of 40 map frescoes painted by the Dominican Ignazio Danti between 1580 and 1592, illustrating the papal territories in Italy up to the time of Pope Gregory XIII Boncompagni (1572–1585), who commissioned the series. The corridor itself is treated as the central Apennine range that divides the Italian peninsula in half. When entered from the far end of the corridor (south), the eastern (Ligurian and Tyrrhenian) and western (Alpine and Adriatic) sides are correctly positioned. Pope Gregory XIII Boncompagni reformed the Julian calendar, still in use since its introduction by Julius Caesar, with the Gregorian calendar that was introduced in Italy in 1582.

The **Papal Apartments** are preceded by the Gallery of Pius V and the Sobieski Room that commemorates John Sobieski, John III of Poland's liberation of Vienna from the Turks who laid siege to the city in 1683. The order of the rooms varies depending on the routes determined by the Vatican staff on that particular day.

The **Raphael Rooms** (Stanze di Raffaello) refer to the apartment rooms built by Pope Nicholas V (1447–1455) and occupied by Pope Julius II della Rovere and then his successor Pope Leo X de' Medici. Pope Julius II chose these rooms since he did not want to live in the apartments located on the floor level below that had been used by his rival, Pope Alexander VI Borgia (1492–1503). **Raphael Sanzio** (1483–1520) received the commission to decorate the rooms on the suggestion of Bramante (most likely based on his trial frescoes in the Room of the Segnatura). The works of the artists who had previously painted the walls of the apartments were mostly destroyed to give Raphael blank walls and include those of some of the leading painters of the day: Baldassarre Peruzzi (1481–1536); Bramantino (Bartolomeo Suardi, c.1456–1530); Perugino (Pietro Vannucci, 1446–1524), the teacher of Raphael; Luca Signorelli (c.1445–1523); Lorenzo Lotto (c.1480–1557); and Sodoma (Giovanni Antonio Bazzi, 1477–1549). Raphael was assisted by his students Giulio Romano (1499–1546), Giovan Francesco Penni (1488–1528) and Perino del Vaga (1501–1547).

In the **Room of the Fire in the Borgo** (Stanza dell'Incendio, 1514–1517) appear frescoes commissioned by Pope Leo X de' Medici, who is depicted in the roles of precursor namesakes. Chronologically, the frescoes in this room were painted after those of the next two rooms that had been commissioned by Pope Julius II della Rovere. The *Fire in the Borgo* alludes to the Fire of 847 that was extinguished when his namesake Pope Leo IV made the sign of the cross from the Loggia of St Peter's Basilica. The mythological figure Aeneas carries Anchises on the left side of the fresco and alludes to the burning of Troy described in Virgil's *Aeneid*. The *Coronation of Charlemagne* commemorates Pope Leo III's coronation of Charlemagne as Holy Roman Emperor in 800 CE. Pope Leo III's portrait is that of Pope Leo X, and the portrait of

Charlemagne is based on Francis I of France. *Victory of Leo IV Over the Saracens at Ostia* alludes to Pope Leo X's proclamation of a crusade against the Turks. The ceiling contains Perugino's *Glorification of the Trinity*, the only work that predates Raphael's commission, perhaps left in homage to his teacher.

The **Room of the Segnatura** (Stanza della Segnatura, 1508–1511) owes its name to its former function as the room used by popes for the signing of bulls and briefs. Pope Leo X de' Medici later used this room as a library, with displays of musical instruments. The allegorical figures of the ceiling decoration correspond to the subjects on the walls that reflect the four branches of Humanist knowledge: *Poetry* over the *Parnassus*; *Philosophy* over the *School of Athens*; *Theology* over the *Disputa*; and *Justice* over the *Cardinal and Theological Virtues and the Law*.

The *Parnassus*, one of Raphael's earliest frescoes in the Apartments, presents Apollo playing the violin (not his customary lyre) on Mount Parnassus beneath his laurel tree surrounded by the nine Muses and famous Greek, Roman and Italian poets. To the viewer's right-hand side of Apollo is the Muse Erato (love poetry), who is seated, and behind her are Clio (history), Thalia (comedy), Euterpe (music/ lyric poetry) and Urania (astromony). Next to them may be Ariosto, Plautus, or Terence, then Ovid, Tibullus and Propertius (Raphael's self-portrait peers out at the viewer behind them, perhaps in the guise of Cornelius Gallus), and below them are Jacopo Sannazaro and Horace, with Pindar seated to his left next to the window that looks onto the Vatican Mount that was believed in antiquity to be sacred to Apollo. To the viewer's left-hand side is the Muse Calliope (epic poetry), who is seated, and behind her are Melpomene (tragedy), Terpsichore (dancing) and Polyhymnia (sacred poetry). Next to them are the poets Virgil, Homer (depicted as blind) and Florentine poet Dante Alighieri, and below them are Alcaeus, Corinna, Petrarch and Anacreon, with Sappho seated to his right, next to the door.

The subjects of the monochrome panels to either side of the door allude to the great epics of Classical antiquity, the *Iliad* and the *Aeneid*. The panel on the viewer's right depicts the Emperor Augustus preventing the burning of Virgil's *Aeneid*, as the poet had instructed in his will. The meaning of the panel to the viewer's left is less certain but seems to depict Alexander the Great either depositing or retrieving a copy of Homer's *Iliad* from the sarcophagus of Achilles. Plutarch claims that after Alexander visited the Tomb of Achilles in Troy, he searched the city for his lyre and sang the glorious deeds of heroes in the *Iliad*.

The *School of Athens* represents the Triumph of Philosophy. It is set in a Renaissance portico whose architectural details (including statues of Apollo and Minerva in the niches) and the placement of the philosophers and other historical persons focus the viewer's eyes on the central figures of Plato and Aristotle, who represent differing schools of philosophical thought. Plato (a portrait of Leonardo da Vinci) points skywards to indicate speculative philosophical inquiry as the source of wisdom. He holds a copy of his *Timaeus* that described the harmony of the universe. Gathered around him to the left are Socrates; Aeschines; Alcibiades as a young general; Xenophon; Chrysippus; Zeno; Epicurus, with vine leaves around his head; Empedocles, looking over Pythagoras' shoulder as he writes, and behind them, in a turban, Averroës (Muslim commentator on Aristotle). The boy to the right of Pythagoras holds a tablet on which is a diagram of the Pythagorean harmonic scale. Heraclitus, sitting on the stairs with his elbow on the table, is a portrait of Michelangelo that was added later to the original composition in homage to him after Raphael caught a glimpse of the Sistine Chapel ceiling. Michelangelo wears sculptor's boots, writes poetry and is depicted as a brooding melancholic figure to portray his personality and artistic genius.

Aristotle, holding a copy of his *Ethics*, gestures towards his ambient environment to indicate scientific inquiry as the source of knowledge. Sitting in front of him is Diogenes. The figures to his left at the foot of the stairs are Archimedes or Euclid (a portrait of Bramante), who bends before his students teaching geometry on the chalkboard; Ptolemy, wearing a crown; Zoroaster, holding a sphere and conversing with Apelles in the black hat, a self-portrait by Raphael. Tradition claims that Raphael placed the artist Sodoma in front of his self-portrait as a tribute since he repainted over the wall that had previously been painted by him.

On the opposite wall is the *Disputa* (*The Disputation of the Most Holy Sacrament*) that depicts the Triumph of the Church in direct response to the Triumph of Philosophy and shows the influence of Perugino's style on the young Raphael. Transubstantiation was a central question of the Church at this time (later contested by Martin Luther). The wall is divided into two planes to represent Heaven centred on the Trinity and Earth. As evidence for the authority and centrality of the doctrine of transubstantiation, the Holy Spirit is represented as a dove with four angels holding the books of the Gospels directly above the monstrance with the Host that is placed on an altar that divides two groups of Church Fathers. On the left side are St Gregory and St Jerome (with the Dominican Fra' Angelico on the far left, with Bramante leaning on the railing), and on the right are St Augustine, St Ambrose, Pope Julius II della Rovere and Pope Sixtus IV della Rovere, to the right of whom in the background are Dante (wearing a laurel crown) and Savonarola, who was executed for heresy and treason by Pope Alexander VI Borgia in 1498.

On the wall with the window is the *Cardinal and Theological Virtues and the Law*. Three of the four Cardinal Virtues are depicted: Fortitude, Temperance and Prudence. Faith, Hope and Charity represent the Theological Virtues. Representations of the 'Law' are on both sides of the window: *The delivery of the Pandects to the Emperor Justinian* and *The Delivery of the Decretals to Pope Gregory IX*, which is a portrait of Pope Julius II della Rovere. Surrounding him are Cardinals Giovanni de' Medici (the future Pope Leo X) and Alessandro Farnese (the future Pope Paul III).

The **Room of Heliodorus** (Stanza d'Eliodoro, 1512–1514) is the second room painted by Raphael, begun for Pope Julius II della Rovere and completed under Pope Leo X de' Medici, and contains frescoes centred on the theme of God's miraculous protection of the Church as inspiration for Pope Julius II's political aims of expelling foreign armies from the Papal States. *The Expulsion of Heliodorus from the Temple at Jerusalem* depicts the Old Testament story of the tax collector Heliodorus who is sent by the Syrian King Seleucus to steal the treasure from the Temple. The theft is thwarted by a horseman and two angels. The masterful perspective forces the viewer's eye into the painting on the left side to the centre with the figure of the Priest Onias praying before the Ark of the Covenant and then out of it on the right with Heliodorus. Pope Julius II della Rovere watches the scene on the left side, carried in his chair (*sedia gestatoria*). The front carriers have been identified as the engraver Marcantonio Raimondi and either Giulio Romano or Baldassarre Peruzzi.

*The Mass at Bolsena* (also known as the *Miracle of Bolsena*) depicts the celebration of Mass at Bolsena by a priest in 1263 (during the reign of Pope Urban IV) that doubted the transubstantiation until the Host produced a drop of blood that fell onto the altar cloth (preserved as a relic in the Cathedral at Orvieto). The portrait of Pope Urban IV is that of Pope Julius II who visited the relic in Orvieto in 1506 on his campaign against Bologna. The group of cardinals behind him includes a portrait of his cousin Cardinal Raffaele Riario (arms crossed against his chest). In the right foreground, a group of five Swiss Guards whom Julius II was the first to appoint also attend the event anachronistically.

On the wall with a window is the *Liberation of St Peter*, presented as a sequence of three scenes that are lit by three different sources of light: an Angel appears to St Peter to free him from his chains, the Angel guides St Peter out of the prison, and the Roman guards awake. The cycle alludes to Pope Leo X's captivity following the Battle of Ravenna (11 April 1512), but it may also have had an earlier connection with Pope Julius II whose titular church as cardinal was S. Pietro in Vincoli (Tour 12). The final fresco in the room is *Leo I Repulsing Attila*. The composition was initially selected by Pope Julius II, but was altered by Pope Leo X to magnify his role in the Battle of Ravenna when he was still a cardinal, including the substitution of Julius II's portrait for that of his own as Leo I. The cityscape of Rome with the Colosseum replaces the landmarks of Ravenna.

The **Room of Constantine** (Sala di Constantino, 1517–1524) is the final room in the series of Raphael Rooms that was painted to Raphael's designs (at least for the *Battle of the Milvian Bridge*) after his death by his assistants Guilio Romano, Giovan Francesco Penni and Raffaellino del Colle. The frescoes were completed under Pope Clement VII de' Medici (1523–1534). The theme of the decoration is the defeat of paganism and the triumph of Christianity illustrated by events in the life of Constantine. *The Battle of the Milvian Bridge* on the long wall depicts the Battle of 28 October 312 CE in which Constantine defeated his co-Emperor Maxentius. The *Vision of the Cross* portended his victory and his conversion to Christianity (*Baptism of Constantine*). The final painting depicts the *Donation of Constantine* in which he handed over authority of Rome to Pope St Sylvester (314–335 CE), represented by a gold statue. On the ceiling is *The Triumph of Christianity* by Tommaso Laureti (1585). From this room there is access (by appointment only) to the **Loggia of Raphael** that was begun by Bramante but completed by Raphael and his assistants and also to the **Hall of the Chiaroscuri** (Sala dei Chiaroscuri), named for the monochrome frescoes that leads to the **Chapel of Nicholas V** that was painted by Fra' Angelico (1447–1449).

The **Borgia Apartment** (Appartamento Borgia) are rooms occupied by Pope Alexander VI Borgia (nephew of Pope Calixtus III) for his private apartment that were shunned by Pope Julius II della Rovere and remained abandoned until Pope Leo XIII (1878–1903) restored them and opened them to the public in 1889. The frescoes are by Pinturicchio (Bernardino di Betto, 1492–1495) and others, namely Antonio da Viterbo and Pier Matteo d'Amelia. The influence of the recently discovered Golden House of Nero is reflected in the *grottesche*. The Borgia family emblems (the bull) are also incorporated in the decoration throughout the rooms. The Room of the Sibyls (Room I) contains 12 lunettes, each painted with a sibyl (paired with a prophet) that was believed to foretell the coming of the Messiah. The room, most likely painted by Pinturicchio's follower Antonio da Viterbo, is in the Borgia tower that was added by Pope Alexander VI to the Palazzo built by Nicholas V. In 1503, Pope Julius II della Rovere imprisoned Cesare Borgia (the son of Pope Alexander VI) here, where in 1500, Cesare Borgia had murdered Alfonso of Aragon, the second husband of his sister Lucrezia Borgia. Lucrezia was then free to marry her third husband, Alfonso I d'Este, the Duke of Ferrara, and it was their son, Cardinal Ippolito II d'Este, who commissioned Pirro Ligorio to design the gardens of the Villa d'Este in Tivoli.

The Room of the Saints (Room V) was painted by Pinturicchio. The frescoes on the walls and vaults are among his greatest works. On the left wall are the *Visitation*, *St Paul the Hermit* and *St Anthony Abbot in the desert*. The next wall contains the *Disputation between St Catherine of Alexandria and the Emperor Maximian*. Speculation once cast the figure of St Catherine as a portrait of Lucrezia Borgia, the daughter of Pope Alexander VI, or of his mistress, Giulia Farnese, the sister of the future Pope Paul III Farnese. The central figures are framed by the arches of the Arch of Constantine in the background in a way that evokes a framed altarpiece. The figure to the left of the throne is a self-portrait by Pinturicchio. On the next wall is the *Martyrdom of St Sebastian* that took place on the Palatine Hill (Tour 6), in close proximity to the Colosseum. The final wall contains *Susanna and the Elders* and the *Legend of St Barbara*.

The Room of the Mysteries of the Faith (Room VI) was painted by Pinturicchio and his students Tiberio d'Assisi and Bartolomeo di Giovanni. The decoration is as lavish as the preceding room and centres on the Mysteries: *Annunciation*, *Nativity*, *Epiphany*, *Resurrection*, *Ascension*, *Pentecost* and the *Assumption of the Virgin*. The *Resurrection* includes the kneeling figure of Pope Alexander VI and perhaps the portrait of his son, Cesare, as the central Roman soldier figure. In 1500 the ceiling collapsed, almost killing Pope Alexander VI, but it was rebuilt by Pope Leo X de' Medici.

The **Gallery of Modern Religious Art** (Collezione d'Arte Religiosa Moderna), with 600 works of modern religious art in various media, was opened in 1973 by Pope Paul VI in the Borgia Apartments and about 50 other rooms. Artists represented include Salvador Dalí, Paul Gauguin, Marc Chagall, Vincent Van Gogh, Odilon Redon, Edvard Munch, Le Corbusier, Wassily Kandinsky, Paul Klee, Henry Moore, Giorgio De Chirico, Max Ernst, Francis Bacon, Pablo Picasso and Diego Rivera.

The **Sistine Chapel** (Cappella Sistina) was commissioned by its namesake Pope Sixtus IV della Rovere in the Jubilee year of 1475. When the construction of the chapel was complete, Pope Sixtus IV commissioned (1481) the leading artists of the day to paint the walls, including Sandro Botticelli, Domenico Ghirlandaio, Cosimo Rosselli, Luca Signorelli, Pinturicchio and Perugino. The chapel was dedicated to Our Lady of the Assumption in 1483. **Michelangelo** di Lodovico Buonarroti Simoni (1475–1564) was commissioned to paint the ceiling in 1508 by Pope Sixtus IV's nephew, Pope Julius II della Rovere, who inaugurated the chapel on 1 November 1512. Twenty-two years later (and seven years after the Sack of Rome in 1527), Pope Clement VII de' Medici commissioned Michelangelo to paint *The Last Judgement* in 1534, but work was interrupted by his death so it was begun in 1536 for Pope Paul III Farnese who unveiled the fresco on 13 October 1541.

The current chapel replaced a medieval hall (Cappella Magna or Maggiore) whose walls were incorporated into the new structure by architect Baccio Pontelli. The inspiration for the Sistine Chapel may have been Solomon's Temple in Jerusalem or the Curia in the Roman Forum (Tour 6), both of which would have signified the succession of the papal Curia over its precursors. Although the entry is now by the altar, the main entry is through the doors of the **Regal Hall** (Sala Regia) opposite, which makes for a more ceremonial entrance with a view of the *Last Judgement* upon entering. The Sala Regia was commissioned by Pope Paul III Farnese and begun by Antonio da Sangallo the Younger in 1540, who also designed the adjacent **Pauline Chapel** (Cappella Paolina) that contains Michelangelo's frescoes the *Conversion of St Paul* and the *Crucifixion of St Peter*.

Since 1492, the chapel has served as the location for the Conclave of the College of Cardinals that elects the Bishop of Rome who becomes the next pope. The secrecy of the proceedings is reflected in the name conclave, derived from Latin, meaning 'with a key', since cardinals traditionally were locked in the chapel until a pope had been elected. The ballots on which successive votes are taken are burned (a stove is set up for this purpose): dark smoke seen from spectators in St Peter's Square means that there is no election yet, white smoke signifies that a new pope has been elected. Upon election, the new pope enters a small red room next to the Sistine Chapel called the Room of Tears for the tears of joy and sorrow that are shed for the office he now fills as St Peter's successor.

The **walls** are divided into three horizontal registers, with simulations of tapestries (*trompe l'oeil*) on the lowest level. The tapestries, based on Raphael's *Acts of the Apostles* for Pope Leo X de' Medici, were hung here on special occasions. The second level has the *Life of Moses* and the *Life of Christ* fresco cycles that emphasise the giving of laws (collaborations and the assistance of students make some of the attributions uncertain); while the third level with windows contains the Gallery of Popes. The lunettes above these were painted by Michelangelo with the Ancestors of Christ. Perugino's frescoes of the *Finding of Moses* and *Nativity* on the altar wall served as the beginning points of the fresco cycles that run along the side walls and balanced the end points of the cycles that remain on the far end of the chapel, but they were covered over for Michelangelo's *Last Judgement*.

For the *Last Judgement*, Michelangelo removed the window and applied plaster over Perugino's frescoes at an angle to keep dust off (in 1535, so painting did not begin until 1536). The vision of the Judgement was inspired by the Book of Revelation but also by Virgil's *Aeneid* and Dante's *Divine Comedy*. Michelangelo's vision of the *Dies irae* is more dramatic and forceful than Luca Signorelli's *Resurrection of the Flesh* in the Chapel of S. Brizio in the Cathedral of Orvieto (1499–1502). The sombre vision also reflects the Counter-Reformation spiritual agenda of Pope Paul III Farnese and Rome in the aftermath of the Sack of 1527. After the Council of Trent, Daniele da Volterra, a student of Michelangelo, was commissioned by Pope Pius IV de' Medici to cover up the nudity with loincloths – a commission that earned him the nickname '*il Braghettone*' (the breeches maker). During the restoration, the loincloths added by da Volterra were retained but later additions commissioned by Pope Gregory XIII Boncompagni and Pope Clement VIII Aldobrandini (1592–1605), who wanted the whole wall white-washed, were removed.

The circular movement of the figures is forceful (and contrasts with the linear cycles of the wall frescoes), as angels awaken the dead with trumpets who regain their bodily form. They rise up on the left for Judgement by a young and beardless Christ who stands in the centre with the Virgin Mary by his side, who adds an element of calm. With a sweeping hand gesture, he saves the faithful but casts sinners down naked to hell on the right-hand side where the Ferryman, Charon, uses his oar to expel them from his boat. Among the damned is the pagan mythological figure of Minos with ass ears that is a portrait of Michelangelo's critic Biagio da Cesena, Pope Paul III's Master of Ceremonies, who criticised the fresco's nudity.

Christ is surrounded by saints bearing instruments of their martyrdoms, including on the left St Andrew with his back to the viewer, holding his x-shaped cross, while below him is St Lawrence with a ladder that symbolises his martyrdom on a grate over hot coals. To the right is St Bartholomew (a portrait of the satirist Pietro Aretino), holding his flesh that contains Michelangelo's self-portrait. To his right is St Peter, holding gold and silver keys, which is a portrait of Pope Paul III Farnese. To his right, below him, is St Blaise, holding iron combs, and in front of him is St Catherine of Alexandria, holding the crescent-shaped spiked wheel. To her right is St Sebastian, holding arrows in his left hand. At the very top in the lunettes are the *Instruments of the Passion*.

The *Life of Moses* cycle begins on the left wall as you face the *Last Judgement*: *Journey to Egypt* (Perugino and Pinturicchio); *Trials of Moses* (Botticelli); *Crossing of the Red Sea*, which alludes to Sixtus IV's victory at the Battle of Campomorto (Rosselli, Ghirlandaio or Biagio d'Antonio); *Receiving the Tablets of the Law* (Rosselli and/or Piero di Cosimo); *Punishment of the Rebels*, with the Arch of Constantine and the

Septizodium in the background (Botticelli); *Death of Moses* (Signorelli); and *St Michael with the Body of Moses* (Matteo da Lecce over Signorelli's original), on the wall opposite the altar wall.

The *Life of Christ* cycle now begins on the right wall as you face the *Last Judgement*: *Baptism of Christ* (Perugino and Pinturicchio); *Temptation of Christ* (Botticelli); *Vocation of the Apostles* (Ghirlandaio); *Sermon on the Mount* (Rosselli); *Entrusting of the Keys to St Peter* (Perugino and Signorelli); *Last Supper* (Rosselli); and the *Ressurection of Christ* (Hendrick van der Broek over Ghirlandaio's original), on the wall opposite the altar wall.

On the **ceiling**, Michelangelo was originally commissioned to paint the 12 Apostles to replace the original ceiling that was blue and studded with stars. The blue paint is made from the expensive semi-precious stone lapis lazuli, that was also liberally used on side walls (and by Michelangelo in the *Last Judgement*), which would have given the chapel a more simple but sumptuous appearance when originally dedicated by Pope Sixtus IV della Rovere in 1483. The painted surface of the ceiling is almost 500 square meters (about 5,000 square feet) and was restored with the *Last Judgement* between 1984 and 1994. The monumentality of the task (considering Michelangelo's experience was as a sculptor and not a painter) and the sublime result is all the more impressive since Michelangelo painted without the help of assistants, whom he fired, and did so standing on a scaffold that he constructed for the purpose. Remarkably, he could not see the finished ceiling until the scaffolding was dismantled. Years of painting under these conditions took a physical toll on the artist.

Michelangelo famously painted as though he were sculpting and the heroic physique of the figures is inspired by the *Belvedere Torso* that was in Pope Julius II della Rovere's antiquities collection, while the pose of Adam in the *Creation of Adam* recalls ancient Roman sculptures of reclining river gods. Raphael, who was painting the *Stanze* at the same time, must have gained access to the chapel by Michelangelo's rival Bramante, since the figures in his own paintings take on the monumentality of Michelangelo's. The portrait of Michelangelo in his *School of Athens* is painted in Michelangelo's heroic muscular style.

The ceiling contains nine scenes from Genesis: *Separation of Light from Darkness*; the *Creation of the Sun and the Moon*; the *Separation of Land from Water*; the *Creation of Adam*; the *Creation of Eve*; *Expulsion from Paradise*; the *Sacrifice of Noah*; *The Flood*; and the *Drunkenness of Noah*. The four corners (pendentives) contain Old Testament scenes: *Punishment of Haman* and *Moses and the Serpent of Brass*, with Jonah in between over the altar wall. At the corners of the opposite wall are *Judith and Holofernes* and *David and Goliath*. The lunettes were painted by Michelangelo with the Ancestors of Christ with alternating Sibyls and Prophets in the spandrels in between. Above the *Life of Moses* cycle from the altar end are Jeremiah, the Persian Sibyl, Ezekiel, the Eritrean Sibyl and Joel. Above the *Life of Christ* cycle from the altar end are the Libyan Sibyl, Daniel, the Cumaean Sibyl, Isaiah and the Delphic Sibyl. Above and in between are nude figures (*Ignudi*) on plinths.

The exit on the left will take you to the Modern Wing through the rest of the Museums along Bramante's long west corridor through the **Museo Cristiano** (Museum of Christian Art) of religious and scientific items. This is preceded by a series of rooms: the **Chapel of St Peter the Martyr** (Cappella di S. Pietro Martire); the **Room of the Addresses** (Sala degli Indirizzi), where the Treasure of the Sancta Sanctorum is displayed; the **Room of the Aldrobandini Wedding** (Sala delle Nozze Aldobrandine), with ancient frescoes from Rome and Ostia Antica; and the **Room of the Papyri** (Sala dei Papiri). If the Sistine Chapel is your final stop, you may attempt to exit by the Group exit on your right to enter directly into St Peter's Basilica.

The **Vatican Picture Gallery** (Pinacoteca Vaticana) was founded by Pope Pius XI (1922–1939), who commissioned the architect Luca Beltrami to design the new building that opened in 1932. The collection was originated by Pope Pius VI (1775–1799), but it fell victim to politics: under the Treaty of Tolentino (1797) paintings were surrendered to Napoleon, but 77 were returned by the terms of the Congress of Vienna (1815), through the intercession of Antonio Canova. The paintings are displayed chronologically (Medieval to 1800) and by schools in 18 rooms.

Among the early treasures is the *Stefaneschi Altarpiece* by Giotto (Giotto di Bondone, 1266/7–1337) in Room II that was commissioned by Cardinal Stefaneschi, the nephew of Pope Boniface VIII, for the confessio of Old St Peter's Basilica. Giotto also painted the Scrovegni Chapel (Arena Chapel) in Padua for Stefaneschi's distant relative Enrico Scrovegni. The altarpiece is painted on both sides. On one side, the centre panel depicts *St Peter Enthroned*. On the other side, the centre panel depicts *Christ Enthroned*, surrounded by angels before whom Stefaneschi kneels. Side panels depict the *Martyrdom of St Peter*, who is crucified upside down, and the *Martyrdom of St Paul*.

Melozzo da Forlì (1438–1494) painted the eight *Angel Musicians* now displayed in Room IV for the apse of Ss. Apostoli (Tour 7) in 1480 and *Sixtus IV Appointing Platina as Prefect of the Vatican Library* that was originally frescoed in the Vatican Library. The painting commemorates Sixtus IV della Rovere's appointment of Bartolomeo Platina as Librarian of the Vatican Library. Platina wrote the first Humanist history of the popes (and was also the author in 1474/5 of the first cookbook printed in his native Italian). The nephews of Pope Sixtus IV look on: Giuliano, the future Pope Julius II della Rovere, with his brother Giovanni and their cousins Girolamo and Raffaele Riario, who constructed Palazzo della Cancelleria (Tour 7).

Room VIII is devoted to Raphael. In the centre of the room are paintings from the beginning and end of his career and show respectively the influence of Perugino and Michelangelo. The *Coronation of the Virgin* was painted in 1503 when Raphael was 20 years old and depicts the discovery of her empty tomb that is filled with flowers as Christ received her in Heaven with a crown. The painting is also known as the *Oddi Altarpiece*, since Maddalena Oddi comissioned it for the family chapel in S. Francesco al Prato in Perugia. The base (predella) of the altarpiece depicts the *Annunciation*, the *Adoration of the Magi* and the *Presenation in the Temple*.

The *Madonna of Foligno* was painted in 1511/12. It was commissioned by Pope Julius II della Rovere's Camerlengo (Chamberlain), Sigismondo de' Conti, for S. Maria in Aracoeli (Tour 5). De' Conti had escaped the Siege of Foligno and attributed his survival (from a cannon ball that was fired into his house) to the intervention of the Blessed Virgin Mary. In 1565, the painting was moved by his descendant Anna de' Conti to the monastery of St Anne in Foligno. Napoleon took it from there to Paris, but it was returned to Italy in 1815 and placed here in the Pinacoteca. Raphael's last work, the *Transfiguration*, dates to the year of his death in 1520 and may have been finished by his students Giulio Romano and Francesco Penni. It was commissioned by Cardinal Giulio de' Medici (the future Pope Clement VII) for the cathedral in Narbonne, but it was placed in S. Pietro in Montorio (Tour 3) and was also taken to Paris by Napoleon.

Along the walls hang valuable 16th-century Flemish tapestries made to designs by Raphael in 1515/16 that depict the *Acts of the Apostles* and scenes from the *Life of Leo X de' Medici*. The tapestries were commissioned by Pope Leo X de' Medici and were displayed in the Sistine Chapel on special occasions. There is also a 16th-century Flemish tapestry that is based on Leonardo da Vinci's *Last Supper*. Leonardo da Vinci's early and incomplete painting of *St Jerome* (*c.*1480) was placed in Room IX after passing through several collections: it was brought to Milan (from France where Leonardo died) by Salaì (Gian Giacomo Caprotti da Oreno), who was Leonardo's student and the beneficiary of several other paintings on his master's death including the *Mona Lisa*. The painting next appears in Rome among possessions of the painter Angelica Kauffmann, the collection of Cardinal Fesch (Napoleon's uncle) and then Pope Pius IX who installed it in the Pinacoteca in the mid-19th century.

The remarkable *Descent from the Cross* (1602) by Caravaggio (Michelangelo Merisi da Caravaggio, 1571–1610) in Room XII was originally painted for the Chiesa Nuova where a copy now hangs (Tour 7). The room also contains works by important artists from the Bolognese School working in Rome in the 17th century: Guercino (Giovanni Francesco Barbieri, 1591–1666), Domenichino (Domenico Zampieri, 1581–1641) and Guido Reni (1575–1642). There is a beautiful view of the Vatican Gardens from this room.

The **Ethnological Missionary Museum** (Museo Missionario Etnologico), founded by Pope Pius XI in 1926, houses a collection of art and historical objects amassed from worldwide missions. **The Historical Museum – Carriage Pavilion** (Padiglione delle Carrozze) is an underground pavilion founded by Pope Paul VI in 1973 for the display of vehicles, including carriages, sedan chairs and saddles, used by popes in the 19th and 20th centuries. A special exhibition features the Fiat 1107 Nuova Campagnola that Pope St John Paul II was riding in when shot. The **Pio-Christian Museum** (Museo Pio Cristiano), founded by Pope Pius IX in 1854, has an important collection of early Christian funerary objects. The sarcophagi, sculpture and inscriptions come mostly from catacombs around Rome dating to the 2nd to the 5th centuries CE. Jewish inscriptions on display are from the Catacombs on Via Portuense (Tour 4). The **Gregorian Museum of Pagan Antiquities** (Museo

Gregoriano Profano), a Classical Antiquities collection, was founded by Pope Gregory XVI (1831–1846) in 1844 in the Lateran Palace and relocated here in 1970 by Pope John XXIII. The collection of sculpture has increased with the addition of archaeological finds from Rome, Ostia Antica, Veio and Cerveteri and includes ancient Greek originals. The **Philatelic and Numismatic Museum** (Museo Filatelio e Numismatico) displays a collection of papal stamps, coins and commemorative medals that have been issued since the Vatican became a sovereign state in 1929.

The **Vatican Library** (Biblioteca Apostolica Vaticana) was established by Pope Nicholas V around 1448 with books from his personal collection and books from earlier papal collections formerly stored in the Lateran Palace and the Palace of the Popes in Avignon during the Schism. To house the growing collection that could no longer be stored in the rooms below the Borgia Apartments, Pope Sixtus V (1585–1590) commissioned Domenico Fontana to build the Salone Sisto (Sistine Hall) across from the Cortile del Belvedere that was completed between 1587 and 1589. The Library that now possesses about 60,000 manuscripts and over 1 million printed books and is open to scholars with prior written permission.

The **Vatican Gardens** (Giardini Vaticani) (by reservation only) cover an area of about 23 hectares (57 acres) and date back to Pope Nicholas III Orsini (1277–80) who planted an orchard (*pomerium*), a lawn (*pratellum*) and a garden (*viridarium*) when he moved his residence to the Vatican from the Lateran Palace in 1279. Christian tradition, however, places the origin with St Helena who brought back soil from Golgotha to symbolically reunite the blood of Christ with the blood of Christians martyred in the Circus of Gaius and Nero. Pope Julius II commissioned Bramante to redesign the gardens which subsequent popes have embellished with fountains and grottoes. Pirro Ligorio designed the **Casina of Pius IV**. Today, the gardens feature the **Audience Hall** that accommodates about 10,000 visitors and the **Old Vatican Radio Station**.

The exit to the Museums is onto Viale Vaticano at the entrance point accessed by the Spiral Ramp designed by Giuseppe Momo in 1932. Exit the Museums and turn right onto Viale Vaticano then turn right on Via di Porta Angelica to walk along the Leonine Walls built by Pope Leo IV (847–855) until you reach the security check-point in the Colonnade of St Peter's Square for entry into St Peter's Basilica (.70km). The stroll passes along the **Borgo**, once a squalid area that was cleared out between the 19th and mid-20th century and inhabitants moved to the suburbs. Borgo is the name for the region but also the word used for streets in the area. The Borgo S. Spirito gives a sense of the medieval appearance and feel of the Borgo. The name is derived from burg or burgh from the Saxon inhabitants who formed the first foreign colony around St Peter's, the Schola Saxonum, visited by King Ine in 725, on the site of the current Ospedale di S. Spirito in Sassia (built by Pope Sixtus IV della Rovere from 1473 to 1478) on Borgo S. Spirito.

The area was reconstructed after the fire and pillage by Saracens in 846. Leo IV (847–855) built the Leonine Walls to contain the city and gives the region its symbol of the lion. The Orsini controlled the area in the 13th century and Pope Nicholas III Orsini (1277–1280) was the first pope to choose the Vatican as his residence (formerly they lived at S. Giovanni in Laterano). Nicholas III added halls and loggias to the fortress built by Innocent III (a tower and hall) near the basilica on a hill called the Mons Saccorum that forms part of the current Sala Ducale and Sala Regia. It was called the *palatium novum*. The Borgo was the 14th regio and was later added as the 14th rione of Rome by Pope Sixtus V Peretti. Architect Domenico Fontana lived at No. 24 Vicolo delle Palline.

In ancient Rome the area was called the *ager Vaticanus*, named after the mount used by Etruscan seers to take the auspices based on the flight of birds. The area contained the villa and garden of Agrippina the Elder. Her son, the Emperor Gaius Caligula, built a private circus that was enlarged by Nero, known as the Circus of Gaius and Nero, the site of Christian persecutions. Nero executed Christians following the Great Fire in 64 CE and in 67 CE. Saint Peter was likely martyred in the circus and buried in the nearby necropolis along Via Cornelia. According to medieval tradition alluded to in Giotto's *Stefaneschi Altarpiece* in the Pinacoteca of the Vatican Museums, he was martyred between two *metae*. A *meta* may refer to a turning post in the circus, a marker, obelisk or pyramid. So the martyrdom was likely remembered to have taken place in the area of the circus between the obelisk in its original location (in the centre of the *spina* or narrow centre island of the circus) in the area of the current sacristy and either the so-called pyramid Tomb of Romulus that stood at the end of Via della Conciliazione (former Via Cornelia) or the Mausoleum of Hadrian, often reconstructed as a conical tomb in medieval and Renaissance depictions. Church tradition formerly placed his martyrdom on the Janiculum Hill (Gianicolo) at S. Pietro in Montorio (Tour 3).

**St Peter's Square** (Piazza di San Pietro) marks the culmination of elements designed by various architects that make it one of the most successful examples of urban planning in Rome. Alexander VII Chigi commissioned Gian Lorenzo Bernini (1598–1680) to design the piazza (1656–1667) that already included the obelisk erected by Pope Sixtus V Peretti. Immediately in front of the basilica is a trapezoidal-shaped area that is framed by two arms that changes into an elliptical shape that is framed by a hemicycle whose ends resemble temple fronts that bear the emblem of Pope Alexander VII. The vast square is 320m deep, 240m across with 284 columns and 88 pilasters to form a four-row colonnade. The 140 statues of saints along the balustrade are 3.2m high and were made by Bernini's students around 1670. The elliptical shape was also used in his design of S. Andrea al Quirinale (Tour 11) and imitated in Giuseppe Valadier's Neoclassical redesign of Piazza del Popolo (Tour 9). Until the demolition of buildings to construct Via della Conciliazione, the full view of St Peter's Square was obscured to visitors approaching from Castel Sant'Angelo.

The centre of the square is defined by an **obelisk** 25m high and is the second tallest in Rome (after the one at S. Giovanni in Laterano). The obelisk was erected by the Emperor Augustus in Alexandria and then brought to Rome by the Emperor Caligula in 37 for his circus. It remained standing (the only one of all the obelisks in Rome not to be toppled in the Middle Ages) in its original position until moved by Domenico Fontana for Pope Sixtus V in 1586. The legend of its raising relates how a Genovese sailor named Bresca (or Breca) upon seeing the ropes strain under the weight shouted for water to wet them ('acqua alle funi'). Pope Sixtus V had forbade anyone to speak while the obelisk was being raised but he rewarded Bresca or his hometown in another version with the honour of supplying palms for Palm Sunday. It is now crowned with the family emblem of Pope Alexander VII Chigi. To either side of the obelisk are markers in the pavement to stand on to see the columns in perspective, another set of markers identifying the names of the winds according to a mariner's compass and two fountains that frame the obelisk. The one on the right when facing the basilica is by Maderno (1614) and the other one is by Bernini (1675).

**Old St Peter's Basilica**, that was originally built by **Constantine**, was added to over the centuries, culminating in the medieval complex that was replaced by the current basilica. This cemetery basilica was built over a necropolis, including pagan tombs whose rooftops were shaved and the tombs in-filled to create a foundation for the basilica. The tombs are still visible in the Vatican Necropolis where St Peter was buried and a shrine erected to mark the location. Construction began *c.*319–322 and the basilica was consecrated on 18 November 326. The construction of the Basilica of S. Giovanni in Laterano began earlier (Tour 13) and is considered the Mother Church and the Cathedral of the Bishop of Rome. Both basilicas were built with the altar facing west rather than east. From the 8th century, the altar end was always considered the liturgical east end of a church even if not geographically accurate. Old St Peter's was the destination of pilgrims since antiquity and the medieval *Einsiedeln Itinerary* (late 8th century) and later Canon Benedict's *Mirabilia Urbis Romae* guided visitors until the 15th century. Pope Boniface VIII's proclamation of the first Jubilee in 1300 that attracted Giotto and Dante and subsequent Jubilees (the name was changed from Jubilee to Holy Year in 1500) spurred the development of the city as a hospitality centre to accommodate the pilgrims. Its medieval appearance contrasts the current majestic basilica: a walled courtyard preceded the basilica that was laid out on a Latin cross plan over 350 feet long with five aisles lined with columns taken from Roman buildings and chapels filled with relics, statues and funerary monuments. Despite issuing a Brief in 1462 calling for the spoliation of ancient monuments to cease, the Humanist Pope Pius II Piccolomini (1458–1464) turned to the surviving materials from the same monuments to rebuild the Loggia of the Benediction to designs by Leon Battista Alberti (1404–1472) and Bernardo Rossellino (Bernardo Gambarelli, 1409–1464).

Pope Julius II della Rovere, whose uncle Pope Sixtus IV had assembled early Renaissance architects and artists in Rome, selected Bramante's design in 1505 and work began on the **New St Peter's Basilica** on 18 April 1506. The basilica was dedicated on 18 November 1626 by Pope Urban VIII Barberini on the 1300th anniversary of the original consecration. His dedication of the basilica was a sign of the Barberini family's rapid rise in Rome when measured against then Cardinal

1. Loggia of the Benediction, St Peter's Basilica, Vatican City

Maffeo Barberini's dedication of the Barberini Chapel in Sant'Andrea della Valle (Tour 7) in 1616. The intended partial renovation of Old St Peter's with the addition of a dome turned into the eventual total demolition (earning Bramante the nickname *il ruinante*) over the course of construction. Martin Luther was in Rome in 1510–1511 and visited the Old Basilica that was mostly intact since work had started only on Bramante's piers for a dome at the end of the former nave of the basilica. The selling of indulgences by Pope Julius II to finance the construction of the New Basilica (and perhaps even the sight of seeing the venerable basilica being demolished) had a profound effect on Martin Luther and contributed to his criticisms of the Church and the series of events that culminated in the Reformation.

Michelangelo destroyed the piers begun by Bramante to make the dome bigger and designed the facade to evoke the Pantheon. Mortar for the dome's construction was mixed in the sarcophagus of Pope Urban VI (1378–1389) that had been in the Old St Peter's. His relics were later restored to the sarcophagus that is now in the Vatican Grottoes. The list of architects who succeeded Bramante as Capomaestro is impressive:

Raphael, Giuliano da Sangallo, Fra' Giocondo, Baldassare Peruzzi, Antonio da Sangallo the Younger, Michelangelo, Gian Lorenzo Bernini and Carlo Maderno. The plan of the basilica would alternate between a Greek and a Latin cross until the construction of Maderno's extension of the nave to form a Latin cross for Pope Paul V Borghese.

Julius II commissioned Michelangelo to design a free-standing monumental tomb over the Tomb of St Peter but Bramante resisted, perhaps out of rivalry with the sculptor. The tomb was never completed and the incomplete monument with the statues of *Moses*, *Rachel* and *Leah* is now in S. Pietro in Vincoli (Tour 12). Julius II is buried in St Peter's Basilica with his uncle Pope Sixtus IV della Rovere whose tomb was destroyed during the Sack of Rome in 1527. Some papal tombs and funerary monuments were moved from the Old Basilica and the atrium to the Grottoes but the relics of others were translated to various churches.

**Carlo Maderno** (1556–1629), the nephew of architect Domenico Fontana (1543–1607), completed the monumental **facade** (about 115m wide and 46m high with columns and pilasters 27m high and about 3m wide). Along the top of the balustrade are statues (almost 6m high) of Christ, St John the Baptist and 11 of the Apostles (including St Matthias on the far right). The statue of St Peter is not on the balustrade but is flanked by one of St Paul at either end of the staircase, with their iconography symbols of key and sword respectively. The Feast Day of Saints Peter and Paul, 29 June, is an important holiday in Rome. The name of St Peter does not appear on the facade but Paul V Borghese's name is centred over the main basilica entrance in the Latin dedication.

The **Loggia of the Benediction** is the balcony where a newly selected pope appears for the *Habemus Papam* ('We have a pope') announcement. The tapestry displayed for the occasion belongs to the former pope. It is also from the loggia that the pope delivers his apostolic blessing to Catholics worldwide, known as the *Urbi et Orbi* ('To the City and to the World'). Bernini's unfinished campanile (only one of two that were commissioned for the far ends of the facade) was demolished when the foundations began to sink. The travertine was used for the facades of S. Maria dei Miracoli and S. Maria in Montesanto in Piazza del Popolo (Tour 9). The clocks on either end are by Giuseppe Valadier (1762–1839).

In the **portico** (narthex/atrium) are five doors that lead into the basilica with the name of Pope Paul V Borghese above each one. The central bronze doors are from Old St Peter's, made by Filarete (Antonio Averulino) for Pope Eugene IV in 1445 with scenes of Christ, the Virgin and the martyrdoms of St Peter and St Paul. The top left panel bears the name of Pope Paul V Borghese who restored the doors for their reinstallation in the new basilica. The **Porta Santa** (the door on the far right) may only be opened by the pope in Holy Years. Just to the left of the Porta Santa is an inscription commemorating Pope Boniface VIII's proclamation of the first Jubilee (Holy Year) in 1300. To the right of the door on the far left is the verse epitaph of Pope Hadrian I attributed to Charlemagne. To the left is an inscription of Pope Gregory II that describes his donation of olive trees to supply oil for the lamps over St Peter's tomb. Vestibules on either end contain equestrian statues: *Constantine the Great* by Bernini (right) and *Charlemagne* by Agostino Cornacchini (left). In the lunette above the main door of the main facade wall is the heavily restored *Navicella* mosaic by Giotto. Commissioned by Cardinal Jacopo Stefaneschi (Pope Boniface VIII's nephew) in 1297, it was formerly displayed in the courtyard of the Old St Peter's but only a fragment of the original mosaic survives. Signs indicate the entrance for the dome.

Upon entering the basilica, it is difficult to get a sense of the scale of the interior and art since proportion gives an impression that the vast size (186m long, 58m wide across the aisles, and 137m across the transepts) and decorative elements seem smaller than they are. The baldacchino equals the height of Palazzo Farnese and the piers that support the dome could contain the church of S. Carlo alle Quattro Fontane (Tour 11). The decoration of the interior is more Baroque and Mannerist than Renaissance and obscures some of Michelangelo's contributions to the architecture. The fusion of elements and styles, however, contribute to the majestic air: the gilded coffered ceiling was designed by Bramante, while the marble decoration on the walls and floor were designed by Giacomo della Porta and Bernini.

The **Chapel of the Pietà** (to your right as you enter) houses the *Pietà* sculpted by Michelangelo in 1499 when he was 24 years old. It was commissioned by Cardinal Jean Bilhères de Lagraulas for the Chapel of St Petronilla. It is signed on the sash of the Madonna (making this the only signed work by Michelangelo) who is represented as younger than

Christ. Dante addresses her as 'Virgin mother, the daughter of your son' in his *Paradiso* (Canto XXIII, line 1). It is now behind bullet-proof glass since it was damaged in 1972. The chapel balances the baptistery on the other side of the nave and echoes the theme of birth and rebirth.

At the start of the **nave** is a large porphyry disc recovered from Old St Peter's on which Charlemagne was crowned Holy Roman Emperor in 800. The metal line markers in the centre aisle indicate the relative sizes of prominent basilicas. Statues of Founder Saints line the nave, the pier and the inner walls of the transepts and Tribune to follow the basilica plan of a Latin cross. Quotations from the New Testament that describe St Peter's apostolic mission line the architrave of the nave, transepts, apse and drum with letters that are 2m high. The inscription on the drum of the dome is from Matthew 16.18–19: 'You are Peter and upon this rock I will build my church … And to you I will give the keys of the kingdom of Heaven.' At the end of the nave is the bronze *Statue of St Peter* seated on a marble throne made by Arnolfo di Cambio (*c.*1296). It was once thought to date to the 5th century CE. The Second Vatican Council that was opened by Blessed Pope John XXIII in 1958 and concluded by Pope Paul VI in 1965 was held in the nave.

The **dome** was designed by Michelangelo and completed up to the level of the drum before his death. The cupola was completed with some design alterations by Giacomo della Porta (assisted by Domenico Fontana) in 1590. Della Porta also added the vault, lantern and two smaller domes. Cavalier d'Arpino completed the mosaics in the dome from 1589 to 1612. The inscription around the oculus records the dedication by Pope Sixtus V Peretti in 1590. The Evangelists are depicted in the pendentives with their symbolic attributes: St Matthew (the ox), St Mark (the lion), whose pen is 1.5m long, St Luke (with the angel) and St John (the eagle).

The piers are named for the statues of St Andrew, St Longinus (the statue by Bernini, 1639), St Veronica and St Helena. Reliefs below the balconies on each pier depict the relics of the saints: the head of St Andrew; the spear of St Longinus; the cloth of St Veronica; and a piece of the True Cross preserved by St Helena. All of the relics are stored in the podium of the pier of St Veronica. The Solomonic columns are from Old St Peter's Basilica. The entrance to the Vatican Grottoes is accessed by a door in the Pier of St Andrew.

The canopy (**baldacchino**) that covers the high altar built above the Tomb of St Peter was designed by Bernini and constructed with bronze taken from the Pantheon (Tour 8). Its design is similar to the original one from the Constantinian Basilica but with angels (by François Duquesnoy) and putti added. The dramatic Solomonic columns refer to the surviving columns from Old St Peter's that are now in the piers. The altar is comprised of a marble slab from the Forum of Nerva (Tour 6) at which only the pope may celebrate Mass. It was unveiled by Pope Urban VIII Barberini in 1633, whose bee emblem appears on the canopy and his crest on the column bases. The **confessio,** the lower level in front of the baldacchino, contains the Chapel of St Peter with perpetually burning lamps. The chapel is above the Tomb of St Peter and was built by Carlo Maderno at the same time that he added the extension to the nave.

The **tribune** is usually cordoned off and reserved for prayer. The monumental composition of the **Cathedra (Cattedra) of St Peter** in the apse was made by Bernini and his assistants Antonio Raggi and Ercole Ferrata between 1658 and 1666 for Pope Alexander VII Chigi. The figures of the four Fathers of the Church support the gilt-bronze throne: St Augustine and St Ambrose of the Latin Church (both wearing mitres), and St John Chrysostom and St Athanasius of the Greek Church (both bare-headed). The wooden chair was once thought to be St Peter's episcopal chair but it was given to Pope John VII in 875 by Emperor Charles the Bald and was formerly displayed in the baptistery. The two porphyry steps in front of the Tribune are from Old St Peter's.

To the right of the chair is the **Monument to Pope Urban VIII Barberini** (1623–1644), completed by Bernini in 1647, with the figures of Justice and Charity. To the right is the **Monument to Pope Clement X** (1670–1676) by Mattia de' Rossi. In the floor in front is the **Tomb of Pope Sixtus IV della Rovere**, who is buried with his nephew, **Pope Julius II della Rovere**.

To the right behind the Pier of St Helena is the **Altar of St Petronilla** that includes a mosaic copy of Guercino's monumental *Burial of St Petronilla*, now in the Pinacoteca Capitolina (Tour 5). The relics of St Petronilla were tranferred here after the round Imperial mausoleum used for her tomb was torn down in the 18th century with another mausoleum, the Rotonda di S. Andrea that served as the old sacristy. Her mausoleum had been converted to the Chapel of St Petronilla and served as the burial place of French kings who claimed kinship with her as the supposed daughter of Peter. She is the Patron Saint of the Dauphins of France. The origin of the French word *dauphin* to signify the heir to the king of France derives from her sarcophagus found in her chapel that contained an image of a dolphin. Cardinal Jean Bilhères de Lagraulas, who commissioned Michelangelo's *Pietà* for the Chapel of St Petronilla as a gift to the French king, is buried here.

The **Monument to Pope Paul III Farnese** (1534–1549) is by Guglielmo della Porta, with the allegorical figures of Justice and Prudence to the left of the chair. The figures of Charity and Abundance also intended for the monument are in the Salone d'Ercole of Palazzo Farnese. To the left of the Monument to Pope Paul III Farnese is the **Monument to Pope Alexander VIII** (1681–1691). To the far left of the Monument to Pope Paul III behind the Pier of St Veronica is the **Cappella della Madonna** (Chapel of Our Lady of the Column) that contains two altars: the **Altar of St Leo the Great** (d. 461) and the **Altar of Our Lady of the Column** that includes a painted image of the Madonna sawn off a column from the old church and incorporated into the altarpiece by Giacomo della Porta for Pope Paul V Borghese. To the left of the Tribune towards the North Transept is the **Monument to Alexander VII Chigi** (1655–1667), sculpted by Bernini in 1678 when he was 80 years old. The monument includes the figures of Charity and Truth between which a figure of Death with an hourglass appears from under a shroud. Opposite inset into the Pier of St Veronica is the **Altar of the Sacred Heart**.

The **North Transept** area is usually cordoned off for the celebration of daily Mass. In the centre is the **Altar of St Joseph**, which incorporates ancient porphyry columns and a sarcophagus that contains the relics of the Apostles Simon and Jude Thaddeus. The ancient antico giallo columns also decorate the South Transept. To the right is the **Altar of St Thomas** that includes the relics of Pope St Boniface IV who consecrated the Pantheon as the first pagan temple converted into a church, S. Maria ad Martyres (Tour 8). To the left is the **Altar of the Crucifixion of St Peter**.

On the **north side**, below the **Monument to Pope Pius VIII** (1829–1830) is the entrance to the **Sacristy and Vatican Treasury Museum** (Museo Storico Artistico), with a list of popes buried in the basilica before the cashier's station. Highlights include the Vatican Cross given by the Emperor Justinian II; the monumental Christian sarcophagus of Junius Bassus (prefect of Rome in 359); the Colonna Santa, one of the Solomonic columns from the Old Basilica; Donatello's Ciborium from the Old St Peter's (1432) that encloses the painting *Madonna della Febbre*, venerated by Romans to protect them from malaria; Antonio del Pollaiuolo's (also known as Antonio Pollaiolo) bronze Monument to Sixtus IV, completed in 1493; and the 9th-century gilt bronze cock that was once on the top of the campanile of Old St Peter's. Opposite the entrance to the Treasury Museum is the **Altar of the Falsehood**.

The **Clementine Chapel** (Cappella Clementina) was designed by Giacomo della Porta who also designed the answering Gregorian Chapel (Cappella Gregoriana) on the other side of the nave. To the right is the **Altar of St Gregory the Great** with his relics. Straight ahead is the **Monument to Pius VII Chiaramonti** (1800–1823) after whom the Chiaramonti Museum in the Vatican Museums is named. The monument is by the Neoclassical sculptor Bertel Thorvaldsen (1823–1831). It is the only sculpture made by a Protestant in the basilica. Pius VII was imprisoned for a time by Napoleon and he supported the US role in the First Barbary War.

Against the Pier of St Andrew is the **Altar of the Transfiguration** with a mosaic copy of Raphael's *Transfiguration*, the original of which is in the Pinacoteca Vaticana. The body of Pope Innocent XI Odescalchi (1676–1689) is below the altar, with a silver mask covering his face. The pope was formerly buried below the Altar of St Sebastian but he was relocated here when it was rededicated to Pope St John Paul II. The new location of Pope Innocent XI Odescalchi's body is within view of the **Monument to Pope Innocent XI Odescalchi** by Pierre-Étienne Monnot. The bas-relief depicts the Battle of Vienna (1683) in which John III Sobieski, the King of Poland, freed the city from the Ottoman Turks. The pope was beatified in 1956. In recent years, the legacy of the pope as a Defender of the Faith has been re-evaluated since his family, the Odescalchi, financed the campaigns of William of Orange that led to his victory over James II at the Battle of the Boyne and the removal of Catholics from the British throne. The **Monument to Pope Leo XI de' Medici** (1605), with the allegorical figures of Fortitude (by Ercole Ferrata) and Generosity (by Allesandro Algardi), is to your right. Pope Leo XI reigned for only 27 days, and the roses carved onto the base with the inscription *sic florui* ('thus did I flourish') allude to his short reign.

The **Chapel of the Choir** (Cappella del Coro) is to your right, with a triumphal arch design and an oval cupola that corresponds to the Chapel of the Blessed Sacrament on the other side of the basilica. The chapel takes its name as the former location of the liturgy of Hours and is dedicated to the Immaculate Conception. Formerly, it was known as the Cappella Sistina since it was dedicated to Pope Sixtus IV della Rovere in 1625 (with Pollaiuolo's Monument to Sixtus IV), who was also buried in the Chapel of the Choir in Old St Peter's. Michelangelo's *Pietà* was displayed here from 1560 to 1609 and again in 1622 by Pope Gregory XV Ludovisi and displayed over the altar (an ancient sarcophagus tub) until it was moved to its present location in 1749. Pope Pius IX celebrated the Dogma of the Immaculate Conception here on 8 December 1854 and added a crown to the Virgin's image in Pietro Bianchi's altarpiece (1740). Pope Pius X added a second crown of nine stars and diamonds to commemorate the 50th anniversary of the dogma. Beneath the altar are the relics of St John Chrysostom and those of St Anthony and St Francis, the saints depicted in Bianchi's altarpiece.

Continuing through the passage, to the left is the **Monument to Pope Innocent VIII Cybo** (also spelled Cibo), the second monument made by Pollaiuolo (1498) in the basilica. In Old St Peter's it was located in the triumphal arch but it was moved here in 1621 when the two elements were reversed: the sarcophagus was situated above the seated portrait of Innocent VIII. It is the first funerary monument that depicts a pope as alive and not only as an effigy lying in state. The pope succeeded Pope Sixtus IV della Rovere and was an ally of his nephew, Pope Julius II della Rovere. Pope Innocent VIII married a son (Franceschetto), whom he fathered before entering the clergy, to a daughter of Lorenzo de' Medici ('*il Magnifico*') and made Lorenzo's son Giovanni a cardinal at the age of 13. Giovanni would become Pope Leo X de' Medici at the age of 38. Franceschetto's remains are interred in the sarcophagus with those of his father.

The **Monument to Pope St Pius X** (1903–1914) is located in a narrow niche to your right. The canonised pope stands with raised arms and head bowed. Scenes from the saint's life are depicted on the surrounding bas-reliefs. Pope St Pius X is buried in the Presentation Chapel just to your right beneath the altar, with his face covered by a silver mask. To the right of the altar is the bronze bas-relief **Monument**

**to Pope St John XXIII** (1958–1963) by Emilio Greco that depicts the pope visiting prisoners in the Regina Coeli Prison, Rome. The pope is buried beneath the **Altar of St Jerome**. To the left is the **Monument to Pope Benedict XV** (1914–1922) by Pietro Canonica (1928), with olive branches and a bas-relief of Mary presenting Christ to the world in flames that allude to the pope's attempts to mediate an end to World War I and then to his humanitarian efforts following the war.

The **Monument to the Stuarts** (1817–1819) is a Neoclassical masterpiece by Antonio Canova. It honours James III, the Old Pretender (1688–1766), and his sons Charles Edward, the Young Pretender (1720–1788), and Henry, Cardinal Duke of York, who called himself Henry IX after the death of his brother (1725–1807). The monument was originally planned for Henry (his portrait is in the centre) and initially funded by his estate but King George III contributed to the cost. James III lived in Piazza dei Ss. Apostoli (Tour 7), where his sons were born. The Stuarts are buried in the Vatican Grottoes in a sarcophagus directly below the monument.

The **Monument to Maria Clementina Sobieski** (1742) honours the wife of James III (1702–1735) and the granddaughter of John III Sobieski, King of Poland, who liberated Vienna from the Turks in 1683. It is one of three monuments in the basilica dedicated to women who have not been canonised. Pope Benedict XIV commissioned the monument from Pietro Bracci (1700–1773) that is situated above the exit of the cupola. Bracci carved the figures of Oceanus, the Tritons and Hippocamps in the Trevi Fountain (Tour 8).

The **baptistery** was designed by Carlo Fontana (1634–1714, no known relation to the family of architect Domenico Fontana) and the main altarpiece is a mosaic copy of Carlo Maratta's *Baptism of Christ*, now in S. Maria degli Angeli (Tour 12). The basin was also designed by Carlo Fontana and is made from an ancient porphyry sarcophagus lid attributed to the Mausoleum of Hadrian (Castel Sant'Angelo, Tour 3) that was later used as the sarcophagus of the Holy Roman Emperor Otto II. This is the third basin in the history of the basilica: the 5th-century basin of Pope Damasus was replaced by Pope Nicholas V with the ancient Christian sarcophagus of Anicius Petronius Probus that was used until replaced by Fontana's basin in 1694.

On the **south side** after the Chapel of the Pietà the **Monument to Pope Leo XII** (1823–1829) is to your right at the door to the **Chapel of**

**the Relics** (normally closed), which contains the heads of St Petronilla, Pope St Damasus and St Mena. The pope's gesture commemorates the delivery of his *Urbi et Orbi* blessing during the Jubilee of 1825.

The **Monument to Queen Christina of Sweden** (1626–1689) to your left is by Carlo Fontana (1702). A portrait medallion of the queen is above a chest with a crown over a skull. The bas-relief on the chest commemorates her conversion to Catholicism and abdication of her throne. She lived in Rome for the remainder of her life where her eccentric behaviour caused the papacy some embarrassment and gave rise to urban legends all over the city.

In the **Chapel of St Sebastian**, Pope St John Paul II is buried under the **Altar of St Sebastian**. His reign (1978–2005) was the third longest after those of St Peter and Pope Pius IX (1846/7–1878). He was the first non-Italian pope since Pope Hadrian VI (Adrian VI, 1522–1523). The body of Pope Innocent XI Odescalchi (1676–1689) that was formerly displayed under the altar was moved to the Altar of the Transfiguration. The altarpiece is a mosaic copy of Domenichino's *Martyrdom of St Sebastian*. To the right is the **Monument to Pope Pius XI** (1922–1929) by Francesco Nagni (1949). Pius XI was the first pope to reign in the Sovereign State of Vatican City that was created in 1929 by the Lateran Treaty. To the left is the **Monument to Pope Pius XII** (1939–1958) who grew up in Rome and was an altar boy at the Chiesa Nuova (Tour 7). His epithet of '*Defensor Civitatis*' (Defender of the City) refers to his efforts in World War II to intervene in the Holocaust. He defined the Dogma of the Assumption in 1950.

Beyond the Chapel of St Sebastian, to your right is the **Monument to Pope Innocent XII** (1691–1700) by Filippo della Valle (1746), who assisted Pietro Bracci in carving figures for the Trevi Fountain. To the left is the **Monument to Matilda of Canossa** (1046–1115) made by Bernini and his workshop between 1633 and 1637.

The **Chapel of the Blessed Sacrament** (Cappella del Santissimo Sacramento) is reserved for Eucharistic Adoration and the celebration of daily Mass (before the location changes in the morning to the Altar of St Joseph in the North Transept). The wrought-iron grill is by Francesco Borromini (1599–1667) but the decoration of the chapel is by Bernini and is his final work in the basilica that he began in 1676, for which he also designed the Ciborium modelled after Bramante's Tempietto (Tour 3).

The **Monument to Pope Gregory XIII Boncompagni** (1572–1585) by Camillo Rusconi (1723) is to your right. The pope sits atop a sarcophagus chest on which is a bas-relief that depicts the pope reforming the Julian Calendar in 1582 when 4 October was followed by 15 October. He also signed the Bull of Foundation of the English College in Via di Monserrato (Tour 3). The **Monument to Pope Gregory XIV** (1590–1591) is by Prospero Bresciano, who is more commonly known for the unsuccessful figure of Moses in the Moses Fountain (Tour 11).

In the **Gregorian Chapel** (Cappella Gregoriana) Pope Gregory XIII Boncompagni commissioned Giacomo della Porta in 1583 to continue the work begun by Michelangelo. Marble plaques from the exterior of the Mausoleum of Hadrian were used that had identified the names of emperors and their family members buried there. In the centre of the chapel is the **Altar of the Madonna del Soccorso** ('Our Lady of Perpetual Help') that contains a venerated image of the Virgin from the Old St Peter's. The relics of St Gregory of Nazianzus (d. *c.*390 CE), an important early theologian, are buried beneath the altar in a porphyry chest. To the right is the **Monument to Pope Gregory XVI** (1831–1846) who founded the Etruscan Museum of the Vatican Museums. Behind the Pier of St Longinus is the **Altar of St Jerome** under which Blessed Pope John XXVIII is buried. Opposite the pier is the **Monument to Pope Benedict XIV** (1740–1758) by Pietro Bracci (1769), paid for by the 64 cardinals whom he created. Across from this monument and built into the pier is the **Altar of St Basil**.

The entire area of the **South Transept** is usually cordoned off and reserved for the Sacrament of Confession. Like the North Transept, the area was designed by Michelangelo as part of his Greek cross design. The decoration was completed by Luigi Vanvitelli (1700–1773), who drastically altered Michelangelo's design for S. Maria degli Angeli (Tour 12). Pope Pius IX held the First Vatican Council here, opening on 8 December 1869, at which the Dogma of Papal Infallibility was proclaimed. The Council ended abruptly on 18 July 1870 when the Italian army began its operation to take the city, which fell on 20 September 1870.

In the centre is the **Altar of St Processus and St Martinian**, the Romans who were guarding St Peter in the Mamertine Prison (Tour 5) and were converted by him. Their relics (found in a necropolis on Via Aurelia) are in the porphyry urn beneath the altar. To the right is the **Altar of St Wenceslas**, the king and patron saint of Bohemia. Beneath the altar are the relics of the Forty Martyrs, St Alexis (Tour 4) and St Mary the Egyptian (Tour 4). The **Altar of St Erasmus** is to your left, which replaced an earlier altar of St Erasmus in Old St Peter's Basilica that was located next to the Porta Santa. The relics of the saint are beneath the altar. Behind the Pier of St Helena to the right above the door is the **Monument to Pope Clement XIII** (1758–1769), a Neoclassical masterpiece by Antonio Canova of 1792. Against the pier is the **Altar of the Navicella**, with the relics of St Mansuetus and St Honestus.

Enter the **Vatican Grottoes** by a door in the Pier of St Andrew. The grottoes occupy the area between the levels of the New Basilica and Old St Peter's. Beyond the **Chapel of Our Lady of Guadalupe** are papal tombs and tombs of prominent figures including the Tomb of Pope Pius VI, the Tomb of Queen Christina of Sweden, the Tomb of the Stuarts, the Tomb of Pope Paul VI and the Tomb of Pope Urban VI (far right) in a reused 3rd-century sarcophagus of a married couple that had been used to mix mortar during the construction of the dome. Along the corridor to your left are four mosaics from Giotto's *Navicella*. The Tomb of Pope Hadrian IV (Adrian IV, Nicholas Breakspear), the only English pope, just beyond to your far right, is a reused ancient pagan sarcophagus in red granite with heads of Medusa and garland decoration. To your left is the Tomb of Pope Innocent VIII who proclaimed the first Jubilee in 1300. Not visible to the far right are tombs including those of Pope Julius III and Emperor Otto II. At the start of the exit corridor are plaques that indicate the level of Old St Peter's and column fragments and bases of the basilica.

The **Vatican Necropolis** (Necropoli della Via Triumphalis) next to the grottoes (by appointment only) preserves the archeological area (scavi) of the 1st-century CE ground level of the city with pagan and Christian brick mausoleum tombs and catacombs among which is the Tomb of St Peter. The mausoleum tombs now with their rooftops shaved off to serve as the foundation of Old St Peter's were secretly excavated when discovered in 1939. They are located along an ancient road parallel to the Via Cornelia that runs under the nave of St Peter's Basilica and its elevation rises towards the Tomb of St Peter. A Christian mausoleum from the 2nd century contains a mosaic on the ceiling of Christ as the Sun (Helios), and Christian scenes of fishermen and Jonah.

The **Tomb of St Peter** consists of an aedicula (known as the 'Trophy of Gaius') and two retaining walls built over his grave within 100 years of his burial, so the site has been associated with his burial since antiquity. Constantine covered the aedicula with a marble and porphyry shrine (Memoria Petri) that is visible from the Niche of the Pallia (the level above the tomb) from the Cappella Clementina (after Pope Clement VIII), also called the Chapel of St Peter, that is directly below the high altar and visible from the Confessio.

To visit the Vatican Museums, exit the basilica, go through St Peter's Square past the obelisk and security check-point in the Colonnade, turn left, and walk along the Walls (Via di Porta Angelica) until you come to Museums entrance on Viale Vaticano. To continue on the tour, exit the basilica into St Peter's Square to the obelisk. Via della Conciliazione is straight ahead but closed off so go through the left side of the barricade into Piazza Pio XII. Walk towards Castel Sant'Angelo (.75km), looking to your left when crossing streets for views of the Vatican Corridor.

The **Vatican Corridor**, the *Passetto del Borgo* or *Corridoio*, a covered passageway that connects the Vatican to Castel Sant'Angelo, was built by Pope Nicholas III from 1277 to 1280 above the Leonine Walls of Pope Leo IV. Pope Clement VII de' Medici escaped the Vatican through the corridor during the Sack of Rome on 5 May 1527 by Spanish, German and Italian troops fighting under Charles V, the Holy Roman Emperor. The attack was only halted by the outbreak of plague in December. A pivotal event in Rome's history, the Sack of Rome was recorded by artist Benvenuto Cellini and signalled the practical end of the Renaissance in Rome when Baldassarre Peruzzi was held for ransom and other artists fled the city. Pope Paul III Farnese's continuation of the Renaissance transformation of Rome depended especially on Michelangelo.

Piazza Pio XII connects St Peter's Square with the **Via della Conciliazione**, named after the Lateran Treaty (La Conciliazione), one of the Lateran Pacts between the state and Church signed in 1929. The Via della Conciliazione corresponds to the ancient Via Cornelia that ran east–west and contained cemeteries including those in the Vatican Necropolis. Funerary monuments survived into later periods such as the Terebinthus Neronis and the **Meta Romuli**, the so-called Pyramid Tomb of Romulus also erroneously identified as the Tomb of Scipio Africanus in the medieval period that corresponded to the Meta Remi, the Pyramid Tomb of Gaius Cestius (Tour 14). The Via Cornelia was rebuilt in 1499 and named Via Alessandrina after Pope Alexander VI Borgia who opened the street for the Jubilee of 1500. Via Alessandrina (also known as the Borgo Nuovo) ran parallel with Borgo Vecchio and led from Ponte S. Angelo to St Peter's Square.

Between these streets was a line of buildings that included the now destroyed **Piazza Scossacavalli**. Palazzo Caprini, designed by Bramante, also called the 'Casa di Raffaello' since he purchased it in 1517 and resided there until his death in 1520, stood at the corner of the piazza and Via Alessandrina. Bramante designed a second palazzo on Via Alessandrina, Palazzo Giraud-Torlonia, that indicates the historical importance of the street to the architecture of the High Renaissance. Another example is Palazzo Jacopo da Brescia designed by Raphael (1515–1519) for the physician of Pope Leo X de' Medici that was demolished and the facade rebuilt on Via dei Corridori.

The construction of Via della Conciliazione in 1937, a Fascist-era project of Mussolini who employed architects Marcello Piacentini and Attilio Spaccarelli, was interrupted by World War II and completed in 1950, requiring the realignment or demolition of some buildings that surrounded the piazza. On the other side of the street, **Palazzo Cesi**, the north facade of which was built by Martino Longhi il Vecchio (1517–1520), was semi-demolished. The famous Cesi ancient sculpture collection was displayed in the courtyard. **Palazzo dei Convertendi** to your left at the corner of Via dell'Erba once faced the piazza on the opposite side from the church of S. Giacomo a Scossacavalli but was demolished and reconstructed here. The building was rotated when it was moved so that the current facade, whose entry portal is attributed to Baldassarre Peruzzi, now faces Via della Conciliazione. Plaques from the old building, now in the courtyard, commemorate Raphael and include street signs and a plan of Piazza Scossacavalli.

On the other side of Via dell'Erba to your left is Palazzo Giraud-Torlonia and across from it on the other side of Via della Conciliazione is the 15th-century **Palazzo dei Penitenzieri** that was modelled after Palazzo di Venezia (also called Palazzo della Rovere and currently a hotel in part). These were spared but Palazzo Branconio and the churches of S. Giacomo a Scossacavalli and Sant'Angelo ai Corridori were demolished. The frescoes from S. Giacomo a Scossacavalli were moved to Palazzo Braschi (Museo di Roma, Tour 7). The fountain now in front of Sant'Andrea delle Valle (installed in 1958) stood in the centre of the piazza since the reign of Pope Paul V Borghese. The destruction of these buildings destroyed the *spina* that was formed by the surrounding buildings that evoked the Circus of Gaius and Nero.

**Palazzo Giraud-Torlonia** was designed by Donato Bramante for Cardinal Adriano Castelli da Corneto around 1500 but only completed at the end of the 15th century by architect and sculptor Andrea Bregno (1418–1506). The palazzo is an example of Renaissance facades (on palaces and churches) that divided the surface into horizontal zones with dividing pilasters. Pope Alexander VI Borgia gave favours to those building palaces along his new road and allowed stones and marble from the Basilica Julia and the Temple of Janus to be used in its construction. The palazzo was home to the representatives of England at the court of Rome before the Reformation, then the Giraud until 1820, before passing to the Torlonia. The garden behind the palazzo was the scene of a dinner hosted on 6 August 1503 by Cardinal Adriano for Pope Alexander VI Borgia and his son Cesare. The guests died a few days later and rumours circulated that Cardinal Adriano Castelli had poisoned them. Pope Alexander VI Borgia and his uncle Pope Calixtus III are buried in S. Maria in Monserrato degli Spagnoli (Tour 3).

The name of **S. Maria in Traspontina** refers to the location of the church 'beyond the bridge' (*trans pontem*), occupying the site of the Meta Romuli pyramid tomb that was demolished by Pope Alexander VI Borgia in 1499 for the construction of Via Alessandrina (Borgo Nuovo). The current church (1566–1587), commissioned by Pope Pius IV (1559–1565), replaced the church built by Alexander VI that was demolished since the dome blocked the line of fire of the cannon of Castel Sant'Angelo. It is the only church in Rome to have no drum to the dome.

Continue walking down Via della Conciliazione to the entrance of Castel Sant'Angelo at the start of the Ponte Sant'Angelo.

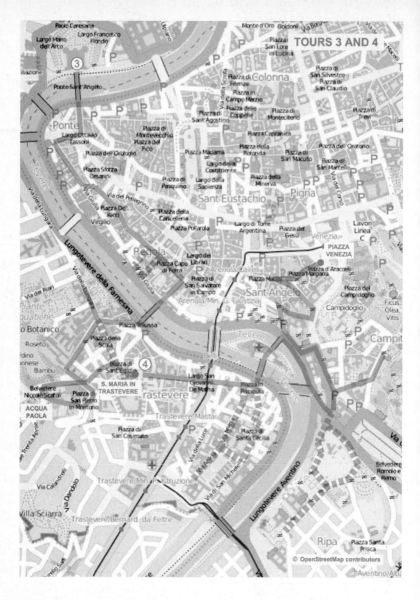

Sites: Castel Sant'Angelo; Ponte Sant'Angelo; S. Giovanni Battista dei Fiorentini; Via Giulia; Via di Monserrato; Palazzo Farnese; Palazzo Spada; Ponte Sisto; Trastevere: Piazza Trilussa; Palazzo Corsini (Galleria Nazionale d'Arte Antica); Botanical Gardens (Orto Botanico); Villa Farnesina S. Pietro in Montorio; Acqua Paola Fountain; Bramante's Tempietto. Optional: Piazzale Garibaldi; Villa Sciarra; Villa Doria Pamphilj.

Distance: 3.5km (1.5km from Castel Sant'Angelo to Ponte Sisto + 2.0km across the Tiber into Trastevere).

# Tour 3

# RENAISSANCE ROME ALONG THE TIBER AND THE JANICULUM HILL

Stroll along the historic streets of Renaissance Rome on both sides of the Tiber with an itinerary that is framed by Castel Sant'Angelo and the Tempietto of Bramante. The urban plans of popes transformed the area into a fashionable Renaissance district with new streets, palaces, churches and fountains. The same artists working on St Peter's Basilica and the Vatican received these commissions including Bramante, Antonio da Sangallo the Younger, Michelangelo, Raphael, Baldassarre Peruzzi, and their successors Maderno, Borromini and Bernini. Optional strolls on the Janiculum Hill include Bramante's Tempietto in S. Pietro in Montorio, Pope Paul V Borghese's Acqua Paola Fountain and several villa parks.

The **Castel Sant'Angelo** (Museo Nazionale di Castel Sant'Angelo), originally the Mausoleum of Hadrian, emperor from 117 to 138, takes its names from the legend of the vision of the Archangel Michael: St Gregory the Great, as he was crossing the Ponte Sant'Angelo (then called the Ponte Elio) leading a procession to seek an end to the plague of 590 CE, saw the apparition of St Michael unsheathing his sword on top of the castle that announced the end of the plague to him.

The Mausoleum of Hadrian (Mole Adriana) evokes the mausoleum of the first Roman emperor, Augustus (Tour 9), with a square base 89m on each side and 15m high, in the centre of which is a circular drum (64m in diameter, 21m high) that supported a second drum perhaps crowned with a tempietto or statue of Hadrian riding a four-horse chariot (*quadriga*). In the Middle Ages, it was imagined as once having a conical-shaped top. The tomb was originally faced in marble, and the

2. Castel Sant'Angelo, view from the Ponte Sant'Angelo

bronze peacocks, now in the Vatican Museums, were from an enclosure attached to the entrance. The tomb included urns of Hadrian's wife Vibia Sabina and his first adopted son Lucius Aelius. The mausoleum was subsequently used for the Antonine emperors (and the Severan emperors to Septimius Severus) since Hadrian had adopted his successor Antoninus Pius who completed the tomb in 139 CE. Many sculptural fragments found inside or immediately surrounding the castel line the entry level of the museum (**Cordonata of Pope Paul III Farnese**).

In the 3rd century CE, the mausoleum was incorporated into the Aurelianic Walls and was converted into a fortress that withstood various sieges by the Ostrogoths: in 537–538, surviving heads of imperial portraits were thrown down on Vitiges and his forces and the fortress remained impregnable against Totila during the Sack of Rome in 546 CE when the rest of the city was plundered, and again in 549 CE when Totila besieged the city for a second time. Pope Gregory VII (1073–1085) sought refuge in the castel from the forces of Henry IV and was rescued by the Normans under Robert Guiscard who then laid siege to the city in 1084 (Tour 13). The conversion of the mausoleum into a fortified papal castle and prison began in the 13th century under Pope Nicholas III (his family, the Orsini, controlled the castel and with it access to Rome from the west since the 12th century), who connected it to the Vatican by the Vatican Corridor. Pope Boniface IX (1389–1404) and Pope Nicholas V (1447–1455) continued work on the castel following the return of the papacy from Avignon with Pope Gregory XI (1370–1378). Pope Clement VII de' Medici sought refuge here in the Sack of 1527 when he fled the Vatican by the Vatican Corridor. The interior remodelling and decoration, like the papal apartments in the Vatican Palace, are defined by the same Renaissance and Baroque-era popes. The outer wall bastions of Pope Pius IV de' Medici that formed a pentagon-shaped enclosure were altered during construction of the embankment of the Tiber (1892–1894) when two were removed. The interior four bastions are named after the Evangelists. The French occupied the castel from 1849 to 1870 and it was used as a barracks and a prison under the new Italian government until 1901 and converted into a museum in 1933.

The **Imperial burial chamber** within the circular drum of the mausoleum was accessed by a circular corridor. Giuseppe Valadier (1822) designed the bridge that takes the visitor past it to the upper floors. The porphyry sarcophagus of Hadrian was reused by Pope Innocent II (1130–1143) and was damaged in a fire at S. Giovanni in Laterano in 1308 where the pope was buried. The lid, however, was reused as the sarcophagus of the Holy Roman Emperor Otto II and is now the baptismal font in St Peter's Basilica (Tour 2). A plaque on the wall of the burial chamber contains a Latin poem, according to tradition, written by Hadrian to his soul as he was dying.

The **Courtyard of the Angel** (also known as the Courtyard of Honour) on the second level is named for the castel's original statue of the Archangel Michael (1536) by Raffaello da Montelupo (Rafaele Sinibaldi, c.1505–1566), an apprentice of Michelangelo. The bronze copy on top of the castel (4m high) was made by Peter Anton von Verschaffelt in 1753. Michelangelo designed the window facade of the Chapel of Pope Leo X de' Medici (1514). Above it is a round niche by Raffaello da Montelupo. The staircase at the end of the courtyard was commissioned by Pope Urban VIII Barberini.

The first two rooms were decorated by Pope Clement VIII Aldobrandini. The next room, the **Hall of Justice**, is part of the ancient superstructure of the mausoleum. From the **Hall of Apollo** there is access to rooms associated with the Medici popes. Off the hall is the **Chapel of Pope Leo X de' Medici**, that he dedicated to the family patron saints of Cosmas and Damian, and a Madonna commissioned from Raffaello da Montelupo. The obese pope also had an elevator installed in the castel (mechanical elements are visible through a grille in the Hall of Apollo). When Clement VII de' Medici fled the forces of Emperor Charles V in the Sack of 1527, he lived in two rooms and a bathroom adjacent to the Hall of Apollo.

The **Courtyard of Alexander VI Borgia** is known as the Courtyard of the Theatre since theatrical performances were staged here. The crossbow and piles of stone cannon balls are reminders of the castel's fortress past. Off the courtyard are storerooms and the papal prison cells whose occupants included Benvenuto Cellini, Giordano Bruno, Beatrice Cenci and Cardinal Carafa.

The terraces on the third level (**Gallery of Pope Pius IV de' Medici**) provide excellent views of St Peter's Basilica. On the north side is the **Loggia of Pope Paul III Farnese**, attributed to Antonio da Sangallo the Younger (1543). The **Loggia of Pope Julius II della Rovere**, designed by Giuliano da Sangallo (1504), overlooks the Ponte Sant'Angelo and the Tiber. From the loggia is the entrance to Pope Paul III Farnese's apartment (**Sala Paolina**) whose fresco decoration was begun by Perino del Vaga. On the ceiling is the motto of the Emperor Augustus shared by the pope: *Festina lente* ('Hasten slowly'). Through several rooms with beautiful frescoes and the **Room of the Treasury** that formed part of the circular superstructure of the mausoleum, the circular staircase continues up to the terrace on the fourth level with sweeping views of Rome. The statue of the Archangel Michael is on a higher terrace. The **Campana della Misericordia** (1758) is the bell formerly rung to announce an execution for capital offences that took place before the Ponte Sant'Angelo. The Papal Court erected scaffolds for public executions that included the beheading of aristocratic Beatrice Cenci in 1599 who was convicted with other family members for the murder of her abusive and incestuous father. Her story inspired Shelley's play *The Cenci*, and legend relates that she haunts the bridge carrying her head. In the finale of Giacomo Puccini's *Tosca*, Floria Tosca leaps to her death from the top of the castel after the execution of Mario Cavaradossi.

Cross the **Ponte Sant'Angelo** to the other side of the Tiber. The three central arches survive from the ancient Pons Aelius that was built by Hadrian in 134 CE to connect his mausoleum with the Campus Martius. In the medieval era, traffic from the Campus Martius side was controlled by the Orsini from their fortress on Monte Giordano. In the Jubilee of 1450, pilgrims crossing the bridge were crushed to death when a panic ensued following the partial collapse of the bridge. The ten angels with the instruments of Christ's passion were designed by Bernini for Pope Clement IX in 1668 (to replace statues of the four Evangelists and the Patriarchs made by Raffaello da Montelupo for Pope Paul III Farnese), but sculpted by his students Antonio Raggi (column), Ercole Ferrata (cross), Pietro Paolo Naldini (dice), Cosimo Fancelli (sudarium), Antonio Giorgetti (sponge), Girolamo Lucenti (nail) and Lazzaro Morelli (whips). Copies of Bernini's two angels holding the titulus of the Crucifixion and the crown of thorns are by Giulio Cartari and Domenico Guidi who also sculpted the angel with the lance. The originals are now in the church of Sant'Andrea delle Fratte (Tour 10). The statues of St Peter by Lorenzetto (Lorenzo Lotti, 1490–1541) and St Paul by Paolo Romano were commissioned by Pope Clement VII de' Medici in 1533–1534 with the toll collected for crossing the bridge.

Once you cross the Tiber, walk across the Lungotevere Tor di Nona and continue on Via del Banco di S. Spirito past the medieval building at No. 61 with reused ancient columns and the Arco dei Banchi to your right until you reach the piazza with **Palazzo del Banco di Santo Spirito** (Bank of the Holy Spirit). Pope Paul V Borghese established the first national bank in Europe here in 1605 that was open to the public for deposits. The bank operated as a papal institution until 1923 when it became a publicly traded company that has since merged with several banks. The palazzo was begun under Pope Leo X de' Medici in 1513 and its corner facade incorporates a triumphal arch design by Antonio da Sangallo the Younger (1520s). It formed the head of banking institutions that lined Via del Banco di S. Spirito that continues on the other side of Corso Vittorio Emanuele II as **Via dei Banchi Vecchi**, where banking families (many from Florence) established their offices in the 15th and 16th centuries. Architect Carlo Maderno lived behind the bank at No. 3 Via dei Banchi Nuovi.

As you face Palazzo del Banco di Santo Spirito, look to your right to see the facade of S. Giovanni Battista dei Fiorentini in Piazza dell'Oro. Cross to the other side of Corso Vittorio Emanuele II then walk down a short flight of steps at the end of Via del Consolato to reach the church.

Pope Leo X de' Medici held a competition for the construction of **S. Giovanni Battista dei Fiorentini** in 1518 that was won by Jacopo Sansovino. His design was selected over those of Raphael, Baldassarre Peruzzi and Antonio da Sangallo the Younger. Following the death of Sansovino, Antonio da Sangallo the Younger continued work on the foundations and the nave that was interrupted by the Sack of Rome in 1527. Construction resumed under Giacomo della Porta, who designed the side chapels (from 1583 to 1602), and then under Carlo Maderno (from 1602 to 1620), who completed the interior including the transept altars and the dome. The facade was designed by the Florentine architect Alessandro Galilei (1734), who won the competition to design the Trevi Fountain but the contract was instead given to Nicola Salvi. Roman branches of powerful Florentine mercantile families such as the Sacchetti and Falconieri already had chapels here and in S. Maria sopra Minerva (Tour 8), so the construction of Sant'Andrea della Valle (Tour 7) gave families such as the Barberini an opportunity to advertise their growing power and wealth.

The chapels contain the works of prominent Baroque artists, and beautiful funerary monuments line the aisles. The high altar, choir and Falconieri Chapel that were designed by Francesco Borromini are important as his last works. On the high altar is Antonio Raggi's *Baptism of Christ* (1669). In the Falconieri Chapel, the left-side funerary monument to Cardinal Lelio Falconieri (Orazio's brother) is by Ercole Ferrata. On the right side is the funerary monument to Orazio Falconieri and his wife Ottavia by Domenico Guidi. Walk behind the altar to visit the Falconieri Crypt, also by Borromini. Two circular staircases descend into a beautiful Baroque crypt with an altar and side niches. The architects Francesco Borromini and Carlo Maderno are buried below the transept floor on the left side of the sanctuary. The chapel to the left of the sanctuary (Cappella del Crocefisso) is the Sacchetti family chapel. Cardinal Giulio Cesare Sacchetti is buried here (Palazzo Sacchetti on Via Giulia is named after him). The chapel was designed by Carlo Maderno and contains frescoes by Giovanni Lanfranco. In the niche next to the chapel is the foot-shaped reliquary that contains the foot of St Mary Magdalene.

The chapel to the right of the sanctuary (Cappella della Madonna) has a fresco of the Madonna and Child by Filippino Lippi, moved here from a street shrine on Vicolo delle Palle in 1640. The south transept altarpiece in the Nerli Chapel, *Sts. Cosmas and Damian at the Stake*, is by Salvator Rosa. In the niche to the left is the bust of Ottavio Corsini (d. 1641) by Alessandro Algardi. In the niche to the right is the bust of Ottaviano Acciaioli (d. 1649) by Ercole Ferrata.

Stroll down the elegant **Via Giulia** named for Pope Julius II della Rovere, who commissioned Bramante to build it in 1508. Following the collapse of Rome and the destruction of aqueducts in the 6th century by the Ostrogoths, the population was centred in the bend of the Tiber. The area at the top of Via Giulia developed into the Florentine quarter in the Renaissance with surrounding areas occupied by Neapolitan, Spanish, Sienese and English communities. The Tiber supplied essential water for consumption and hygiene but it was also the source of commerce, with watermills on floating pontoons near S. Giovanni dei Fiorentini. Gristmills were located along the opposite bank of the river. Many of the cross-streets are named after the guilds that once flourished in the area.

To your right at No. 79 is the 16th-century **Palazzo Medici Clarelli** (formerly called Palazzo Sangallo since it was designed by Antonio da Sangallo the Younger as his residence). An inscription above the door bears the name of Cosimo de' Medici II. The palazzo at No. 85 across the street was also designed by Antonio da Sangallo the Younger. An inscription above three windows claims that Raphael owned the palazzo in 1520; however, Raphael lived on Via Alessandrina in Palazzo Caprini, designed by Bramante (also called the 'Casa di Raffaello'), that he purchased in 1517 and resided in until his death in 1520 (Tour 2). The name of the cross-street to your left, Vicolo dei Cimatori, records the location of the cemetery guild.

The emblem of Pope Paul III Farnese is on the 16th-century palazzo to your left at No. 93. To your right at No. 66 is **Palazzo Sacchetti**. The inscription to the left of the balcony reads 'The house of architect Antonio da Sangallo – 1543', referring to Antonio da Sangallo the Younger. The architect built the house for himself but the building has also been assigned to Nanni di Baccio Bigio and Annibale Lippi, though they may have only had a hand in completing construction since da Sangallo died before completion. The fountain at the far left corner of the facade at the corner of Vicolo del Cefalo dates from the 16th century.

The palazzo passed into the possession of Giovanni Ricci di Montepulciano who made additions to it and then to Cardinal Giulio Cesare Sacchetti whose Florentine family was allied to the family of Pope Urban VIII Barberini and the Sacchetti (his sister Ottavia married Orazio Falconieri) in 1649 and is still owned by the family. The interior was sumptuously decorated and once contained the Classical themed paintings of Pietro da Cortona. The paintings were acquired by Pope Benedict XIV who installed them in Palazzo dei Conservatori to form the nucleus of the Pinacoteca Capitolina of the Capitoline Museums. Cardinal Sacchetti maintained close ties with the French as did later members of the family including Scipio Sacchetti, who accompanied Pope Pius VII to Paris for the coronation of Napoleon. Across the street is the 15th-century **Palazzo Donarelli**.

To your right are the 'sofas of the Via Giulia', rounded travertine blocks that were intended for Pope Julius II della Rovere's Law Court that was never built. The foundations were reused for several buildings including the church of S. Biagio, the Armenian Church in Rome. The area around this part of the Via Giulia was occupied by Neapolitans and is reflected in the name of the church Spirito Santo dei Napoletani. Also to your right is the **Carceri Nuove** that was designed as the New Prison in 1655 by Antonio del Grande for Pope Innocent X Pamphilj. Today it houses Ministry of Justice offices including the Direzione Nazionale Antimafia that is the national office for efforts to combat the Mafia. The adjacent prison was designed by Giuseppe Valadier in 1827 and now houses the **Museo Criminologico** (the entrance is at No. 29 Via del Gonfalone). The name of the side street Vicolo della Prigioni preserves the name of the Carceri.

Turn left on Vicolo Malpasso to reach **Largo della Moretta** (where Benvenuto Cellini killed the Milanese goldsmith Pompeo in 1534) at the intersection of Via dei Banchi Vecchi and Via del Pellegrino (named for the medieval pilgrim route, the Via Peregrinorum) for the start of Via di Monserrato. As you stroll through the intersection, look at the marble plaque on No. 145 that preserves the inscription from the ancient boundary marker from the reign of the Emperor Claudius. On your right are the half-demolished buildings that surround the ruins of the church of S. Filippo Neri. A street planned in 1940 was never completed.

Begin your stroll down Via di Monserrato. **Palazzo Incoronati** (16th century) at No. 152 is to your right. Also to your right is the16th-century **Palazzo Ricci** at the end of Piazza Ricci with a view through the courtyard to the Via Giulia. The facade was painted by Polidoro da Caravaggio (around 1525) and is one of the few surviving examples in Rome of painted Renaissance facades that often took Classical or triumphal military themes as inspiration. Raphael designed the church of **S. Eligio degli Orefici** for the Goldsmiths (1514) on Vicolo S. Eligio (a continuation of Via della Barchetta to your right) on a Greek cross plan with a cupola. Baldassarre Peruzzi completed the work following Raphael's death. Flaminio Ponzio restored the facade (following a collapse) for Pope Paul V Borghese to Raphael's design.

To your right is the church of **S. Maria di Monserrato degli Spagnoli**. The Spanish national church in Rome was built on the site of a Spanish hospice established in 1506. Palazzo del Collegio Spagnolo is adjacent. The church was begun by Antonio da Sangallo the Younger (1518), but the facade was completed later by Francesco da Volterra. The first chapel on the south side contains Annibale Carracci's altarpiece *San Diego de Alcalà* and the tombs (19th century) of the Borgia Popes Calixtus III and the notorious Alexander VI. King Alfonso XIII of Spain (d. 1941) is also buried here. Bernini's bust of Monsignor Pedro de Foix Montoya in the monument to Orazio Torriani (*c.*1621) was transferred here from S. Giacomo degli Spagnoli at the end of the 19th century. The courtyard contains 15th-century tombs by Andrea Bregno and Luigi Capponi.

The house at No. 111 to your right with an open loggia on three levels and a medallion of Romulus and Remus is part of complex of buildings affiliated with the church of **S. Caterina da Siena a Via Giulia**. Baldassarre Peruzzi's 1526 church was rebuilt by Paolo Posi in 1766–1775, vying for the accolade of the last Baroque church in Rome with S. Paolo Primo Eremita (Tour 12) that is directly behind it facing Via Giulia. The facade was rebuilt in 1912 and imitates the house in Siena in which St Catherine was born. The symbol of Siena is the she-wolf suckling Romulus and Remus. According to medieval legend, the city was founded by Senius (Senio in Italian) who was the son of Remus. Opposite at No. 94–97 is the palazzo that once served as the **Corte Savella**, the court established by the Savelli, that was later replaced by the Carceri Nuove, in which Beatrice Cenci was tried and imprisoned.

Piazza di S. Caterina della Rota is to your right with the church of **S. Caterina della Rota** at the far end. Opposite the piazza to your left at No. 45 is the church of **St Thomas of Canterbury** and the **Venerable English College**. This site, in ancient Rome, originally held the barracks and stables of the 'Blue' team of charioteers (*Factio Veneta*) and two ancient columns were later incorporated into the hospice building. John Shepherd, a London merchant, and his wife Alice bought several houses on Via di Monserrato to found the English Hospice of the Most Holy Trinity and St Thomas in 1362 for English travellers and pilgrims, including the mystic Margery Kempe (1416). The Schola Saxonum in the Borgo had welcomed English visitors to Rome, including Alfred the Great in 854, but Pope Innocent III converted it into a hospital (on the site of the current Ospedale di S. Spirito in Sassia founded by Pope Sixtus IV della Rovere in 1473–1478). Thomas Cromwell visited in 1514. The hospice was pillaged during the Sack of Rome in 1527. Following King Henry VIII's break with Rome, Pope Paul III Farnese took over the hospice and placed it under the direction of Cardinal Reginald Pole (Henry VIII's cousin). The college was founded by William Allen for English and Welsh seminarians and was formally recognised by the Bull of Foundation (1579) that was signed by Pope Gregory XIII Boncompagni. It is the oldest English institution outside of England. Entries in the guest book include Thomas Hobbes (1635), William Harvey (1636), John Milton (1638), John Evelyn (1644) and Richard Cranshaw (1646). Philip Howard, Cardinal Protector of Great Britain, 1682–1694, rebuilt part of the college as a palazzo.

The church of St Thomas of Canterbury was rebuilt from 1866 to 1888 to the Romanesque designs of Virginio Vespignani (1808–1882) over 11th–12th-century church buildings and an ancient Roman road. Pope Pius IX laid the foundation stone in 1866. The relics of St Thomas are believed to be in the church of Sant'Alessio on the Aventine Hill (Tour 4). A central focus of the church is Durante Alberti's *The Martyr's Picture* (1580), with the Trinity and St Thomas à Becket of Canterbury and St Edmund of East Anglia, that is also associated with the 44 Martyrs (1581–1679) who were commemorated before it when news arrived of their deaths. The Martyrs' Chapel contains a ceiling fresco of the *Assumption* by Andrea Pozzo (*c.*1701), who also painted *The washing of Christ's feet at the house of the Pharisee* that hangs in the refectory. The church contains the effigy Tomb of Cardinal Christopher Bainbridge, the Bishop of York, who was King Henry VIII's first ambassador to the Holy See (d. 1514). Ferdinando Fuga designed the funerary monument to Thomas Dereham (d. 1739). Pope St John Paul II celebrated Mass in the church in 1979 to mark the 400th anniversary of the college.

Across the street with its side facing the piazza is the church of **S. Girolamo della Carità** with a facade by Carlo Rainaldi (1660). The church is mostly visited for the Cappella Spada, the first chapel to the right from the main entrance that may be the work of Cosimo Fanzago with the collaboration of Francesco Borromini. The chapel, with the effigy tombs of Orazio Spada by Ercole Ferrata (right) and Tommaso Spada by Cosimo Fancelli (left), is decorated with polychrome marble that imitates a tapestry over which hang portrait medallions. Two kneeling angels holding a marble cloth serve as the balustrade. In the south transept is the funeral monument to Count Asdrubale di Montauto designed by Pietro da Cortona (1629). On the north side, a marble plaque contains a Latin inscription that relates the tradition that the church was built on the site where St Jerome stayed in 382.

The 16th-century **Palazzo Fioravanti** is to your right at No. 61 just before you enter **Piazza Farnese**. In the centre of the piazza are two ancient Egyptian granite basins from the Baths of Caracalla (Tour 13) that were converted into fountains in 1626 with the Farnese emblem of the fleur-de-lys. The basins also served as platforms from which the Farnese would watch spectacles in the piazza, but on other occasions, in the 18th century, the piazza itself served as a stage and Palazzo Farnese as the backdrop for monumental temporary set pieces (*chinea*). To your left as you enter is the church of **S. Brigida di Svezia** who lived in the adjacent house for 19 years and who died here on 23 July 1373. The Swedish Hospice located here was contemporaneous in date with the English Hospice around the corner on Via di Monserrato. To the right of the church is **Palazzo Fusconi Pighini** begun by Jacopo Barozzi da Vignola but whose entry portal is attributed to Baldassarre Peruzzi (*c.*1524).

**Palazzo Farnese** is one of the most beautiful Renaissance palaces in Rome and rivals the immense Palazzo della Cancelleria built by Bramante for Cardinal Riario, the nephew of Pope Sixtus IV della Rovere (Tour 7). It is currently the seat of the French Embassy (since 1871) and may only be visited by appointment. Pope Paul III Farnese began construction of the palazzo in 1514, while he was still a cardinal, and commissioned Antonio da Sangallo the Younger to build it but he only completed the facade, the colonnaded atrium with a triple row of granite columns and the first two-thirds of the courtyard. After his death in 1546, Michelangelo took up the project and completed the third level of the courtyard and added the loggia over the main entrance facing the piazza. The palazzo was still incomplete at the time of Pope Paul III's death in 1549 and was only finished in 1589 by Giacomo della Porta. The design called for a bridge to span the Tiber for access to the Villa Farnesina. The viaduct (the Arco Farnese) that spans the Via Giulia was commissioned by Odoardo Farnese in 1603 and intended to connect to the bridge. The palazzo was the first residence of Queen Christina of Sweden in 1655 and she was called the tenant from hell.

The famous Farnese collection of ancient sculpture, many pieces found in the Baths of Caracalla, also included art collections acquired by purchase, confiscation and marriage (part of the Medici collection was added to the Farnese collection through the marriage of Margaret of Parma, the daughter of the Holy Roman Emperor Charles V, to Alessandro de' Medici and, upon his death, to Ottavio Farnese, the grandson of Pope Paul III Farnese). The collection is now in the National Archeological Museum in Naples since the collection passed to the Bourbons of Naples through Elisabetta Farnese, the wife of Philip V of Spain, then to their son Charles who became King of Naples in 1734. In 1787, his son Ferdinand IV of Naples moved the collection from Rome to Naples. The *Farnese Bull* group that depicts the punishment of Dirce was displayed in the centre of the portico with other sculptures now in Naples.

In the **Salone d'Ercole** the famous *Farnese Hercules* (the statue is a copy of the original now in Naples) was displayed beneath frescoes depicting the Labours of Hercules. The original marble statue of the mythological hero who leans against his club holding the apples of the Hesperides behind his back is a Roman copy of the bronze original by Lysippus (4th century BCE). Remarkably, the statue discovered in the

Baths of Caracalla in 1546 was reassembled from three pieces, but the original legs from the knees to the ankles were discovered only after the restoration by Guglielmo della Porta. The statue was much admired and copies of it overlook the magnificent gardens of the 17th-century Château de Vaux-le-Vicomte in Maincy, the Château de Versailles, France, and the Hercules Garden in Blair Castle, Scotland. The reclining statues of the allegorical figures of Charity and Abundance are by Guglielmo della Porta and were intended to accompany the figures of Justice and Prudence on Pope Paul III Farnese's funerary monument in St Peter's Basilica.

Long galleries that face the courtyard lead to the magnificent **Galleria dei Carracci** (Annibale was assisted by his brother Agostino and so the name of the room refers to both Carracci) that was commissioned by Odoardo Farnese in 1598–1602. Farnese required the artist to live in residence for his monthly payment, the last of which was delivered to Carracci by a servant on a saucer. The ceiling fresco is by Annibale Carracci (1597–1607/8) and depicts the *Loves of the Gods* based on the ancient Roman poet Ovid's *Metamorphoses*, with the *Triumph of Bacchus and Ariadne* in the centre. Domenichino (1608) assisted in the painting of the frescoes on the lower walls above the doors and niches. The themes of the ceiling correspond to the ancient statues in the niches that line the room. The marriage between Rannucio I Farnese, the Duke of Parma, and Margherita Aldobrandini (the niece of Pope Clement VIII Aldobrandini) was celebrated here in 1600 when she was 11 years old.

To walk around the palazzo to see the garden facade by Vignola and courtyard loggia by Giacomo della Porta through the gate, take Vicolo dei Farnesi (the street to the right of the palazzo when facing it) to Via Giulia. Before turning left to walk under the viaduct (Arco Farnese), take a few steps to your right to see the winged skull in the facade of **S. Maria dell'Orazione e Morte**, designed by Ferdinando Fuga (1733–1737) to replace an earlier church. The plaque to the right of the entrance has a slot for alms surrounded by more death imagery where money was collected to provide a burial for unclaimed corpses that were buried in a cemetery behind the church (removed when the Tiber Embankment was constructed). The palazzo next to the church on the right-hand side is **Palazzo Falconieri**, enlarged by Francesco Borromini (1646–1649) for Orazio Falconieri, that has the distinctive herm pilasters at each end of the facade of falcons with female breasts.

Retrace your steps and walk along Via Giulia until Via del Mascherone to see the **Fontana del Mascherone**, an ancient mask displayed over an ancient porphyry basin, and take Via del Mascherone to return to Piazza Farnese. Turn right onto Vicolo dei Venti (the continuation of Via di Monserrato) with Renaissance houses at Nos 5–9. Continue past Via dei Polverone ('Street of the Crushers'), a street name that speaks of the trade, here and by the Colosseum, devoted to crushing ancient marbles and other stones where the name changes again to Via Capo di Ferro.

Continue to the charming Piazza della Quercia. The small church in the corner with the Rococo facade is **S. Maria della Quercia dei Macellai** by Filippo Raguzzini (1727–1731) that has been the home of the guild of butchers (Confraternita dei Macellai di Roma) since 1532. Pope Clement VII de' Medici gave them this church in exchange for their former church Ss. Sergio e Bacco al Foro Romano that he had demolished since it had been built against the Arch of Septimius Severus that he wanted to free (Tour 6). The name derives from an earlier dedication of the church by Pope Julius II della Rovere to horse traders from Viterbo who named it for the sanctuary of S. Maria della Quercia near Viterbo. The oak tree planted in honour of S. Maria is also the emblem of the della Rovere family. In the adjoining Piazza Capo di Ferro is the **Fontana delle Mammelle**, opposite Palazzo Spada, that takes its name after the bare-breasted nymph placed over an ancient sarcophagus to a design by Borromini. Above, on the wall of the tower, is a clock with fleur-de-lys markers. The contiguous piazze reveal Classical quotations from the facade of Palazzo Spada to a surviving segment of an ancient frieze with lotus flowers from the reign of Trajan or Hadrian that was meticulously inserted above the entrance to **Palazzo Ossoli** at No. 1 Piazza della Quercia, facing the church, that is attributed to Baldassarre Peruzzi (*c.*1525).

**Palazzo Spada** was built in 1548–1550 for Cardinal Girolamo Capodiferro, but was acquired by Cardinal Bernardino Spada in 1632, who, with his brother Cardinal Virgilio Spada, assembled the art collection that was added to by their grandnephew Cardinal Fabrizio Spada. The highly ornate stucco facade (by Giulio Mazzoni) for Capodiferro frames him within the context of ancient Roman military, political and religious figures. From left to right are the Emperor Trajan, Pompey the

Great, Fabius Maximus, Romulus, Numa, Julius Caesar and the Emperor Augustus. Francesco Borromini designed the colonnaded gallery called the 'perspective gallery' that leads from the courtyard to the garden in only 9m, but which gives the illusion of a much longer space. The palazzo was bought by the Italian state from the Spada family in 1927, and today houses the Italian Council of State. Displayed in the State Rooms is the statue once identified as Pompey the Great that stood outside of the Curia of his theatre (Tour 7), in front of which Julius Caesar was assassinated. It was given to Cardinal Capodiferro in 1552–1553 after its discovery in the area of Via dei Leutari. The art is typical of 17th-century contemporary collections that blended ancient and contemporary sculpture with paintings on Classical and religious themes. The collection is the last of the smaller family collections and is displayed in its original setting over four rooms according to 17th-century tastes.

From Palazzo Spada, continue on Via Capo di Ferro towards Via dei Pettinari. At No. 7 is **Palazzetto Spada** attributed to Baldassarre Peruzzi. The medieval building to your left at the end of the street (No. 31) has spoliated columns embedded into the wall. The church of **SS. Trinità dei Pellegrini** at the end of Via di Capo Ferro once served as a hostel for pilgrims. Turn right and walk along Via dei Pettinari, a medieval pilgrim route once lined with pawnshops that now sell jewellery, to reach the **Ponte Sisto**.

The bridge is named after Pope Sixtus IV della Rovere who commissioned the architect Baccio Pontelli to construct it (between 1473 and 1479) as a replacement for the ancient Pons Aurelius. This is the first bridge constructed across the Tiber since antiquity. Until the end of the 19th century, the banks of the Tiber contained swimming beaches, La Rimella, with cabins on floating decks to allow for the modest to swim unseen by others. As you cross the pedestrian bridge into **Trastevere** (in the Rione Trastevere), look up the Janiculum Hill to see the Acqua Paola Fountain that would have been the terminus point of the Ponte Sisto if a planned street had been built in the early 17th century under Pope Paul V Borghese. The Italian name Trastevere is derived from the Latin *trans Tiberim*, meaning 'across the Tiber'. The ancient Etruscans controlled the Trastevere side of the Tiber (right bank) until the Romans occupied it. The area contained the garden estate of Julius Caesar, perhaps where his mistress Cleopatra was lodged (with their son Caesarion) during her stay in Rome from 46 to 44 BCE. The estate was later the site of the Naumachia of Augustus where mock naval battles were staged. In the medieval period, the area was squalid and prone to malaria.

In the centre of **Piazza Trilussa** is the **Fontana dell'Acqua Paola** (also called the Fontanone di Ponte Sisto) that is the answering fountain to the monumental Acqua Paola Fountain on the Janiculum Hill commissioned by Pope Paul V Borghese. This smaller fountain used to be incorporated into the facade of the Casa dei Mendicanti, a building that abutted the left side of the bridge at the end of Via dei Pettinari and Via Giulia. The fountain served as a visual terminal point to the Via Giulia. It was demolished during the construction of the Embankment and the Lungotevere (1898–1892) and moved here in 1898. The building facing the fountain at an angle playfully references it with a Latin quote that begins 'The fountain sings ...' The piazza is dedicated to the famous poet Carlo Alberto Salustri (1873–1950) (his pen name Trilussa is an anagram), who wrote sonnets in the Trastevere dialect.

Take Via di Ponte Sisto (the right-side of the fountain) straight through Piazza di S. Giovanni della Malva to Via di S. Dorotea (the church of S. Dorotea is to your right). At the end of the street at No. 20 to your right is the **Casa della Fornarina** (currently a restaurant), the supposed house of Raphael's mistress and model for *La Fornarina*. Continue to your right onto Via di Porta Settimiana (where Via Garibaldi begins with the Scuola Ufficiali dei Carabinieri) and walk through the **Porta Settimiana** (built by Pope Alexander VI Borgia in 1498) to **Via della Lungara** that was built by Pope Julius II della Rovere at the same time as the Via Giulia to connect the Borgo to Trastevere. To your left just before Palazzo Corsini is **Palazzo Torlonia alla Lungara**. The ancient **Tomb of the Platorini** was discovered in the area in 1880 and is now on display in the Museo Nazionale Romano delle Terme di Diocleziano (Tour 12). A little beyond to your left is Palazzo Corsini and to your right is the Villa Farnesina.

**Palazzo Corsini**, formerly known as Villa Riario, was renamed for Cardinal Neri Maria Corsini, the nephew of Pope Clement XII Corsini (1730–1740), who acquired it from the Riario family in 1736 and commissioned Ferdinando Fuga to design the long facade. Queen Christina of Sweden resided here from 1659 until her death here

(Room 5) in 1689. It was the proposed home for James Stuart (James III, the 'Old Pretender'), who was given Palazzo Balestra (Palazzo Muti Papazzurri) in Piazza dei Ss. Apostoli instead (Tour 7). In 1883, the Corsini sold the palazzo to the state and donated the collection of art (mostly early Renaissance to late 18th century paintings on religious and Classical subjects including Flemish landscapes and genre scenes that were popular in Rome). The collection is now the **Galleria Nazionale d'Arte Antica** that is displayed in its original setting in eight rooms with views of the Botanical Gardens including Nicolas Poussin's *Triumph of Ovid* and Salvator Rosa's *Prometheus' Torment* and a bronze of the *Baptism of Christ* by Alessandro Algardi (Room 2); Bernini's *Terra Cotta bust of Pope Alexander VII Chigi* (Room 5); Pietro Bracci's *Portrait of Pope Clement XII Corsini* (Room 6); and Caravaggio's *St John the Baptist* (Room 7). The palazzo also houses the Biblioteca Corsiniana, the Accademia Nazionale dei Lincei and the Fondazione Caetani.

The **Botanical Gardens**, once the gardens of Palazzo Corsini, were donated to the state by Tommaso Corsini in 1883. The collection of native and exotic plant species are grouped together to illustrate various ecosystems. The gardens include a fountain by Ferdinando Fuga and a monumental Baroque staircase with a tiered fountain in the centre called a catena d'acqua ('chain of water') from the top of which the Corsini could show their guests panoramic views of their garden and Rome. The 18th-century Teatro di Verzura, an open-air theatre created with hedges, does not survive. The Concerti all'Orto Botanico are held here in July.

Agostino Chigi commissioned Baldassarre Peruzzi to design and build the suburban **Villa Farnesina** from around 1505 to 1510, with decoration added until 1520. The villa was originally called the Villa Chigi but the name changed to the Villa Farnesina when the Farnese bought it around 1580. Guests at the villa included Cardinal Richelieu and Queen Christina of Sweden. The villa subsequently passed to the Bourbon of Naples in 1714 (through Elisabetta Farnese's marriage to Charles V of Spain) and then to the Spanish Ambassador Salvador Bermúdez de Castro y Díez, the Duke of Ripetta, who restored the interior. The Italian state acquired the villa in 1927. Today it is the seat of the Accademia dei Lincei and the Gabinetto dei Desegni e delle Stampe. Roman ruins of an Augustan-era building were found below the villa, whose frescoes are now in Palazzo Massimo (Tour 12).

The design of a central block and extended wings, based on a mathematically precise adaptation of ancient architecture, influenced Renaissance villa design in Rome. The interior is famous for its decoration and frescoes whose themes on the ground and first floors centre on the manipulation and union of the senses and intellect. In the **Loggia of Galatea**, Peruzzi painted the ceiling with a zodiac representing Agostino Chigi's birthday. The *The Triumph of Galatea* is by Raphael and the figure of Polyphemus is by Sebastiano del Piombo who also painted the lunettes with scenes from Ovid's *Metamorphoses*. The large monochrome head is attributed to Peruzzi.

The festive **Loggia of Cupid and Psyche**, situated along the side facing the garden, once included a stage area between the wings of the house for the production of theatrical performances against the backdrop (*scaenae frons*) of the facade. Theatricality extended to a famous dinner party in which Agostino Chigi threw silver plate into the Tiber that was later retrieved by nets. Raphael designed the illusionistic frescoes that were completed in 1517 by Giulio Romano, Francesco Penni, Giovanni da Udine and Raffaellino del Colle. The frescoes are based on the story of Cupid and Psyche in Apuleius' *Metamorphoses* (also referred to as the *Golden Ass*), in which Venus torments Psyche with tasks until she relents and consents to her marriage to Cupid. On the first floor, Peruzzi painted the **Salone delle Prospettive** that was used for Chigi's marriage banquet to Francesca Ordeaschi in 1519. There is a fusion of realism and illusion in the frescoes that play on the senses in which known sites such as the Torre delle Milizie are set against an idealised landscape. The adjoining room is the **Sala delle Nozze di Alessandro e Rossana** (Room of the *Marriage of Alexander and Roxane*), named after the fresco by Sodoma for the honeymoon of Chigi and his bride.

Retrace your steps on Via della Lungara and pass through Porta Settimiana. To continue on the tour, turn right to walk up the winding Via Garibaldi to reach S. Pietro in Montorio at the top of the Janiculum Hill. Just beyond a fountain on your right that has a Roman sarcophagus for a basin that was installed by Pope Urban VIII Barberini in 1627, look for a gate with steps (Via di S. Pietro in Montorio) that leads to the Royal Academy of Spain and the church of S. Pietro in Montorio. As you make the walk up, take in the sweeping views. If the gate is closed, continue walking on Via Garibaldi until you reach the church on your right.

To proceed to Tour 4 instead of climbing the hill, then from the Porta Settimiana continue straight on Via della Scala past **S. Maria della Scala** whose Carmelite Order rejected Caravaggio's *Death of a Virgin* (1601), through Piazza di S. Egidio and then turn left on Via della Paglia to Piazza S. Maria in Trastevere.

**San Pietro in Montorio** is a titular church founded around the 9th century that was rebuilt in 1481 by King Ferdinando II of Aragon and Queen Isabella I of Castille who funded Christopher Columbus's 1492 voyage to the New World. They were the parents of Catherine of Aragon, the first wife of King Henry VIII, and also the grandparents of the Holy Roman Emperor Charles the V, whose forces sacked Rome in 1527. The apse and campanile were damaged in 1849 but restored in 1851.

Raphael's *Transfiguration* hung in the apse from 1523 until it was taken to Paris by Napoleon. It was placed in the Pinacoteca Vaticana of the Vatican Museums when returned in 1815. Guido Reni's *Crucifixion of St Peter* was hung as a replacement but that too is now in the Pinacoteca Vaticana and the copy here is by Vincenzo Camuccini. In the pavement to the left of the high altar are the Irish Chieftains' Tombs associated with the Flight of the Earls (14 September 1607) of Hugh, Baron of Dungannon, son of Hugh O'Neill, the Earl of Tyrone, who is also buried here with Rory O'Donnell, the 1st Earl of Tyrconnell, and his brother Cathbharr, the brothers of Red Hugh O'Donnell.

Important works by prominent artists in the south chapels include the second chapel (Raimondi Chapel) that contains an early altar by Gian Lorenzo Bernini (*c.*1640). Giorgio Vasari painted the ceiling of the fourth chapel, where legend claims Beatrice Cenci is buried (no epitaph). The altarpiece *Conversion of St Paul* is also by Giorgio Vasari (1552) in the fifth chapel. Vasari was responsible for the decoration of the Del Monte Chapel at the end of the south side. The funerary monuments with reclining effigies to Cardinal Antonio Maria Ciocchi Del Monte (1461/2–1533, the uncle of Pope Julius III) to the left and Fabiano Del Monte (the great uncle of Pope Julius III) to the right and the balustrade with putti are by Bartolomeo Ammannati (1550–1555) and were commissioned by Pope Julius III, who selected Ammannati over Raffaello da Montelupo on the recommendation of Michelangelo.

Ammannati is more popularly known for his *Fontana del Nettuno* (1563–1565) in Piazza della Signoria, Florence. Michelangelo was later less favourable in his opinion of the figure of Neptune and claimed that Ammannati had ruined a beautiful piece of marble. Pope Julius III (Giovanni Maria Ciocchi Del Monte) is buried in the Vatican Grottoes, but these tombs have been attributed to him and his scandalous lover, Innocenzo Ciocchi Del Monte, who was adopted by the pope's brother, Cardinal Baldovino Ciocchi Del Monte, and made a 'cardinal nephew' and favoured for promotion and influence.

Bramante's **Tempietto** is in the convent courtyard next to the church (to the right facing the facade of the church and behind the iron gate). The tempietto is a martyr shrine that marks the location where church tradition formerly placed the location of St Peter's martyrdom that is now accepted to be in the area of the Circus of Gaius and Nero close to the Tomb of St Peter below the Basilica of St Peter (Tour 2). If the door is open, enter and look down to see the ancient Roman level.

This is one of Bramante's earliest works in Rome (*c.*1502) that launched Renaissance architecture as a systematic approach (to religious and secular architecture) based on ancient architectural principles of Vitruvius that were popularised by Leon Battista Alberti. Filippo Brunelleschi made earlier contributions with the facade of the Spedale degli Innocenti in Florence. The name tempietto, 'little temple', for a martyr shrine alludes to the transformative process of adapting its inspiration, the pagan Temple of Vesta (Tour 6), into a Christian martyr shrine. Bramante did the same on a larger scale in his designs for the new St Peter's Basilica and the Cortile del Belvedere of the Vatican Museums (Tour 2).

Exit S. Pietro in Montorio right and make a sharp right to walk around the church and then follow Via Garibaldi up to the Acqua Paola that is visible straight ahead. To your left is the **Mausoleo dei Garibaldini** (also called the Mausoleo Ossario Gianicolense) by Giovanni Jacobucci (1941) that commemorates the fallen during the Risorgimento (1849–1870). The Janiculum Hill was the site of important battles in the First Italian War of Independence (as was the Quirinal Hill in the Second Italian War of Independence) that are commemorated with the sites at the end of the tour. For a full history of the Risorgimento and the founding of the Italian Republic, visit the Museo Centrale del Risorgimento Italiano al

Vittoriano in the National Monument to Vittorio Emanuele II (Tour 7). The French dead are commemorated in the church of S. Luigi dei Francesi (Tour 8).

Pope Paul V Borghese used materials from the Temple of Minerva in the Forum of Nerva to create the **Acqua Paola** Fountain that is the terminus of the restored Aqueduct of Trajan from Bracciano. As with many of his projects, he was following Sixtus V's lead who had built the Acqua Felice aqueduct and constructed the Fontana dell'Acqua Felice (Moses Fountain) on the Quirinal Hill (Tour 11). The fountain, built between 1608 and 1612 by Flaminio Ponzio and Giovanni Fontana, evokes a Roman triumphal arch and theatre backdrop (*scaena frons*) like the Moses Fountain, but its scale and manipulation of water is a precursor to the Trevi Fountain as a *mostra*, a theatrical spectacle. Carlo Fontana added the large granite basin in 1690. The dragon and eagles are Borghese family emblems. A theatre now occupies the adjoining building. There are sweeping views from here as far as the Villa Medici and Basilica of S. Maria Maggiore. The fountain is a popular backdrop for Roman wedding photos.

To proceed to Tour 4 from the Acqua Paola, note that next to the Gates of the Passeggiata del Gianicolo is a flight of stairs that leads to a continuation of Via di S. Pancrazio past the Liceo Español 'Cervantes' Roma. At the bottom of the hill you will pass the Roman sarcophagus fountain again. Cross to the other side of Via Garibaldi to take a second flight of stairs just to your right. At the foot of the stairs, follow the winding Vicolo del Cedro. At the intersection where Vicolo del Cedro becomes Vicolo del Cinque, turn right on Via della Scala (you will see an 18th-century fresco of a Madonna with a bronze canopy) to Piazza S. Egidio. Walk through the piazza and turn left on Via della Paglia to Piazza S. Maria in Trastevere.

To linger on the Janiculum Hill, there are several options to explore with directions from the Acqua Paola Fountain: Piazzale Garibaldi for a scenic overlook of the city, the charming Villa Sciarra, or the vast grounds of the Villa Doria Pamphilj. Return to the Acqua Paola after the optional tours and follow directions above to proceed to Tour 4.

From the Acqua Paola, take the **Passegiatta del Gianicolo** that is accessed through gates on the right side of the Acqua Paola Fountain. In the centre of **Piazzale Garibaldi** is the **Equestrian statue of Giuseppe Garibaldi** by Emilio Gallori (1895) around which are statues of the Garibaldini (the name given to the Partigiani who fought on behalf of the Risorgimento). Four bronze statue groups are around the base (the Charge of Manara's Bersaglieri, Rome, 1849 and the Battle of Calatafimi, Sicily, 1860, with Europe and America at the sides) that bears his slogan, *Roma o Morte* ('Rome or Death'). Every day at noon, a cannon fires a blank shot. Garibaldi was a Ligurian but he lived in Uruguay and Brazil, after he fled Europe in 1836, where he met his remarkable wife Anita (Ana Maria de Jesus Ribeiro di Garibaldi). The **Equestrian statue of Anita Garibaldi** by Mario Rutelli (1932), who also designed the Fontana delle Naiadi in Piazza della Repubblica (Tour 12), is located near her husband's on Viale Aldo Fabrizi across from the Renaissance **Villa Lante al Gianicolo** that was built by Giulio Romano (1518–1527) and is now home to the Institutum Romanum Finlandiae. The statue was a gift by the Brazilian government in recognition of her Brazilian origin. She is depicted charging on horseback with pistol raised as she holds her infant son. The adventures of Garibaldi and Anita on campaign quickly became the stuff of romantic novels set against the backdrop of the Risorgimento. She died in Garibaldi's arms at the age of 28, pregnant and with malaria, during their retreat following the fall of Rome to French forces on 29 June 1849.

The Passeggiata continues past the **Manfredi Lighthouse** (built by Manfredo Manfredi in 1911 as a gift from Italian immigrants in Argentina) to **Sant'Onofrio** (with the Museo Tassiano dedicated to the poet Torquato Tasso, 1544–1595) and down to the Borgo.

For the **Villa Sciarra**, from the Acqua Paola Fountain, walk up the hill to the left of the fountain on Via Giacomo Medici. The Irish Embassy to the Holy See is to your left in the **Villa Nobili Spada** (1639). From Via Angelo Masina, you are walking alongside the **American Academy in Rome**, designed by McKim, Mead and White between 1912 and 1914 (the entrance is at No. 5 Via Angelo Masina), to your right that was founded as the American School of Architecture in Rome in 1894 and merged with the American School of Classical Studies in Rome in 1911. It was formerly housed in the Villa Aurora (Tour 11). Continue along the Aurelianic Walls on Via Pietro Roselli to the entrance to the Villa Sciarra on the opposite side of Via Calandrelli.

The **Villa Sciarra** was originally part of the vast vigna of Cardinal Antonio Barberini (the nephew of Pope Urban VIII Barberini) that stretched down the hill to Porta Portese. On the slopes, the ruins of the so-called Syrian Sanctuary (4th century CE) were discovered in 1906 (accessed from the steps on Via Dandalo next to No. 47). In antiquity, the gardens were the site of the grove dedicated to the water nymph Furrina where, in 121 BCE, the populist Tribune Sempronius Gaius Gracchus committed suicide. The Barberini Colonna di Sciarra acquired the villa in 1811. The casino suffered damage in 1849 and was rebuilt soon after. Prince Maffeo Sciarra Colonna went bankrupt in 1880, at which time the villa property was divided. Half was sold for residential development and the other half with the casino was later acquired by George Wurts and his wife Henrietta in 1902, who added the aviaries and gardens that they decorated with 18th-century sculpture from a Lombard villa near Milan. Henrietta donated the villa to the Italian state in 1930 as a public park. The casino was rebuilt in 1932 to house the Istituto Italiano di Studi Germanici. Return to the Acqua Paola to continue to Tour 4 or visit the Villa Doria Pamphilj by exiting the park left onto Via Calandrelli and crossing through the opening of the Aurelianic Walls and turning right to follow the Viale delle Mura Gianicolensi to Porta S. Pancrazio and follow directions below.

For the **Villa Doria Pamphilj**, from the Acqua Paola Fountain, walk up the hill to the right of the fountain to Porta S. Pancrazio. The **American Academy in Rome** on Via Angelo Masina is to your left and the **Villa Aurelia** to your right, built for Cardinal Girolamo Farnese in 1650, damaged in 1849 when it served as Garibaldi's headquarters. It is now the property of the American Academy in Rome (since 1909). The **Porta S. Pancrazio** in Piazzale Aurelio (on the site of the ancient Porta Aurelia) was built by Pope Urban VIII Barberini but was destroyed in 1849 by the French and rebuilt by Virginio Vespignani in 1854. The Porta Aurelia provided access from the west through the Aurelianic Walls from which the earlier consular road, the Via Aurelia, left the city and continued north to Pisa and later, with the addition of a network of roads, led to Arles in France, and Cadiz in Spain. To the right of the arch is the alternate entrance to the Passeggiata del Gianicolo. Immediately to the left inside the entrance is the **Casa di Michelangelo**, the house of Michelangelo that was moved here in 1941 (to serve as the facade of a water storage facility) from the area to the right of the Cordonata of Piazza del Campidoglio, after its demolition

near S. Maria di Loreto al Foro Traiano (Tour 6) for the construction
of the modern Piazza Venezia.

Continue on Via di S. Pancrazio. The entrance to the **Villa Doria
Pamphilj** is visible straight ahead past Viale delle Mura Gianicolo in
between where the road forks with the Via Aurelia Antica in Largo
Tre Giugno 1849. The site known as **il Vascello** is to your right and
is named for a Baroque villa that was destroyed in 1849. Enter the
Villa Doria Pamphilj and continue to a monumental gate in Piazzale
dei Ragazzi del 1849, known as the **Arco dei Quattro Venti** ('Arch
of the Four Winds'), that is built on the site of the **Villa Corsini**
that was also destroyed in 1849 and the property added to the Villa
Doria Pamphilj. The Casino del Bel Respiro is visible in the distance
to your right.

The Villa Doria Pamphilj is the largest public park in Rome and is
filled with copies of Roman sculpture and fountains that give a sense of
the luxury of ancient Horti. The park is popular as a fitness destination
with a soccer field and a grass running track. It was originally built for
Prince Camillo Pamphilj (the nephew of Pope Innocent X Pamphilj)
between 1644 and 1652 on part of the grounds of an older Villa Vecchia
and passed to Giovanni Andrea IV Doria in 1763 when Pope Clement
XIII appointed him heir to the Pamphilj since Girolamo Pamphilj
had died childless in 1760. The **Casino del Bel Respiro** (closed to the
public) was designed by the sculptor Alessandro Algardi (1644–1652)
and assisted by Giovanni Francesco Grimaldi to house the Pamphilj
collection of antiquities. Algardi made the stucco decoration and
designed the exterior to serve as a display area for sculpture in niches
and on balustrades. The garden parterre with formal gardens extended
down into an exedra-shaped grotto that contained Algardi's Fountain of
Venus, now in the Villa Vecchia.

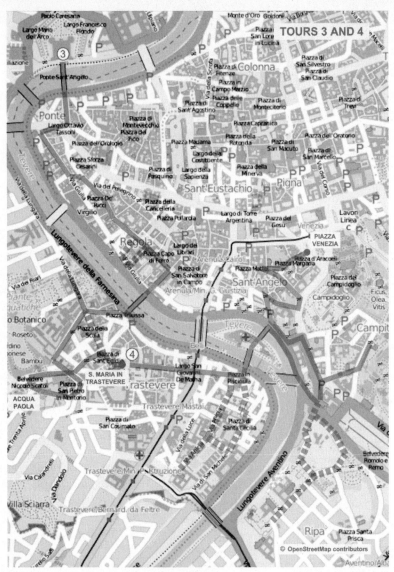

Sites: S. Maria in Trastevere; S. Crisogono (Option: S. Francesco a Ripa; Porta Portese Flea Market on Sundays; S. Cecilia in Trastevere; Medieval Synagogue); S. Benedetto in Piscinula; Tiber Island; Synagogue; Republican Temples; Casa dei Crescenzi; S. Maria in Cosmedin/Bocca della Verità (Optional stroll on the Aventine Hill: Parco Savello; S. Sabina; Sant'Alessio; Ordine dei Cavalieri di Malta; Roseto Comunale); Arch of Janus; S. Giorgio in Velabro; S. Teodoro; Area Sacra di Sant'Omobono; S. Nicola in Carcere; Ghetto; Porticus of Octavia, Theatre of Marcellus; S. Maria in Portico in Campitelli; Fontana delle Tartarughe in Piazza Mattei; Piazza Aracoeli.
Distance: 3.5km.

# BYZANTINE AND MEDIEVAL ROME IN TRASTEVERE AND AROUND THE GHETTO

Explore medieval Rome on both sides of the Tiber with a stroll that begins in the heart of Trastevere and continues over the Tiber into the historic areas of the Velabrum and former Ghetto. The tour focuses on the making of medieval Rome, with several churches built over ancient ruins that you can explore. The church interiors feature beautiful mosaics and frescoes by Pietro Cavallini that anticipate the naturalism of the Renaissance. Fascist reworking of the area centred on ancient monuments make explicit connections to Imperial Rome. Optional strolls in Trastevere and on the tranquil Aventine Hill offer more opportunities to explore Rome's early Christian and Jewish history.

The Basilica of S. Maria in Trastevere is in Piazza S. Maria in Trastevere. In the centre is the **Fontana in Piazza S. Maria in Trastevere**, an ancient fountain with wolf heads added at a later period and a basin that was redesigned many times by famous architects: Bramante, Giacomo della Porta, Girolamo Rainaldi, Bernini and Carlo Fontana (1692). In 1873, the Comune di Roma restored the fountain to its 1692 appearance. Facing the piazza is the 17th-century **Palazzo di S. Callisto**.

**Santa Maria in Trastevere**, founded by Pope Innocent II (between 1140 and 1143) as S. Maria trans Tiberim, was preceded by a 4th-century church on the site of an even earlier titular church of Pope St Calixtus I (217–222) that incorporated a hostel for retired soldiers (*taberna meritoria*). This earlier church (*titulus Callisti*) is one of the earliest in Rome and believed to be the earliest with open worship indicating that early Christians and their former Jewish communities lived in the area. The 4th-century church built by Pope Julius I (the name of *titulus Calixti* was changed to *titulus Julii*) is considered a possible forerunner to S. Maria Maggiore (Tour 12) as the first church dedicated to St Mary in Rome. Medieval legend held that the church is built on the spot where a stream of olive oil (*fons olei*) flowed either in 38 BCE or on the day of Christ's birth and is marked by a little opening (*finestrella*) between the altar and the Paschal candlestick. The nearby Via della Fonte d'Olio preserves this tradition.

The 12th-century mosaic on the facade depicts the Madonna enthroned nursing the infant Christ flanked by ten women, some with crowns, holding lamps. On the Romanesque campanile is a 17th-century mosaic of the Madonna and Child. In 1702, the facade was restored by Carlo Fontana who also replaced the medieval porch with the current portico with the statues of popes on the balustrade. Inside the portico are inscriptions, sarcophagi and sculptural fragments embedded in the walls from earlier buildings on the site and in the area.

The majestic interior recalls the grandeur of S. Maria Maggiore. Pope Innocent II acquired ancient Roman elements from various sites including the 22 columns of different heights and diameter, column bases and the elaborately carved marble slabs of the architrave. Eight of the Ionic capitals with the faces of Isis, Serapis and Harpocrates in the scrolls and volute are from the Baths of Caracalla (Tour 13). Ancient elements fared less well under Pope Pius IX who commissioned Virginio Vespignani to rework the church (1866–1877) including the 13th-century cosmatesque pavement. The gilded ceiling with a fresco of the *Assumption of the Blessed Virgin* (1617) is by Domenichino (1581–1641). The beautiful 12th-century mosaics in the triumphal arch and apse were completed after the death of Innocent II (1143). The apse mosaic, *Coronation of the Virgin* with St Mary seated next to Christ, is earlier than the mosaic with a similar theme in S. Maria Maggiore. Below a band of lambs representing the Apostles is Pietro Cavallini's important mosaic cycle on the *Life of the Virgin* (1291), commissioned by Bertoldo Stefaneschi. The panels extend onto the triumphal arch under the prophets. His frescoes in the Benedictine Convent of S. Cecilia in Trastevere show the same realism. Centred below this cycle behind the altar is a mosaic

(1290) of the Madonna with St Peter and St Paul who present the donor Bertoldo Stefaneschi. Over the altar is the venerated *Madonna della Clemenza* (6th/7th century).

Under the baldacchino with ancient porphyry columns by Virginio Vespignani are the relics of Pope St Calixtus I. The church also has relics of S. Apollonia and a piece of the Holy Sponge. The Paschal candlestick is by the Cosmati (13th century). The Chapel of the Winter Choir to the right of the sanctuary was completed to designs by Domenichino and restored by Henry Stuart, Cardinal Duke of York, who was titular head of the church from 1759 to 1761. His royal arms appear on the shield on the west wall above the main doors. The Avila Chapel (fifth on north side) by Antonio Gherardi (1680) plays with perspective and natural light to spectacular effect from an oculus held up by angels. The Chapel of S. Cecilia in S. Carlo ai Catinari (Tour 7) is another Gherardi masterpiece. The Tomb of Innocent II (1130–1143), who was from Trastevere, is by Virginio Vespignani. The ruins of a Roman house were discovered under the floor of the baptistery.

Walk through the piazza to your left and continue along **Via della Lungaretta** which corresponds to a section of the ancient Via Aurelia Vetus that remained the main thoroughfare in medieval Rome (known as the Via Transtiberina), leading from Porta S. Pancrazio on the Janiculum Hill to the Ponte S. Maria (the ancient Pons Aemilius) over the Tiber, now known as the Ponte Rotto. An arch known as the 'Arco dei Cavalieri' spanned the Via della Lungaretta until it was demolished in 1603. Along the street were the most fashionable medieval houses on this side of the Tiber, with workshops and the homes of tradesmen located on the crowded side streets. In the piazza at the intersection of Viale di Trastevere (Largo S. Giovanni de Matha), adjacent to the larger Piazza Sonnino, is the church of **Sant'Agata** to your left that contains the image of the *Madonna de' Noantri* that is venerated in Trastevere in a festival every July called the Festa de' Noantri.

**San Crisogono** to your right was built in 1129 by Giovanni da Crema on the foundations of an earlier 5th-century titular church (titulus Crisogoni) over 2nd-century Imperial-era ruins that were discovered in 1907. The Romanesque campanile with the distinct pyramid top was added in the 12th century. The current Classical facade is part of the 17th-century reconstructions for Cardinal Scipione Caffarelli Borghese, the nephew of Pope Paul V Borghese. The Borghese family emblems of the dragon and eagle, incorporated into the exterior and interior decoration, is also reflected in the name of Piazza del Drago that once faced the church but is now across the street behind the row of buildings along the Viale di Trastevere (formerly called the Viale de Re, 'Boulevard of the King') that was opened in 1888.

The solemn interior has 22 ancient columns with stucco Ionic capitals that were added in the 17th century. Two monumental ancient porphyry columns support the triumphal arch. Columns of various stones were sliced to make the medallions in the cosmateque pavement (13th century). Four ancient columns of yellow alabaster support the baldacchino by Giovanni Battista Soria over the high altar that contains the relics of St Chrysogonus. The apse contains a 13th-century mosaic of the *Madonna and Child between St James and St Chrysogonus* by Pietro Cavallini or his school. The design of the chapel to the right of the sanctuary is attributed to Bernini. On the north side is a cosmatesque tabernacle from the 5th-century church and inscriptions relating to the church's history. The ceiling fresco is a copy of the *San Crisogono in Glory* (1622) by Guercino, a nickname ('squinter') that he received since he was cross-eyed. The original was removed in 1808 to Stafford House, London.

The **Archaeological Area** (scavi) beneath the church is accessed through the sacristy off the north transept. The apse at the bottom of the entrance stairs contains the fragments of 8th-century frescoes in the annular crypt (that contained the relics of St Chrysogonus), depicting St Chrysogonus with St Anastasia and St Rufus. Basins discovered beneath the floor of the church suggest that the titular church was originally founded on a laundry site (*fullonica*) and the basins were adapted for baptism. Along the south wall of the church are fragments of an 11th-century fresco cycle of St Sylvester and a fresco of St Benedict curing a leper.

Exit the church and cross Viale di Trastevere. To your left as you cross is the 13th-century **Palazzetto dell'Anguillara** with one of the few remaining medieval towers along the bank of the river. It now houses the **Casa di Dante** with a library including the finest Dante collection in Italy. The barracks (*excubitorium*) of the **VII Cohort** of the fire and police brigade (*Cohortes Vigilum*) that date to the reign of Augustus are to your right as you walk through Piazza del Drago.

Continue walking along Via della Lungaretta to the end of the street in Piazza in Piscinula. To your right is the small Benedictine church of **S. Benedetto in Piscinula**. Inside the atrium is the room of St Benedict. The restored interior has beautiful frescoes, cosmatesque floor and ancient columns. At the end of the piazza to your left is the medieval **Casa Mattei** with ancient sculptural fragments embedded into the walls. Climb the short flight of steps to cross the Lungotevere degli Alberteschi and walk across the **Ponte Cestio** to Tiber Island (described after optional tour). The Ponte Cestio was demolished when the Tiber Embankment was constructed (1888–1992) and rebuilt with a longer span and only one of the original arches, the centre one. The National Monument to Vittorio Emanuele II rises above S. Bartolomeo, and to your right are the ruins of the **Ponte Rotto** (Pons Aemilius) from which the body of Emperor Elagabulus was thrown in 222 CE.

To linger in Trastevere before crossing to the other side of the Tiber for an optional itinerary to see Bernini's *Blessed Beata Ludovica Albertoni* in S. Francesco a Ripa, S. Cecilia in Trastevere built on the site of her house, and medieval sites associated with Jewish history, then continue on Via della Lungaretta to just before Piazza in Piscinula. Turn right on Via dell'Arco de' Tolomei. Walk under the arch and continue on Via Anicia past the church of **S. Maria dell'Orto** to your right into Piazza di S. Francesco d'Assisi. This piazza contains a Column monument (from Veii) erected by Pope Pius IX in 1847 to commemorate his restoration of the area centred on Piazza Mastai, named for the pope's family.

**San Francesco a Ripa** was built in 1231 by Onorio Longhi on the site of an earlier hospice where St Francis stayed in 1219 and a church dedicated to S. Biagio (St Blaise). As part of the demolition of the earlier church, Pietro Cavallini's St Francis fresco cycle was destroyed. The cell that St Francis occupied above the present sacristy was preserved and is shown by request. In addition to the saint's relics, a copy of Margaritone d'Arezzo's portrait of him is displayed. The original is now in the Pinacoteca Vaticana (Tour 2). The interior is richly decorated. In the Paluzzi Albertoni Chapel in the north transept is Bernini's masterful sculpture of the *Blessed Beata Ludovica Albertoni* (1671–1675) that recalls his earlier *Ecstasy of St Teresa* in S. Maria della Vittoria (Tour 11). The altarpiece is by Baciccia (Giovanni Battista Gaulli). The third chapel on the north side contains the tomb of artist

Giorgio de Chirico (1888–1978). The church was used as a barracks by the Bersaglieri from 1873 to 1943.

From S. Francesco a Ripa, retrace your steps on Via Anicia to Via della Madonna dell'Orto that faces the front of the church. Turn right and continue to Via di S. Michele then turn left and follow into Piazza di S. Cecilia in Trastevere. Facing the church at No. 19 in Piazza dei Mercanti is a restored medieval building with ancient columns and the remnants of a turret.

To visit **Porta Portese**, exit the church of S. Francesco a Ripa left to walk a short distance around the left side of the complex on Via di Porta to reach Porta Portese. The vast **Isituto S. Michele a Ripa** complex that includes the Ministry of Cultural Assets and the Environment that stretches along the Porto di Ripa Grande dominates Piazza di Porta Portese. On the Tiber side of the building is the **Fontana del Timone** ('Fountain of the Helm') by Pietro Lombardi (1927) to commemorate the Ripa Grande. The ancient Porta Portuensis that was the entry point into Rome of Genseric and the Vandals in 455 was demolished in 1643 and rebuilt by Pope Urban VIII Barberini. Porta Portese was rebuilt by Pope Pius IX in 1849 when destroyed by the French during the campaign that also destroyed many buildings on the Janiculum Hill (Tour 3). A flea market is held here on Sundays. Outside of the walls, ancient Jewish catacombs discovered in 1602 were destroyed in the construction of Pope Urban VIII Barberini's walls. After the move to the area of the former Ghetto, Jews continued to bury their dead in the *Ortaccio degli Ebrei*, the plain outside of the walls of Porta Portese to the foot of the Janiculum Hill that was also called the *Campus Iudaeorum* until the Comune granted burial in the Roseto Comunale on the slope of the Aventine Hill from 1645 to 1934. Like all burials, ancient Jewish catacombs and funerary monuments were located outside the city walls including the area of Monteverde on the southern slope of the Janiculum Hill overlooking the *Campus*. Titular inscriptions from the Catacomb from the Via Portuense Necropolis are now dispersed in museum collections in Naples and Rome including the Vatican Museums (Tour 2) and the Capitoline Museums. From Porta Portese retrace your steps to S. Francesco a Ripa and follow the directions (above) to S. Cecilia in Trastevere.

Pope St Paschal I (817–824) built the current **S. Cecilia in Trastevere** over the site of an earlier 5th-century titular church (*titulus Caeciliae*) located on the site of the house of St Cecilia and her husband St Valerian. Saint Cecilia, the patron saint of music, belonged to the aristocratic family of the Caecilii and she was martyred with her husband in 230 under the Emperor Alexander Severus. In front of the church is a large courtyard with an ancient Roman urn (cantharus) in the centre. In the choir of the **Benedictine Convent** (the building in the courtyard to the left of the church entrance) is the beautiful fresco of the *Last Judgement* (*c.*1290) by Pietro Cavallini. The fresco was rediscovered in 1900 during renovations to the choir and is a rare example of pre-Giotto painting in Rome that shows an emerging realism from stylised iconic Byzantine art.

The facade by Ferdinando Fuga (1741–1742) with spoliated ancient columns and a mosaic frieze opens into a portico with pavement tombs, medieval sculpture and inscription fragments embedded into the walls. Inside, 19th-century stucco covers the ancient columns to form an arcade of piers with screens above the side aisles that allowed nuns to attend services. The ceiling fresco is Sebastiano Conca's *Coronation of St Cecilia*. On the west wall is the funerary monument to Cardinal Niccolò Forteguerri (d. 1473) attributed to Mino da Fiesole. On the other side of the entrance is the Tomb of Cardinal Adam Easton of Hertford (d. 1398).

The apse mosaic (9th century) depicts Christ the Redeemer in the centre with saints including Pope St Paschal I holding a model of the church (left). The square blue nimbus signifies that Paschal I was still alive at the time of the mosaic's creation. He is similarly represented in the apse mosaics of other churches that he rebuilt: S. Prassede (Tour 12) and S. Maria in Domnica (Tour 13). Under the baldacchino (1293) signed by Arnolfo di Cambio is the high altar with Stefano Maderno's effigy of S. Cecilia (1600) that recreates the position of her body at its discovery in 1599 in the presence of Maderno in the Catacombs of San Callisto (Tour 14). Her gesture with three fingers represents the Trinity. Pope Clement VIII Aldobrandini translated her relics here.

A corridor from the south aisle with landscapes by the Flemish painter Paul Bril leads to the *caldarium* (hot water room of a Roman bath) that was the site of her martyrdom: after surviving a scalding here, she was taken to another room to be beheaded but she survived the botched execution and lived for three more days. Over the altar is Guido Reni's *Beheading of St Cecilia*. Opposite is his *Mystical Marriage of St Cecilia and St Valerian*. The **Archaeological Area** (scavi) is accessed at the end of the north side through a small gift shop. Below the church are the ruins of a house (*domus*) whose atrium contained a pool and a wall shrine (*lararium*) with a terra cotta relief of Minerva and two panels of bacchic offerings and an apartment building (*insula*) from the early 2nd century CE. Other elements of the site are difficult to identify but span the late Republic to the 4th century CE.

Exit the church and walk left on Via di S. Cecilia to Via de' Genovesi. Turn left and look to your right for **Vicolo dell'Atleta**. This charming alley with medieval buildings that incorporate fragments of ancient sculpture is named after the statue of the *Apoxyomenos*, now in the Vatican Museums but found here in 1844. The medieval building to your left at Nos 13 and 14 is the **Medieval Synagogue** founded by Rabbi Nathan ben Jachiel (1035–1106), the lexicographer and scholar of the Talmud who wrote a dictionary called the *Arukh*. The central column holding up the arch has faint traces of Hebrew.

The Jewish community in Rome is over 2,000 years old and is the oldest of the Diaspora to Europe, but ties to Rome predate the arrival of slaves brought by Pompey the Great in 63 BCE and later freed by Julius Caesar: Judah Maccabee sent an embassy to the Senate in 161 BCE to seek friendship with Rome. Their numbers increased when Jewish slaves were brought to Rome following Vespasian's Sack of Jerusalem in 70 CE. The main ancient synagogue was in the area around S. Cecilia in Trastevere but it burned down in the fire of 1268. The date of its destruction and the active cemeteries in the area of Porta Portese indicate that Jews continued to have ties to this side of the Tiber after their move to the area of the former Ghetto in 1084 following Robert Guiscard's destruction of the area. Other ancient Jewish communities were located outside the Porta Capena (Tour 13) and Ostia Antica (Tour 15).

At the end of the vicolo, turn left on Via dei Salumi then turn right on Via in Piscinula and follow into Piazza in Piscinula. To your immediate left is the church of **S. Benedetto in Piscinula**. At the end of the piazza straight ahead is the medieval **Casa Mattei**. Climb the short flight of steps to cross the Lungotevere degli Alberteschi and walk across the **Ponte Cestio** to Tiber Island.

On the boat-shaped **Tiber Island** was the ancient Temple of Aesculapius, the god of healing, that was dedicated in 293 BCE to commemorate the arrival in Rome from Epidaurus by boat (trireme) of his symbol, the sacred serpent, that rid the city of plague. According to legend, the serpent escaped upon his arrival but was found on the island and so the cult of Aesculapius was established here. On the prow end of the island is a relief of the snake around the staff that the god holds. The remnants of the boat structure date to a reconstruction in the first century BCE.

To your right in the piazza that contains a spire monument by Ignazio Jacometti (1869) is the church of **S. Bartolomeo all'Isola** that was built in the 10th century in honour of St Adalbert, the Bishop of Prague, over the site of the Temple of Aesculapius. The Latin inscription on the facade states that the church contains the relics of St Bartholomew. Ancient elements preserved in the church include 14 columns, an ancient column that was carved into a wellhead (11th century) and placed on the sanctuary steps to mark the location of a spring sacred to the temple, and a porphyry tub from the Baths of Caracalla (Tour 13) that serves as the high altar.

To your left are the **Ospedale dei Fatebenefratelli** (founded in 1548), part of the legacy of the island as a place of healing isolated from the rest of the city, and the church of **S. Giovanni Calibita**, with its distinctive campanile. Opposite is the **Torre Caetani**, part of a Caetani family stronghold, acquired when Pope Boniface VIII Caetani was pope, and one of the few remaining medieval towers to survive along the Tiber. It originally belonged to the Pierleoni, a Jewish banking family founded in the 11th century that eventually converted to Christianity and produced Pope Anacletus II, the antipope to Innocent II. Fragments of sculpture are embedded into the exterior, including the head of a woman who appears to be looking out of a window.

Cross the second footbridge, the **Ponte Fabricio** (the ancient Pons Fabricius built by Lucius Fabricius in 62 BCE), the oldest bridge to survive from ancient Rome. Buidlings to either side of the bridge were cleared for the construction of the Embankment and the Lungotevere. On the parapet are two distinctive four-headed marble herms that give the bridge the alternate name of Ponte Quattro Capi. The bridge was renamed the 'Pons Judaeorum' following the migration of Jews from the Trastevere side of the Tiber to the area of the former Ghetto site in Rione Sant'Angelo. The square dome of the Great Synagogue is visible ahead just to your left. The synagogue is included in the itinerary below but if you wish to proceed immediately to the former Ghetto, cross to the other side of the street and follow the tour from that point.

Once across the bridge, turn right to walk along the Tiber side of Lungotevere dei Pierleoni for a view of Tiber Island and the Ponte Rotto to your right. In the medieval era, the grain mills of the Cenci family that extended out into the river were located here. Cross to the other side of the street when you reach the Ponte Palatino (the exit point of the 6th-century BCE sewer, the Cloaca Maxima, is visible below from the other side of the bridge) to enter into **Piazza Bocca della Verità** in Rione Ripa and walk down the steps to enter the piazza.

The **Republican Temples of the Forum Boarium** survive in the area of the ancient Cattle Market (Forum Boarium), an area once lined with temples that indicates the importance of the harbour (Portus Tiberinus) that was located between the Temple of Portunus and the temples below S. Nicola in Carcere. The vegetable and oil market (Forum Holitorium) extended from the Forum Boarium to the base of the Capitoline Hill. In the medieval era, the area was home to Byzantine rite churches for the Greek and Middle Eastern Catholic communities, many of whose members were refugees from iconoclastic persecution in Constantinople. They brought with them the worship of saints important to the Eastern Orthodox Church, such as St Nicholas (S. Nicola in Carcere) and St Valentine (S. Maria in Cosmedin). The association of the area with Greeks goes back to the legendary Arcadian Evander who settled the Palatine Hill where according to an earlier legend Hercules had defeated the monster Cacus and set up the Ara Maxima in the Forum Boarium to mark his victory. The area at the foot of the Palatine Hill is the Velabrum where according to legend a she-wolf discovered and nursed the infant Romulus and Remus. This area was significantly altered in the Fascist era along with the area of the Forum Holitorium.

The two Republican temples in the piazza survive because they were converted into churches. They were restored and later additions were removed under the direction of Mussolini's main cultural consultant, the archaeologist and architect **Antonio Muñoz** (1884–1960), who served as Superintendent of the Monuments of Lazio (1914–1928) and Inspector General of Antiquities and Fine Arts of the Government of Rome (1928–1944). He renovated many of the medieval churches on this tour and was responsible for renovating the city's ancient sites as part of the propaganda of Fascist ideology that altered the city's urban core.

The round temple formerly known as the Temple of Vesta because of its similarity to the temple in the Roman Forum (Tour 6) is actually the **Temple of Hercules Victor** (2nd century BCE) and is the oldest marble building in the city. The cult of Hercules in the area is due to the proximity of the **Circus Maximus** at one end of which was the **Ara Maxima of Hercules** in the area directly behind the church of S. Maria in Cosmedin. The god's associations with suffering and the reward of fame and immortality appealed to athletes competing in the circus. The roof gives the temple a distinctive look because it is missing the entablature level. The temple was converted into the church of S. Stefano delle Carozze in 1132 and later into S. Maria del Sole in the 17th century. Like the Temple of Vesta in the Roman Forum, the temple influenced Bramante's design of his Tempietto (Tour 3).

The **Temple of Portunus** (formerly known as the Temple of Fortuna Virilis) is dedicated to the god of harbours and dates from the 2nd century BCE with some reconstruction from the 1st century BCE. The temple serves as a reminder of how important the ports along the Tiber were to the ancient and medieval city. The Roman temple in the Ionic order stands on a high podium orientated to the front portico and is one the best-preserved temples to survive antiquity. The cella that contained the cult statue is enclosed with engaged columns. The temple was converted to the church of S. Maria Egiziaca (St Mary the Egyptian) in 872. The 9th-century fresco fragments are now in Palazzo Massimo (Museo Nazionale Romano, Tour 12). The Armenian church of S. Lorenzo dei Cavalluzzi was relocated here when Pope Paul IV Carafa segregated the former Ghetto from the rest of the city in 1555. The Temple of Harmony (1767) at Haiswell House, Goathurst, Somerset, is a replica.

Across the street is the medieval **Casa dei Crescenzi** (built between 1040 and 1065), with ancient elements built into the exterior. Over the door is an inscription that states that the house was built by Nicholas Crescenzi to restore the glory of ancient Rome. The house was also known as the **Casa di Pilota** since it was used as the house of Pontius Pilate for re-enactments of the Via Crucis on Good Friday due to the similarity of the area to the Holy Land.

Walk through the piazza past the **Fontana dei Tritoni** (Fountain of the Tritons) by Carlo Bizzaccheri (1717) for Pope Clement XI that imitates Bernini's Fontana del Tritone in Piazza Barberini. A trough that was also commissioned by the pope was moved to a nearby park along the Lungotevere opposite the Clivo di Rocca Savelli. An entry point to the Cloaca Maxima is visible under a square travertine lid near the fountain.

**Santa Maria in Cosmedin**, an 8th-century minor basilica church of Greek-Melkite rite, incorporates two ancient buildings: the side portico walls of a Christian centre for charitable works (*diaconia*) that dates to around 600 CE and the colonnaded gallery connected to the Ara Maxima of Hercules (formerly thought to be the *Statio Annonae*, the office of the market inspector). Columns from these structures are incorporated into the church and below are fragments of the Ara Maxima of Hercules. Robert Guiscard destroyed an oratory, a sacristy and an adjoining papal residence in 1084. Cardinal Alfano (Camerlengo of Pope Calixtus II) restored the church around 1123 and added the schola cantorum and campanile. The 18th-century facade by Giuseppe Sardi (1715–1719) was removed in 1894–1899 and returned to its original medieval appearance. In the portico is the **Bocca della Verità**, an ancient fountain head with the face of a river god placed here in 1632 that is legendary for testing the truthfulness of those who put their hand into its mouth (*bocca*). Against the wall is the canopy funerary monument to Cardinal Alfano.

The restored medieval interior is of three naves, separated by an arcade, all of which end in an apse with fresco decoration throughout from the 8th to the 12th centuries. The columns come from the adjacent ancient buildings that are of different granite varieties, heights, diameter and capitals. The schola cantorum is by the Cosmati who designed the screen, episcopal throne, paschal candelabrum and the pavement. Over the high altar made from an ancient porphyry tub is a baldacchino (1294) by the family of the Cosmati (Deodatus, the third son of Cosma). An altar on the north side contains the reliquary of St Valentine with a floral crown around his skull. The **Archaeological Area** (scavi) below the church contains the Crypt of Pope Hadrian I and a portion of the tufa block wall from the Ara Maxima of Hercules. In the gift shop (formerly the sacristy) is a mosaic fragment of the *Adoration of the*

*Magi* (706) originally from the Oratory of Pope John VIII in Old St Peter's Basilica.

To continue with the tour itinerary, exit the church and turn right and walk along the sidewalk (past the building that Muñoz opened as the Museo di Roma until it was moved to the current Palazzo Braschi) until you reach Piazza Bocca della Verità. You will see the **Arch of Janus** to your right through which S. Giorgio in Velabro is visible (described after optional tour).

To take the optional stroll (approximately 2.5km to return to S. Maria in Cosmedin) on the serene Aventine Hill to visit the Parco Savello with a panoramic view of the city and more sites associated with early Christianity and Jewish Rome, exit S. Maria in Cosmedin, turn left and cross to the other side of Via della Greca. Walk about 90m along Via di S. Maria in Cosmedin until you see steps at the base of a lane to your left called **Clivo di Rocca Savelli**. Climb the steps that become a lane that winds past the ruin walls of the Savelli palace fortress.

At the top, turn right onto Via di S. Sabina and walk along the wall for the entrance into Parco Savello. If the main entrance is closed, continue around the corner for the side entrance facing the church of S. Sabina with the **Fontana del Mascherone di S. Sabina** designed by Giacomo della Porta. The mask was originally added to the round basin found in the Roman Forum, now in Piazza del Quirinale (Tour 11). When the basin was moved, the mask was placed above a trough along the right bank of the Tiber before being placed here in 1936. **Parco Savello**, also called the Giardino degli Aranci (Garden of Oranges), is a walled orange grove providing panoramic views of the city on the site of the Savelli palace fortress (12th century) that was later given to the Basilica of S. Sabina.

The Basilica of **S. Sabina all'Aventino** was founded by Peter of Illyria (422–432) on the site of the original titulus of the Roman matron Sabina. In 1219, Pope Honorius III Savelli gave the basilica to St Dominic to found his Order. In the adjoining convent, the room in which St Dominic lived and had a meeting with St Francis is now a chapel (closed to the public). The convent is also associated with St Thomas Aquinas who taught there. Antonio Muñoz restored the church in 1919 and 1937 and reversed earlier modifications made by Domenico Fontana and Borromini. In the Sack of 410, Alaric and the Visigoths destroyed the aristocratic enclave on the Aventine Hill (formerly associated with plebeians under the Roman Republic) where Trajan lived before becoming emperor. Imperial-era temples and bath complexes in the area provided building materials for the basilica's construction. It is one of the best examples of early Christian basilicas to survive.

In the atrium, along with fragments of Christian inscriptions and sarcophagi, are 5th-century door panels with scenes from the Old and New Testament including one of the earliest representations of the crucifixion. The stark interior focuses the eye on the 24 Corinthian columns that support the clerestory in an arcade to form three aisles. Surviving the restoration are 5th-century inlay decoration along the arcade and the mosaic Latin inscription in hexameter verse over the main entrance that records the foundation of the church and declares the universal power of the Bishop of Rome. It is framed by two female figures representing conversions to Christianity by Jews (*Excircumcisione*) and pagans (*Exgentibus*). In the centre of the nave is the pavement Tomb of Fra Muñoz de Zamora (d. 1300). The schola cantorum, the apse and the bishop's throne were made in 1936 from ancient materials. The original apse fresco by Taddeo Zuccari was repainted by Vincenzo Camuccini (1836). There is a replica of the baldacchino in Forest Lawn Cemetery, Glendale, California. A small museum (Museo Domenicano di S. Sabina all'Aventino) requires prior appointment.

Continue along Via di S. Sabina. The church of **Sant'Alessio all'Aventino** is to your right though the entrance gate at No. 23. The church fronted by a quadriporticus was originally dedicated to St Boniface but is now commonly referred to as Ss. Bonifacio e Alessio. The origins of the church's foundation are obscure but Pope Honorius III Savelli rebuilt it in 1217 on the original *titulus* of St Boniface. In 1750, the Baroque interior was added but a few Romanesque elements such as the campanile and crypt survive. The Cappella di S. Alessio by Andrea Bergondi (the first chapel on the north side) contains a gesso portrait of St Alessio. Above him is a theca made of glass containing the stairs under which he lived and died. Formerly, the space held the cenotaph of Pope Honorius IV Savelli who died in the nearby family palace fortress in 1287. Stairs below the main altar lead to the crypt that is believed to contain the relics of St Thomas à Becket of Canterbury

At the end of the street in Piazza dei Cavalieri di Malta is the monumental entrance to the **Ordine dei Cavalieri di Malta** (Order of the Knights of Malta), designed in 1765 by the engraver Giovanni Battista Piranesi (1720–1778) who also designed the church of **S. Maria del Priorato** on the grounds where he is buried. These are his only architectural works. The Knights of Malta were founded in 1113 by the Blessed Gerard following the First Crusade as the Order of the Knights of St John of Jerusalem or the Knights Hospitallers by papal bull of Pope Paschal II to assist pilgrims to the Holy Land. Prior to their residency in Rome, the Order was based on the Island of Rhodes (1310–1522) and the Island of Malta (until 1798). The Military Order of Malta is considered the world's smallest sovereign state. Look through the portal keyhole to see the dome of St Peter's Basilica. Opposite are the Benedictine seminary designed by Francesco Vespignani (1892–1898), the church of **Sant'Anselmo** where Mass is celebrated with Gregorian Chant. Adjacent is a Benedictine shop.

Retrace your steps on Via di S. Sabina and continue past the entrance to the Clivo di Rocca Savelli for the entrance to the **Roseto Comunale** (Via di Valle Murcia, No. 6), a beautiful rose garden facing the Circus Maximus. This was the site of the Jewish Cemetery (Orto degli Ebrei) from 1645 to 1934, when it was moved to Campo Verano Cemetery (Tour 11). The rows of roses are planted in the shape of a Menorah and there is a view of the synagogue's dome from the grounds. In antiquity, it was the location of the ancient Murcia valley that included a Temple of Flora. The area below the Roseto, with a monument to Giuseppe Mazzini (1805–1872), was designed by Antonio Muñoz (1935).

Descend the Aventine Hill by the Clivo dei Publicii, an ancient road, to return to Via della Greca. The Circus Maximus and the Palatine Hill beyond it are within view ahead and then to your right as you descend down the Hill. Cross to the other side of the street at the intersection to return to S. Maria in Cosmedin. Walk past the church and follow the curve of the sidewalk. Cross the busy Via dei Cerchi. The Arch of Janus is to your right through which S. Giorgio in Velabro is visible.

The **Arch of Janus** is a quadrifons (four-fronted) triumphal arch with two orders of niches from the beginning of the 4th century that may be in honour of Constantine the Great or his son Constantius II. The keystones above each arch contain reliefs of two seated goddesses: Roma and Juno; and of two standing: Minerva and possibly Ceres. It survives since it had been converted into a Frangipane family stronghold.

In 1830, the attic level was removed because it was thought to be a medieval addition.

Continue past the arch and walk up the short flight of stairs to Via del Velabro that leads to S. Giorgio in Velabro. The street at the top of the stairs that intersects Via del Velabro is called **S. Giovanni Decollato** (St John the Beheaded) and is named for the little church that is rarely opened. At the corner is the medieval **Casa dei Pierleoni** that was relocated here by Antonio Muñoz. He lived here overlooking the piazza that he designed as a terminal point to Piazza Venezia.

The church of **S. Giorgio in Velabro** dedicated to St George (martyred *c*.300) preserves in its name a reference to the ancient Velabrum area. Built on the site of a Christian diaconia of the 5th–6th centuries, the church was originally dedicated to St Sebastian by Leo II in the 7th century. It received its Romanesque appearance in the 12th century. The interior was restored by Antonio Muñoz (1923–1926) to its medieval appearance with reopened windows of the clerestory. A 13th-century baldacchino covers the altar that contains a reliquary with the skull of St George that was brought to Rome by Pope Zacharias in the 8th century. The apse fresco, *Christ with the Virgin and Saints George, Peter, and Sebastian*, is by Pietro Cavallini (*c*.1296), but was restored in the 16th century. The latest restoration of the church followed the destruction of part of the external wall and the portico by a Mafia car bomb on 27 July 1993, with ancient materials used for the rebuilding.

The **Arch of the Argentarii**, next to S. Giorgio, was not damaged by the bomb. The arch was erected to the Emperor Septimius Severus by moneychangers and cattle merchants of the area in 204 and may have been at the head of an ancient street that led into the Roman Forum. The dedication inscription mentions Septimius Severus, his wife Julia Domna and their son and future Emperor Caracalla. The names of Caracalla's brother Geta, Plautilla, the wife of Caracalla, and her father Plautianus, all of whom were put to death by Caracalla, were removed in an act intended to erase their existence from memory. Further signs of erasure are evident in the two reliefs on the interior of the arch. The Arch of Septimius Severus in the Roman Forum (Tour 6) shows similar signs of erasure. Across the piazza at No. 3 is an arch opening of the Cloaca Maxima.

Exit left from S. Giorgio in Velabro and turn left on Via di San Teodoro. The street corresponds to the ancient Vicus Tuscus. The church of **S. Teodoro al Palatino** is just ahead to your right below the current street level, with the building foundations of the Palatine Hill towering above. The church dates to the 6th century and was restored under Pope Nicholas V (*c.*1453), possibly by the Florentine architect Bernardo Rossellino. It is dedicated to St Theodore Amasea (also known as St Theodore Tyro) who was martyred in 311 CE in Turkey and is venerated as a Great Martyr in the Eastern Orthodox Church. The circular church was built on the site of the granary of Agrippa (Horrea Agrippiana) that was later used as a Christian diaconia. The courtyard with a pagan altar in the centre and double staircase was designed by Carlo Fontana (1642–1645). The *Capitoline She-Wolf* now in the Capitoline Museums was found next to the church. The apse contains a much-restored 6th-century mosaic of Christ (seated on an orb) and saints.

Retrace your steps to S. Giorgio in Velabro and return to the staircase at the end of Via del Velabro. At the foot of the steps, continue straight (with the Temple of Portunus directly in front of you). Turn right on Via Luigi Petroselli. It was named Via del Mare, together with its extension Via del Teatro di Marcello, by the Fascists when constructed to designate the route to Porta S. Paolo and to Ostia Antica from Piazza Venezia. To your right are an ancient travertine pedestal and altar with a wreath and a fragmentary inscription that is dedicated to *Concordia Augusta* discovered near the Temple of Portunus in 1939. Continue on Via Luigi Petroselli. The plaque on the Fascist-era building to your left, **Palazzo dell'Anagrafe** designed by Cesare Valle (1936–1937), with the She-Wolf nursing Romulus and Remus and inscription with Mussolini's name, references the twin's association with the Velabrum and alludes to Mussolini's refounding of Imperial Rome.

The archaeological area known as the **Area Sacra di Sant'Omobono** is at the corner to your right. Excavations of the site below and surrounding the church of Sant'Omobono begun in 1937 continue today. The site contains a series of ancient temples (seven construction phases that span the archaic to the early Imperial period, though evidence of cult activity goes back to the 9th century BCE) including two temples of the archaic period dedicated to Fortuna and Mater Matuta believed to have been founded by King Servius Tullius (578–535 BCE). The terracotta pediment decoration of Hercules and Minerva from one of the Republican-era temples (3rd century BCE) is now in the Capitoline Museums.

Cross to the other side of the Vico Jugario, the ancient Vicus Jugarius that exited the Republican Walls through a double arch gate called the **Porta Carmentalis**. At the corner is a late Republican porticus that consists of two parallel arcades that may have been part of the **Porticus Triumphalis** that was situated along the initial route of the triumphal procession between the Circus Flaminius and the **Porta Triumphalis**. To your far right is the church of **S. Maria della Consolazione** with a facade by Martino Longhi (1583–1606). Cross to the other side of Via del Teatro di Marcello. At the corner is S. Nicola in Carcere.

The 11th-century church of **S. Nicola in Carcere** (St Nicholas in Prison) is dedicated to St Nicholas of Myra, the St Nick of later Santa Claus tradition. Contrary to the name of the church, he was not imprisoned here, but rather the titular church (possibly 7th century) was built over the ruins of three **Roman Republican Temples in the Forum Holitorium** that had been built side by side, and later used as a prison: the Temple of Janus, the Temple of Juno Sospita (in the Ionic style) and the Temple of Spes ('Hope') in the Doric style. A fourth temple (the Temple of Pietas) that stood in a row with these three temples was demolished for the construction of the Theatre of Marcellus under the Emperor Augustus. The interior dates to 1128 and contains ancient elements: mismatched spoliated columns and capitals along the central nave and a green porphyry tub beneath the high altar and baldacchino (1856). It was remodelled by Giacomo della Porta (1599) who also designed the facade but left the medieval campanile unchanged. The *Trinity* (west wall) is attributed to Guercino. The church was renovated in 1808 by Giuseppe Valadier, in 1865 (apse frescoes) and again in 1932 when later additions to the building were removed including the medieval house with a tower across the street that was moved from this area. The **Archaeological Area** (scavi) is accessible on a guided tour of the subterranean area with the ancient temple foundations.

Walk along Via del Foro Olitorio (with a good view of the Temple of Spes ruins along the outer wall of the church) and then along the right side of Lungotevere dei Cenci past **Piazza di Monte Savello** and the archaeological area to your right next to **Palazzo Orsini** (formerly owned by the Pierleoni and Savelli families), with charming bears in reference to the family name on the gate posts. Turn right at the next corner on Via di Portico d'Ottavia. The small 12th-century church at the corner is **S. Gregorio a Ponte Quattro Capi** (also called S. Gregorio

della Divina Pietà) that takes its name from the alternate name for the
Ponte Fabricio. Originally located next to one of the main entry gates
into the former Ghetto, Jews were forced to attend Mass here. Over the
entrance is a passage from Isaiah 65.2 in Hebrew and Latin that was
used to justify the conversions. The fresco of the crucifixion in the oval
frame is by Étienne Parrocel.

The **Great Synagogue of Rome** (Tempio Maggiore di Roma) is
opposite in Piazza Gerusalemme. Built between 1901 and 1904 by
Vincenzo Costa and Osvaldo Armanni in an Art Nouveau style with a
distinctive square dome (the only one in Rome), the synagogue occupies
the area of the ancient Circus Flaminius (220 BCE) where the triumphal
processions of victorious generals were assembled. On 13 April 1986,
Pope St John Paul II visited the synagogue, the first known visit by a
pope to a synagogue. The **Museo Ebraico** traces the history of Jews in
Rome and offers guided tours of the former Ghetto.

Continue on Via del Portico d'Ottavia that was the main street of the
former **Ghetto**. Spanish Jews joined the Roman community in 1492
following their expulsion from Spain. Pope Paul IV Carafa ordered Jews
to be enclosed in the Ghetto in 1555, but they were already there, having
made the transition to this side of the Tiber over the previous centuries
from their earlier communities in Trastevere. Pope Pius IX removed
the walls in 1848 and the area was largely demolished, including the
bakeries that once lined Via delle Azimelle, and was rebuilt from 1888.
The ancient buildings were isolated from 1926 to 1932, but the area was
enclosed again in World War II. A plaque on the wall of the building
facing **Largo 16 Ottobre 1943** at the entrance to the archaeological area
of the Porticus of Octavia commemorates the date when Nazi trucks
parked in the largo and threatened to round up Jews to be transported
to concentration camps unless 110 pounds of gold were delivered in 24
hours. Jews and non-Jewish Romans raised the amount but the Nazis
returned later and took more than 2,000 Jews away.

Before descending into the archaeological area of the Porticus
of Octavia and the Theatre of Marcellus, continue on Via di Portico
d'Ottavia beyond Largo 16 Ottobre 1943 a short distance. The street
is lined with restaurants that make traditional dishes such as *Filetti
di Baccalà* (fried cod) and *Carciofi alla Giuda* (fried artichokes) that
apparently lured Pope Pius IX to the area in disguise. At the end of
the block is the famous Pasticceria Il Boccione. The Scuola Ebraica is

to your left and opposite are medieval (No. 25, formerly the Torre dei Grassi, 13th century) and Renaissance houses (Nos 8 and 13, the Casa dei Fabi, 15th–16th century). Via della Reginella to your right gives a sense of the narrow streets prior to the demolition of the area.

At the end of the block to your right is the **Casa di Lorenzo Manili or Manilio** (1468) whose Latinised name is given as Laurentius Manlius in the dedicatory inscription. Embedded into the facade are fragments of ancient sculpture including a relief from an ancient tomb with portrait busts of freedmen who seem to be looking out of an apartment window. Lorenzo Manili was one of the first to reference the Classical past on the facade of his home (the Casa dei Crescenzi is earlier). The inscription states that he built the house in year 221 since the foundation date of Rome in 753 BCE. Along the side of the building, *Have Roma* (Hail Rome) is inscribed above three of the windows. At the semicircular **Tempietto del Carmelo** (1759), Jews were subjected to sermons aimed at their conversion.

The central area of the former **Piazza Giudea**, once the large entry point into the former Ghetto before the demolition and realignment of streets, is the heart of the vibrant Jewish community. In the centre of the piazza is an outline of the **Fontana di Piazza Giudea** by Giacomo della Porta (*c*.1593) that was demolished in 1905 and rebuilt in **Piazza delle Cinque Scole** in 1930, the long piazza to your left (with the Porticus of Octavia behind you) on the outside of the wall that was constructed in the middle of the piazza to isolate the ghetto. The piazza takes its name from a building demolished in 1908 that housed five synagogues that were called schools (scole), since it was prohibited for members of the various Jewish communities to have more than one synagogue: these were the Scola Tempio for Roman Jews; the Scola Nuova for Jews from Lazio; the Scola Siciliana for southern Italian Jews; and the Scola Catalana and Scola Castigliana for Spanish Jews. Immediately to your right in the piazza is one of the entrances into **S. Maria del Pianto** (formerly S. Salvatore de Cacaberis and Sant'Andrea). **Palazzo Cenci** is at the far end of the piazza where Beatrice Cenci murdered her abusive father in 1598.

Retrace your steps back to the **Porticus of Octavia** and walk down into the archaeological area. The porticus was built by Augustus (27–23 BCE) who dedicated it in the name of his sister Octavia in the location of the earlier Porticus of Metellus. It was restored after a fire in 80 CE and was rebuilt by Emperor Septimius Severus in 203 CE following fire damage in 191 CE. The vast quadriporticus (119m x 132m) enclosed the Temple of Juno Regina and the Temple of Jupiter Stator, two libraries (one Greek and the other Latin) and a curia. One of the two monumental entrances (propylaea) survives that stood on opposite ends of the porticus that faced the Circus Flaminius. It was incorporated into the church of **S. Angelo in Pescheria** (founded in 755 and rebuilt in the 16th century). From 1584 to the reign of Pope Pius IX, Jews were forced to attend sermons here intended for their conversion. The Via di S. Angelo in Pescheria runs along the front of the porticus and was the location of Rome's fish market in the medieval era. The entire area of the archeological zone was cleared in 1888 to isolate the ancient monuments that continued with the construction of Via del Teatro di Marcello under the Fascists.

The **Theatre of Marcellus** was built by the Emperor Augustus (between 13 and 11 BCE), and named for his nephew Marcellus (son of his sister Octavia), on land bought by Julius Caesar for the construction of a theatre. It could seat 15,000–20,000 spectators and consisted of 41 arches framed by 42 piers with three storeys decorated with Doric, Ionic and Doric pilasters. At the official opening of the theatre, Augustus's chair collapsed. In the 12th century, the Pierleoni used the theatre as a fortress until the Savelli (Pope Honorius III Savelli, 1216–1227, and Pope Honorius IV Savelli, 1285–1287) took control of the theatre and the area of the Aventine Hill. It was converted into a palazzo by Baldassarre Peruzzi (1523–1527). The Orsini family acquired the theatre in 1716 from which time it was known as Palazzo Orsini and became part of their complex of buildings in Monte Savello.

Opposite the theatre are three Corinthian columns that survive from the **Temple of Apollo Medicus** that were discovered when the area around the former Piazza Montanara was demolished. The temple was built by C. Sosius but dedicated by Augustus in 34 BCE on the site of an earlier Temple of Apollo that was dedicated in 431 BCE (the first dedicated to the god in Rome) and restored several times (353 BCE and 179 BCE). Decorating the pediment were sculptures of Athena presiding over an Amazonomachy (mid-5th century BCE) that were taken from a Greek temple that are now in the Museo Centrale Montemartini (Tour 14). Adjacent to the temple was the **Temple of Bellona**, another of the many dedicatory temples erected in the area of the Circus Flaminius that was originally dedicated by Appius Claudius Caecus (after 296 BCE) but rebuilt in the Augustan period.

Exit the archaeological area up the ramp and turn left on Via Montanara. Piazza Montanara was demolished for the construction of the street. At the corner is **S. Rita de Cascia** designed by Carlo Fontana for Pope Alexander VII Chigi (1665) that was relocated here by Antonio Muñoz in 1928 from the left side of the steps leading to S. Maria in Aracoeli on the Capitoline Hill. **Santa Maria in Portico in Campitelli** is ahead of you to the left, just beyond the fountain by Giacomo della Porta (1589) that formerly stood directly in front of the church. The church was designed by Carlo Rainaldi (1659–1667) for Pope Alexander VII Chigi whose name appears on the monumental facade above the entrance. The opulent high Baroque interior contains the icon of the Virgin from the Oratory of S. Galla over the high altar that stood behind the church in the Porticus of Octavia.

Continue on Via Montanara. Veer left through Via dei Funari ('Rope makers') with spoliated columns in **Palazzo Patrizi a S. Caterina** to your right. Continue on Via dei Funari past **Palazzo Mattei di Giove** and **Palazzo Mattei Paganica** into Piazza Mattei. In the centre of the piazza is the charming **Fontana delle Tartarughe** designed by Giacomo della Porta (1584) and constructed by Taddeo Landini. The tortoises seem integral to the design but they were added later when the fountain was restored in 1658 (possibly by Bernini). Originally, the fountain was maintained at the expense of the Mattei and is one of the earliest fountains in the area. Opposite the fountain is **Palazzo Costaguti**, with ceilings painted by Guercino.

To explore the Campo de' Fiori area at this point, take Via di Falegnami across to Via Arenula then cross to the other side of the street to Via Giubbonari to join Tour 7 at S. Carlo ai Catinari. To continue on the tour, retrace your steps on Via dei Funari to **S. Caterina dei Funari**. At the corner of Via Michelangelo Caetani, a memorial between Nos 8 and 9 commemorates the location where the body of former Prime Minister **Aldo Moro** was discovered after his kidnapping by the Red Brigade (1978). Veer left onto Via de' Delfini. Go straight through Piazza Margana to Via Margana (spoliated columns and frieze fragments are embedded into the walls of the medieval **Torre dei Margani**), then veer right a few steps later onto Via di Tor Margana when the street forks a short distance into **Piazza d'Aracoeli** that occupies a corner of Piazza Venezia.

3. Fontana delle Tartarughe, Piazza Mattei

To your right as you enter the piazza is the **Cordonata** of Michelangelo that leads to Piazza del Campidoglio (Tour 5). Medieval buildings such as the church of S. Venanzio dei Camerinesi, the Torre del Mercato and the Torre del Cancelliere that surrounded the piazza – that once served as a market until moved by Pope Sixtus IV della Rovere to Piazza Navona in 1477 – were demolished in 1928 for the construction of this section of Piazza Venezia. In the centre is the **Fontana di Piazza d'Aracoeli** (1589) designed by Giacomo della Porta (constructed by Andrea Brasca, Pietro Gucci and Pace Naldini) for Pope Sixtus V with four putti pouring water. When the piazza was demolished, the original oval basin was replaced with the current round one.

Facing the Campidoglio, continue past Via della Tribuna di Tor dè Specchi. At No. 3 to your right is **Palazzo Pecci Blunt** (formerly Palazzo Ruspoli) by Giacomo della Porta (end of the 16th century) and at No. 1 **Palazzo Massimo di Rignano** by Carlo Fontana (end of the 17th century) with a Triton fountain in the courtyard. At the end of the block, cross Via del Teatro di Marcello to walk up the Cordonata to the Campidoglio to continue to Tour 5 or cross the street and turn left to the National Monument to Vittorio Emanuele II to begin Tour 7.

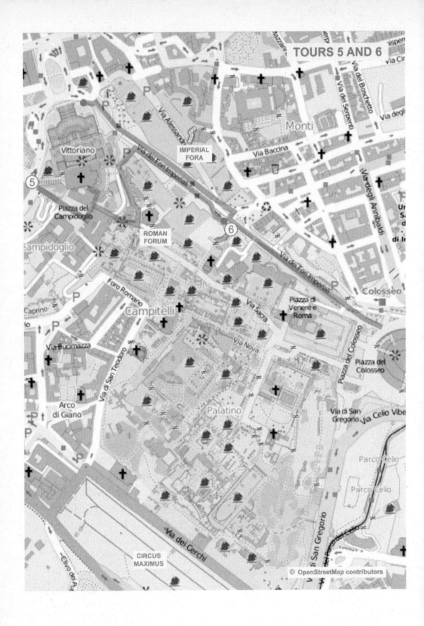

Sites: Piazza del Campidoglio; Palazzo Senatorio; Capitoline Museums (Musei Capitolini): Palazzo dei Conservatori and Palazzo Nuovo; S. Maria in Aracoeli; Temple of Juno; S. Giuseppe dei Falegnami (Mamertine Prison); Ss. Luca e Martina; Forum of Caesar.

Distance: 1.5km (+ 1.5–2.0km for Capitoline Museums visit).

Tour 5

# Capitoline Hill

## Piazza del Campidoglio and Capitoline Museums

The Capitoline Hill once dominated by the Capitolium was the civic heart of medieval Rome, with Palazzo Senatorio and the church of S. Maria in Aracoeli towering above the city. Michelangelo's stately redesign of the famous Piazza del Campidoglio in anticipation of the arrival of Charles V, the Holy Roman Emperor, reoriented the Hill with the Cordonata. Facing the piazza are the Capitoline Museums, the world's first public museum with a quality collection of antiquities including the *Capitoline She-Wolf*, the *Capitoline Venus*, and the *Dying Gaul* and paintings in the Pinacoteca Capitolina. Stunning views of the Roman Forum all the way to the Colosseum are visible from Palazzo Senatorio, which remains a vital civic centre of the Comune di Roma.

**Piazza del Campidoglio** is approached by the **Cordonata** designed by Michelangelo next to the steep steps leading to S. Maria in Aracoeli that reoriented access to the Capitoline Hill towards St Peter's Basilica. Giacomo della Porta modified the design and added the basalt Egyptian lions from the ancient Iseum (Temple of Isis) in the Campus Martius to serve as fountains (1588). When Via del Teatro di Marcello (originally Via del Mare) was constructed, the Cordonata was shortened (1929).

Before walking up the Cordonata, take a few steps to your left just beyond the steep flight of stairs leading up to S. Maria in Aracoeli to see the ruins of an ancient Roman apartment building (**Insula dell'Aracoeli**) from the 2nd century CE and the campanile from the 11th-century church of S. Biagio de Mercato or S. Biagio in Campitello. The faint fresco of Christ descended from the cross between St Mary and St John the Apostle is from the church of S. Rita de Cascia that was demolished and moved to Via Montanara (Tour 4) for the construction of Via del Teatro di Marcello. Other buildings that lined the Cordonata and the base of the hill including the Torre di Paolo III were also demolished for the construction of the National Monument to Vittorio Emanuele II (Tour 7).

Walking up the Cordonata, the **Statue of Cola di Rienzo** (1313–1354) erected in 1887 is to your left. The tribune and dictator who advocated an end to the pope's temporal power and the unification of Italy was assassinated in 1354 and his cause made him a hero in the 19th century. To your right on Via delle Tre Pile, the **Casa di Michelangelo** was moved from Via Macel de' Corvi, formerly on the other side of Piazza Venezia (Tour 6), but was moved again to the Passeggiata del Gianicolo (Tour 3). On the balustrade designed by Michelangelo and modified by Giacomo della Porta are the late Imperial statues of **Castor and Pollux** (known collectively as the Dioscuri) and their horses that were found in the nearby Via delle Botteghe Oscure and added in 1585. Michelangelo's design called for the Castor and Pollux statues now in Piazza del Quirinale. Next to them are the so-called Trophies of Marius, statues of Constantine the Great and his son Constantius II from the Baths of Constantine and two milestones (first and seventh) from the Via Appia Antica.

Facing **Piazza del Campidoglio** are **Palazzo Senatorio** (centre), **Palazzo dei Conservatori** (right) and **Palazzo Nuovo** (left). The piazza corresponds roughly to the ancient site of the **Asylum** in the valley area between the hill's two peaks, the **Capitolium** and the **Arx**, founded by Romulus to attract inhabitants to his new city. The area of the Asylum with the **Temple of Veiovis** was later occupied by the **Tabularium** in the area of Palazzo Senatorio. The **Scalae Gemoniae** descended to the Mamertine Prison. The colossal **Temple of Jupiter Optimus Maximus** (also called the Temple of Jupiter Capitolinus) that dominated the skyline facing the Forum Boarium was the end point of the Triumphal Procession route that climbed the Hill from the Roman Forum by the **Clivus Capitolinus**. The **Tarpeian Rock** (precipice at the eastern corner) was named after the Vestal Virgin Tarpeia who betrayed Rome to the Sabines and was thrown from it to her death as punishment. On the peak of the Arx was the **Temple of Juno Moneta** and the Mint, where now stands S. Maria in Aracoeli. Edward Gibbon conceived *The History of the Decline and Fall of Roman Empire* on the Capitoline Hill:

'It was at Rome, on the 15 October, 1764, as I sat musing amidst the ruins of the Capitol, while the barefooted friars were singing Vespers in the Temple of Jupiter, that the idea of writing the decline and fall of the city first started to my mind ...'

In the medieval period, the Capitoline Hill served as the grazing grounds for goats and was known as Monte Caprino until it emerged as the civic centre of Rome. In the 12th century, the Senate of the Comune di Roma met in Palazzo Senatorio and later (from the 14th century) in Palazzo dei Conservatori. Santa Maria in Aracoeli is the civic church of Rome, a role that goes back to the 8th century when the Roman Council held meetings there. The Capitoline Hill remains the civic centre of the Comune di Roma, and Palazzo Senatorio is the official seat of the Mayor of Rome.

Pope Paul III Farnese commissioned Michelangelo to redesign the piazza in 1536 for the ceremonial reception of the Holy Roman Emperor Charles V whose troops were responsible for the Sack of Rome in 1527. The piazza was incomplete (construction continued into the 17th century) when he celebrated a triumphal procession in the ancient Roman tradition through the Roman Forum and arrived at the Campildoglio where the newly installed **Equestrian Statue of Marcus Aurelius** (1538) greeted him as Marcus Aurelius's modern-day successor. The statue survives because it was mistaken for Constantine the Great and was formerly displayed outside S. Giovanni in Laterano from the 8th century until relocated by the pope. A copy is now on display in the piazza with the original inside Palazzo dei Conservatori.

Michelangelo designed a trapezoidal-shaped piazza (Antonio Muñoz carried out Michelangelo's pavement design in 1940) and reworked the medieval facades of Palazzo Senatorio and Palazzo dei Conservatori and designed Palazzo Nuovo in matching style. The pilasters occupying two storeys further unite the facades thematically and became an influential architectural style. Michelangelo's redesigned facade for **Palazzo Senatorio** covered a loggia on the right-hand side with further modifications by Giacomo della Porta, Girolamo Rainaldi and Martino Longhi the Elder, who remodelled the campanile (1592). The clock formerly on the facade of S. Maria in Aracoeli was added in 1806. The original ramp entrance was replaced by the double staircase with a statue of Minerva adapted as Roma by Martino Longhi the Elder in the centre niche flanked by two River Gods: the Tiber (from a recarved

4. Equestrian Statue of Marcus Aurelius, Piazza del Campidoglio

statue of the Tigris river) on the right and the Nile on the left. They were found on the Quirinal Hill and installed here in 1589. For a sweeping view of the Roman Forum, walk along the right of Palazzo Senatorio to the Overlook. J. M. W. Turner painted his *Campo Vaccino*, now in the J. Paul Getty Museum, Los Angeles, from this area.

The **Capitoline Museums** (Musei Capitolini), comprised of several palaces, were founded by Pope Sixtus IV della Rovere who donated Classical sculpture (including the *Capitoline She-Wolf*, the *Spinario* and bronze head of Constantine the Great) in 1471 that formed the nucleus of the Museums as the world's oldest public collection. The site of the world's first 'blockbuster' exhibition occurred in front of Palazzo Senatorio in 1485 when a sarcophagus discovered on the Via Appia contained a perfectly preserved woman identified erroneously as Tulliola, the daughter of the orator Cicero. Long lines of visitors formed to touch the pliant skin of the girl, to pull out her tongue and play with her eyelids, nose and ears. To quell popular excitement and superstition, Pope Innocent VIII secretly had the body dumped into the Tiber or buried it outside the Porta Salaria. In 1566, Pope Pius V added to the collection the Gilded Bronze statue of Hercules from the Forum Boarium, the marble statue fragments of Constantine the Great and the *Brutus*. Centuries later, the Museums were a must-see site on the Grand Tour and the sculpture displays and wall decorations have changed little since then, especially in Palazzo Nuovo inaugurated by Pope Clement XII Corsini in 1734 with pieces from the extensive collection of Cardinal Alessandro Albani (nephew of Pope Clement XI Albani) that he purchased and donated to the Museums.

In the **courtyard** the marble statue fragments of Constantine the Great came from a monumental acrolith statue (about 12m high) found in the apse of the Basilica of Maxentius in the Roman Forum in 1486. The head shows signs of reworking and may have been a portrait of Maxentius. Opposite are large relief panels of Provinces from the Temple of Hadrian (Tour 8) and a large dedicatory inscription from the Arch of Claudius set up in 51 CE to commemorate the conquest of Britain that formerly spanned the Via del Corso at S. Maria in Via Lata. In the niche a Hadrianic-era statue that was adapted into Roma is flanked by two statues of Barbarian Captives (2nd century CE) formerly displayed in the gardens of Palazzo Cesi (Tour 2).

After clearing security, go up the staircase to your right. On the first floor landing are three reliefs of Marcus Aurelius from a triumphal arch from the area near Ss. Luca e Martina that depict the emperor dispensing clemency, celebrating a triumph and burning incense in front of the Temple of Jupiter Optimus Maximus prior to a sacrifice. The fourth relief (to your left) is of the Emperor Hadrian's ceremonial entry into Rome that came from the Arco di Portogallo that was formerly on the Via del Corso at Via delle Vite (Tour 9). There are two more panels from the arch: one to the left of the entrance to the Sala degli Orazi e Curiazi of the Appartamento dei Conservatori (Hadrian dispensing charity); and the other on the second level to the left of the entrance to the Pinacoteca Capitolina (Apotheosis of Vibia Sabina, Hadrian's wife).

The **Apartment of the Conservators** (Appartamento dei Conservatori) is a series of rooms in the oldest part of the palace decorated with scenes from Rome's legendary history. The first room is the **Hall of the Horatii and Curiatii** (Sala degli Orazi e Curiazi), named for the fresco (1613) of the early Roman legendary *Battle between the Horatii and Curiatii* by Cavalier d'Arpino (Giuseppe Cesari). At either end are Bernini's marble statue of Pope Urban VIII Barberini (1635–1639) and Alessandro Algardi's bronze statue of Pope Innocent X Pamphilj (1645–

1650). Other papal statues now in S. Maria in Aracoeli were removed in 1876. The Mayor of Rome uses the room for official state functions: the Treaty of Rome was signed here in 1957 and the Constitution of the European Union was ratified here in 2004.

The Apartment rooms continue through the **Hall of the Captains** (Sala dei Capitani), named after the five statues of generals from Roman patrician families who fought on behalf of the Church. The frescoes by Tommaso Laureti (from 1594) depict scenes from Roman history from the ancient historian Livy. A stone plaque records the moving of Pope Nicolas III's (1277–1280) residence from the Lateran Palace to the Vatican and his construction of gardens. From here there is access to your left to the **Hall of Hannibal** (Sala di Annibale), with frescoes that commemorate Hannibal and the Second Punic War, the **Cappella** (decorated in 1578) and the **Hall of the Tapestries** (Sala degli Arazzi).

The **Hall of the Triumphs** (Sala dei Trionfi) is named for the frieze of a Roman triumph ascending the Capitoline Hill. Here begins the series of rooms that include the nucleus of the collection opened to the public by Sixtus IV della Rovere in 1471. In the centre of the room is the *Spinario*, a bronze Hellenistic sculpture (1st century BCE) of a seated boy removing a thorn from the bottom of his foot. By the entrance door is the so-called *Brutus*, an early bronze portrait (*c.*3rd–1st century BCE) that was added to a modern bust. The bronze vase is inscribed with the name of King Mithridates from Pontus and probably arrived in Rome as war booty from the Mithridatic War in 63 BCE. The painting *Victory of Alexander the Great over Darius* is by Pietro da Cortona (1635).

In the **Hall of the She-Wolf** (Sala della Lupa) is the famous symbol of Rome, the *Capitoline She-Wolf* that was found in the area of the church of S. Teodoro (Tour 4). The date of the bronze sculpture is controversial, ranging from an Etruscan piece from the 5th century BCE to a date in the medieval period. Cicero mentions that a statue of the She-Wolf on the Capitoline Hill was struck by lightning in 65 BCE and this one shows signs of damage. The twins were likely added by Antonio del Pollaiuolo at the end of the 15th century. On the wall are the *Fasti Capitolini* fragments from the *Fasti Consulares*, containing the names of ancient Romans who served as one of two consuls (up to the year 13 BCE) that were used to date each year, and the *Fasti Triumphales*, listing the triumphing generals (up to the year 12 BCE). The Fasti panels come from the inner wall of the Arch of Augustus in the Roman Forum and were installed in the marble frame by Michelangelo.

The **Hall of the Geese** (Sala delle Oche) is named after the ancient sculptures of bronze Geese. The marble head of Medusa (1630) is by Bernini. The bronze bust of *Michelangelo* by his student Daniele da Volterra is from the artist's death mask. The **Hall of the Eagles** (Sala delle Aquile) is named for the ancient Roman Eagles displayed on columns with a 17th-century frieze attributed to Antonio Gherardi. In the final three rooms of this section are pieces from the **Castellani Collection** of antiquities donated to the Comune di Roma in 1867 by Augusto Castellani. These were acquired from excavations of Etruscan tombs north of Rome in Lazio and southern Etruria in the 1860s. In the third room, the krater vase from ancient Caere (modern Cerveteri) contains a scene of *Odysseus' Blinding of the Cyclops Polyphemus* (*c.*650 BCE) and is signed by the artist Aristonothos.

The **Gallery** along the rear wall of Palazzo dei Conservatori includes the *Esquiline Venus* and *Commodus as Hercules* found in the Lamian Gardens (Horti Lamiani), named after Lucius Aelius Lamia (consul in 3 CE), during excavations in 1874. The gardens, located on the Esquiline Hill in the area of Piazza Vittorio Emanuele II and Stazione Termini (Tour 12), later passed into Imperial possession in the reign of the Emperor Caligula.

The **Exedra of Marcus Aurelius** (Esedra di Marco Aurelio) is a glass-enclosed courtyard that was designed by Carlo Aymonino (1991, inaugurated in 2005) for the display of the original **Equestrian Statue of Marcus Aurelius** (emperor from 161 to 180 CE) and the Capitoline bronzes. Its location in ancient Rome (prior to its display at S. Giovanni in Laterano) is unknown, but it is the only one to survive out of over 20 known equestrian statues. Donatello's *Equestrian Statue of Gattamelata* (*Erasmo da Narni*) from 1453 in Piazza del Santo, Padua, was the first full-scale bronze equestrian statue since antiquity. The bronze head and foot of Constantine the Great and orb come from a colossal statue. The gilded bronze statue of Hercules was found in the Forum Boarium near the Ara Maxima of Hercules (Tour 4).

A portion of the substructure of the **Temple of Jupiter Optimus Maximus** occupies the area beyond the Hall of Marcus Aurelius. The original temple was built on a monumental scale under the kings but it was dedicated after the expulsion of the last king, Tarquinius

Superbus ('Tarquin the Proud'), and symbolised the founding of the
Republic in 509 BCE. The temple was dedicated to the Capitoline
Triad of Jupiter Optimus Maximus, Juno Regina and Minerva.
Originally Etruscan in appearance (about 62m x 54m), the temple
burned down three times: in 83 BCE during the dictatorship of Sulla,
69 CE and 80 CE and was rebuilt with more expensive materials with
each rebuilding, especially the last version by Domitian. His temple
stood for about 400 years until the Sack of Rome in 455 by Genseric,
King of the Vandals, and was systematically quarried for building
materials in the medieval era. Very little of the superstructure survived
into the modern era but a capital was discovered at the base of the
hill and furnished the marble for the decoration of the Cesi chapel in
S. Maria della Pace (Tour 8) and the *Medici Lion* by Flaminio Vacca
that now stands at the entrance to the Loggia dei Lanzi in Piazza della
Signoria, Florence.

The terra cotta pediment decoration from the archaic **Temple of
Mater Matuta** was excavated at the site of S. Omobono in the Forum
Boarium (Tour 4). The figures of Hercules and Minerva and the archaic
volutes stood on top of the pediment. Other finds from the area on
display in the cases illustrate the Etruscan presence in Rome in the archaic
period including the earliest Etruscan inscription discovered in Rome.

Along the Exedra of Marcus Aurelius is the **New Wing** (Braccio
Nuovo) that contains a **Gallery** with portraits (including a rare portrait
of Domitian) from the various aristocratic gardens (horti) on the
Esquiline Hill that passed into Imperial possession. Off the Gallery are
rooms with ancient Greek sculpture, Roman copies of Greek originals,
and original Roman compositions from the horti that were excavated
in 1874. At the end of the gallery are the Modern Fasti (Fasti Moderni)
lists of Roman magistrates since 1640. The **Medieval Room** by the
first floor landing contains the portrait and fragments of Arnolfo di
Cambio's honorary monument to Charles I of Anjou, King of Sicily
and Senator of Rome (1226–1285), formerly in Palazzo Senatorio. The
bronze orb (1st century CE) is from the Obelisk in St Peter's Square that
was removed for the current crucifix mounted on the emblem of Pope
Alexander VII Chigi.

Take the stairs up to the second floor to the **Pinacoteca Capitolina**
picture gallery of medieval, Renaissance and Baroque masterpieces
arranged in nine rooms. The nucleus of the collection was founded by

Pope Benedict XIV in 1749 and was increased by the addition of several private collections including those of Cardinal Sachetti, Prince Gilberto Pio di Savoia and Count Giuseppe Cini (1881).

The **Hall of Saint Petronilla** (Room VII) is named after the monumental altar painting, the *Burial of Saint Petronilla* by Guercino, commissioned by Pope Gregory XV Ludovisi in 1623 for St Peter's Basilica around the same time that Guercino painted the *Aurora* fresco in the Villa Aurora (Tour 11) for Cardinal Ludovico Ludovisi, the pope's nephew. The painting was removed from St Peter's Basilica in 1730 and replaced by a mosaic copy. In 1797, the painting was requisitioned by French troops, brought to Paris and exhibited in the Louvre. The painting returned to Rome by the terms of the Treaty of Vienna (1815), when it was recovered by Antonio Canova and placed permanently in the Museums in 1818. In addition to other works by Guercino, Domenichino and Peter Paul Rubens' *Romulus and Remus nursed by the She-Wolf* (1617–1618), are Caravaggio's *The Fortune Teller* and *St John the Baptist* (1602).

Room VIII, the **Hall of Pietro da Cortona** (Sala di Pietro da Cortona), designed by Ferdinando Fuga (1748), is named for the important artist and architect of the Counter-Reformation, Pietro da Cortona (1596–1669), whose works including the *Rape of the Sabines*, the *Triumph of Bacchus*, the *Sacrifice of Polyxena* and *Portrait of Urban VIII* are prominently displayed here. The paintings formerly hung in Palazzo Sachetti (Tour 3). The hall was called the Sala d'Ercole after the gilded bronze statue of Hercules in the Exedra of Marcus Aurelius that was formerly displayed here with the Classical-themed paintings.

Exit the Pinacoteca Capitolina and descend the stairs to the ground floor landing. Continue down the stairs to the Galleria Lapidaria that connects to the Tabularium and Palazzo Nuovo. To visit Palazzo Clementino-Caffarelli beforehand, return to the Cortile with the marble portrait of Constantine the Great and take the stairs to **Palazzo Clementino-Caffarelli** that contains the **Caffè Capitolino**, with beautiful views from its terrace (Terrazza Caffarelli) and more exhibition space including the Capitoline Numismatics Collection and the **Hall of the Pediment** (Sala del Frontone), with terra cotta pediment statues from a Roman temple (2nd century BCE) that was uncovered on Via di S. Gregorio.

The **Galleria Lapidaria** is an epigraphy collection in the corridor (Galleria di Congiunzione) built by Mussolini in 1939 that runs below

Piazza del Campidoglio and joins Palazzo dei Conservatori to Palazzo Nuovo. The inscriptions on dedicatory and funerary objects in the various languages of the Empire are arranged thematically. Among the fascinating inscriptions that document facets of everyday life in ancient Rome are those on the Corinthian capitals at the entrance that were reused for modern Jewish funerary markers including one (1560–1576) that was found near Stazione Trastevere in 1889. Funerary objects include stele grave markers, cinerary urns, grave and burial marker plaques (tituli), some with drainage holes for libations, and Jewish epitaphs from the Via Portuense Necropolis (Tour 4). The dedicatory inscription with the footprints pointing in different directions is a votive offering to the goddess Caelestis for a safe return trip (3rd century CE).

Take the stairs to your right towards the end of the Galleria Lapidaria for the area below Palazzo Senatorio. The **Temple of Veiovis** was originally built in 192 BCE but rebuilt by the Dictator Sulla following the fire of 83 BCE. The colossal statue of the god Veiovis (1st century CE) was discovered in the cella of the temple in 1939. The obscure god is connected with healing and associated with the sacrifice of goats. The temple was squeezed into the tight space between the vaults of the Tabularium substructure. Along the corridor are the Altar of the Vicomagistri (136 CE) that contains a dedicatory inscription to the Emperor Hadrian; next to it is a statue base dedicated to Cornelia, the daughter of Scipio Africanus and the mother of the Gracchi; and opposite is the pedestal base for the cinerary urn of Agrippina, the granddaughter of Augustus and the wife of Germanicus. At the end of the corridor are copies of sections of the cornices from the Temple of Concord, with beautiful rosettes, and from the Temple of the Deified Vespasian, with sacrificial instruments. Also displayed here is the original relief from the Lacus Curtius in the Roman Forum.

The structure below Palazzo Senatorio is called the **Tabularium** but what survives is the substructure complex that filled in the valley of the Capitoline Hill (under the Tabularium where state archives were stored). This provided an open gallery facing the Roman Forum between the Capitolium and the Arx above a closed gallery (the lowest level of the retaining wall with square windows) that provided access to the complex from the Roman Forum. The entrance to the Tabularium was from Piazza del Campidoglio from a colonnaded portico corresponding to the location of the double staircase today. In the Middle Ages, these substructure rooms were used for the storage of salt and as a prison. From the open gallery (three arched openings are best seen from the Roman Forum) are spectacular views of the Roman Forum.

Retrace your steps to the Galleria Lapidaria then turn right at the bottom of the stairs a short distance to walk up another flight of stairs that lead to **Palazzo Nuovo**. At the ground floor landing is the monumental statue of the god Mars from the Flavian era that was identified as *Pyrrhus* (the son of the mythological warrior Achilles, also known as Neoptolemus) when discovered in the area of the Imperial Fora (Forum of Nerva) in the 16th century. It gave the common name of *il Pirro* to Palazzo Massimo alle Colonne (Tour 7) since it stood in the courtyard before moved here.

Turn right to enter into the **courtyard**. The reclining statue of a river god is the famous *Marforio* (Oceanus), one of the talking statues in the Renaissance, like *Pasquino* (Tour 7) who 'conversed' with the statue called *Madama Lucrezia* (Tour 7) via messages left attached to the statue often hostile to the papacy and prominent figures. It was found at the base of the Capitoline Hill near the Arch of Septimius Severus and displayed near S. Giuseppe dei Falegnami until 1587 when Pope Sixtus V moved the statue to Piazza di S. Marco and displayed on its namesake street, Salita di Marforio, that cut through the current area of the steps of the National Monument to Vittorio Emanuele II. In 1592 it was moved to its present location (enclosed when the palace was built) and placed in the fountain designed by Giacomo della Porta. The two *Pans* are attributed to the Theatre of Pompey (Tour 7) and were once in the collection of Cardinal Andrea della Valle.

The gallery off of the courtyard contains Egyptian and Egyptianising Roman art from the Iseum (Temple of Isis) in the Campus Martius in the area near the present day Collegio Romano (Tour 8). The sphinxes, crocodile, hawk and dog-faced baboons were found on Via del Beato Angelico near the apse of S. Maria sopra Minerva and likely decorated the portico. In the **atrium** is a colossal statue of Minerva, a copy of a 5th-century Greek original that was initially intended for the niche of the Palazzo Senatorio staircase in Piazza del Campidoglio by Pope Paul III Farnese, but was replaced by the current seated figure.

Walk up to the first floor. On the landing is a marble krater (1st century CE) from the Tomb of Caecilia Metella (Tour 14) displayed on a wellhead from the Villa of Hadrian at Tivoli that is decorated with a procession of the 12 Olympian gods (Dii Consentes). The **Galleria** is lined with 200 sculptures, dedicatory inscriptions, altars, funerary art, burial plaque markers recovered from the Via Appia Antica (Tour 14) from the Columbarium of freedmen and slaves of the Empress Livia discovered in 1726, sarcophagi and cinerary urns. The display preserves the original placement by the Marquis Alessandro Capponi and Pope Clement XII Corsini from the inauguration of Palazzo Nuovo in 1734. The *Hercules* (2nd century CE) was restored by Alessandro Algardi as the Labour of the Hydra instead of the original Labour of the Hind. The *Wounded Gladiator* was carved by Pierre-Étienne Monnot (1657–1733) and incorporates the torso from a copy of Myron's *Discus Thrower*. It was intended to complement the famous *Dying Gaul* and was donated to the Museums by Pope Clement XII.

The **Hall of the Doves** (Sala delle Colombe) is named for the doves at a fountain in the mosaic (2nd century CE) found at the Villa of Hadrian at Tivoli that was modelled after an original by Sosus from Pergamum. In the centre of the room is the statue of a *Young Girl with Dove* that is a copy of a 3rd–2nd-century BCE Hellenistic original in which the girl protects the dove from the snake at her feet. In the display case is a fragment of the *Tabula Iliaca Capitolina* (*c.*15 BCE), a plaque that depicts Aeneas' departure from Troy.

Returning to the Galleria, the famous *Drunken Old Woman* with her wine jug is after a Hellenistic original. The *Flavian Woman as Venus* with provocative pose was found in an area of the Basilica of S. Sebastiano on the Via Appia that suggests a funerary context. Opposite is the celebrated *Capitoline Venus* in the **Cabinet of Venus** (Gabinetto della Venere) that was designed to give visitors a view of her entire 6' 6" body. It is a copy of a 4th-century BCE original by Praxiteles for the Shrine of Aphrodite on the island of Cnidos, the first freestanding fully nude female statue on a large scale. She is of the *Venus Pudica* ('modest') statue type since she attempts to cover up her body as though surprised by the arrival of a stranger while at her bath. It was discovered by the Basilica of S. Vitale (Tour 12) between 1667 and 1670 and donated to the Museums by Pope Benedict XIV in 1752. The nose and some fingers are 17th-century repairs. One of the most famous pieces in the collection, it has long attracted admirers including visitors to Rome on the Grand Tour and Napoleon who took the statue to Paris in 1797. It was returned to this cabinet in 1816.

The **Hall of the Emperors** (Sala degli Imperatori) contains portrait busts of emperors and Imperial women in chronological order. The series begins at the top shelf by the door that leads to the Hall of the Philosophers with the Dictator Julius Caesar, although his adopted son Augustus (born Gaius Octavius and known as Octavian to history before his name change to Augustus in 27 BCE) was the first emperor who transitioned Rome from the Republic to the Empire and established Imperial protocols. On pedestals in front of the windows are portraits of *Marcus Aurelius as a boy* and the *Flavian Woman*, known as the *Fonseca Bust* famous for her delicate features and elaborate hairpiece that was typical of the late 1st century CE. In the centre of the hall is the seated statue of St Helena, the mother of Constantine the Great, that may be a reworking of an earlier portrait of Livia, wife of the Emperor Augustus.

The next room is the **Hall of the Philosophers** (Sala dei Filosofi) that contains 79 portrait busts of Greek and Roman philosophers, poets, doctors, orators and historians. The portrait of Socrates (the third and fourth busts on the top shelf from the left) is based on the version of Lysippus that was made 50 years after Socrates' death from descriptions found in Plato's dialogues. At the end of the shelf are busts of Homer who is depicted as blind according to Greek legend. The bust of Cicero is on the bottom shelf in the right-hand corner. On the walls are Roman sarcophagus reliefs that show the carrying of Meleager's corpse, thought to have inspired Raphael's *Deposition* in the Galleria Borghese (Tour 10).

The **Great Hall** (Salone) was lavishly decorated by Pope Innocent X Pamphilj. In the centre is a colossal statue of the *Infant Hercules* (3rd century CE) in green basalt with attributes of his future labours: the lion skin and the apples of the Hesperides that was added to the Museums in 1570. The pair of *Centaurs* in black marble were found at the Villa of Hadrian at Tivoli and added to the Museums by Pope Clement XIII in 1765. The Centaurs are signed by Aristeas and Papias from Aphrodisias in Asia Minor and are allegories of love.

The **Hall of the Faun** (Sala del Fauno) is named for the *Laughing Faun* or *Silenus* in rare red marble that comes from the Villa of Hadrian at Tivoli and was donated to the Museums by Pope Benedict XIV. The *Lex de Imperio Vespasiani* (69–70 CE) is a bronze plaque with the ending of the decree by the Senate that outlines the transfer of specific powers to the emperor. It was cited by Cola di Rienzo in defence of the sovereignty of the Roman people from the papacy and displayed in S. Giovanni in Laterano after he claimed that Pope Boniface VIII tried to hide it under an altar. By the door is a collection of brick stamps used to date the production of bricks in the Roman world.

The last room is named the **Hall of the Gladiator** (Sala del Gladiatore) for the famous statue of the *Dying Gaul* that is a figure of a Celtic warrior and not a gladiator as originally named. It was a must-see piece on the Grand Tour that Byron described as 'butcher'd to make a Roman holiday'. It was part of a monument on the grounds of the Villa Ludovisi (ancient Gardens of Sallust) that included the *Suicidal Gaul* now in Palazzo Altemps Museum (Tour 8) and by 1623 it was displayed in the famous Boncompagni Ludovisi ancient sculpture collection in the Palazzo Grande di Villa Ludovisi (Tour 11) until Pope Clement XII Corsini acquired it for the Capitoline Museums. Napoleon brought the statue to Paris but it was returned to Rome in 1816. The right arm was restored when found but its position was corrected in a 1986 restoration. The original sculpture group in bronze was built for Attalus I of Pergamon to commemorate his victory over the Gauls in 239 BCE. It was much copied in English gardens including at Iford Manor and Rousham House. The *Resting Satyr* is a copy of an original by Praxiteles found at the Villa of Hadrian at Tivoli. This is the same statue (in the same room and surrounded by the same statues) upon which Nathaniel Hawthorne based his novel the *Marble Faun*. According to Hawthorne, 'The whole statue [...] conveys the idea of an amiable and sensual creature, easy, mirthful, apt for jollity, yet not incapable of being touched by pathos.' Exit Palazzo Nuovo and turn left to climb the steps that lead to the Il Vittoriano Museum in the National Monument to Vittorio Emanuele II and to the side entrance of S. Maria in Aracoeli to your left.

**Santa Maria in Aracoeli al Campidoglio** is a titular church founded in the 6th century on the site of the ancient Temple of Juno Moneta and formerly known as S. Maria in Capitolio. The name change is related to the legend preserved in Canon Benedict's 12th-century *Memorabilia* of the Emperor Augustus receiving a revelation from the Tiburtine Sibyl from which the name of the church is derived: *Haec est ara filii Dei* – 'This is the altar of the Son of God.'

The earlier church was demolished and reconstructed in the 13th century (1285–1287) and inaugurated by Cola di Rienzo in 1348. It remains the church of the Comune di Roma. The unfinished brick facade bears clamp holes for an intended marble facade that was not completed. The centre bears traces where Rome's first public clock was installed in 1412. The 124 steps leading to the front entrance from Piazza d'Aracoeli were constructed as a thanks-offering to the Madonna d'Aracoeli for the end of the plague of 1348. In the 17th century, Prince Caffarelli rolled barrels filled with rocks down the stairs to keep foreigners from sleeping on the steps. Raphael's *Madonna di Foligno* was displayed in the church until it was moved to the Monastery of St Anne in Foligno in 1565. During the French occupation of Rome, the church was deconsecrated and used as stables. The adjoining convent was torn down to build the National Monument to Vittorio Emanuele II.

The side entrance is through the former Cappella della Madonna and contains the funerary monument to Pietro Manzi by Andrea Sansovino and the funerary monument to Cecchino Bracci by Francesco Amadori to a design by Michelangelo. The 22 spoliated columns are from various Roman buildings: on the north side, the third column is inscribed *a cubicolo Augustorum* ('from the room of the Augustuses'). On the fourth, fifth ('Madonna and Child') and seventh columns are 15th-century fresco fragments. The 13th-century cosmatesque pavement contains numerous pavement tombs. The ceiling decoration by Sermoneta (Girolamo Siciolante da Sermoneta) and Cesare Trapassi (1572–1575) commemorates the defeat of the Turks in the Battle of Lepanto (1571). For this feat, the victorious admiral Marcantonio II Colonna was given a 'triumph' celebration in the church that capped a triumphal procession through the Roman Forum modelled after ancient Roman triumphs. He was also granted an honourary statue in the Sala dei Capitani in Palazzo dei Conservatori.

In the sanctuary, the ambones and cosmatesque decoration survive from the earlier church. Over the high altar is a painting of the *Madonna d'Aracoeli* (10th–11th century) that is credited with ending the 'Black Death' plague of 1348 and to whom the steps leading to the church from Piazza d'Aracoeli is dedicated. The apse with frescoes by Pietro Cavallini was destroyed in the renovation of Pope Pius IV de' Medici (1564) when the schola cantorum was also demolished. The Chapel of

the Blessed Sacrament (Cappella del Sacramento) to the right of the
high altar was designed and decorated by Antonio Gherardi (1675). In
the south transept is the Savelli Chapel with two funerary monuments
by Arnolfo di Cambio: the one on the left to Luca Savelli incorporates
an ancient sarcophagus (3rd century CE). The monument to the right
with cosmatesque decoration is to his wife Vana Aldobrandesca with
an effigy of their son, Pope Honorius IV Savelli (d. 1287), originally
part of a trefoil canopy monument in Old St Peter's that was Arnolfo di
Cambio's first papal tomb.

On the north side of the sanctuary is the Chapel of St Helena that is
a little temple (17th century) with eight columns over a porphyry urn
altar with the relics of St Helena. On the cosmatesque altar beneath the
urn, the foundation legend of the church is depicted with the Emperor
Augustus kneeling before the apparition of the Virgin. The medieval
trefoil canopy funerary monument in the north transept contains the
recumbant effigy of Cardinal Matteo d'Acquasparta and is attributed to
Giovanni di Cosma. The fresco behind the canopy of the *Madonna and
Child Enthroned with St Matthew, St John and Cardinal d'Acquasparta* is
attributed to Pietro Cavallini. From here there is access to the Cappella
del Santo Bambino, with a venerated statue of the Infant Christ.
Hidden from view is the unflattering statue of Pope Leo X de' Medici by
Domenico Aimo (*c.*1520). On the wall along the steps an ornate epitaph
commemorates Felice de Fredi who discovered the *Laocoön* sculpture
group now in the Vatican Museums. The epitaph above it records the
death by drowning (1778) of Octavio Buccapadulio, described as a
youth erudite in Greek and Latin.

The aisle chapels were patronised by prominent families including
on the north side, the Cappella della Valle/Orsini ('Chapel of the
Ascension'), with a remarkable portrait bust of Marchessa Vittoria della
Tolfa Orsini (d. 1582). On the south side, the first chapel, the Bufalini
Chapel (also known as the Cappella di S. Bernardino de Siena), contains
frescoes on the *Life of St Bernardino* (1486) by Pinturicchio, painted
soon after his frescoes for the Borgia Apartment at the Vatican (Tour 2).
In the second chapel (Cappella della Pietà) are frescoes on the *Passion*
by Pomarancio (Cristoforo Roncalli) of 1582. The last chapel (Cappella
di S. Rosa da Viterbo) contains recently discovered fresco fragments of
Pietro Cavallini that depict a *Madonna and Child Enthroned with Saints*
and *Christ between Two Angels*.

On the west wall (facade wall), the dedication by the Roman Senate to Pope Urban VIII Barberini, inscribed on a scroll held by two angels, is by Bernini who incorporated a window with the Barberini bee emblem within the heraldic shield. Bernini also designed a monumental catafalque for the funeral of Carlo Barberini against this wall in 1633. The pavement monument to Giovanni Crivelli (d. 1432), now set upright in the left-hand niche facing the doors, is by Donatello (his name is inscribed on the left-hand side border). Next to it is the funerary monument of Cardinal Ludovico d'Albret (d. 1465), with a reclining effigy by Andrea Bregno (1465). On the other side of the door is the funerary monument to the astronomer Lodovico Grato Margani by the studio of Andrea Sansovino, but Sansovino carved the Christ figure at the top of the monument.

Exit the church by the side entrance and turn left at the bottom of the stairs to walk on Via S. Pietro in Carcere. At the corner of Palazzo Senatorio are commemorative plaques and a column with the *Capitoline She-Wolf* with Romulus and Remus. Opposite on your left is a section of the Capitoline Hill (Arx) where part of the **Temple of Juno Moneta** and the Mint sanctuary was located. According to Roman legend, the Gauls tried to storm the Hill at this location in 390 BCE, but their presence was betrayed by the sacred geese that warned of their attack. The incident accounts for the word Moneta in the name of the temple: the verb *monere* in Latin means to warn, and the association of the Mint to the temple is the origin of the English word 'money'. From the small park with architectural fragments there is a view of the Forum of Julius Caesar with the Imperial Fora on the other side of Via dei Fori Imperiali.

Follow Via S. Pietro in Carcere and take the staircase by the Overlook of the Roman Forum that descends along the side of the church of **S. Giuseppe dei Falegnami** in the location of the ancient Gemonian Steps ('Steps of Mourning'). According to tradition, this is the **Mamertine Prison** where St Peter and St Paul were held before their martyrdoms and was formerly called S. Pietro in Carcere. In ancient Rome, the prison was called the Tullianum and may have had its origin as an Etruscan cistern (6th century BCE) since there is still a spring on the site. On the upper level is a list of Christian martyrs who were imprisoned here and another list of prominent political prisoners and the method of execution, including Jugurtha, the King of Numidia, the Gallic leader Vercingetorix, members of the Catilinarian conspiracy and Sejanus,

Prefect of the Praetorian Guard under the Emperor Tiberius. Access to the round lower level in antiquity was by the hole in the floor of the upper level. The saints were chained to the column next to the altar, with the upside down cross that alludes to St Peter's crucifixion.

Cross the piazza (formerly the level of the Forum prior to excavations) with an excellent view of the Arch of Septimius Severus to the entrance of **Ss. Luca e Martina**. The Arch of Marcus Aurelius, whose reliefs are in Palazzo dei Conservatori, stood nearby. The Curia (Senate House) is to the right of the church. The church with its beautiful facade of convex shapes is a masterpiece by Pietro da Cortona who is buried here. The church was built in 1640 for Cardinal Francesco Barberini, the nephew of Pope Urban VIII Barberini (whose bee emblem is repeated all over the exterior). It is on the site of an earlier church dedicated to S. Martina that was founded in the 7th century by Pope Honorius I and given to the Accademia di S. Luca by Pope Sixtus V Peretti in 1588. The Accademia relocated from their adjacent building in 1932, when it was demolished for excavations, to their current location near the Trevi Fountain (Tour 8).

Pietro da Cortona designed a church with two levels in honour of each saint. The upper church references St Luke as an artist with a painting over the high altar – *St Luke Painting the Virgin* (a copy after an original now in the Accademia di S. Luca attributed to Raphael) – but the interior is more defined by architectural elements. The centre of the lower church contains an altar to S. Martina with tabernacle by Pietro da Cortona, the artist's crypt and a chapel decorated by Alessandro Algardi.

Follow the ancient **Clivus Argentarius** (Clivo Argentario), named for the moneylenders (Argentarii) operating here. At the top of the hill to your left is the entrance to the Complesso del Vittoriano with the **Museo Centrale del Risorgimento**. Continue to your right and walk around the **Forum of Caesar** with a view of the rear wall and apse of the **Temple of Venus Genetrix**. The Forum was built by Julius Caesar in 54 BCE and later reworked by Domitian. It comprised a forum square in front of the temple (inaugurated in 46 BCE) that was surrounded by a porticus. Its construction had been planned for some time to increase the area of the Roman Forum near the meeting venues of the Curia and Comitium that Caesar also revised in 46 BCE. The temple explicitly linked Caesar with his putative mythological ancestress, the goddess Venus, through her son Aeneas and grandson Ascanius (also called

5. Colosseum

Iulus) from whom the Julians claimed descent. The temple was set on a high podium from which Caesar would sit towering before the senators assembled in the forum square. An equestrian statue of Caesar stood in the centre and artwork was displayed in the temple precinct including a statue of Cleopatra who lived in Rome as Caesar's mistress.

Turn right on Via dei Fori Imperiali for a better view of the Forum of Julius Caesar and the ruins of buildings, from the medieval era to the 19th century, demolished as part of the Fascist-era reworking of the area. Just below the didactic sign is pavement from the **Forum of Nerva** and to the left is the pavement from **Vespasian's Forum of Peace**. Both fora extended to the other side of Via dei Fori Imperiali to the **Torre dei Conti** (Tour 6). The ticket office entrance to the **Roman Forum** is to your right, next to S. Lorenzo in Miranda in Largo della Salara Vecchia at the intersection of Via Cavour.

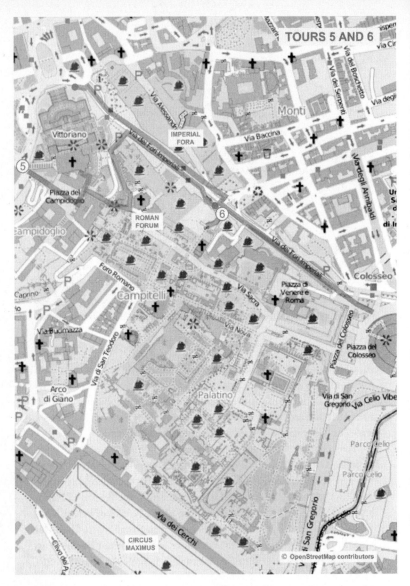

Sites: Roman Forum; Arch of Titus; Palatine Hill; View of Circus Maximus; Arch of Constantine; Temple of Venus and Roma; Colosseum (Option: Ludus Magnus; Nero's Golden House; S. Clemente); Ss. Cosma e Damiano; Vespasian's Temple of Peace; S. Lorenzo in Miranda; Imperial Fora (Forum of Nerva; Forum of Augustus; Forum of Trajan: Basilica Ulpia; Column of Trajan; Trajan's Markets); SS. Nome di Maria; S. Maria di Loreto al Foro Traiano.

Distance: 1.5km (Roman Forum) + 1.75km (Palatine Hill) + 1.3km (Colosseum and Imperial Fora).

Tour 6

# ANCIENT ROME

## Roman Forum, Palatine Hill, Colosseum and Imperial Fora

Rome was the capital and centre of the Roman Empire and at its heart was the Roman Forum. Walk in the footsteps of ancient Romans like Julius Caesar, triumphing generals, or the Vestal Virgins as you stroll the heart of the Roman Forum whose monuments witnessed triumph and bloodshed. A climb up the Palatine Hill that overlooks the Forum from the Renaissance garden of the Farnese and the Circus Maximus gives a glimpse of Imperial life with the House of Augustus, Rome's first emperor, and with the ruins of Domitian's once sumptuous palace where emperors could live like gods. The iconic Colosseum, whose history of blood lust still haunts its ruins, draws thousands of visitors to its arena.

The entrance to the **Roman Forum** is on Via dei Fori Imperiali in Largo della Salara Vecchia next to S. Lorenzo in Miranda. At the current time, the admission ticket covers admission to the Forum, the Palatine Hill and the Colosseum. Individual ticket holders (no group tickets) may enter the Colosseum directly. A site map is provided at the entrance.

The legendary foundation of Rome is assigned to Romulus, following his contest with his twin brother Remus. Tradition relates that his demarcation of the religious boundary of his new city (*pomerium*) traversed the area of the future Forum and included the Capitoline and Palatine Hills. The development of the Roman Forum occurred under the kings who drained the marshlands of the area and transformed Rome from a farming village to a city. Through the Forum ran the Sacred

Way (Sacra Via), commonly called the Via Sacra, the route taken on triumphal processions that entered the Forum from the direction of the Arch of Titus and then up to Capitoline Hill to the Temple of Jupiter Optimus Maximus. Due to fires, the area saw successive construction and reconstruction of buildings and monuments under the Republic and Empire that often served the propaganda goals of prominent public figures and, later, of Imperial dynasties.

Despite the historical importance of the Roman Forum, it was not always preserved as an open site to commemorate ancient Rome. The area was long known as the Campo Vaccino, a grazing area for cattle amidst the ruins, a paradox for the civic centre of a once great empire. The ancient ruins survive despite the systematic destruction of monuments (hastened by the earthquakes of 443, 847 and 1349) when the Fora, Palatine Hill and Colosseum served as a quarry for building materials into the Renaissance and Counter-Reformation, often at the hands of popes who disregarded papal bulls that forbade their destruction. Interest in the ancient monuments and development of archaeology coincided with the Grand Tour whose participants searched for sites from Rome's glorious past encountered in Classical texts. Charlotte Anne Eaton recounts her first visit to the Forum (1817–1818): 'I stood in the Roman Forum! Amidst its silence and desertion, how forcibly did the memory of ages that were fled speak to the soul! How did every broken pillar and fallen capital tell of former greatness!' The surviving monuments are mostly Fascist-era restorations with ongoing archaeological excavations that have taken the area down to the ancient stone pavement.

At the bottom of the entrance ramp, turn right. Immediately to your left is the **Temple of the Deified Julius Caesar** (*Divus Julius*) that was dedicated by Augustus in 29 BCE. The temple was erected at the site of his impromptu cremation during his funeral when the crowd of mourners set fire to his funeral bier in a show of anger against his assassins. The podium of the temple extended into an orator's platform called the Rostra to the Divine Julius. The Latin word *rostra* refers to the beaks of ships that were displayed on the front of the orator's platform following naval victories, as Augustus did here to mark his naval victory over Mark Antony and Cleopatra in 31 BCE.

Julius Caesar as Dictator was responsible for a series of construction projects that transformed the Republican Roman Forum, continued by

Augustus and subsequent emperors. The temple stood at the long end of the **Roman Forum** and faced the Capitoline Hill. This is the once open space of the Forum where orators gave speeches and aristocratic funerals were held that could include gladiatorial combats under the Republic. The once open space was later filled in with dedicatory monuments. Here was the **Golden Milestone** (*Miliarium Aureum*) set up by the Emperor Augustus to mark the symbolic centre of the world from which the roads that left the city to various parts of the empire were measured.

Continue towards the Arch of Septimius Severus. Along the **Basilica Aemilia** to your right ran the **Porticus of Gaius and Lucius**, the grandsons and adopted sons of Augustus that included shops (*Tabernae Novae*). The basilica was first built in 179 BCE by the Censors M. Fulvius Nobilior and M. Aemilius Lepidus on the location of an earlier structure. It was rebuilt from 55 to 34 BCE by later generations of the Aemilius family and again by Augustus who dedicated it in the name of M. Aemilius Lepidus. The final reconstruction of the basilica was at the beginning of the 5th century CE after Alaric's sack of Rome. Basilicas served as civic buildings for the hearing of law cases and other public meetings and their utilitarian form was adopted by early Christians in Rome who shunned buildings associated with pagan idolatry.

Between the basilica and the Curia was the **Argiletum**, the route that connected the Roman Forum to the Subura district (transformed into the Forum Transitorium that was later renamed the Forum of Nerva). The **Cloaca Maxima**, the monumental sewer system attributed to the 6th-century BCE kings Tarquinius Priscus and Tarquinius Superbus, entered the Forum along this route and was commemorated by the round **Temple of Venus Cloacina** whose base survives to your right. At the corner of the basilica near the entrance to the Curia is an area that was planted with trees (fig, olive and grape vine) in 1958 to mark the location of the ancient grove where a statue of the mythological figure Marsyas was displayed as a symbol of liberty, but its location may have been in the area of the Lacus Curtius to your left.

The original **Curia** (Senate House), the Curia Hostilia, was located in the area of the church of Ss. Luca e Martina and stood next to Rome's earliest basilica, the Basilica Porcia (184 BCE). Both buildings burned down following the impromptu cremation of P. Clodius Pulcher (52 BCE), the notorious brother of Clodia associated with the Lesbia of Catullus' poetry, when supporters set fire to his funeral bier that was displayed in the Curia. Julius Caesar began a reconstruction of the Senate House as the Curia Julia in conjunction with his Forum that was completed by the Emperor Augustus in 29 BCE. During its reconstruction, the Senate met at the Curia of the Theatre of Pompey complex (Tour 7), where Caesar was assassinated on the Ides of March in 44 BCE. The current building was restored by the Emperor Diocletian after a fire in 283 CE (under the Emperor Carinus) destroyed all of the buildings between the Forum of Caesar and the Basilica Julia. In 630 CE, Pope Honorius I converted the Curia into the church of S. Adriano. The original bronze doors were moved to the Basilica of S. Giovanni in Laterano by Pope Alexander VII Chigi in 1660. The church interior was removed between 1935 and 1938 and was mostly destroyed, though some fresco fragments survive in the niches on the west wall and others are displayed at the Crypta Balbi Museum (Tour 7).

Under the Republic, the area in front of the Curia once served as the **Comitium**, an open-air area of tiered steps used for political assemblies. A rostra formed part of the consecrated complex (perhaps including the Volcanal, the sanctuary of Vulcan) that also included a black stone (**Lapis Niger**) in front of the Arch of Septimius Severus behind a square railing. The stone is inscribed with a ritual text that is difficult to decipher and was thought to be a grave marker in the late Republic of one of Rome's early figures including Romulus but may actually commemorate the spot where, according to one tradition of his death, he was murdered by senators. Julius Caesar rebuilt the area at the same time that he rebuilt the new Curia Julia. The Comitium was paved over and the rostra moved to its current location as the Imperial Rostra facing the Forum against the backdrop of the monuments on the Capitoline Hill.

The **Arch of Septimius Severus** (203 CE) commemorates Septimius Severus and his sons Caracalla and Geta (whose name was erased from the dedicatory inscription in 212 CE after he was murdered by Caracalla). The decoration of the arch commemorates Septimius Severus's victory over the Parthians who are depicted as captive barbarians. The arch survives because it was reused as a fortress in the medieval era. In 1532, Pope Clement VII de' Medici demolished the adjoining church of Ss. Sergio e Bacco al Foro Romano. The Confraternity of Butchers in exchange received S. Maria della Quercia in Piazza della Quercia (Tour

3). The Decennalia base in front was one of five honorary columns set up by the Emperor Diocletian on the Imperial Rostra to commemorate the tenth year of the Tetrarchy.

Walk through the arch and turn left. Immediately to your left is the cylindrical brick structure identified as the **Umbilicus Urbis** (navel or centre of the city). In front of it may be the Altar of Saturn. Directly behind it is the **Imperial Rostra** that was originated by Julius Caesar but enlarged and extended by Augustus. After being proscribed in 43 BCE by Mark Antony (who formed part of a political alliance called the Second Triumvirate with Octavian, the future Augustus, and M. Aemilius Lepidus), Cicero's head and hands were cut off and attached to it.

To your right opposite the arch is the **Temple of Concord**. The earliest temple on this site was attributed to Camillus in 367 BCE but it is more likely that the temple was built in 121 BCE. Cicero delivered his fourth Catilinarian oration here in 63 BCE. Tiberius rebuilt the temple from 7 BCE to 10 CE and dedicated it as the Temple of Concordia Augusta where Senate meetings were held. Greek art was displayed in the central hall.

Next to the temple are the three surviving columns from the **Temple of the Deified Vespasian and Titus**, dedicated by the Emperor Domitian. It was restored by architect Giuseppe Camporese in 1811. To your far right is the **Portico of the Dei Consentes** (rebuilt in 367 CE), dedicated to the Consenting Gods that formed the Roman pantheon of 12 gods. It lines the **Clivus Capitolinus**, part of the Via Sacra route by which triumphal processions ascended the Capitoline Hill.

Straight ahead with eight standing columns with Ionic capitals is the **Temple of Saturn** that served as the state treasury whose deposits were stored under its high podium. The earliest temple may have been inaugurated on 17 December 498 BCE, the feast day of the Saturnalia. The temple was rebuilt in 42 BCE and restored several times in the following centuries. The inscription records its restoration following a fire. Cicero delivered his speech the *Pro Milone* in the area of the temple.

Turn left to walk along the Via Sacra past where the **Arch of Tiberius** (16 CE) stood connected to the Basilica Julia. The arch commemorated the victories of the Emperor Tiberius and his nephew Germanicus over German tribes. To your right is the stepped podium of the **Basilica Julia**. The basilica, built on the site of the Basilica Sempronia (169 BCE) and the house of Scipio Africanus, who defeated Hannibal in 202 BCE, was dedicated in 46 BCE by Julius Caesar but completed by Augustus. The two-storey basilica was destroyed by fire but rebuilt in 12 CE and restored by Domitian in 94 CE. It was rebuilt again after the fire of 283 CE as a vast three-storey basilica (101m x 49m) by the Emperor Diocletian. Shops lined the area along the far long side and a commercial area where the **Temple of Divus Augustus** may have been located on the site of his first house. The basilica was used as a law court and for business meetings and the gaming boards etched onto the steps and pavement suggest that some visitors faced a long wait. Surviving elements were demolished for the construction of Palazzo Giraud-Torlonia on Via della Conciliazione (Tour 2).

The fluted Corinthian **Column of Phocas** (608 CE) to your left is one of seven commemorative columns that lined the south side of the Forum that was dedicated to the Byzantine emperor by Smaragdus, the exarch of Italy. The column is from the 4th century, spoliated from an earlier monument. Emperor Phocas gave the Pantheon to Pope St Boniface IV who converted it into the church of S. Maria ad Martyrs (Tour 8). The column was the last monument erected in the Forum and one of the first excavated. The Duchess of Devonshire (the former Lady Elizabeth Foster) excavated the column during her funding of the Forum excavations from 1816 to 1824 that also saw the restoration of the stones along the Via Sacra.

Just to the right of the column is the area of the **Lacus Curtius**. The relief sculpture (a copy of the original in the Capitoline Museums) commemorates the location of a lake or pond where legend claims Marcus Curtius sacrificed himself before a battle in 362 BCE by plunging with his horse into the lake that closed up after him. The grove of Marsyas planted with an olive, a fig and grape vine may have been located here. According to Pliny the Elder, the grove contained the sacred fig tree (*ficus Ruminalis*) that marked the centre of the Forum. A base to the right of the Lacus Curtius once supported a statue of Constantine and a colossal Equestrian Statue of Domitian was also erected in this area.

Turn right at the corner of the Basilica Julia onto the Vicus Tuscus between the basilica and the Temple of Castor and Pollux. Processions passed along the vicus during the Ludi Romani ('Roman Games') when images of the gods were conveyed on wagons from the Capitolium to the Circus Maximus. To your right down a short flight of steps is an entrance door to the Cloaca Maxima. To your left on the other side of the Vicus Tuscus immediately behind the Temple of Castor and Pollux is the **Domitianic Hall** (*c.*90 CE).

Beyond is the **Oratory of the Forty Martyrs** and next to it on an angle is the white marble shrine of the **Lacus Juturnae** (Lake or Pool of Juturna the nymph of spring water and healing) on the site where the spring of Juturna provided fresh water to the residents of the Palatine Hill, who could access it from a ramp behind S. Maria Antiqua. To the right and behind the Domitianic Hall is the church of **S. Maria Antiqua** that is preceded by a forecourt. The church was built in the mid-6th century but was abandoned in the mid-9th century. An early fresco of the Madonna from here is now displayed in S. Francesca Romana (S. Maria Nova). Further along the Vicus Tuscus are the **Horrea Agrippiana** warehouses, named for Marcus Agrippa, into which the church of S. Teodoro (Tour 4) was built.

Retrace your steps on the Vicus Tuscus to the Via Sacra and turn right at the **Temple of Castor and Pollux** where three Corinthian columns and a fragment of the entablature rise over the cement core of the podium. The earliest version of the peripteral temple was dedicated by Aulus Postumius in 484 BCE following the Roman victory over the Etruscans in the Battle of Lake Regillus (499 or 496 BCE), since the twins were seen watering their horses during the battle at the Lacus Juturnae behind the temple. Castor and Pollux are known collectively as the Dioscuri and the twins of Gemini. They are the precursors to the marine phenomenon known as St Elmo's fire. They represent the first foreign cult (Greek) introduced to Rome and became the patron gods of the knights class (*Equites*) at Rome who celebrated the twins with a procession past the temple on 15 July each year.

A triple **Arch of Augustus** stood at this corner of the Forum in the area of the current steps. The arch likely commemorated Augustus' Parthian victory in 19 BCE when the legionary battle standards lost by M. Licinius Crassus in 53 BCE were returned to Rome, but it has also been identified with another arch erected in the Forum in 29 BCE to celebrate Augustus' victory over Mark Antony and Cleopatra at the Battle of Actium and victories in Dalmatia and Egypt. The *Fasti Consulares*, the list of Roman Consuls now in the Capitoline Museums, was found here when the ruins of the arch were demolished in 1546.

6. Statues of Vestal Virgins from the House of the Vestals, Roman Forum

Walk up the short flight of stairs to continue to the eastern end of the Forum to the round **Temple of Vesta** straight ahead that is at the corner of the vast **House of the Vestals** complex. This complex was part of the sacred area of the Forum together with the Regia and the Domus Publica. The surviving elements of the temple that dates to a reconstruction by Julia Domna, the wife of Septimius Severus, after the fire of 191 CE are largely reconstructions from 1930. A ramp connected the temple to the Palatine Hill. Vesta was the goddess of the hearth whose sacred fire in her temple was constantly tended by a College of Vestal Virgins who would collect the ashes and ceremoniously throw them into the Tiber on 15 June. The Vestals were from aristocratic families and served until the age of 30 during which time they were highly honoured by the state. They took a vow of chastity that if violated was punishable by execution (buried alive). The sacred flame of the Vestals was extinguished by order of Theodosius I in 394 three years after his edict by Coelia Concordia, the last Vestal Virgin in history who converted to Christianity later in life. The statues of Vestals that lined the porticus were found in a pit to be burned for lime. The statues do not correspond to the names preserved on the bases.

Exit the House of the Vestal Virgins and walk straight ahead towards the church of S. Lorenzo in Miranda, next to the entrance ramp of the Forum. The sites associated with the Pontifex Maximus, the **Regia** (office) and **Domus Publica** (house), are in the triangular-shaped area behind the Temple of Deified Julius Caesar to your left. The official office of the Pontifex Maximus and the Rex Sacrorum included a Shrine of Mars, a sanctuary of Ops the harvest goddess and the sacred shield (*ancilia*) that was carried in procession by the Salian priests. At the corner of the Regia spanning the Via Sacra was the Fornix Fabianus, the oldest triumphal arch erected by Q. Fabius Maximus (121 BCE) commemorating his victory over the Allobroges tribe in Gaul.

The Baroque facade of the church of **S. Lorenzo in Miranda** (1602) rises behind the portico of the **Temple of the Deified Antoninus Pius and Faustina**. The temple originally faced with marble was first dedicated to his wife, the Deified Faustina the Younger, by Antoninus Pius in 141 CE, but after his own death and deification, his successor Marcus Aurelius altered the inscription to include his name. Carystian green marble columns (14m high), also called cipollino in Italian for its resemblance to a sliced onion, line the facade and the sides of the porch. The cause of the grooves in the columns is unknown but they may be related to attempts to pull down the temple for building materials. A brick altar is displayed on the brick steps that are not original to the temple. Access to the church is from Via dei Fori Imperiali.

Facing the church, continue on the Via Sacra to your right as it ascends towards the Velia, the northern ridge of the Palatine Hill that occupies the area of the Basilica of Maxentius. The Porta Mugonia, the gate that led to the Palatine Hill, was in this area. Immediately to the right of the temple steps, archaeological excavations revealed an **Archaic Necropolis**. Burials, cremation and inhumation, from the early Iron Age to the 6th century BCE, in a variety of methods from large jars, cinerary urns, tree trunks, pits and trenches closely resemble those discovered on the Palatine Hill.

Just beyond and to your left is the so-called **Temple of Romulus**, a round brick temple with a dome built in the early 4th century with ancient bronze doors and porphyry columns flanked by a brick exedra. The temple is attributed to Maxentius in honour of his son Romulus who died in 309 at the age of four, but Constantine may have rededicated the temple. The architectural elements come from various buildings dating back to the reign of Augustus including the bronze doors (*c.*200). The temple was incorporated into the church of Ss. Cosma e Damiano that was built into Vespasian's Forum of Peace. The entry door was raised in 1632 by Pope Urban VIII Barberini but returned to its current and original location in 1879. If closed, a glass window inside the church gives a view of interior.

Keep to your left along a medieval brick portico to the **Basilica of Maxentius**. The Temple of Jupiter Stator, the first temple or shrine constructed in Rome by Romulus, was located in the area. Walk up the ramp to your left to get a closer look at the open area of the central nave (80m x 25m), three cross-vaults and the three surviving barrel-vaulted niches along the north wall whose coffered ceilings are now without their stucco. The vast basilica (100m x 65m x 35m high), also known as the Basilica Nova and the Basilica of Constantine, was started by Maxentius in 306 but completed by Constantine after his victory at the Battle of the Milvian Bridge. The axis was changed with an entry along the south wall facing the Via Sacra that was approached by steps and four porphyry columns. The apse in the central niche along the north wall was also added at this time. The marble head and other body parts of Constantine's statue now in the Capitoline Museums were found in the apse on the west side. The commercial area between the basilica and the Temple of Peace was known as the **Carinae**, where the City Prefecture (*Praefectura Urbana*) was located and whose official judicial and administrative functions were carried out in the basilica. Pope Paul V Borghese removed the surviving Corinthian column to Piazza S. Maria Maggiore in 1613 for the Column of the Virgin monument (Tour 12). The basilica was mistakenly identified as Vespasian's Temple of Peace until correctly identified in the 19th century. Currently, this is an exit point of the Roman Forum area. Exit here to proceed immediately to the Colosseum.

Opposite on the other side of the Via Sacra are the ruins of the **Horrea Vespasiani** warehouses built by Domitian that replaced a monumental colonnade built by Nero that lined the Via Sacra. In the area are the ruins of early Republican houses that likely included the luxurious House of Marcus Aemilius Scaurus that contained 50 bedrooms for slaves at the basement level, and a section of an 8th-century BCE wall that is called the **Wall of Romulus** since it corresponds in date to the legendary founding of the city in 753 BCE.

The entrance to **S. Francesca Romana** (S. Maria Nova) is by Via dei Fori Imperiali. Next to the church on the right-hand side is the entrance to the **Forum Antiquarium** museum in the former convent of the church (usually closed) that is built into the **Temple of Venus and Roma**. The surviving architectural elements here are best viewed from the front facing the Colosseum.

Continue left on the Via Sacra to the **Arch of Titus** that was erected after 81 CE and dedicated to the Deified Titus. It commemorates his and his father Vespasian's victory in the Jewish War (70–71 CE). The original dedication is on the east side attic (facing the Colosseum). On the interior panel on the south side, the spoils of Jerusalem are carried in a triumphal procession that were later deposited in Vespasian's Temple of Peace in his Forum of Peace. On the north side panel, Titus rides in triumph on a chariot through the Porta Triumphalis that was at the start of the triumphal procession. Another arch dedicated to Titus at the curved end of the Circus Maximus (Tour 13) contained a scene of his apotheosis. In the medieval period, the arch was incorporated into the stronghold of the Frangipane who controlled the Palatine Hill and was later controlled by the Annibaldi. Giuseppe Valadier heavily restored the arch for Pope Pius VII (1822) by removing later additions, including adjoining structures and using travertine to distinguish his reconstruction from the original marble elements.

At this point there are several tour options. Currently, the exit at the Arch of Titus winds along the side of the Palatine Hill to the ticket entrance and exit of the Palatine Hill on Via di S. Gregorio. Exit left and resume the tour at the Arch of Constantine for entry directions to the Colosseum.

To explore the Palatine Hill, turn right at the arch and continue straight up the slope of the **Clivus Palatinus**. Signs point to the Museo Palatino straight ahead and to the entrance to the Cryptoporticus of Nero to your right. Enter the Cryptoporticus to continue on the tour. If you would like to visit the Grotto below the Farnese pavilions first, turn right onto the Via Nova past the warehouses of Vespasian and shops to your right. The arches that span the road are Severan in date. The entrance to the **Grotto** (known as the Nymphaeum of the Rain) is to your left and is approached by steps. From the Grotto (facing the fountain) walk up the steps to your left and follow signs to the Cryptoporticus of Nero. The Farnese Gardens covered the area of the hill (the Germalus) towards the Capitoline Hill, where the substructure foundations of the House of Tiberius are visible, descending to the Via Nova in terraces, and were accessed from the Forum through a monumental gate now on the other side of Hill at the Via di S. Gregorio entrance.

The **Palatine Hill** is one of the Seven Hills of Rome associated with Romulus in the legendary period, the Roman elite under the Republic, and Imperial palaces under the Empire. The central peak of the hill was named for the ancient settlement called Palatium. After the transfer of the capital to Constantinople, the Imperial palace complexes were sporadically occupied: in the 6th century, Theodoric the Great used the Palatine as his residence and Pope John VII (705–707) moved the papal residence here, but this was moved back to the Lateran by Pope Gregory II (715–731). In the Middle Ages, the structures fell into ruin and in the following centuries were systematically destroyed for building materials.

The **Cryptoporticus of Nero** (covered corridor) survives from his **Domus Transitoria**, the house that he was building before the Great Fire of 64. The Domus Transitoria was replaced by Nero's infamous **Golden House** (Domus Aurea) that stretched from here to the Oppian Hill on the other side of the Colosseum (at the completion of which he supposedly remarked, 'Finally, I can live like a human being'). Towards the exit are plaster copies of the original ceiling decoration.

As you leave the Cryptoporticus on the south-west part of the hill, the so-called **House of Livia**, the wife of the Emperor Augustus, is to your left. Augustus forced her husband, Tiberius Claudius Nero, to divorce her in 39 BCE (her son Tiberius was a child and she was pregnant with her second child Drusus). The marriage lasted until his death in 14 CE but they had no children and his hopes for succession were focused on his daughter Julia from his marriage to Scribonia whom he divorced the day his daughter was born. After other candidates related by blood died, Augustus married Julia to Tiberius whom he reluctantly adopted and named as heir. The entrance faced east and the house included bedrooms on the basement level of the atrium for slaves. The interior contains frescoes with mythological and landscape themes of the Second Style from the 1st century BCE.

With the House of Livia to your left, continue to the **House of Augustus** that incorporated earlier houses including the house originally owned by the orator Hortensius. It was joined to the House of Livia and was adjacent to Augustus' Temple of Apollo. Augustus cultivated an image of austere simplicity and lived here throughout his reign, but luxurious elements betray the conceit. To visit the rooms with beautiful Second Style frescoes (*c.*30 BCE), continue past the house and descend the steps to enter the house through an area that was the peristyle. The steps are known as the **Steps of Cacus** (*Scalae Caci*). According to Roman legend, the monster Cacus, who was defeated by Hercules, occupied the Palatine Hill that was subsequently inhabited by the Arcadian Evander, who founded the ancient city of Palatium.

To your right in the area covered by roofing are Iron Age Huts (9th and 8th century) where Roman legend placed the **Hut of Romulus**. The traditional area of the lupercal where the She-Wolf (*lupa*) suckled the twins Romulus and Remus was at the base of the slope in the area of the Velabrum (Tour 4), where the twins were discovered by the shepherd Faustulus. The historian Livy preserves an alternative version of the myth that the She-Wolf referred to a whore (also called *lupa*) named Laurentia. The purification and fertility ritual of the Lupercalia (13–15 February) took place here in which Priests of Faunus (the Luperci) sacrificed two goats and a dog. Two patrician members of the Luperci were selected to run around the border of the ancient Palatium dressed in goatskins and striking women with whips made from the sacrificed goatskins (*februa*, from which the name of the month of February is derived). Augustus located his house next to the Hut of Romulus to connect his refounding of the Golden Age with Rome's legendary founder whose name he contemplated adopting.

From the House of Augustus, retrace your steps past the House of Livia then turn left and climb the first flight of steps. For a better view of the Iron Age huts area, take the path to your left at the top of the first landing to view the **Temple of the Magna Mater** (also known as Cybele) whose cult was introduced to Rome in 205 BCE from Phrygia (modern Turkey) when her headless image was drawn along the Tiber by the Vestal Virgin Claudia Quinta. The original temple built in 191 BCE was rebuilt around 111 BCE and in 3 CE following fires. The *Ludi Magalenses* were held in her honour (11 April), which included scenic entertainment devoted to comedy on stages set up in front of the temple at which the plays of Plautus and Terence were performed. To the left, with its long side along the Houses of Livia and Augustus, was the **Temple of Victory** dedicated by Lucius Postumius Megellus in 294 BCE. In between these temples was the small **Shrine of Victoria Virgo.**

Return to the first landing then continue up the stairs to your left to tour the **Farnese Gardens** (Horti Farnesiani) designed by Vignola in the mid-16th century for Cardinal Alessandro Farnese, the grandson of Pope Paul III Farnese, in the grounds of the **Palace of Tiberius** (Domus Tiberiana) and monumental Julio-Claudian gardens. Augustus' friend Gaius Martius is credited with the invention of topiaries in shapes that included hunting scenes and naval fleets. From this part of the hill are beautiful views of the Forum. In the centre of the rose garden is the tomb of Italian archaeologist Giacomo Boni (1859–1925), who excavated the Forum and Palatine Hill. He replanted the garden here and in the areas by Vignola's pavilions (used as aviaries by the Farnese) where he lived from 1907 to 1925 while conducting his excavations.

With the pavilions to your back, take the broad path into the open area of Domitian's Palace. The ruins of the **Temple of Apollo** are straight ahead. The temple complex, that also included two libraries, was built by Augustus and dedicated in 28 BCE with an ode from the poet Horace. The cella contained original 4th-century Greek statues of Apollo, Diana and Leo. The sanctuary portico enclosure was decorated with the myth of the Danaids. The *Ludi Apollinares* were held in Apollo's honour (13 July) and celebrated with scenic entertainment from tragedies.

Continue to the left of the Temple of Apollo (east) to enter the area of **Domitian's Palace** that comprised both official (**Domus Flavia**) and private (**Domus Augustana**) areas. The magnificently lavish palace complex was built by the architect Rabirius between 81 and 92 CE on an immense scale and on multiple levels, on top of Republican houses and Nero's Domus Transitoria, to fill in the valley between the Palatium and Germalus ridges. The House of Augustus complex was preserved and the palace soared beyond the current elevation of the ruins. He was the first emperor who was called *dominus et deus* ('lord and god'). Mussolini aimed to take his own place in the hierarchy of Rome's founders with the restoration of ancient monuments throughout the city that included the palace complex first excavated in 1926–1928 and restored from 1934 to 1936 for Hitler's visit.

The entrance to the **Domus Flavia** was probably through this west side of the palace that led to the first large peristyle **Court** that was lined with marble and a portico of yellow marble columns that surrounded a lake with an octagonal island in the centre. On the north side of the large court (to your left) was a **Basilica** at the north-west corner, built over an earlier house known as the Aula Isiaca, an **Audience Hall** in the centre and at the north-east corner a Lararium that was built over a Republican house known as the 'House of the Griffins', after the decoration of the Second Style frescoes (*c.*100 BCE). To your right the ruins of a monumental oval-shaped fountain, the **Elliptical Nymphaeum**, adjoined the **Dining Hall** that faced the courtyard and was built over two of Nero's dining rooms. The poet Statius was a guest at the official opening reception and he describes a magnificent room worthy of Jupiter. To the right of the fountain is the Mills Tower, a restored tower built by the Frangipane that is named after Charles Mills, whose 19th-century villa with turrets and an ogee arcade occupied this corner of the hill. Underneath the tower is a colour marble pavement (opus sectile) that was laid above a nymphaeum fountain from Nero's Domus Transitoria.

Retrace your steps to the Domus Flavia and walk around the monumental fountain in the peristyle court to enter the **Museo Palatino**. The museum was established in 1936 in the former Convent of the Sisters of the Visitation with objects found on the Hill in the 19th century by archaeologist Pietro Rosa. The ground floor contains reconstructions and archeological artifacts of the Hut of Romulus and burials from the Iron Age settlement of the Hill to objects from the late Republic. The first floor displays Imperial-era sculpture and architectural fragments from the reign of Augustus to the 4th century CE including sculptural and decorative elements from the Temple of Apollo.

Continue past the museum to stroll around the ruins of the **Domus Augustana**, part of the palace complex that contained Domitian's bedroom where he was assassinated in 96 CE. Continue straight through the second large peristyle **Court** and past the ruins to your right, marked with the sign *Domus Augustana*, to reach the so-called **Stadium of Domitian** that is a **Garden** in the form of a sunken Stadium or Hippodrome. This is the site of the martyrdom of St Sebastian who was tied to a column and pierced by arrows perhaps as part of a hunting-theme (*venatio*) form of execution. His body was thrown into the Cloaca Maxima and buried in the catacombs named after him under the Basilica S. Sebastiano ad Catacumbas (Tour 14). The church of S. Sebastiano al Palatino commemorates his martyrdom. The ruins visible on the other side of the Stadium belong to the **Domus Severiana**, the palace extension built by the Emperor Septimius Severus and members of his dynasty at the beginning of the 3rd century.

Turn right at the Stadium to view the lower levels of the Domus Augustana with a third peristyle **court** and for a view of the Circus Maximus from the terraced side of the Palatine Hill that contained a semicircular exedra and the Imperial Viewing Box, with levels that descended to the seats of the Circus.

Exit the Palatine Hill by walking around the north end of the Stadium, with ruins of baths that date to the reign of Maxentius and a view of the interior of the Colosseum. From here a sign points left for the current exit into the Roman Forum by way of the Clivus Palatinus to the Arch of Titus exit. To your right as you descend is a door marked with a sign for the **Vigna Barberini** if you would like to extend your stroll to the churches of **S. Bonaventura** and **S. Sebastiano al Palatino** by Luigi Arrigucci (1624) for Pope Urban VII Barberini with his signature bees on the facade, the ruins of the **Temple of Elagabalus** that was dedicated to Deus Sol Invictus (El-Gabal) and to the terrace with the best views of the Colosseum.

Or you may descend the double staircase and turn right to tour the areas of the **Domus Severiana** with views from a platform of the Circus Maximus, the Caelian Hill (Tour 13) and a line of cypress trees at the base of the Hill to your left that mark the location of the Septizodium (Tour 13). From there you may return to this point and reclimb the double staircase to follow the exit sign into the Roman Forum or exit the Hill immediately by following the winding path to the Via di S. Gregorio exit for views of the Domus Severiana exterior (and entry to the Severan Arcades and Bath complex when open) and the ruins of **Aqueduct Arches**. Turn left at the exit and resume the tour at the Arch of Constantine.

The **Arch of Constantine** was dedicated by the Senate and the Roman People (SPQR) on 25 July 315, with inscriptions that commemorate Constantine's defeat of his co-ruler Maxentius (called 'tyrant') at the Battle of the Milvian Bridge on 28 October 312. Other inscriptions commemorate the 10th and 20th anniversaries of Constantine's reign. The arch takes its design cues from the Arch of Septimius Severus. On all sides are original and earlier reused (spoliated) architectural elements and sculpture. Original elements are the column bases with reliefs of captives and victories, spandrels on the arches, roundels with the sun

(Sol) and moon (Luna) on the sides, and the narrow friezes along the front and sides whose narrative is read counter-clockwise, beginning with the west side. Lorenzino de' Medici, the nephew of Pope Clement VII de' Medici, earned the nickname 'Lorenzaccio' for decapitating the heads of Constantine on the contemporary friezes as an act of defiance against his papal uncle. He later assassinated Alessandro de' Medici and was condemned to death by Cosimo I de' Medici who succeeded him as Duke of Florence and then as Grand Duke of Tuscany.

Spoliated sculpture was specifically selected from monuments of the so-called Good Emperors: Trajan (eight statues of Dacian captives; friezes on the interior walls of the central arch from the Great Trajanic Frieze and the reliefs at the sides of the attic), Hadrian (eight roundels with some portraits recarved as Constantine and Licinius) and Marcus Aurelius (four tall reliefs on the attic that are the same size as the three in Palazzo dei Conservatori). The portraits were recarved as Constantine. The source of the yellow marble (giallo antico) Corinthian columns is unknown. One replaces the column removed by Pope Clement VIII for S. Giovanni in Laterano (1597). Little survives of the polychrome decoration of red and green porphyry. Although it commemorated Constantine's triumph of 312 and was situated along the triumphal route, the monument only witnessed a single triumph: that of 403 CE to commemorate Stilicho's victory over Count Gildo.

A marker in the pavement on the north side of the arch identifies the location of the **Meta Sudans**, a fountain erected by Domitian between 89 and 96 CE and restored by Constantine that marked the boundaries of Regions II, III, IV and X of the Augustan city. The fountain name referred to the similarity of its shape to a turning post (*meta*) in a circus and function at the location that marks the turning point of triumphal processions towards the Via Sacra. The fountain appeared to sweat (*sudans*) water from many small openings. It was destroyed by Mussolini in 1936.

The **Temple of Venus and Roma** was built and designed by the Emperor Hadrian and dedicated in 135 CE. The vast area of the precinct (1.5 hectares) was formerly occupied by the atrium of Nero's Golden House. The temple consisted of two frontal porticoes of ten columns facing opposite directions with back-to-back apses in the centre with seated cult statues of Venus Felix facing the Colosseum and Roma Aeterna (Eternal Rome) facing the Forum and incorporated into the convent of S. Francesca Romana. The temple was rebuilt by Maxentius after a fire in 307, at which time the cement coffered ceiling was added. Following his victory over Maxentius, Constantine appropriated the cella of Venus for his family, the second gens Flavia, and he rededicated the temple as the Temple of Roma and of the Flavian Gens. The temple was at the centre of a vast area appropriated by Constantine with his own and earlier Flavian monuments as the Colosseum, the Colossal statue of Sol, Vespasian's Forum of Peace and the Arch of Titus. The Piazza del Colosseo is the location of the Good Friday service of the Stations of the Cross (*Via Crucis*).

Opposite, the raised bed with an oak tree marks the base on which the **Colossal Statue of Nero/Sol** stood after being moved by Hadrian for the construction of the Temple of Venus and Roma. The statue (30–35m high) originally depicted Nero nude as the sun god Sol (Helios in Greek), but after his death the features were changed to those of Sol. Prior to Constantine's conversion to Christianity, he worshipped the pagan Sol Invictus, whose own cult was associated with the worship of Christ through the cult of Christ-Helios. The arch's proximity to the Colossal statue of Sol along the triumphal route acknowledges the god's transformative role in Constantine's conversion to Christianity and his victory over the pagan Maxentius.

The **Colosseum** is one of the most iconic buildings in the world. Charles Dickens visited its ruins in 1844 and wrote: 'As it tops the other ruins: standing there, a mountain among graves: so do its ancient influences outlive all other remnants of the old mythology and old butchery of Rome, in the nature of the fierce and cruel Roman people.' The name Colosseum is medieval in origin and derives from the colossal statue of Nero/Sol. The official name is the Flavian Amphitheatre (Amphitheatrum Flavium). The Colosseum was a symbol of empire and a monument to bloodlust for entertainment but it was also an informal parliament or congress where the public could communicate their views to public officials and a law court where the punishment of criminals became part of the spectacle, often with mythological allusions and role-playing.

Construction started under the Emperor Vespasian in 70 CE with Jewish slaves that he brought to Rome by draining the lake from Nero's Golden House. Only three storeys were complete at the time of Vespasian's death in 79. The upper level was completed and dedicated by the Emperor Titus in 80 CE with opening games that lasted 100 days during which 5,000 animals were killed. The Colosseum was the largest amphitheatre ever constructed with vast dimensions (189m long by 156m wide and 48m high) over four levels defined by various architectural orders: Tuscan, Ionic, Corinthian and Corinthian pilasters on the fourth level with corbels on which poles (240) were positioned for the awning (*velarium*). Stones (*cippi*) circled the exterior to attach the ropes used for the operation of the awning by sailors from the naval headquarters at Misenum. Some are preserved at the north-east corner. It could accommodate about 50,000 spectators who were seated according to social rank: the emperor and Vestal Virgins sat opposite each other at the north and south ends; the senators seated on the same level at the east and west ends; the next levels were occupied by Knights (Equites) and citizens (plebs); and women, slaves and the poor were placed in the highest seats furthest from the arena. They entered through 80 entrance arches according to their seating area whose number was indicated above the arches (numbers 23 (XXIII) to 54 (LIV) survive) providing direct routes (*vomitoria*) that allowed for rapid entrance and exit.

Spectacle entertainments took immense planning and stagecraft to produce and were called gifts (*munera*) to the people by Titus, but gladiatorial combats were originally performed at funerals by prisoners of war as gifts to the dead until Julius Caesar held games in memory of his daughter. Soon after, the state sponsored games, including Augustus who supplied 10,000 gladiators for public entertainment. This became part of the 'bread and circuses' formula used to control the urban populace in Rome and other major cities in the empire. Events featured the hunting of wild and exotic animals (*venationes*), animals hunting unarmed prisoners as a form of public execution, and the main spectacle: gladiatorial combats. There were four types of gladiators with their own distinct weapons: Samnite (long shield and sword), Thracian (round shield with curved sword), Myrmillo (long shield and sword and named for the fish on his helmet) and Retiarius (net and trident). Gladiators are often associated with the entrance address of *Ave Caesar, nos morituri te salutamus* ('Hail Caesar, We about to die salute you'), but it is only attested once for a mock naval battle under the Emperor Claudius. The ruins of the Ludus Magnus gladiator school and barrack that was connected to the Colosseum by tunnels are on the north-east side of the Colosseum. Below the arena named for the sand (*harena*) that was used to sprinkle over the blood between acts is an underground labyrinth of holding pens (for fighters and animals) and trap doors. The crew that cleared the arena of corpses and carcasses were dressed as Hades, the god of the Underworld. Ancient sources mention that the Colosseum was filled with water for mock naval battles but this is problematic considering that there are wooden substructures below the arena and other venues known as *naumachia* were designed for such entertainment.

Constantine did not ban gladiator games, just crucifixion as a form of execution, so the bloody entertainments continued under the Christian emperors for an audience that was just as bloodthirsty. Gladiatorial combats were banned after the 5th century (last mentioned in sources in 434/435), but animal hunts continued at least until 523 when the Emperor Theodoric granted the request of the consul-elect Maximus to celebrate his appointment. Church tradition observes the Colosseum as the site of Christian martyrs. Pope Clement XI (1700–1724) consecrated an archway to the Chapel of S. Maria della Pietà al Colosseo, and prior to the excavation of the arena, Pope Benedict XIV (1740–1758) erected a crucifix at its centre with chapels devoted to the Stations of the Cross around its perimeter where Good Friday services were held.

The Colosseum survives despite natural disasters and intense quarrying. It was restored several times and needed more repairs after the fires of 217 and 250 CE, after being struck by lightening in 320 CE and after the earthquakes of 429 and 443 CE. In the medieval period, it served as a cemetery and became the stronghold of the Frangipane and the Annibaldi families. In 1312, Emperor Henry VII gave the Colosseum to the Senate and People of Rome. The earthquake of 1349 took down the south wall but the systematic destruction had already begun and the Colosseum served as the quarry of Rome for centuries. Giuseppe Valadier constructed the buttress support walls in 1820 for Pope Pius VII to shore up what remained of the outer wall. The floor of the arena was removed under Mussolini. Restorations are ongoing.

To continue the tour to the Imperial Fora, turn right after you exit the Colosseum past the Temple of Venus and Roma and turn left onto Via dei Fori Imperiali and continue to the Basilica of Ss. Cosma e Damiano. Along the way, the entrance to **S. Francesca Romana** (S. Maria Nova) is up the ramp to your left as you walk past the Temple of Venus and Roma into which the 11th-century church was built. The 5th-century fresco of the *Madonna Glycophilusa* from S. Maria Antiqua in the Roman Forum is in the sacristy. Behind a grate in the south transept is the basalt stone that church tradition identifies as the imprint of St Peter, who prayed for the fall of Simon Magus flying over the Roman Forum. On the feast day of S. Francesca, taxis drive past the church for the annual blessing of taxicabs.

To take an optional stroll east of the Colosseum to explore sites connected to the Colosseum and the 1st century CE, the Ludus Magnus, Nero's Golden House (Domus Aurea), the Baths of Trajan and the Basilica of S. Clemente before continuing to the Imperial Fora, then from the Temple of Venus and Roma, continue around the north side of the Colosseum to the corner of Via Labicana and Via di S. Giovanni in Laterano. Cross to other side of the street with railings around the block for the half-excavated ruins of the **Ludus Magnus**, the gladiator school and barracks for which the buildings that once occupied the area were torn down in 1937 and from 1957 to 1961. Only half of the arena has been excavated. Cross to the other side of Via Labicana for the entrance to **Nero's Golden House** that was built after the Great Fire of 64 CE and inspired the Villa of Hadrian at Tivoli. The **Baths of Trajan** were built over the house and its ruins are visible in the Parco del Colle Oppio. From the Ludus Magnus, continue for two blocks on Via di S. Giovanni to the **Basilica of S. Clemente** (Tour 13) for Byzantine mosaics and an opportunity to go under the current church to visit the earlier church destroyed by Robert Guiscard in 1084 and the street level of the Colosseum. Retrace your steps back to the Colosseum and continue on Via dei Fori Imperiali to Ss. Cosma e Damiano.

As you approach the Basilica of Ss. Cosma e Damiano, to your left beyond S. Francesca Romana are marble maps showing Italian empires in various historic periods and the ruins of the Basilica of Maxentius. Across the street in the niche of the retaining wall is the **Fontana del Nicchione** ('Fountain of the Great Niche') that was formerly in Palazzo di Montecitorio (Tour 8) but was moved here during construction of Via dell'Impero. On the ancient brick wall to the left of the entrance clamp holes show where the **Severan Marble Plan** (*Forma Urbis Romae*), a marble map of Rome, was displayed.

The **Basilica of Ss. Cosma e Damiano** was founded by Pope St Felix in 527 on the site of two halls from Vespasian's Forum complex known as the Temple of Peace. Saints Cosmas and Damian were the patron saints of the Medici so Pope Leo X de' Medici renovated the interior. The ancient halls from the Temple of Peace are to your right as you enter, where the fragments of the Severan Marble Plan were found. The church is accessed through a cloister. Pope St Felix commissioned the mosaics in the apse and triumphal arch. The Classical-style apse mosaic depicts Christ's Second Coming (*Parousia*) against a mystical orange-blue background. The church was rebuilt and renovated by Pope Urban VIII (1632). A glass window at the end of the nave faces the interior of the Temple of Romulus that served as the vestibule of the church with access from the Via Sacra of the Roman Forum. In the vestibule is an 18th-century Neapolitan *Presepio* or Nativity scene that is open all year.

Exit the basilica and continue on Via dei Fori Imperiali. To your left just beyond the entrance to the Roman Forum are ruins from **Vespasian's Temple of Peace**, a large square forum (108m x 108m) enclosed by a porticus that was dedicated by Vespasian in 75 CE. It stretched from the area in front of the Basilica of Ss. Cosma e Damiano to the **Torre dei Conti** on the other side of the street and along the Forum of Nerva. It was once part of the complex of buildings that made up the Imperial Fora. The temple complex with a temple built along the east wall facing west commemorated his victory in the Jewish War (70–71 CE). The **spoils from the Temple of Jerusalem** carried in the triumphal procession and depicted on the Arch of Titus were displayed here. The temple became a pilgrimage site for Jews. The spoils seem to have been spared from the fire of 191 CE in the reign of Commodus that damaged the temple, since it is later attested that Genseric seized them in his sack of Rome in June 455 and brought them to Carthage where they disappear from history. The temple complex also contained a library and an art gallery where the statues and paintings seized by Nero from Greece and Asia Minor for his Golden House were displayed. These included statues of Gauls (Galatians) from Pergamum and works by Myron, Phidias and Polyclitus.

Exit the church and continue on Via dei Fori Imperiali to the church of **S. Lorenzo in Miranda** that was built into the ruins of the Temple of the Deified Antoninus Pius and Faustina in the 7th–8th century but first recorded in the 12th century. The church was rebuilt from 1601 to 1614 when Orazio Torriani added the facade on the Roman Forum side (1602). The art on display includes a painting of the *Martydom of St Lawrence* by Pietro da Cortona (1646) and an altarpiece of the *Madonna and Child* by Domenichino (*c.*1626).

Cross to the other side of Via dei Fori Imperiali at the intersection of Via Cavour to the **Torre dei Conti** and then make a sharp left to walk along the other side of Via dei Fori Imperiali to view the excavations of the Imperial Fora. The Torre dei Conti was part of the 12th-century stronghold of the Conti, the family of Pope Innocent III (1198–1216), from where they controlled traffic between the Lateran and the Vatican. The top of the tower fell in the earthquake of 1349 when Rome and the rest of Europe was recovering from the outbreak of the Black Death the previous year. The tower marks the adjoining corner of the Forum of Vespasian and the Forum of Nerva. The area now called the **Imperial Fora** was created when entire neighbourhoods of medieval to 19th-century buildings in the Rione Monti were removed for archaeological excavations. The fora are only half excavated on the north side of the Via dei Fori Imperiali that bisects them and divides them from the Forum of Julius Caesar and the Roman Forum when all were interconnected in antiquity. Modern copies of ancient statues of the emperors stand in front of their respective fora.

The **Via dei Fori Imperiali** was originally named **Via dell'Impero** ('The Avenue of Empire') and also known as the **Via dei Monti** and was constructed by the Fascists between 1931 and 1933 to provide a ceremonial route between the Colosseum and Piazza Venezia. The Fascist-era revision of the city made explicit reference to Imperial Rome, casting Benito Mussolini as a modern day Augustus restoring the Golden Age of Empire – a role he made explicit in 1925: '*Tra cinque anni Roma deve apparire meravigliosa a tutte le genti del mondo; vasta, ordinata, potente, come fu ai tempo del primo impero di Augusto*' ('Within five years, Rome must appear marvellous to all of the peoples of the world; vast, orderly, powerful, just as it was at the time of the first Empire under Augustus'). Mussolini's founding of EUR (Esposizione Universale di Roma) in 1938 demonstrated his urban ideal of a Fascist revival of Imperial Rome (Tour 14). Although the name has changed, the street is still used for a military parade on 2 June for the Festa della Repubblica, when viewing stands are erected.

The **Forum of Nerva** was built by Domitian, but he was assassinated before its completion so it was dedicated by Nerva in 97 CE. The forum is an ingenius use of a narrow space (45m wide x *c.*150m long to the Roman Forum) that transformed the route called the **Argiletum** (now Via Madonna dei Monti) that provided access to the Roman Forum from the Subura district between the Viminal and Esquiline Hills, hence it was also known as the **Forum Transitorium** ('Access Forum'). The Cloaca Maxima runs along its course. The **Temple of Minerva** stood at the north end of the forum, built against an apse of the Forum of Augustus on the west side and the entry point for the Argiletum on the east side. Surviving materials were used by Pope Paul V Borghese to build the Acqua Paola Fountain (Tour 3) and the Cappella Paolina in S. Maria Maggiore (Tour 12). The two surviving Corinthian columns from the colonnade that hold up the attic frieze with depictions of Minerva teaching domestic arts and punishing her mythological rival Arachne received the nickname **Colonnacce** ('ugly columns') when, prior to the construction of Via dell'Impero, they were incorporated into a house that faced a street that ran over the current archaeological site.

The **Forum of Augustus**, the first Imperial forum, was connected to the Forum of Julius Caesar. It included porticoes along the long walls with the **Temple of Mars Ultor** ('the Avenger') in the centre, flanked by two exedras. The temple was vowed in 42 BCE at the Battle of Philippi in which Caesar's assassins Brutus and Cassius were defeated, but it was inaugurated much later in 2 BCE. The temple was in the Corinthian style in white Luna marble. Inside, the Parthian standards retrieved by Augustus in 19 BCE and commemorated with his arch in the Roman Forum were displayed at the entrance to the cella that contained a statue of Mars, perhaps associated with the *Pyrrhus* statue now in the Capitoline Museums that was uncovered in this area in the 16th century.

The forum decoration advertised Augustus' divine lineage and his military triumphs. Niches with statues that traced Augustus' Julian ancestry from Venus and the pivotal figures of Republican history beginning with Romulus that lined the back walls of the porticoes and exedras presented his reign as the culmination of prophecy that promised a return to the Golden Age of Saturn. Under Augustus, the forum became the focus of military business and ceremonies: he shifted Senate business here relating to declarations of war and the awarding of triumphs. It was the place where the sons of the elite assumed their togas of adulthood that signalled they had passed to military age, and it served as the point from which military commanders would leave the city to take up their provincial commands.

The outer wall of the forum was built of Gabine tufa that has fire-resistant properties, so it survived the Great Fire of 64 CE. The arch in the wall, later called the **Arco dei Pantani**, provided access to the Esquiline Hill from a street that passed over the current archaeological site that was lined with houses and buildings. Wheel marks left on the Roman pavement are visible to the right of the temple. On the other side is the **Casa dei Cavalieri di Rodi**, the House of the Knights of Rhodes, the property of the Order of the Knights of Malta whose sovereign territory is on the Aventine Hill (Tour 4), built against the exedra on the west side of the forum with a beautiful loggia. To your left as you continue on Via dei Fori Imperiali are the substructures of medieval to 19th-century buildings that were removed for archeological excavations that have not been extended to reach the ancient level of the fora. During World War II, vegetables were grown here in areas called Orti di Guerra ('Wartime Gardens').

The **Forum of Trajan** ran parallel to the modern Via dei Fori Imperiali and perpendicular to the Forum of Augustus, with two two-storey exedras along the long sides. The forum complex comprised the Basilica Ulpia (the gens or family name of Trajan), the Column of Trajan, Libraries, the Temple of the Deified Trajan and Trajan's Markets. The vast forum was built from 107 to 112 CE and designed by the architect Apollodorus of Damascus. The decoration of the forum commemorated Trajan's Dacian triumph (107 CE), with the frieze on his column and statues of Dacian prisoners similar to those on the Arch of Constantine that were placed above the portico that lined the forum and alternated with marble panels with reliefs of Dacian trophies and portraits of previous emperors and empresses on shields. In the centre was a colossal equestrian statue of Trajan.

The **Basilica Ulpia**, with five aisles and apses at either end, was the largest basilica constructed in ancient Rome (*c.*170m x 60m) and was used for judicial functions. Access was from the forum side through a porch comprised of three sections with statue groups on the roof and three statues of Trajan in the areas between the sections. The marble cipollino columns along the central nave (the ceiling was *c.*25m high) were larger than the columns of the side aisles. Sections of the colourful marble pavement survive.

Access to the **Column of Trajan** was through the basilica and it stood in the small area between two **libraries**. Trajan's cremated remains and those of his wife Pompeia Plotina were stored in a vault within the base that is decorated with a relief of Dacian trophies, garlands and eagles. The magnificent reliefs (200m long) run counter-clockwise along the column of Luna marble and depict several scenes of Trajan on his Dacian campaign that were originally painted. Plaster casts of the reliefs are in the Museo della Civiltà Romana, EUR (Esposizione Universale di Roma). A spiral staircase inside the column leads outside to the platform where there was a statue of Trajan until the bronze was melted for the current statue of St Peter in 1588 by Domenico Fontana for Pope Sixtus V. The pope also commissioned Fontana to melt the statue of Marcus Aurelius on his column for the current statue of St Paul (Tour 8).

Behind the column in the area of **Palazzo Valentini**, now a museum that preserves the ruins of Roman houses (accessed from Via Cesare Battisti in Piazza Venezia), was the **Temple of the Deified Trajan** built by his adopted successor Hadrian that faced the Forum of Trajan but also formed a bookend with Vespasian's Temple of Peace at the opposite end of the Imperial Fora. The **Athenaeum** of Hadrian (after 123 CE), an academy for literary and scientific studies, was discovered under Piazza Venezia during excavations for the construction of Metro line C.

Along the northern exedra of the forum is the red brick hemicycle of **Trajan's Markets**. This is actually comprised of several distinct buildings on three different ancient Roman street levels of shops including the **Via Biberatica** and the alcove shops along the hemicycle and a 2nd-century CE apartment block (*insula*). A large number of buildings that had been built into the ruins over the centuries, including the Convent of S. Caterina da Siena a Magnanapoli, were demolished in 1912 when the area was restored under Antonio Muñoz. Muñoz also restored the **Torre delle Milizie** built by the Frangipane in the 12th century that passed to the Conti and Caetani families. It towers at an angle behind the markets even in its ruined state that was caused by the earthquake of 1349. To stroll around the ground level of the Forum of Trajan and visit the **Museo dei Fori Imperiali** in Trajan's Markets, turn right at the column and walk up the stairs (Scalinata di Magnanapoli) that lead to Largo Magnanapoli for the entrance to your right.

In the centre of **Largo Magnanapoli** are tufa blocks that formed part of the Republican Walls. To your left down Via XXIV Maggio is the **Obelisk** in Piazza del Quirinale (Tour 11). To your right is the church of **S. Caterina da Siena a Magnanapoli** and straight ahead is the church of **Ss. Domenico e Sisto** (with Antonio Raggi's *Noli me tangere* sculpture group). Above the largo is the retaining wall of the **Villa Aldobrandini** with views of the Forum of Trajan and beyond from the garden (to visit, walk up Via Panisperna to the right of the Villa and turn left on Via Mazzarino past the church of **S. Agata dei Goti**, 'St Agatha of the Goths'). From Largo Magnanapoli you may begin Tour 12 by walking up Via Nazionale to Palazzo delle Esposizione. If continuing to Tour 7, retrace your steps to the Column of Trajan.

Across the street from the Column of Trajan are the churches of **SS. Nome di Maria** (18th century) and **S. Maria di Loreto al Foro Traiano** that was designed by Antonio da Sangallo the Younger around 1507, with a dome and lantern added later in the 16th century by Jacopo del Duca. The cupola frescoes are by Pomarancio (Cristoforo Roncalli). The interior is on a hexagonal plan and contains statues of four women martyrs including Saint Susanna by François Duquesnoy.

The **Casa di Michelangelo,** his home and studio for 30 years in which he died in 1564, was on Via Macel de' Corvi in the current area between the church and **Palazzo delle Assicurazioni Generali di Venezia**. It was demolished in 1871 but the facade was saved and rebuilt on Via delle Tre Pile to the right of the Cordonata of Piazza del Campidoglio (Tour 5). However, it was demolished again in 1930 and moved in 1941 to its current location on the Passeggiata del Gianicolo near Porta di S. Pancrazio (Tour 3).

Cross Via dei Fori Imperiali to the National Monument to Vittorio Emanuele II in Piazza Venezia. At the base of the monument to your left is the facade wall of the **Tomb of Bibulus** that was incorporated into the side wall of a building that bordered Piazza di Macel de' Corvi. The tomb commemorates C. Publicius Bibulus, tribune in 209 BCE, but the monument was rebuilt around 100–50 BCE. The doorway of the monument is visible but most of the podium is now buried. Its ancient location was outside the Porta Fontinalis in the Republican Walls at the start of the Via Lata that is now Via del Corso.

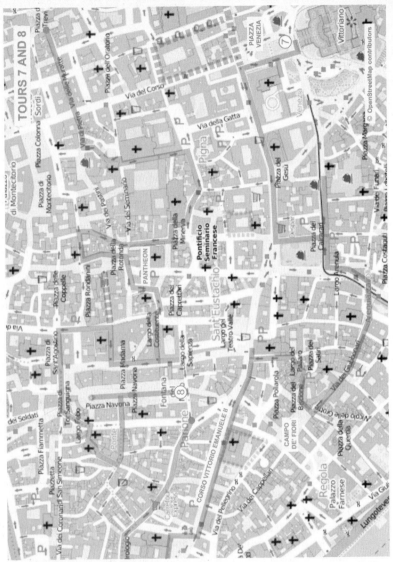

Sites: Piazza Venezia; National Monument to Vittorio Emanuele II (il Vittoriano); Roman Apartment Building; *Madama Lucrezia*; S. Marco; Museo Nazionale del Palazzo di Venezia; Galleria Doria Pamphilj; il Facchino; Ss. Apostoli (Optional visit to Galleria Colonna); The Gesù; Largo di Torre Argentina; Crypta Balbi; Via de' Giubbonari; S. Carlo ai Catinari; S. Barbara dei Librai; Campo de' Fiori; Theatre of Pompey; Corso Vittorio Emanuele II; Sant'Andrea della Valle; Abate *Luigi*; Palazzo Massimo alle Colonne; Piccola Farnesina; Palazzo della Cancelleria; Chiesa Nuova (S. Maria in Vallicella); *Pasquino*; Palazzo Braschi (Museo di Roma).
Distance: 3.25km.

# PIAZZA VENEZIA
# AND CAMPO DE' FIORI

Stroll through the winding and busy streets of medieval and Renaissance Rome in the areas of Piazza Venezia now dominated by the National Monument to Vittorio Emanuele II and Campo de' Fiori. The tour features important Renaissance palaces such as Palazzo di Venezia and Palazzo della Cancelleria, the Baroque palaces of the Doria Pamphilj and Colonna families with important private art collections and the palace of the Jacobite Court at Rome in Piazza dei Ss. Apostoli. Important Counter-Reformation churches line Corso Vittorio Emanuele II.

The vast **Piazza Venezia** is dominated by the National Monument to Vittorio Emanuele II and Palazzo di Venezia in the heart of historic Rome. This was the medieval core of the city that had developed around the Comune on the Campidoglio that was demolished when Rome was made the capital of Italy on 2 July 1871 (a position briefly held by Torino and Florence). Previously, the city had been decentralised with a series of piazze that interconnected neighbourhoods. The demolition of the area was brutal. The Palazzetto di Venezia, moved to the other side of the Basilica di S. Marco (c.1910), was formerly connected to Palazzo di Venezia to frame one side of the original Piazza Venezia. The other side of the palazzetto enclosed part of Piazza di S. Marco with Via di S. Marco where the architect Giulio Romano lived. The Arco di S. Marco that was attached to the palazzetto and linked to the Torre di Paolo III on the Campidoglio was demolished in the area in front of the National Monument to Vittorio Emanuele II. Towards the

Cordonata was the house of the Counter-Reformation architect and artist Pietro da Cortona.

Mussolini moved his office to Palazzo di Venezia from Palazzo Chigi and used the piazza for Fascist rallies that he addressed from the framed balcony portal on the first floor of the Sala del Mappamondo. The piazza was the terminal point of the processional route along the new Via dell'Impero that connected it to the Colosseum and the hub of a nexus of roads that led out of the city.

The **National Monument to Vittorio Emanuele II** (Monumento Nazionale a Vittorio Emanuele II), also called **il Vittoriano** and the **Altare della Patria** (Altar of the Fatherland), is dedicated to Vittorio Emanuele II from the House of Savoy, the first king of the unified Italy (1861–1878). He did not adopt the title of Vittorio Emanuele I of Italy; rather, his title of Vittorio Emanuele II referred to his kingdoms of Sardinia-Piedmont. The other royal houses in Italy and their supporters in Europe shunned him for his role in the Risorgimento. The modern monarchy of Italy was short-lived. He was succeeded by his son Umberto I (1878–1900) and his grandson Vittorio Emanuele III (1900–1946), whose tumultuous reign spanned two world wars, the signing of the Lateran Treaty (1929) and the rise and fall of Fascism. His son Umberto II was king from only 9 May to 12 June 1946. A plebiscite dispensed with the monarchy in favour of the Italian Republic.

The Monument designed by Giuseppe Sacconi (begun in 1885 and inaugurated in 1911) in the ostentatious Academic Neoclassical style has earned it the nicknames of the 'wedding cake' and 'typewriter'. The **Altare della Patria** by Angelo Zanelli serves as Italy's sacred site of the Tomb of the Unknown Soldier (Milite Ignoto) that is under constant guard. On the second level with a view up Via del Corso to the obelisk in Piazza del Popolo (*c.*1.5km away) is the colossal Equestrian Statue of Vittorio Emanuele II with allegories of Italian towns on the base and military trophies on the pedestal. The **Portico** at the top of the monument contains colossal statues representing the provinces of Italy. Two bronze quadrigas are on top of the temple fronts (propylaea) of the portico: *Unity* by Carlo Fontana to the left, and *Liberty* by Paolo Bartolini to the right. The **Museo Centrale del Risorgimento** traces the history of the Risorgimento and the role played by Garibaldi. Special exhibitions are held in the **Complesso del Vittoriano**, accessed from Via S. Pietro in Carcere behind the monument. The sky deck **Roma**

**dal Cielo**, 'Rome from the Sky', accessed at ground level to the right of the monument next to the ruins of an ancient **Roman Apartment Building** (Tour 5), offers spectacular views of the city.

Cross the street into **Piazza di S. Marco** in front of the Basilica di S. Marco. The Piazza di S. Marco served as the market area of Rome before it was moved to Piazza Navona. The pine cone shaped fountain, the **Fontanella della Pigna** by Pietro Lombardi (1926), indicates this corner of the piazza is in the Rione Pigna but the rest is in Rione Campitelli. In the corner of the piazza to the left as you approach the Basilica di S. Marco is the marble statue (2nd–3rd century CE) known as *Madama Lucrezia*, likely from the nearby Iseum (Temple of Isis), and may represent Isis or one of her priestesses. She was placed in front of the basilica by Cardinal Lorenzo Cybo in 1500 but subsequently moved to this corner. She is one of four 'talking statues' on this tour and often 'communicated' with *Marforio* in the Capitoline Museums with notes posted anonymously.

The **Basilica di S. Marco** was founded by Pope St Mark in 336 and is the first church dedicated to the Evangelist St Mark in Rome, who is the patron saint of Venice. Pope Paul II, who was from Venice, built the Renaissance loggia for papal benedictions and portico facade with travertine from the Colosseum and the Theatre of Marcellus. In the atrium, fragments from ancient sculpture are displayed with two lions, the iconographic symbol of St Mark, flanking the entrance door with reliefs by Isaia da Pisa (1464). The interior of the basilica was reworked for the Jubilee of 1750 but earlier features survive from the renovations of Pope Gregory IV in 833 and Pope Paul II between 1465 and 1470 including the 9th-century mosaics, the cosmatesque pavement from 1478 in the sanctuary, and the Renaissance coffered ceiling. Under the sanctuary is the Tomb of Martyrs whose relics were moved here from suburban cemeteries by Pope Gregory IV. The relics of Pope St Mark are in the porphyry urn under the altar. To the right of the altar in the Chapel of the Sacrament designed by Pietro da Cortona is a portrait of *Pope St Mark* by Melozzo da Forlì. Antonio Canova's monument to Leonardo Pesaro (d. 1796) in the form of an ancient stele is to the right of the steps leading to the choir. In the third chapel on the south side is the *Adoration of the Magi* by Carlo Maratta (1625–1713), one of the most important Counter-Reformation artists in the late 17th century.

Exit the basilica and turn left and then left again to walk across the front of **Palazzo di Venezia** to Via del Plebiscito. Turn left for the entrance to the Museo Nazionale del Palazzo di Venezia. You may enter now or return after a short stroll north of Piazza Venezia to visit the Galleria Doria Pamphilj, the Jacobite sites in Piazza dei Ss. Apostoli or the Galleria Colonna.

Palazzo di Venezia, built between 1455 and 1464, is the most important building in 15th-century Rome. It was built for Pope Paul II (beginning when he was still Cardinal Pietro Barbo) as his papal residence with materials from the Colosseum that was also quarried for his renovations to the Basilica di S. Marco. The design suggests the influence of Leon Battista Alberti, but the architect is unknown and the building has been attributed to Giuliano da Maiano, Bernardo Rossellino or Francesco del Borgo. The palace gave the pope an excellent vantage point to watch the dramatic finish of the annual riderless horse race (Palio or Corsa dei Barberi) during the Carnevale that he relocated to the Via del Corso in 1467 (then called Via Lata). The race started in Piazza del Popolo and ended in front of his palace in Piazza Venezia and the race gives the Via del Corso its present name. Vittorio Emanuele II abolished the race in 1874. In 1564, Pope Pius IV de' Medici transferred ownership of the palace to the Republic of Venice for their embassy (hence its name, Palazzo di Venezia). From 1797 to 1916 the palace passed to Austria for its Ambassador to the Vatican until its expropriation by King Vittorio Emanuele III. Mussolini used the palace as the seat of the Fascist government from 1929 to 1943. Across the piazza is **Palazzo delle Assicurazioni Generali di Venezia** that was built from 1902 to 1904 to match the appearance of Palazzo di Venezia.

The **Museo Nazionale del Palazzo di Venezia** opened in 1921 with Renaissance restorations directed by Federico Hermann and comprises 27 rooms in Palazzo di Venezia and Palazzetto di Venezia. The nucleus of the collection are the decorative arts assembled in 1916 from the Kircher collection of the Museo Kircheriano, the Galleria Nazionale d'Arte Antica and the pieces exhibited in the International Art Exhibition in 1911. Several private art collections of ceramics, porcelain, armour, paintings and sculpture were added to the museum. The Altoviti Hall has ceiling frescoes of the myth of Ceres and *grottesche* by Giorgio Vasari (1553) from Palazzo Altoviti dal Tevere in Piazza di

Ponte at the end of the Ponte Sant'Angelo that was demolished for the construction of the Tiber Embankment in 1888.

Continue on Via del Plebiscito to arrive at the Gesù. To your right is the new wing of Palazzo Doria Pamphilj. Once you cross Via degli Astali, you are walking along the side wall of the church whose entrance faces Piazza del Gesù. Also facing the piazza on Via del Plebiscito is **Palazzo Altieri**, the family palazzo of Pope Clement X (1670–1676) that is currently owned by a bank. At No. 45 Piazza del Gesù (to the right of the church facade) is the entrance to the rooms where Saint Ignatius lived from 1554 to 1556.

To visit the sites north of Piazza Venezia, return to the corner of Palazzo di Venezia and Via del Plebiscito, cross to the other side of Via del Plebiscito to walk up Via del Corso. Napoleon's mother, Letitia Ramolino, lived in the 17th-century **Palazzo Bonaparte** (Palazzo D'Aste Rinuccini Bonaparte) at the corner after his removal from power. At the end of the first block to your left is **Palazzo Doria Pamphilj** (15th–18th century) with the dove and fleur-de-lys emblems of the Pamphilj, the family of Pope Innocent X Pamphilj, on the facade designed by Gabriele Valvassori (1731–1734). The nucleus (Palazzo Aldrobrandini) of the immense palace that faces both Via del Corso and Via del Plebiscito (1748–1749, extension by Paolo Ameli) is connected to the church of S. Maria in Via Lata that was built in 1435. Across the street is Palazzo Mancini-Salviati by Carlo Rainaldi (1662). The vast palazzo has served as the residence of the Doria Pamphilj family since the 17th century and, like the Galleria Colonna, contains one of the most important intact private art collections (protected by the state since 1816) open to the public.

The nucleus of the **Galleria Doria Pamphilj** collection was started by Pope Innocent X Pamphilj with art from his Palazzo Pamphilj in Piazza Navona. The collection was bequeathed to his nephew Camillo Pamphilj who added to it after his marriage (1647) to Olimpia Aldobrandini, whose family owned the original palazzo connected to S. Maria in Via Lata. Painting and sculpture mostly from the 17th century and ancient sculpture mainly from the Villa Doria Pamphilj (Tour 3) are displayed in several rooms, including Raphael's *Portraits of Andrea Navagero and Agostino Beazzano*; Caravaggio's *Rest on the Flight to Egypt* and *Penitent Magdalene*; the *Portrait of Innocent X* by Diego Velázquez (1650); a marble *Bust of Pope Innocent X* by Bernini; the *Portrait of Donna Olimpia*

*Maidalchini Pamphilj*, the sister-in-law of Pope Innocent X Pamphilj, by
Alessandro Algardi (*c.*1650); and Quinten Massy's *The Usurers*.

Continue up Via del Corso past Palazzo Doria Pamphilj and the
church of **S. Maria in Via Lata** with a facade by Pietro da Cortona
(1658–1662). The **Arch of Diocletian**, called the Arcus Novus
(303–304), that spanned the Corso, was demolished in 1491 for the
construction of the church that occupies the site of an ancient church
and Roman ruins below it. Two pedestals from the arch were brought to
the Boboli Gardens, Florence, by the Medici. At the corner of Via Lata
to your left is one of the talking statues, *il Facchino*, holding a cask from
which water pours.

At Via Lata, cross to the other side of Via del Corso in the Rione
Trevi. The church of **S. Marcello al Corso** is to your far left with a
concave facade by Carlo Fontana (1683). Continue straight through
onto Via dei Ss. Apostoli to enter **Piazza dei Ss. Apostoli** to your right.

The Stuarts of Scotland and England once owned **Palazzo Balestra**
(1644) at No. 49 at the north end, behind you as you enter, also
known as Palazzo Muti e Santuario delle Madonna dell'Archetto and
part of the **Palazzo Muti Papazzurri** complex in Piazza Pilotta that
was also known as 'Palazzo del Re' (Palace of the King). Pope Clement
XI gave the palazzo as a wedding present to James Stuart (James III,
the 'Old Pretender', 1688–1766) and Maria Clementina Sobieski. It
was in this palazzo that their sons were born: Charles Edward ('Bonnie
Prince Charlie', the 'Young Pretender') in 1720, who also died here
in 1788; and Henry Benedict, Cardinal Duke of York (1725–1807),
whose elevation to Cardinal York (1747) was celebrated by his father
in front of an elaborate temporary facade attached to the palace by
Clemente Orlandi. The event is commemorated in a painting ascribed
to Giuseppe Valeriani, now in the Scottish National Portrait Gallery in
Edinburgh. Walk into the vestibule to see the plaque high on the wall
that commemorates the Stuarts' occupancy.

**Palazzo Chigi-Odescalchi** is to your right. The renovation of
the palazzo, originally owned by the Colonna, was started by Carlo
Maderno for the then owner Cardinal Ludovico Ludovisi, nephew of
Pope Gregory XV Ludovisi. He sold it back to the Colonna who sold
it to Cardinal Flavio Chigi who commissioned Bernini to design the
facade (1661). The palace was acquired by the family of Pope Innocent
XI Odescalchi in 1745, who commissioned additions to the palazzo by

Nicola Salvi and Luigi Vanvitelli (1750). The Stuarts did not know that the family of Pope Innocent XI had secretly financed the campaigns of William III of Orange in the Glorious Revolution and the Battle of the Boyne in which he defeated his father-in-law James II, thereby removing Catholics from the British throne.

The Basilica of **Ss. Apostoli** is to your left. The 6th-century church was restored by Pope Martin V Colonna and again by Pope Sixtus IV della Rovere who added the double loggia. Pope Clement XI commissioned further renovations from Francesco Fontana (1702–1708) that his father Carlo Fontana completed in 1714 after his son's death. The Neoclassical facade is after a design by Giuseppe Valadier (1827). The balustrade with statues of Christ and the Apostles is by Carlo Rainaldi (1674–1675), who also closed in the upper loggia and added the windows. James Stuart lay in repose in the basilica in 1766 before burial in St Peter's Basilica.

The adjoining Palazzo dei Ss. Apostoli (to the left when facing the church) was started by the nephew of Pope Sixtus IV, Cardinal Pietro Riario (1445–1474), who was titular cardinal of the basilica, but it was completed by Giuliano da Sangallo (1478–1480) for his other nephew, Pope Julius II della Rovere, when he was still Cardinal Giuliano della Rovere. His father Raffaele lived here and is buried in the basilica. The palazzo is also associated with Michelangelo who lived nearby. In 1564, Michelangelo's body was temporarily kept in the cloister until it was secretly removed in a bale of fabric and brought to Florence for his funeral and burial in the Basilica of Santa Croce. Ring for admission at No. 51 to view his cenotaph, the funerary monument to Cardinal Bessarion and a fountain by Domenico Fontana.

In the portico, the bas-relief of an eagle holding an oak wreath in its talons is from the Forum of Trajan. The inscription records Pope Julius II della Rovere's role in preserving it. Below it is a 12th-century lion by Pietro Vassalletto. The two marble lions flanking the entrance are also from the 12th century. The Colonna funerary monument against the facade wall with a portrait bust within a tondo below the Colonna symbol of a column is not identified but is perhaps Lorenzo Oddone Colonna, who as a Ghibelline, the political faction in Italy that supported the Holy Roman Emperor over the papacy that was supported by the Guelphs, was executed in 1484 by Pope Sixtus IV for the murder of an Orsini, a long-standing rival aristocratic family loyal to the papacy. Pope Sixtus IV confiscated their palazzo but it was returned to them as a wedding gift when Lucrezia della Rovere, the niece of Pope Julius II della Rovere, married Marcantonio I Colonna. To your left is Antonio Canova's Neoclassical funerary monument to the engraver Giovanni Volpato (1807), who helped him secure the commission for the portrait and mausoleum monument to Pope Clement XIV inside the basilica.

The vast gold gilt Baroque interior contains the nave frescoes of the *Triumph of the Order of St Francis* (1707) by Baciccia that was painted after his ceiling fresco for the Gesù with the *Evangelists* and *Angels* by Luigi Fontana (1875). The first chapel (south side) contains the *Madonna and Child* by Antoniazzo Romano for Cardinal Bessarion, who was a member of the Greek Emperor John Palaeologus' mission to Rome to unite the Greek and Roman churches. On the second pillar is the funerary monument to Maria Clementina Sobieski, wife of James Stuart. There is another monument to her in St Peter's Basilica. The Chapel of Cardinal Bessarion contains his mausoleum and is decorated with frescoes by Antoniazzo Romano depicting the *Life of Archangel St Michael*. The Chapel of the Crucifix contains eight columns from the 6th-century church.

The *Fallen Angels* fresco over the high altar is by Giovanni Odazzi. The Riario family funerary monuments include that of Cardinal Pietro Riario by the School of Andrea Bregno, with a *Madonna* by Mino da Fiesole. An ancient Roman sarcophagus serves as the tomb of Alessandro Riario. The apse frescoes by Melozzo da Forlì, *Christ in Glory with Angels* (1480), were moved to Palazzo del Quirinale (Tour 11) and the Pinacoteca Vaticana (Tour 2). The confessio leads to the crypt with the relics of St Philip and St James the Younger and the funerary monument to Raffaele della Rovere (d. 1477), the brother of Pope Sixtus IV della Rovere and the father of Pope Julius II della Rovere. At the end of the north side is Antonio Canova's monumental *Portrait and Mausoleum of Pope Clement XIV*, his first work in Rome (1789). In mourning are allegories of Humility and Modesty. On the second pillar is the medallion funerary monument to Cardinal Bessarion. The chapels on the north side contain many funerary monuments to the Colonna family.

To continue directly to the Gesù, exit the basilica and retrace your steps to Piazza Venezia and cross Via del Plebiscito to Palazzo di

Venezia, turning right to continue on Via del Plebiscito to arrive at the Gesù. To visit the Galleria Colonna beforehand, exit the basilica and turn left to exit the piazza and then turn left onto Via IV Novembre to walk around the Galleria Colonna to its entrance on Via della Pilotta to your left.

The **Galleria Colonna** is a must-see private art collection displayed in a magnificent Baroque interior. Palazzo Colonna was started by Pope Martin V (Oddone Colonna) and was expanded in 1484 by Pope Julius II della Rovere when still a cardinal and by Antonio del Grande for Cardinal Girolamo I Colonna in 1654, with further additions in the 18th century. The palazzo was not destroyed in the Sack of 1527 because of the alliance between the Colonna and Charles V, the Holy Roman Emperor. Only a part of the brick staircase survives of the ruins of the **Serapeum** (Temple of Serapis) that were sold by the Colonna for building material. A marble pilaster capital and a cornice fragment displayed in the garden are the only elements that survive from the largest temple in Rome.

The **Sala della Colonna Bellica** ceiling fresco *The Apotheosis of Marcantonio II Colonna* by Giuseppe Bartolomeo Chiari commemorates his naval victory at the Battle of Lepanto in 1571 for Pope Pius V and the Holy League over the Ottoman Empire. Steps with a cannon ball that landed here on 24 June 1849 during Garibaldi's defence of the city against the French lead down into the sumptuous **Sala Grande** (Great Hall) that is lined with mirrors decorated with putti by Carlo Maratta and flowers by Mario de' Fiori, antique sculpture and paintings, including Salvator Rosa's *St John the Baptist*, Guercino's *Martyrdom of St Emerenziana*, and *Adam and Eve* by Francesco Salviati.

The **Sala dell'Apoteosi di Martino V** (Hall of the Apotheosis of Martin V) takes its name from the ceiling fresco depicting the *Apotheosis of Pope Martin V Colonna* by Benedetto Luti, with panels *Time discovering Truth* by Pompeo Batoni and *Fame crowning Glory* by Pietro Banchi. Paintings include works by Guercino, Jacopo Tintoretto, Domenico Tintoretto, Paolo Veronese, Bronzino and Francesco Salviati and the *Bean Eaters* by Annibale Carracci. From here there is an excellent view of the cortile.

Exit and turn right on Via Cesare Battista then cross to the other side of Via del Corso. Cross to the other side of Via del Plebiscito to Palazzo di Venezia and turn right to continue on Via del Plebiscito to arrive at the Gesù.

**The Gesù** (SS. Nome di Gesù), the most important Jesuit church in Rome, played a pivotal role in the development of the lavish style associated with the order. It is the first of three important 16th-century Counter-Reformation churches on this itinerary including Sant'Andrea della Valle and Chiesa Nuova (S. Maria in Vallicella) that were founded by influential new religious orders. All feature a vast richly decorated Baroque interior with an aisleless nave with side chapels that could accommodate large numbers of worshippers. Their architectural plans, like theatre set designs, focus attention on the high altar for the celebration of the Eucharist. The whole architectural effect advertised the strength of the Catholic Church to Protestant Europe. The Gesù was built between 1568 and 1584 with the financial assistance of Alessandro Farnese, the nephew of Pope Paul III Farnese, whose name appears above the central entrance. The two-order facade (1571–1577) was designed by Giacomo della Porta who also completed the cupola and the interior and dome by Vignola. The monogram of the Name of Jesus above the main entrance is by Bartolomeo Ammannati (1574).

In the interior, the magnificent ceiling fresco *Triumph of the Name of Jesus* (1679) is by Baciccia, who also designed the stucco angels and decoration, executed by Antonio Raggi and Leonardo Retti, that add a three-dimensional quality. It adds another theatrical element that breaks the planes of the ceiling and wall and explodes into the space of the worshipper and brings Heaven into the church within sight and reach of the worshippers. In the south transept is the altar to St Francis Xavier designed by Pietro da Cortona and Carlo Fontana. The altarpiece by Carlo Maratta is based on a design by Pietro da Cortona (1679). The arm of the saint, in the silver reliquary, was brought to Rome from Goa in 1614. To the left in the Cappella del Sacro Cuore is the *Sacred Heart of Jesus* by Pompeo Batoni (*c.*1760).

The construction of the high altar by Antonio Sarti (1840–1843) caused the destruction of the funerary monument to S. Roberto Bellarmino or St Robert Bellarmine (1542–1621), whose bust, to the left of the altar, is by Bernini (1621–1624). Bellarmine served many roles in the Church including Cardinal Inquisitor and was a member of the jury that convicted Giordano Bruni of heresy, for which he was burned at the stake. He also condemned James I of England's Oath of

Allegiance and summoned Galileo Galilei to warn him of the decree of the Congregation of the Index. His relics are in S. Ignazio (Tour 8). Baciccia painted the frescoes of the tribune and cupola (1672–1685). In the north transept, the altar tomb of St Ignatius of Loyola, the founder of the Jesuit Order, is by Andrea Pozzo (1696–1700). The altar is decorated with lapis lazuli and gilded bronze reliefs with scenes from the Life of S. Ignatius. The reliefs on the sarcophagus urn are by Alessandro Algardi. To the right is the Cappella di S. Maria della Strada with the 15th-century fresco *Madonna della Strada*.

Exit the piazza straight ahead and continue on the left side of Corso Vittorio Emanuele II until you reach the **Largo di Torre Argentina**. Turn left onto the pedestrian-only street of Via di S. Nicola dè Cesarini to view the ruins. The largo is named for the Torre Argentina that is connected to the Casa del Burcado on Via del Sudario. Facing the piazza is **Palazzo Ruggeri** (No. 24) by Giacomo della Porta (1588–1591). The entire block was demolished (in 1885 and from 1926 to 1929), including the church of S. Nicola de' Cesarini, for the excavation of the archaeological area known as the **Area Sacra di Largo Argentina** after the four Republican temples built side by side and facing east that were incorporated into the Theatre of Pompey complex. Along Via Arenula in front of the **Teatro Argentina** are traces of the **Porticus of the Theatre of Pompey** that had been turned into latrines. Behind the round **Temple B** (after 100 BCE), part of the porticus contained the **Curia Pompeiana** that was the site of Julius Caesar's assassination on the Ides of March 44 BCE. Marble fragments of the colossal acrolith cult statue are in the Capitoline Museum's Museo Centro Montemartini (Tour 14). The appearance of the temples and the level of the pavement were altered several times in antiquity. Antonio Muñoz restored the site in 1933, including the medieval tower and loggia in the corner known as the Torre del Papito ('Tower of the Little Pope') after the antipope Anacletus II Pierleoni. The archaeological area is famous for the feral cats that live amid the ruins and are cared for by women known as *Gattare*.

From the tower at the end of the block, cross to the other side of Via Florida and make a sharp left past Piazza dei Calcarari to walk on the other side of the street on Via delle Botteghe Oscure. The **Crypta Balbi Museum** (Museo Nazionale Romano Crypta Balbi) is just ahead to your right. Across the street are ancient columns and ruins identified as the **Temple of the Via delle Botteghe Oscure**, uncovered when the street was excavated in 1938. The church of S. Lucia alle Botteghe Oscure was demolished earlier in 1936. The Crypta Balbi refers to the porticus that adjoined the **Theatre of Balbus** complex dedicated by L. Cornelius Balbus. At the opening games of the theatre in 13 BCE, the Tiber flooded the area and guests had to arrive by boat. The museum is built over the ruins of the porticus and contains material devoted to daily life in medieval Rome, especially the 6th–9th centuries when the ruins of the theatre housed bronze, ceramics and glass production workshops. Fresco fragments and other objects removed from the church of S. Adriano were moved here from the Curia in the Roman Forum.

Retrace your steps along Via delle Botteghe Oscure to Via Florida past Largo di Torre Argentina to your right and turn left on Via Arenula. The name of the street derives from the Latin word for a little grain of sand (*harenula*) from the bank of the Tiber that is also the derivation of the Renella beach (1886–1888) that was located at the end of the street and the Regola district that runs along the Tiber. Cross Via Arenula at the first street, **Via de' Giubbonari**, once part of the pilgrim route, the Via Peregrinorum. The trendy and lively street with a variety of clothing and artisan shops has long been associated with the garment industry that leads to Campo de' Fiori. The Piazza dei Branca (named for the prominent Jewish family, the Branca di Clausura, that flourished in the 14th century) was destroyed during construction of Via Arenula in 1887.

Continue through Piazza Benedetto Cairoli to **S. Carlo ai Catinari**. This 17th-century Counter-Reformation church, dedicated to St Charles Borromeo, was built from 1612 to 1620 by its Milanese congregation of basin makers (*Catinari*) on an earlier site of Roman ruins and later houses owned by the Orsini family. The imposing facade is by Giovanni Battista Soria (1636). The interior, on a Greek cross-plan with a dome in the centre, was renovated by Virginio Vespignani (1857–1861). The *Cardinal Virtues* in the pendentives of the dome are by Domenichino (1627–1630). Above the high altar designed by Martino Longhi is Pietro da Cortona's altarpiece, *St Charles Carrying the Sacred Cross Nail to the Plague-Stricken* (1650). Behind in the choir is Guidi Reni's *St Charles at Prayer* (1636). The apse fresco, *St Charles Received into Heaven*, is by Giovanni Lanfranco. The third chapel (south side), Cappella di S. Cecilia, is by Antonio Gherardi (1692–1700). Like his Avila Chapel in S. Maria in Trastevere (Tour 4), architecture is used to fill the chapel with light and create the illusion of space as the figures of angels ascend to the dome.

Continue on Via de' Giubbonari. Opposite the church at No. 6 is **Palazzo Santacroce** by Carlo Maderno (1598–1602). A short distance ahead, turn left on Via della Pietà into Piazza del Monte di Pietà for a view of the facade of **Palazzo del Monte di Pietà** by Carlo Maderno (from 1604), for Pope Clement VIII Aldobrandini, who enlarged an earlier design of Ottaviano Nonni. The bell tower and clock are by Borromini (from 1623 to 1631). In 1539, Pope Paul III Farnese established a public bank for lending money on pledge and a pawn shop for pilgrims in need of money on Via dei Banchi Vecchi that was relocated here in 1603.

Return to Via de' Giubbonari. At the intersection with Via del Arco del Monte is the narrow **Largo dei Librai**, named for the booksellers who used to fill the largo with their stalls. At the end of the largo is the church of **S. Barbara dei Librai**. The facade designed by Giuseppe Passeri (1680) appropriately honours the patron saint of architecture by creatively using its narrow space (originally a support vault of the Theatre of Pompey) to charming effect. Behind the church is Piazza dei Satiri where the two Pan statues now in the atrium of Palazzo Nuovo of the Capitoline Museums were uncovered.

Opposite the largo is **Palazzo Barberini ai Giubbonari**, also known as the Barberini Case Grande, where Pope Urban VIII lived as a cardinal (Maffeo) with his uncle, Cardinal Francesco Barberini (1528–1600), who acquired the house in 1581. Architects Flaminio Ponzio and Carlo Maderno worked on the palace (the original entrance of which is at No. 41) that was given to Carlo Barberini by his brother Maffeo when he became Pope Urban VIII in 1623. Maderno then began construction of Palazzo Barberini on the Quirinal Hill (Tour 11) in 1624. Taddeo Barberini extended the palace to Via del Arco del Monte (1640–1644), where the family emblem of bees is visible on the coining and capitals of the pilasters of the belvedere. In 1734, the Barberini sold the palazzo to the Carmelites who in turn sold it to Monte di Pietà in 1759. Continue on Via de' Giubbonari. At No. 46 to your left is a painted facade, and at No. 63 to your right is the spoliated columns of a medieval building.

At the end of the street is **Campo de' Fiori** in the Rione Parione. As you enter, **Palazzo Pio Righetti** is to your right behind store fronts. The campo derives its named from the meadow that once occupied the area. Today it is a lively outdoor market (since 1869) in the morning and popular gathering spot in the evening. In the centre is the statue of the Dominican Friar **Giordano Bruno** (*c.*1548–1600), marking the spot where he was burned at the stake for his heretical polytheistic theories by order of Pope Clement VIII Aldobrandini, who had condemned Beatrice Cenci to death the previous year (Tour 4). The statue was erected in 1889 by Freemasons who supported the unification of Italy as a protest against Pope Leo XIII's encyclical called the *Humanus Genus*. A plaque in the pavement behind the statue marks the location where the Talmud was burned in 1553. The fountain, known as the 'soup tureen', that is now in front of the Chiesa Nuova was moved to make room for the statue. The matching fountain remains in the campo behind the flower stalls at the western end.

After a stroll through the campo, return to the end from which you entered but exit on the left side (facing the corner of Palazzo Pio Righetti) onto Via del Biscione. Almost immediately you enter into Piazza del Biscione with a Renaissance building with a painted facade and *Madonnella* with a fresco known as the *Madonna del Latte*. To your right is the Ristorante Pancrazio on the ground floor of Palazzo Pio Righetti (also known as Palazzo Orsini Pio Righetti) that allows visitors (between meal-serving hours) to go into their cellar to view foundation ruins and a model of the **Theatre of Pompey**, the first stone theatre in Rome inaugurated by Pompey the Great in 55 BCE with spectacular games and theatre entertainment. The theatre complex, which also included a Porticus and Curia, covered the area now occupied by Sant'Andrea della Valle as far as Largo Argentina. In 1865, the gilded bronze statue of *Hercules Righetti*, now in the Circular Hall (Sala Rotonda) of the Vatican Museums, was discovered in the grounds of the palace.

Walk through the arch at the right end of the piazza and follow the alley that emerges onto Via di Grotta Pinta. If the archway gate is closed, retrace your steps to Via del Biscione and turn right into Piazza del Paradiso, following the street to your right that leads to Via dei Chiavari and turn right into Largo del Pallaro to Via di Grotta Pinta. The Orsini family owned buildings built over the ruins of the theatre complex including the **Cappella Orsini** to your right and a tower called the Torre Arcapata. The buildings preserve the curved shape of the spectator's seats (*cavea*) of the Theatre of Pompey.

Follow Via di Grotta Pinta left (with the Cappella Orsini behind you) through Largo del Pallaro and look up to see the dome of Sant'Andrea della Valle. Turn left onto Via dei Chiavari to walk along the side of the church until you reach the entrance that faces onto Corso Vittorio Emanuele II in Rione Sant'Eustachio. The fountain in the piazza opposite Sant'Andrea della Valle is another moving fountain. It formerly stood in Piazza Scossacavalli that was demolished for the construction of the Via della Conciliazione (Tour 2). **Palazzo Valle** next to the piazza was built by Cardinal Andrea della Valle (his name appears over the entrance), who sold his ancient art collection to Cardinal Ferdinando de' Medici who used it in the decoration of the Villa Medici (Tour 10). The **Corso Vittorio Emanuele II** was formerly called Via Papalis since it formed part of the route taken by popes after their coronation between St Peter's and S. Giovanni in Laterano. The street was widened at the end of the 19th century. Buildings on the south side were demolished, such as Palazzo degli Truglia that stood next to Sant'Andrea della Valle, or had their facades removed and rebuilt at a greater distance from the street.

The construction of the Counter-Reformantion church of **Sant'Andrea della Valle** began in 1591 for the Theatine Order on the site donated to the order by Donna Costanza Piccolomini d'Aragona, the Duchess of Amalfi, that originally included a palace and a church of S. Sebastiano. The new church was rededicated to Sant'Andrea, who is the patron saint of Amalfi. The tombs of the Duchess's ancestors, the Piccolomini Popes Pius II (d. 1464) and Pius III (d. 1503), were relocated here from the Old St Peter's Basilica. Construction was first financed by Cardinal Alfonso Gesualdo, who hired the architects Giacomo della Porta and Pier Paolo Olivieri. The nephew of Pope Sixtus V Peretti, Cardinal Alessandro Peretti di Montalto, hired Carlo Maderno to continue the construction of the church but not the facade – that is by Carlo Rainaldi and was completed in 1665. Only one of Ercole Ferrata's angels survives. Cardinal Alessandro Peretti di Montalto was himself an architect who designed the second casino of the Villa Lante at Bagnaia (near Viterbo) when he was 17 years old. The basilica has the second tallest dome after St Peter's. The cupola is by Carlo Maderno (1622). The church is the setting for Puccini's *Tosca*, Act 1, but the Attavanti Chapel is Puccini's creation.

The interior evokes the Gesù and contains works by leading artists for important patrons, many from prominent and ambitious banking and guild families from Florence who vied for chapel space (and ancient marbles) after the chapels in S. Giovanni Battista dei Fiorentini (Tour 3) were already assigned to other families. The tombs of the Humanist Piccolomini Popes Pius II and Pius III are set high up at the mid-point of the nave. The cupola fresco *Glory of Paradise* (1625–1628) is by Giovanni Lanfranco but the pendentives are by his rival Domenichino from the Bolognese School with the *Evangelists* and *Virtues* (1621–1628). The high altar was designed by Carlo Fontana with centre apse frescoes by Mattia Preti (1650–1651), who follows tradition by depicting Saint Andrew's crucifixion on an x-shaped cross. The side wall frescoes are by Emilio Taruffi (right side) and Carlo Cignani (left side). The vault frescoes, *Scenes from the Life of St Andrew*, are by Domenichino. In the Chapel of St Andrew Avellino (south transept) is the *Death of the Saint* (1625) by Giovanni Lanfranco.

On the south side, the Ginetti Chapel (first) is by Carlo Fontana (1670) with relief sculpture by Antonio Raggi, *Angel Instructs Sacred Family to Flee to Egypt* (1675). The Strozzi Chapel (second), likely designed by Michelangelo, has bronze copies of his *Pietà* and the figures of *Leah* and *Rachel* from the Tomb of Pope Julius II della Rovere in S. Pietro in Vincoli (Tour 12). On the north side, the Barberini Chapel (first) is the first major commission by Cardinal Maffeo Barberini, the future Pope Urban VIII. The altar *Assumption* and side wall paintings *Visitation* and *Lucia Collects the Body of St Sebastian* are by Passignano (Domenico Cresti) from around 1616. *St John the Baptist* (1616) to the left is by Pietro Bernini, the father of Gian Lorenzo Bernini.

Walk around to the other side of the church into Piazza Vidoni to see another of the talking statues, **Abate Luigi** (Abbot Luigi). The street facing the statue, Via del Sudario, contains the original 16th-century facade of **Palazzo Vidoni Caffarelli** (1513–1536) attributed to Raphael but more likely the design of one of his students who was influenced by Bramante's Palazzo Caprini. Across the street is **SS. Sudario de' Savojardi** (sudario is Italian for shroud and alludes to the House of Savoy's connection with the Shroud of Turin). The facade is by Carlo Rainaldi (1687) with a relief with angels holding the Shroud of Turin. At No. 44 is the **Casa del Burcado** (1503) built by Johannes Burckardt who was nicknamed Argentarius since he was from Strasbourg (Argentoratum in Latin). The casa complex contains the tower that gives Largo di Torre Argentina its name.

Retrace your steps to Corso Vittorio Emanuele II and turn left past Sant'Andrea della Valle into Rione Parione and continue to the curve in the street. On the other side of the street is **Palazzo Massimo alle Colonne**, an important late work by the Renaissance architect Baldassarre Peruzzi (1532–1536) upon his return to Rome after being ransomed following the Sack of Rome in 1527. The palazzo preserves the convex curve of **Domitian's Odeon**, a roofed theatre for musical performances and recitations. The palazzo is built on the site of earlier palazzi owned by the Massimo family that were destroyed in the Sack of Rome in 1527. The family still resides in the palazzo today.

The adjacent palazzo to the left is commonly called *il Pirro* after the statue of Pyrrhus that was found near the Forum of Augustus that was on display here, but which is now in the Capitoline Museums (Tour 5). A column from Domitian's Odeon is preserved on the rear side of the palazzo in Piazza dei Massimi, which is accessed by walking around either side of the block. Also visible there is the adjoining Palazzetto Massimi (or Palazzetto Istoriato) that has a painted Renaissance facade from the School of Daniele da Volterra like the nearby Palazzo Ricci (Tour 3).

Continue on Corso Vittorio Emanuele II and on the other side of Via dei Baullari is the **Piccola Farnesina** (or Farnesina ai Baullari) to your left. It was designed by Antonio da Sangallo the Younger (1523) for Thomas Le Roy, a French cleric who assisted Pope Leo X de' Medici in his negotiations with Francis I of France in 1516. Excavations beneath the palazzo revealed the ruins of a 3rd–4th-century CE colonnaded courtyard of a Roman house and a street. The facade facing the corso (1898–1901) required reconstruction when buildings on the palazzo's north side were demolished for the widening of the corso. The orientation also changed at this time (it formerly faced south) towards Piazza dei Baullari, with the addition of the steps and balustrade. The palazzo houses a collection of ancient sculpture, the **Museo di Scultura Antica Giovanni Barracco**, that was bequeathed to the city of Rome by Senator Giovanni Barracco in 1902.

Just beyond through Piazza della Cancelleria to your left is the immense Renaissance **Palazzo della Cancelleria**. The palazzo was built between 1489 and 1513 for Cardinal Raffaele Riario, the son of Pope Sixtus IV's niece, when he was appointed titular head of the Basilica of S. Lorenzo in Damaso that he demolished together with the adjoining residence for the palazzo's construction. Marble and travertine from the Colosseum were used for its construction and spoliated red Egyptian granite for the columns of the loggia and cortile. Architects associated with its construction include Andrea Bregno, Francesco di Giorgio Martini or Baccio Pontelli. Donato Bramante probably joined the work in progress to complete the courtyard. The Florentine-inspired facade was completed only 15 years after the construction of Palazzo di Venezia and its design shows a more proportioned and balanced Renaissance approach, so that it is called the first Renaissance palace in Rome. The grand entry portal was by Domenico Fontana (1589) for Cardinal Alessandro Peretti di Montalto, the nephew of Pope Sixtus V Peretti. Cardinal Riario was responsible for bringing Michelangelo to Rome. He commissioned his *Bacchus* for his sculpture collection but he rejected it. The banker Jacopo Galli acquired it and displayed it in the garden of his nearby palazzo. The Medici, in turn, acquired it and in 1572 it was moved to Florence, now on display in the Museo Nazionale del Bargello.

Cardinal Riario's uncle, Girolamo Riario (nephew of Pope Sixtus IV della Rovere), was in league with the leaders of the Pazzi conspiracy and the pope against the Medici in Florence. In 1517, Cardinal Riario was aware of but did not participate in a plot against Pope Leo X de' Medici. Nonetheless, the pope, mindful of the earlier conspiracy, took possession of the palazzo and gave it to his cousin, Cardinal Giulio de' Medici, the future Pope Clement VII, for use as the Papal Chancery, which gives the palazzo its name of Cancelleria. The palazzo was damaged in the Sack of Rome in 1527 and restored by Pope Paul III Farnese, whose grandson, Cardinal Alessandro Farnese, served as Vice-Chancellor of the Holy Roman Church. Henry Benedict Stuart, Cardinal Duke of York (1725–1807) and the final Jacobite heir, occupied the palazzo from 1753 in his role as Vice-Chancellor. The French took possession of the palazzo during their occupation of the city and used the basilica as stables, but it was returned to the Vatican in 1800. After a brief repossession of the palazzo as the parliament of the Roman Republic in 1849, it was restored to the Vatican in 1870 and remains the Apostolic Chancery.

**San Lorenzo in Damaso**, entered by the portal on the right side of the palazzo, was originally the site of the Green Charioteer team (*Factio Prasina*) and Mithraeum. Pope Damasus built the basilica and an archive on the site in 366 and 384, but the structures were levelled in 1486 for the construction of the palazzo and replacement basilica. Excavations in the cortile of the palazzo have revealed the ruins of the basilica and a cemetery that was active from the 8th to the 15th century. In earlier excavations, the Cancelleria Reliefs in the Vatican Museums, commissioned by the Emperor Domitian, were found leaning against the enclosure to the **Tomb of Aulus Hirtius** (consul in 43 BCE), which is on display here in the museum. The interior of the basilica was reworked several times: the apse area by Bernini for Cardinal Francesco Barberini, the nephew of Pope Urban VIII (1638–40); and the basilica by Giuseppe Valadier in 1807 following the French occupation, though many of his renovations were reversed by Virginio Vespignani for Pope Pius IX (1868–1882).

Continue on Corso Vittorio Emanuele II for four blocks to reach the Chiesa Nuova (S. Maria in Vallicella) in Piazza della Chiesa Nuova. Cross to the other side of the street. The fountain in the piazza, called the **Fontana della Terrina** ('soup tureen'), was originally installed in the centre of Campo de' Fiori but was moved here in 1924 after the statue of Bruno Giordano was erected in its place in 1889. The original fountain by Giacomo della Porta (*c.*1590) was given the cover in 1622 to keep out the waste of the vegetable merchants. The piazza was much smaller before the construction of Corso Vittorio Emanuele II (from 1883), when the fronts of buildings across the street were demolished and the facades rebuilt.

The **Chiesa Nuova** or S. Maria in Vallicella, is the third major Counter-Reformation church on the itinerary. Saint Filippo Neri (1515–1595) founded the Oratorian Order in 1551 and is known as the 'Apostle of Rome'. Pope Gregory XIII Boncompagni gave him the 12th-century church of S. Maria in Vallicella in 1571 for his order that was replaced by the Chiesa Nuova. Cardinal Pier Donato Cesi and his brother Antonio provided financial assistance. The original design of Matteo da Città di Castello (from 1575) was altered by Martino Longhi the Elder (1586–1590). The facade is by Fausto Rughesi (1594–1606) and shows the influence of the Gesù. The adjacent palazzo that contains the **Oratorio dei Filippini**, named for the followers of S. Filippo Neri, was designed mostly by Borromini (between 1637 and 1650) with a distinctive concave facade that anticipates the architectural tension and drama of his facade for Palazzo di Propaganda Fide (Tour 10).

The interior is as lavish as the Gesù, whose vault, *Miracle of the Madonna della Vallicella* (1664–1665), is a masterpiece of the Counter-Reformation by Pietro da Cortona, who also painted the apse *Assumption* (1655–1660) and cupola *Glorification of the Trinity* (1647–1651) with prophets in the pendentives (1659–1660). Stucco decoration is also by da Cortona and executed by Ercole Ferrata and Cosimo Fancelli (1662–1665). Above the high altar, Peter Paul Rubens (1606–1608) painted the central panel *Madonna and Angels*. Behind it is the icon of *Madonna and Angels* from the earlier church and the two side paintings with saints. The Chapel of S. Filippo to the left of the sanctuary contains his relics and mosaic copy of Guido Reni's *S. Filippo and the Virgin*. *Scenes from the Life of S. Filippo* on the walls are by Pomarancio (Cristoforo Roncalli).

In the north transept is the entry door to the sacristy with *S. Filippo Neri and Angel* and bust of *Pope Gregory XV Ludovisi* by Alessandro Algardi (1640). There is access from here to the rooms of S. Filippo Neri and a chapel with *S. Filippo Neri* by Algardi in silver; *Madonna and Child with S. Martina* by Pietro da Cortona; the original *S. Filippo and the Virgin* by Guido Reni (1615); and *S. Filippo and the Angel* by Guercino. The Cappella Spada to the right of the sanctuary, begun by Camillo Arcucci in 1662 but completed by Carlo Rainaldi in 1667, contains Carlo Maratta's *Madonna and Child with Saints Carlo Borromeo and Ignatius of Loyola*. In the second chapel (south side) is a copy of Caravaggio's *Descent from the Cross* (1602–1603). The original painting was taken by the French in 1797 and substituted by this copy painted by Michele Koeck. The original is now in the Pinacoteca Vaticana. On the north side (fifth chapel) is an *Annunciation* by Passignano, *Adoration of the Shepherds* by Durante Alberti (third chapel) and Cavalier d'Arpino's *Presentation in the Temple* (first chapel).

Exit the church and turn right then another sharp right to walk around the Oratorio dei Filippini to Piazza del Orologio to see Borromini's **Orologio** clock tower. The mosaic *Madonna della Vallicella* (1657) is perhaps to the design of Pietro da Cortona. Turn right on Via del Governo Vecchio, once part of the Via Papalis. Continue past **Palazzo del Governo Vecchio** (1473–1477), also called Palazzo

7. Pantheon

Nardini, to your left with 15th-, 16th- and 17th-century palazzi to your right including **Palazzetto Turci** or the Piccola Cancelleria (*c.*1500) at No. 123, formerly attributed to Bramante.

Proceed into Piazza di Pasquino, named for the famous talking statue of *Pasquino* at the corner wall of the immense **Palazzo Braschi** (Museo di Roma), the Palace of Pope Pius VI and the last of the papal palaces in Rome. It was built by Cosimo Morelli (1791–1796) in a design that recalls the architectural style of 16th-century palazzi. It faces both Piazza di Pasquino and Piazza Navona with distinctive lion and pine cone decoration. After the French occupation, Giuseppe Valadier restored the palazzo that became the property of the Italian state in 1871. Currently it houses the **Museo di Roma** whose collection is devoted to the history of the city with a focus on the 16th to the 19th centuries.

*Pasquino* is named for a tailor for whose shop it served as a doorstop. The name is the origin of the term *pasquinade*, referring to irreverent satires posted anonymously aimed at prominent public figures and critical of the papacy. The statue is a fragment of a sculpture group of Menelaus holding the dead Patroklos, more commonly seen in the copy in the Loggia dei Lanzi in Piazza della Signoria, Florence. Turn left at the statue to walk into Piazza Navona for the start of Tour 8.

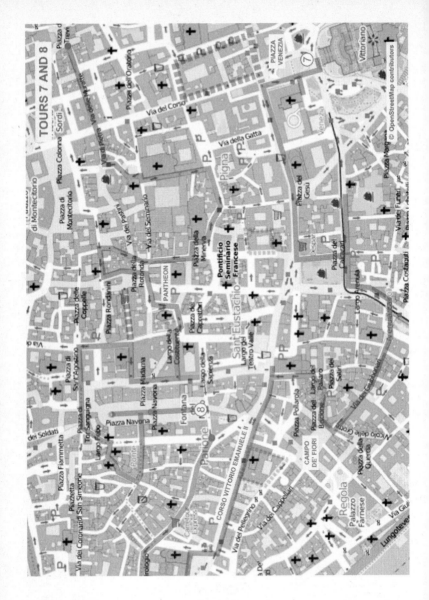

Sites: Piazza Navona; Sant'Agnese in Agone; S. Maria della Pace; S. Maria dell'Anima; Domitian's Stadium; Palazzo Altemps; Sant'Agostino; S. Luigi dei Francesi; Palazzo Giustiniani; Palazzo Madama; Palazzo della Sapienza; Sant'Ivo alla Sapienza; Sant'Eustachio; Piazza della Rotonda; Pantheon; S. Maria Maddalena; S. Maria sopra Minerva; Collegio Romano; Sant'Ignazio; Temple of Hadrian; Trevi Fountain.
Distance: 2.75km.

Tour 8

# Piazza Navona, Pantheon and the Trevi Fountain

A tour of spectacular Baroque art and architecture begins in Piazza Navona with Bernini's 'Four Rivers Fountain' and winds through the area of the iconic Pantheon to the dramatic Trevi Fountain. Must-see Renaissance churches include S. Maria della Pace with the Chiostro del Bramante, Sant'Agostino, S. Maria sopra Minerva and S. Luigi dei Francesi with Caravaggio's *Scenes from the Life of St Matthew* cycle and the dramatic Counter-Reformation churches Sant'Agnese in Agone and Sant'Ivo alla Sapienza by Francesco Borromini.

**Piazza Navona** is a Baroque gem in Rione Parione famous for its fountains, artist booths and street performers that attracts large crowds day and night. The piazza has a long history as the location of spectacle entertainment going back to ancient Rome and it preserves the outline (curved north end and straight south end) of **Domitian's Stadium**, called an *agon* from the Greek word for a contest, inaugurated in 86 CE, which featured nude Greek athletic contests. Surviving architectural elements of the stadium are visible at the outer side of the north end. In time, the word *agon* became corrupted into Navona. The word also develops the meaning 'agony' from the physical location of the legend of St Agnes who suffered her martyrdom in the stadium (*in agone*). Gladiatorial contests were held here when the Colosseum was struck by lightning in 217 CE. The annual **Christmas Fair** (Mercantino di Natale a Piazza Navona) from mid-December to Epiphany (6 January), dedicated to 'La Befana', an old witch figure associated with 'Mother Christmas', is a reminder of the piazza's commercial past when the mercato was moved here from Piazza di S. Marco in 1477 by Pope

Sixtus IV della Rovere. It was moved again to Campo de' Fiori (Tour 7) in 1869.

To the left as you enter the piazza from Via di Pasquino at the south end is **Palazzo Pamphilj a Piazza Navona**. A marble plaque at the left-hand corner of the palazzo indicates the flood level of the Tiber in 1870 (about 6.5 feet). The palazzo, currently the Brazilian Embassy,

8. Piazza Navona

was begun by Girolamo Rainaldi but completed by Borromini who designed the Sala Palestrina that contains busts by Alessandro Algardi and the Galleria with a Classical themed fresco by Pietro da Cortona (*The Story of Aeneas*). As an exaltation of the Pamphilj family, the piazza was also called the Forum Pamphilium, referencing the central role played by ancient fora in civic life.

In front of the palazzo is the **Fontana del Moro** (Fountain of the Moor). The first of three monumental fountains in the piazza is named after the Ethiopian in the centre by Giovanni Antonio Mari (1654). Bernini designed the figures for Olimpia Maidalchini, the sister-in-law of Pope Innocent X, who lived in the palazzo. The fountain basin was originally designed by Giacomo della Porta (1576) for Pope Gregory XIII Boncompagni. The original statues were replaced with copies by Luigi Amici (1909). Facing the fountain from the south end of the piazza next to Palazzo Braschi is **Palazzo Lancellotti**, built by Pirro Ligorio (1552) for Ludovico de Torres and acquired by the Lancellotti in the following century.

On the other side of the piazza facing the fountain is the church of **Nostra Signora del Sacro Cuore** that was built for the Jubilee in 1450 on the site on a 12th-century church. The church was formerly called S. Giacomo degli Spagnoli and was replaced as the Spanish national church in Rome after the construction of S. Maria in Monserrato degli Spagnoli (Tour 3), where many of the interior monuments were transferred. In 1879, the facade, possibly by Bernardo Rossellino for Pope Alexander VI Borgia, was moved to this side of the building by Luca Carimini for Pope Leo XIII, but only the bottom half of the original survives. The nave and apse of the church were demolished for the construction of Corso del Rinascimento (1938). The shell and pin decoration that appears on the church and above the doors and windows of nearby buildings associated with the Spanish community represents the *xenodochion* worn by pilgrims to Santiago di Compostela. The Spanish community in the area reflects its support for Pope Innocent X in contrast to the French community that had supported his precursor Pope Urban VIII and the Barberini family, the rivals of the Pamphilj.

In the centre of the piazza, the spectacular **Fontana dei Quattro Fiumi** (Fountain of the Four Rivers) by Bernini (1651) rises to the height of the obelisk moved here from the Circus of Maxentius on the Via Appia Antica (Tour 14), but originally erected by Domitian elsewhere in the city. At the time of the design competition for the fountain that Innocent X wanted to include the obelisk, Bernini was out of favour with the pope so he submitted his design anonymously. The pope's family emblems of the dove and olive branch at the top are also part of the decorative motif of the palazzo and church of Sant'Agnese in Agone.

The composition of the fountain forces spectators to walk around it to view the rivers and their animal symbols. The figures at the base are personifications of the most famous four rivers from the then known continents sculpted by Bernini's pupils: the Danube (Antonio Raggi) touches the papal crest as the closest river in proximity to the Vatican; the Ganges (Claude Poussin) holds an oar for its navigability; the Nile (Giacomo Antonio Fancelli) with covered head symbolises the hidden source of the river; and the Rio de la Plata (Francesco Baratta) sits next to coins to signify the wealth of the New World. According to urban legend, the Rio de la Plata is holding up his hand to block out Borromini's church of Sant'Agnese in Agone, but the story is apocryphal since the fountain, completed in 1651, predates Borromini's contribution to the construction of the church (1653–1657).

All three fountains in the piazza are supplied with water from the Acqua Vergine (ancient Aqua Virgo) that was restored by Pope Nicholas V in 1453 and ends at the Trevi Fountain. The low level of the aqueduct results in gentle water flows rather than forceful sprays, but the spectacular sculptural effects of the Four Rivers Fountain draws attention away from the less dramatic flows of water. As the source of spectacle entertainment, the fountain was also the focal point for staged events in the piazza. In the 18th century, the piazza was flooded for *lago* (lake) spectacles for mock naval displays seen by spectators, including James Stuart and Maria Clementina, from viewing stands erected along the piazza.

The church of **Sant'Agnese in Agone** is an architectural masterpiece by Francesco Borromini built for Pope Innocent X Pamphilj. Work on the church was started by Girolamo Rainaldi and his son Carlo in 1652 but Borromini took over the project and worked on it from 1653 until 1657 when he fell out of favour with Pope Innocent X's successor, Alexander VII Chigi. Giovanni Maria Baratta completed work on Borromini's concave facade and twin bell towers.

The interior is on a Greek cross-plan under a beautiful cupola that gives a smaller scale impression of the effect of Bramante's original Greek cross design for St Peter's Basilica. The cupola fresco, *Glory of Paradise*, is by Ciro Ferri (1689) with pendentives illustrating the *Cardinal Virtues* (1665) by Baciccia. There are no paintings in the church but reliefs and statues above the seven altars, including the south side altar with the statue of *St Agnes in the flames* and relief *Martyrdom of St Emerenziana*, are by Ercole Ferrata. The high altar relief, *Two Sacred Families*, is by Domenico Guidi. The relief to the left of the sanctuary, *Martyrdom of St Cecilia*, is by Antonio Raggi. Through a door inscribed *Testa di S. Agnese* ('Head of St Agnes'), a corridor leads to a chapel with the skull of S. Agnes in a reliquary. Other relics are in Sant'Agnese fuori le Mura (Tour 11). Above the main entrance is the monument to Pope Innocent X by Giovanni Battista Maini, who is buried in a family crypt below the church. The Oratory of St Agnes, built in a vault of Domitian's stadium in 800, contains Alessandro Algardi's last work, *Miracle of St Agnes* (1653).

Continue towards the **Fontana di Nettuno** (Fountain of Neptune) at the curved north end of the piazza. The basin is by Giacomo della Porta (1576) but it was remodelled to match the Fontana del Moro. The fountain was not finished until 1878, with the addition of the figures of Neptune (by Antonio della Bitta) and Nereids, sea horses and putti (by Gregorio Zappalà).

Exit the piazza by Via di S. Agnese in Agone alongside the church. A sign on the opposite side of the piazza indicates the direct route to the Pantheon. Proceed to the charming Via della Pace. Turn right and the church of **S. Maria della Pace** is straight ahead. Pope Sixtus IV della Rovere rebuilt and renamed an earlier church, San Andrea de Aquarizariis (1480–1484), and possibly commissioned Baccio Pontelli for its construction. The elegant portico with a semicircular portico was designed by Pietro da Cortona for Pope Alexander VII Chigi (1656–1657). The piazza allowed carriages an opportunity to turn around, and the procession of carriages became a form of street theatre.

The Baroque exterior houses Renaissance and Mannerist masterpieces inside. The Chigi Chapel (first on south side) contains Raphael's fresco *Sibyls* for Agostino Chigi (1514), the great uncle of Pope Alexander VII, below the fresco of *Prophets* by Timoteo Viti. On the tablet next to the Cumaean Sibyl is a quote from Virgil's *Fourth Eclogue* that was later interpreted as her prophecy of the birth of Christ. The altar relief *Deposition* is by Cosimo Fancelli with statues by Antonio Raggi in the niches. Next to it, the Cesi Chapel designed by Antonio da Sangallo the

Younger (1525) contains the funerary effigies of Angelo Cesi and his wife Francesca Carduli Cesi by Vincenzo de Rossi, who also carved the chapel arch facade and the statues of Saints Peter and Paul. The exterior lunettes are by Rosso Fiorentino (1524). The marble for the sphinxes, attributed to Simone Mosca (1550–1560), came from a surviving capital from the Temple of Jupiter Optimus Maximus. Ironically, the Emperor Domitian, who rebuilt the temple, ordered the contents of a tomb built by one of his freedmen with stones intended for the temple thrown into the sea.

The cupola (also by Sangallo), with fresco by Francesco Cozza, rises above an octagonal tribune area with stucco decoration by Pietro da Cortona that includes the *Visitation* by Carlo Maratta (1655) and Baldassarre Peruzzi's *Presentation of the Virgin* (1524). The high altar by Carlo Maderno (1611) incorporates the 15th-century icon of the *Madonna della Pace*. To either side are the *Nativity* and *Annunciation* by Passignano. The series of *Saints* are by Lavinia Fontana (1611–1614). In the chapel to the right of the high altar is the *Baptism of Christ* by Orazio Gentileschi (1603). In the north side chapel is Sermoneta's *Adoration of the Shepherds* (1565). In the Ponzetti Chapel (first on north side) is Baldassarre Peruzzi's fresco *Madonna and Child with Saints Bridget and Catherine* (1516).

On the left side of S. Maria della Pace is the entrance to the **Chiostro del Bramante** (1500–1504), built for Cardinal Oliviero Carafa. The elegant cloister was Bramante's first work in Rome followed soon after by his Tempietto (Tour 3). Today, the cloister hosts exhibitions but the courtyard may be visited free of charge. On the first floor, the Sala delle Sibille of the Cafe has a window with a view of Raphael's fresco when the church is closed.

If the doors to the adjacent church of **S. Maria dell'Anima**, the German national church in Rome, into the piazza are closed, walk through the arch (to the right of S. Maria della Pace) and turn right to walk along the side of the church on Via dei Lorensi to the front entrance to your right on Via di S. Maria dell'Anima. Above the main entrance of the church (1500–1523; consecrated 1542), the *Madonna and Child between two souls in Purgatory* is a cast of a group attributed to Andrea Sansovino. The Gothic interior, restored in 1843, retains earlier architectural elements by Sansovino and distinct funerary monuments. Over the high altar, the *Sacred Family and Saints* is by Giulio Romano (1522). The Tomb of Hadrian VI (1522–1523) was designed by Baldassarre Peruzzi. The pope's cessation of artistic patronage led artists to leave Rome at the height of the Renaissance. On the south side (first chapel) is Carlo Saraceni's *St Benno receiving the keys to Meissen Cathedral from the Fisherman* (1618) and (fourth chapel) a copy of Michelangelo's *Pietà* begun by Lorenzetto and completed by Nanni di Baccio Bigio (1532). On the north side (first chapel) is Carlo Saraceni's *Martyrdom of St Lambert* (1618).

Exit by the front entrance and continue left on Via di S. Maria dell'Anima through Largo Febo to walk along the outer curve of buildings that enclose Piazza Navona. Turn right on Via di Tor Sanguigna. Immediately to your right are the surviving (visible) substructures of **Domitian's Stadium**, accessed from the museum. The ruins were exposed when buildings were demolished (1936–1938) for a sight line to the river, but the project was never completed. When replacement buildings were constructed, access and a view of the ruins were retained.

To continue on the tour, cross to the other side of the street to the medieval tower, **Tor Sanguigna**. Palazzo di Giustizia is visible on the other side of the Tiber. On Via Giusseppe Zanardelli that was opened in 1902 is the **Museo Mario Praz** at No. 2 in Palazzo Primoli. The house museum preserves the apartment of the famous essayist. The palazzo also houses the **Museo Napoleonico**. Turn right into Piazza di Sant'Apollinare for the entrance to Palazzo Altemps. The 16th-century **Teatro Goldoni** (accessed from Piazza di Sant'Apollinare), named for the 18th-century playwright Carlo Goldoni, is one of the oldest private theatres in Rome.

To linger in the area to explore more of Renaissance Rome, turn left on Via dei Coronari (with the ruins behind you). Lining the beautiful **Via dei Coronari** (named after rosary makers) are antique shops and palazzi including **Palazzo Lancellotti ai Coronari** by Carlo Maderno in Piazza di San Simeone (No. 5) where a Roman copy of Myron's *Discobolus* now in Palazzo Massimo (Tour 12) was displayed and removed to Berlin by Hitler. The **Fontana di Piazza di San Simeone** by Giacomo della Porta (1589) was moved here in 1973 from Parco Savello (Giardino degli Aranci) on the Aventine Hill, though it was originally in Piazza Montanara that was demolished during the construction of Via del Mare (Tour 4). Other palazzi include the 16th-century **Palazzi del Drago** at Nos 33–44 and the 16th-century **Palazzo Fioravanti** at No. 45. Farther along to your right in the piazza is the church of **San Salvatore in Lauro** with a beautiful Neoclassical interior. On the opposite side of the street is the Via di Monte Giordano with the 15th-century **Palazzo Taverna** on Monte Giordano at No. 36 that incorporates the former Orsini palace fortress with Baroque and 19th-century additions. Continue straight ahead when the street name changes to Vicolo del Curato. Turn left on Via del Banco di S. Spirito and join Tour 3 at the Banco di S. Spirito or retrace your steps to rejoin Tour 8.

**Palazzo Altemps** (Museo Nazionale Romano Palazzo Altemps) in Rione Ponte occupies the site of an ancient dock along the Tiber. Girolamo Riario, the nephew of Pope Sixtus IV della Rovere, began construction of the palazzo (1477) the year before his involvement in the Pazzi conspiracy against the Medici in Florence. For a time, the palazzo was the residence of Cardinal Innocenzo Cybo, the son of Franceschetto (illegitimate son of Pope Innocent VIII Cybo), and Maddalena di Lorenzo de' Medici, the sister of Pope Leo X de' Medici and cousin of Pope Clement VII de' Medici after whose death he lost the papal election to Pope Julius III. Possession of the palazzo passed to Cardinal Francesco Soderini who continued work on the palazzo as did Cardinal Marco Sittico Altemps (Mark Sittich von Hohenem Altemps), the nephew of Pope Pius IV de' Medici, who hired the architect Martino Longhi the Elder who added the belvedere with four obelisks. The palazzo was restored by Virginio Vespignani (1837) and Antonio Muñoz (1949) and acquired by the Italian state in 1982.

The museum focuses on famous pieces of ancient sculpture (Egyptian, original Greek and Roman copies) collected by Roman aristocratic families and restored by Bernini and Algardi primarily from the **Boncompagni Ludovisi Collection** assembled by Cardinal Ludovico Ludovisi, the nephew of Pope Gregory XV Ludovisi, for the decoration of the gardens of the Villa Ludovisi that occupied the area between the Porta Pinciana and Porta Salaria, originally part of the Gardens of Sallust in ancient Rome (Tour 11). The villa was sold in 1885 and the sculpture collection of 104 pieces was bought by the Italian state in 1901. Visitors on the Grand Tour bought engravings of the collection (on display) and commissioned copies and plaster casts. Antonio da Sangallo the Elder began construction of the courtyard (1513–1517) but the project continued under Baldassarre Peruzzi and was completed by Martino Longhi the Elder. On display here are statues from the Mattei and Altemps collections. Beginning with the atrium off of the portico are ancient and 17th-century sculptures from the Boncompagni Ludovisi collection.

On the **first floor**, the *Hermes Ludovisi* is a Roman copy of a 5th-century original that was restored by Algardi. The **Room of the Sideboard** with frescoes celebrating the wedding of Girolamo Riario to Caterina Sforza in 1477 contains masterpieces from the Boncompagni Ludovisi collection that continue into the following rooms: *Ares Ludovisi*; *Achilles*, restored by Bernini; *Orestes and Electra*, signed by a Greek artist named Menelaus who trained under Stephanos; *Ludovisi Throne*, with the birth of Aphrodite considered an original Greek work from the 5th century BCE or a fake; and *Juno Ludovisi*, considered a Greek work by the 18th-century art historian and archaeologist Johann Joachim Winckelmann who was influential in defining Greek and Roman aesthetics, though today the colossal head is identified as Antonia Minor, the younger daughter of Octavia, the sister of the Emperor Augustus, and Mark Antony. She was the mother of the Emperor Claudius and grandmother of the Emperor Caligula. Goethe made a cast for his house on Via del Corso (Tour 9).

The **Great Hall of the Galatian** (Sala Grande del Galata) is named after the *Suicidal Gaul* (also known as the *Suicidal Galatian* and *Ludovisi Gaul*) in the centre of the room. It is a Roman copy of an original bronze sculpture group for Attalus I of Pergamon that also included the *Dying Gaul* in the Capitoline Museums. Both sculptures were found on the grounds of the Villa Ludovisi. The Ludovisi Sarcophagus (mid-3rd century CE) was discovered near the Porta Tiburtina in 1621. The Great Hall also leads to the church of **Sant'Aniceto** and Loggia with a pergola fresco.

From Piazza di Sant'Apollinare, walk through the arch at the left-hand corner of Piazza delle Cinque Lune. Immediately to your left on Via delle Coppelle is the church of **Sant'Agostino** with one of the earliest Renaissance facades in Rome by Giacomo da Pietrasanta (1479–1483) for Cardinal Guillaume d'Estouteville. The travertine is from the Colosseum. The interior, reworked by Luigi Vanvitelli (1756–1761), is devoted to St Augustine of Hippo and his mother St Monica whose relics are here. In the early Renaissance, the church was visited by courtesans including Fiametta de Michaelis, the mistress of Cesare Borgia. Giorgio Vasari's *Deposition* (1534–1544) was displayed here until purchased by Camillo Pamphilj in 1661.

The statue of the *Madonna del Parto* at the entrance by Jacopo Sansovino (1521) seems to be a reworked ancient statue of Apollo. The chapel contains votive offerings to St Mary for her intercession with fertility and childbirth. The two statues of angels holding the holy water basins (stoups) are by Antonio Raggi. The fresco of the Prophet Isaiah on the third pillar of the north side of the nave is by Raphael (1512). Beneath it is Andrea Sansovino's sculpture *Madonna and Child with St Anne* (1512). The other prophets were painted by Pietro Gagliardi (1855).

The high altar was designed by Bernini (1627) with a Byzantine icon of the Madonna. The Chapel of St Augustine (south transept) altarpiece is by Guercino. To the left is the funerary monument to Cardinal Renato Imperiali with sculpture by Pietro Bracci (1741). To the left of the sanctuary is the Chapel of St Monica attributed to Isaia da Pisa, containing her tomb. St Monica died at a hostel in Ostia Antica (Tour 15) in 387 on her journey back to Africa. In the adjacent chapel, the cupola, lunettes and walls were painted by Giovanni Lanfranco (1616). In the first chapel (north side) is Caravaggio's *Madonna di Loreto* or the *Madonna dei Pellegrini* (named after the kneeling pilgrims) that was painted for this altar (1604–1606) for Ermete Cavalletti.

Next to the church at No. 8 is the **Bibliotheca Angelica**, Rome's first public library, founded in 1614 by Angelo Rocca. Continue on Via delle Coppelle to the next intersection at Via della Scrofa. Look ahead on Via delle Coppelle to your left at No. 35 for **Palazzo Baldassini** by Antonio da Sangallo the Younger (1514–1520). Giuseppe Garibaldi lived here in 1875. Turn right onto Via della Scrofa. The church of S. Luigi dei Francesi is ahead to your right in Piazza di S. Luigi de' Francesi opposite **Palazzo Patrizi** at No. 37.

**San Luigi dei Francesi** is the French national church in Rome. Catherine de' Medici (Queen of France) donated land next to Palazzo Madama to enlarge the church and build a hospital on the site of the ancient Baths of Nero that extended beyond Palazzo Giustiniani. The facade was designed by Giacomo della Porta and Domenico Fontana (1589), showing the influence of Michelangelo. The interior design of marble and stucco is by Antoine Dérizet (1756–1764).

The Contarelli Chapel (the fifth chapel on the north side) attracts visitors for Caravaggio's *Scenes from the Life of St Matthew* cycle (1599–1602), painted for the heirs of Cardinal Matthieu Cointrel (d. 1585) who shared the saint's name and whose own name was Italianised as Matteo Contarelli. The light source in the paintings imitates the direction of light coming into the chapel. On the left is the *Calling of St Matthew* in which St Peter forms the link between Christ and St Matthew. In the centre is the second version of *St Matthew and the Angel* in which the Angel startles St Matthew at work on his Gospel. The original version was rejected by the Church and sold to Vincenzo Giustiniani. On the right is the *Martyrdom of St Matthew*. The frescoes on the dome are by Cavalier d'Arpino (Giuseppe Cesari), in whose studio Caravaggio had trained. Against the pier at the beginning of the north side is the funerary monument to the painter Claude Lorrain, known simply as Claude, who died in Rome in 1682. The former draw of visitors to the church was the Cappella S. Cecilia (south side, second chapel) with frescoes by Domenichino (*c*.1614): *St Cecilia distributing alms* to the right, and *St Cecilia and her betrothed St Valerian are crowned by Angels* to the left. The altarpiece by Guido Reni is a copy of Raphael's *Ecstasy of St Cecilia*, now in the Pinacoteca Nazionale di Bologna. Against the pier at the beginning of the south side is the Monument to the French dead in the Siege of Rome (1849).

Exit the piazza to Via Giustiniani. Across the street to the right is the rear of Palazzo Madama and to the left is **Palazzo Giustiniani** begun by Giovanni and Domenico Fontana (1585–1587) but continued under Carlo Maderno, Girolamo and Carlo Rainaldi and completed by Borromini (1678), who designed the main entrance. Vincenzo Giustiniani (1564–1637) acquired the palazzo in 1590 where he displayed his famous collection of ancient sculpture. Giustiniani was a friend of Cardinal Francesco Maria Del Monte (1549–1627), the first patron of Caravaggio, who lived opposite in Palazzo Madama as representative of Grand Duke (formerly Cardinal) Fernando I de' Medici. Giustiniani owned 300 paintings, 15 of which were by Caravaggio, including the original version of *St Matthew and the Angel* that was taken to Berlin but destroyed in World War II. The palazzo is now the official residence of the President of the Italian Senate that convenes in Palazzo Madama.

To go directly to the Pantheon, turn left on Via Giustiniani into Piazza della Rotonda and resume the tour itinerary there. To continue on the tour, turn right on Via Giustiniani and walk along the side of the church of San Luigi dei Francesi and the side of Palazzo Madama to Corso del Rinascimento. Turn left to walk along the front of Palazzo Madama. The dome of Sant'Andrea della Valle is visible straight ahead.

**Palazzo Madama** was originally owned by the Crescenzi family whose earlier palace on the site incorporated part of the Baths of Nero. In the 16th century, the palazzo came into the possession of the Medici as part of Alfonsina Orsini's dowry when she married Piero de' Medici, the brother of Pope Leo X de' Medici, who incorporated the original medieval palace complex into a new palazzo (1503) that was enlarged in 1512. The ornate Baroque facade is by Paolo Marucelli (1637–1642). After the Medici were expelled from Florence in 1527, Catherine de' Medici lived with her grandmother Alfonsina at the palazzo until she married Henry II of France at the age of 14 and later became Queen of France when his brother Francis died. The palazzo gets its current name from 'Madama' Margaret of Parma, the illegitimate daughter of the Holy Roman Emperor Charles V who married Alessandro de' Medici and next Ottavio Farnese. In 1740, Pope Benedict XIV acquired the palace but it passed from papal possession when it became the residence of the Governor of Rome and the seat of the Ministry of Finance (1852–1870). It has served as the seat of the Italian Senate since 1871. The right wing of the palazzo on Via della Vecchia Dogana was added between 1926 and 1931.

Continue past Palazzo Madama and cross Via degli Staderari to the entrance of Palazzo della Sapienza whose steps jut out onto the sidewalk mid-block. **Palazzo della Sapienza** was begun by Guidetto Guidetti and Pirro Ligorio but work on the facade and courtyard was continued by Giacomo della Porta (from 1577) for Pope Gregory XIII Boncompagni and Pope Sixtus V Peretti. Borromini (1632–1667) completed work on the courtyard, interior halls and the church of Sant'Ivo alla Sapienza. La Sapienza University was founded by Pope Boniface VIII Caetani in 1303 as the *Studium Urbis*. It was located here during the reign of Pope Eugenius IV (1431–1447), where it remained until 1935 when it moved to the current location of the Città Universitaria and is now called the Sapienza Università di Roma. The inscription on the west side of the courtyard ('Fear of God is the beginning of wisdom') is a reminder of its papal foundations.

The church of **Sant'Ivo alla Sapienza** is at the end of the courtyard with a facade of concave and convex curves that continues the pattern of arches from the courtyard and rises to a spiral lantern distinct in the skyline of Rome. The church is a masterpiece by Borromini (1642–1660) begun for Pope Urban VIII Barberini but completed under Pope Alexander VII Chigi whose family emblems of mountains and star figure prominently in the decoration and convey the visitor's gaze towards the lantern. The theatrical interplay between the concave and convex shapes gives the white and gold interior a sense of lightness. The altarpiece is by Pietro da Cortona (1661).

Retrace your steps on Corso del Rinascimento and turn right on Via degli Straderari. Walk past the **Fontana dei Libri** (Book Fountain) to your right by Pietro Lombardi (1927) that references the University of La Sapienza and the stag emblem of the Rione Sant'Eustachio (St Eustace). The monumental ancient Aswan granite basin fountain to your left, the **Fontana di Via degli Straderari**, is from the Baths of Nero and was excavated in 1985 in the adjacent Palm Courtyard that is bordered by Palazzo Madama, the portico that connects it to **Palazzo Carpegna**, and the **Torre dei Crescenzi a Palazzo Madama**. It was given to the Comune di Roma by the Italian Senate to mark the 40th anniversary of the Italian Constitution. Veer right to enter into Piazza di Sant'Eustachio. To your right at No. 83 is **Palazzo Cenci a Sant'Eustachio** (also called Palazzo Stati Cenci Maccarani di Brazzà) designed by Giulio Romano (*c.*1516). On the ground level is the famous Sant'Eustachio il Caffè. Next to it is **Palazzo Medici-Lante** whose design is attributed to Giuliano da Sangallo and was once owned by Pope Leo X de' Medici.

At the end of the piazza is the 16th-century **Palazzo Tizio di Spoleto** with a painted facade by Federico Zuccari that depicts the coat of arms of Pope Pius IV de' Medici. Above it, the fresco relates the legend of the 'Miracle of Sant'Eustachio' who was a Roman soldier who converted to Christianity when he saw the sign of the cross on the forehead of a stag. The church of **Sant'Eustachio** with a 12th-century campanile is to your left, with the head of a stag at the top of its facade. Continue through the piazza and turn left at the church onto Via di Sant'Eustachio. To your left are two surviving columns from the **Baths of Nero**. Two other columns were used to repair the columns of the Pantheon porch and to create the Porta Pia on Via XX Settembre (Tour 11). The marble plaque on the wall (1717) forbids anyone from littering the piazza.

Turn right on Salita de' Crescenzi to enter **Piazza della Rotonda** that is named after the rotunda of the Pantheon whose porch is visible straight ahead. The piazza, in the Rione Pigna, was the location of a fish and vegetable market until it was moved to Piazza Navona in 1804. The modern level of the piazza is higher than the level of the Pantheon's porch floor, but in antiquity it was approached by a flight of stairs that would have made the facade more imposing upon entering. The **Fontana di Piazza della Rotonda** (1575) was modelled after a design by Giacomo della Porta. The obelisk that was originally from the nearby Iseum (Temple of Isis) dates to the reign of Ramesses II and was added by Pope Clement XI in 1711.

The iconic **Pantheon** is one of the best-preserved temples that survives from Classical antiquity. The inscription on the facade records Marcus Agrippa as the builder ('Marcus Agrippa, son of Lucius, built this in his third consulship'), but what survives is a later version. The original building built by Agrippa between 27 and 25 BCE was destroyed by fire and was rebuilt by the Emperor Domitian (after the fire of 80 CE) and rebuilt again by the Emperor Hadrian, between 118 and 125 CE, who dramatically altered the appearance and orientation of the original but restored the original dedication inscription. Restorations were carried out under Antoninus Pius, Septimius Severus and Caracalla. The Pantheon survives today as **S. Maria ad Martyres** (also known as S. Maria della Rotonda) and was the first pagan temple in Rome converted into a church in 609 CE after the Byzantine Emperor Phocas gave it to Pope Boniface IV. The Temple of Concordia in Agrigento was converted into a church a decade earlier in 597. The Corinthian Order of the Pantheon complemented that order's association with St Mary.

Canon Benedict in his medieval guide to Rome (*Mirabilia Urbis Romae*) claimed (erroneously) that the pine cone now in the Vatican Museums in the Cortile della Pigna and the namesake of the area, the Rione Pigna, once capped the oculus. Architect Filippo Brunelleschi, in Rome with the sculptor Donatello (Donato di Niccolò di Betto Bardi) from 1402 to 1404, studied Roman architecture including the dome of the Pantheon, which influenced his design for the dome of the Duomo (S. Maria del Fiore) in Florence.

The name Pantheon refers to a temple dedicated to all gods, but the name also implies that it also served as an Augusteum, a sanctuary devoted to the ruler in the Hellenistic tradition. Statues of the gods occupied the niches inside including those with particular significance to the Emperor Augustus: Venus, Mars and the Deified Julius Caesar. Statues of Augustus and Agrippa occupied the niches on either side of the entrance doors and the pediment likely included an eagle and wreath bronze decoration. Eight monolithic columns (*c.*13m high) support the facade of the porch, originally all grey with two more grey columns at the sides and four pink columns in the centre to form three aisles. The Corinthian capitals and bases are white marble. It seems that even taller columns were planned that would have reached the level of the second pediment. Porticoes that flanked the area in front of the temple obscured the shape of the rotunda and the impressive dome (43.30m in diameter) that was cast from a single mold with an oculus that bathes the interior with light, but also allows rainwater to enter the building.

The appearance of the Pantheon has been altered since antiquity. On the east side of the porch are three replacement monolithic columns of pink Egyptian granite from Aswan with restored Corinthian capitals: Pope Urban VIII Barberini replaced one with a column from Domitian's villa in Castelgandolfo (1626); the other two were taken from the Baths of Nero by Pope Alexander VII Chigi (1666) to replace the originals that were removed in the medieval period. At this time, Pope Alexander VII also cleared the adjoining medieval buildings to the left of the Pantheon when facing the facade. Pope Urban VIII Barberini removed the bronze from the ceiling of the porch for the construction of the baldacchino in St Peter's Basilica and 80 cannon for Castel Sant'Angelo. The famous pasquinade composed against the pope was written in response to his abuse of ancient monuments: *Quod non fecerunt barbari, fecerunt Barberini* (*What the barbarians did not destroy, the Barberini destroyed*). To replace a medieval campanile that stood on the porch roof (1270), Pope Urban VIII commissioned Bernini to add two cupolas (1626–1627) that were derisively known as 'ass ears', but these were not removed until 1881–1883. The bronze doors are not original to the building and were installed by Pope Pius IV de' Medici (1563).

The proportions of the interior result in a perfect sphere as tall as its radius inside a cylinder (temple walls). Upon entering, the Emperor Constans II compared the vast interior to a piazza. The pavement design of geometric shapes in a grid pattern is original. Chapels in the alcoves alternate between square and semicircular shapes between the aedicules that alternate between triangular and curved pediment shapes. To either side of the shrines are oval niches intended to honour members of the *Virtuosi al Pantheon* arts academy established in 1543. The large alcove that is on an axis with the entrance and now serves as the high altar and apse of the church occupied the place of honour in the ancient temple.

The high altar was designed by Alessandro Specchi for Pope Clement XI Albani with the 7th-century Byzantine icon of *Madonna and Child*. The first chapel on the left serves as the Chapel of the Virtuosi al Pantheon with a funerary epitaph commemorating members: Perino del Vaga (1547), Taddeo Zuccari (1566) and Flaminio Vacca (1605). The composer Arcangelo Corelli is also buried here (1713). The aedicule to the right contains the Tomb of Baldassarre Peruzzi, with his bust in the oval niche. In the aedicule to the right of the Tomb of King Umberto I and Regina Margherita is the Tomb of Raphael. In 1833, Pope Gregory XVI verified the existence of Raphael's remains since a skull at the Accademia di San Luca was believed to belong to the artist and was an object of veneration. Raphael's remains were intact and the skull ceased to be displayed at the Accademia. Pope Gregory XVI placed Raphael's remains in an ancient sarcophagus that contains a Latin couplet by Italian Humanist Pietro Bembo: 'Here lies Raphael by whom alive the great parent of things [Nature] feared to be surpassed and at his death feared her own.' In the altar above is Lorenzetto's *Madonna del Sasso* (1523–1524) and to the right is the Tomb of Annibale Carracci that is marked by a plaque. Another plaque commemorates Raphael's fiancé Maria Bibbiena.

The Tomb of King Vittorio Emanuele II is on the right. His funeral was held here in 1878 and the exterior was transformed into a temple in his honour, with Imperial Roman referents: the inscription of M. Agrippa was covered and replaced with '*Vittorio Emanuele II Padre della Patria*' ('Victor Emmanuel II Father of the Fatherland'), an Italian adaptation of the Latin title *Pater Patriae* that was conferred upon the Emperor Augustus and Cosimo de' Medici the Elder after his death in 1464. The design of the eagle and wreath of his mausoleum by Manfredo Manfredi was based on the Trajanic relief in Ss. Apostoli (Tour 7).

With the Pantheon behind you, walk straight through the piazza. A plaque on the facade of the building facing the Pantheon commemorates Pope Pius VII's demolition of unsightly taverns. Take Via del Pantheon to your right one block into Piazza della Maddalena to the church of **S. Maria Maddalena (La Maddalena)** of the Camillan Order. The interior was completed in 1699 (Carlo Fontana contributed to the design) but the facade was finished around 1735 in the exuberant Rococo style. Giuseppe Sardi is believed to have been the architect of the facade but it may have been Manuel Rodriguez Dos Santos who directed the completion of the church's construction. Via delle Colonnelle to the right of the facade leads to Piazza Capranica, with the mid-15th century **Palazzo Capranica** to your left and the church of **S. Maria in Aquiro** that was given to the Confraternity of Orphans (Orfani) by Pope Paul III Farnese in 1540. The facade was designed by Carlo Maderno. At No. 95 is the **Casa Giannini** that served as the seat of the Democratic League founded by Giuseppe Garibaldi. The **Temple of Matidia**, dedicated by the Emperor Hadrian to his mother-in-law (d. 119 CE) whom he deified, was in the area of the piazza with surviving columns incorporated into the house at No. 76.

Exit the piazza on Via degli Orfani past the famous La Casa del Caffè Tazzo d'Oro al Pantheon into Piazza della Rotonda with a view of the upper second facade of the Pantheon from this higher ground vantage point. Continue straight to walk along the east side of the Pantheon on Via della Minerva a short distance into Piazza della Minerva. The ruins of a frieze with maritime decoration behind the Pantheon on Via della Palombella are from the **Basilica of Neptune**. The **Baths of Agrippa** were also in the area.

In the centre of **Piazza della Minerva** in front of the basilica of S. Maria sopra Minerva is the charming statue designed by Bernini and sculpted by Ercole Ferrata (1667) of an elephant supporting an obelisk known as *il Pulcino della Minerva*. Pope Alexander VII Chigi commissioned Bernini to design a base for the obelisk from the Iseum (Temple of Isis) that would honour divine wisdom. Bernini chose the elephant as the representation of wisdom (reflected in the playful inscription on its base that refers to the hieroglyphics on the obelisk). The theological meaning of the obelisk and its location relative to the cult of St Mary is indicated by the other inscription: 'Alexander VII dedicated this ancient obelisk, a monument of the Egyptian Athena unearthed from the ground and erected in the piazza once dedicated to Minerva but now to the Mother of God, to divine wisdom in the year of Salvation 1667.'

To the left of the basilica is **Palazzo del Domenicani**, the Dominican Convent of Minerva (Convento della Minerva) that was the seat of the

Congregation of the Holy Office and the Roman Inquisition, where Galileo Galilei was tried for heresy on 22 June 1663. The palazzo is now the Collegium Pontificium Americanum. Opposite the basilica is **Palazzo dell'Accademia Ecclesiastica** where Vatican diplomats receive their training. To the right of the church is the 16th-century **Palazzo Fonseca a Pigna** (currently the Grand Hotel de la Minerve) that was converted into the hotel known as the Minerva (1832) where many visitors on the Grand Tour resided including Stendhal (1834–1836). José de San Martín, the Liberator of Argentina, Chile and Peru, resided here in 1846. The Fonseca family once owned the famous portrait of the *Flavian Woman* also known as the *Fonseca Bust* in the Capitoline Museums.

**Santa Maria sopra Minerva,** built by the Dominicans in 1280, replaced an earlier Greek oratory that was built on the site of the ancient Temple of Minerva as was the church of S. Maria sopra Minerva in Assisi. It was rebuilt in the Gothic style for the Florentine congregation before the construction of S. Giovanni Battista dei Fiorentini (Tour 3). The nave and facade were completed for Count Francesco Orsini (1453) but work continued in the 16th century under Giuliano da Sangallo and Carlo Maderno, who added the Baroque interior and reworked the facade in an early Renaissance style. To the right of the entrance on the outer wall are the surviving Tiber flood mark plaques from 1530, 1557 and 1598 at the highest levels and 1422, 1495 and 1870 at the lower levels.

The interior was reworked in the 19th century in the Neo-Gothic style that contrasts with the Renaissance and Baroque sculpture, painting and funerary monuments to prominent Florentine families whose chapels are found here. On the south side, Carlo Maderno designed the fifth chapel that contains Antoniazzo Romano's *Annunciation* altarpiece (1500) commissioned by Cardinal Juan de Torquemada, the uncle of the Inquisitor Tomás de Torquemada. The Aldobrandini Chapel (sixth), designed by Giacomo della Porta (1600), Maderno and Girolamo Rainaldi, contains the funerary monuments of Pope Clement VIII's parents by Giacomo della Porta (1600–1602).

The Carafa Chapel (south transept) contains a Filippino Lippi masterpiece (1488–1493) for Cardinal Oliviero Carafa in honour of St Thomas Aquinas. Carafa lured the artist away from Florence where he was working on the Filippo Strozzi Chapel in S. Maria Novella (begun in the late 1480s but completed in 1502). On the altar wall is the *Assumption* and over the altar is the *Annunciation* with St Thomas Aquinas presenting Cardinal Carafa to the Virgin. The chapel contains the Tomb of Pope Paul IV Carafa, his kinsman, by Pirro Ligorio and Giacomo and Tommaso Cassignola (1566), and once held the relics of St Thomas Aquinas until moved to Naples in 1511. To the left is the 13th-century canopy funerary monument to Guillaume Durand, the Bishop of Mende (d. 1296), signed by Giovanni di Cosma with an effigy of the deceased between two angels and a mosaic *Madonna Enthroned and Saints*.

The relics of **St Catherine of Siena** (1347–1380), a tertiary of the Domenican Order, are preserved below the high altar by Giuseppe Fontana (1857) in a sarcophagus with a statue of the saint lying in repose (1430). Her skull was given to the Sienese in 1385 and is preserved in the Basilica of S. Domenico, Siena. She died in a nearby house on Via di S. Chiara but the room was removed and relocated here beyond the sacristy. Saint Catherine, one of the patron saints of Italy, convinced Pope Gregory XI to return the papacy to Rome from Avignon. Behind the altar in the apse, Antonio da Sangallo the Younger designed the triumphal arch inspired tombs of the Medici Popes Leo X (statues by Raffaello da Montelupo) and Clement VII (statues by Nanni di Baccio Bigio), with statues of the Prophets in the niches by Baccio Bandinelli. In the centre of the choir behind the altar is the Tomb of Innocenzo Cybo, the nephew of Pope Leo X and the cousin of Clement VII. The tomb of the Humanist Pietro Bembo, who was Pope Leo X's secretary and wrote Raphael's epitaph, is also here.

To the left of the high altar is Michelangelo's *Christ the Redeemer* (1519–1520), also known as the *Cristo della Minerva*, for Metello Vari that was sent to Rome from Florence unfinished. Michelangelo's apprentice Pietro Urbano worked on it but was replaced after damaging the statue. The drapery is a later addition. This is the second version of the statue. The original version (1514–1515) was started by Michelangelo in his house at Via Macel de' Corvi (Tour 6) but abandoned when a black vein appeared on Christ's face. Vari asked for this version as well and displayed it in his nearby Palazzo Vari-Porcari. Today it is in the church of S. Vincenzo Martire in Bassano Romano, Viterbo. Giuseppe Obici was commissioned to create the statue of St John the Baptist (1858) for the right side to balance Michelangelo's statue.

To the left of the sanctuary is the vestibule (1600) that was formerly the Rustici and Cenci Chapels. To your immediate left is the Pavement Tomb of Fra' Angelico (*c.*1395–1455), also known as '*il Beato Angelico*', who died in the adjoining convent, by Isaia di Pisa. The effigy portrait was modelled after his death mask. Fra' Angelico was a Dominican friar and painter who produced influential frescoes for the convent of S. Marco, Florence, where Cosimo de' Medici the Elder and Savonarola had cells. On the right wall is the funerary monument to Cardinal Domenico Pimental designed by Bernini with sculptures by Ercole Ferrata (portrait of the Cardinal) and Antonio Raggi (*Charity*).

Next to the vestibule is the Frangipane Chapel with a 15th-century *Madonna and Child* altarpiece and the 15th-century tomb of Giovanni Alberini attributed to Agostino di Duccio or Mino da Fiesole that incorporates a relief panel from a Roman sarcophagus of *Hercules and the Nemean Lion*. To the left of the chapel is the corridor that leads to the sacristy and from there to the Room of St Catherine with frescoes by Antoniazzo Romano (1482–1483). The funerary monument to Pope Benedict XIII (1730) in the north transept is by Carlo Marchionni with the portrait of the pope and *Purity* by Pietro Bracci. On the west wall of the north transept is the funerary monument to the sculptor Andrea Bregno (1418–1506), who died in Rome, with a portrait attributed to Luigi Capponi and reliefs of his drafting tools.

On the north side, on the second pillar from the sanctuary is Bernini's funerary monument to the Dominican nun Maria Raggi (1643), whose portrait is in a gilt medallion against a backdrop of billowing black marble drapery. The funerary monument to Giovanni Vigevano between the 3rd and 4th chapels is also by Bernini (1630). Opposite is the funerary monument to Fabio and Ippolito De Amicis designed by Pietro da Cortona (1631). The Tomb of Cardinal Gregorio Naro (second chapel) is attributed to Bernini with portraits of Naro family members in oval niches. At the end of the aisle is the Tomb of Francesco Tornabuoni by Mino da Fiesole (1480). Above it is the Tomb of Cardinal Tebaldi by Andrea Bregno and Giovanni Dalmata (1466). On the west wall is the funerary monument to Diotisalvi Neroni (1482) by the School of Andrea Bregno. Neroni was involved in the plot (1462) against Piero di Cosimo de' Medici, the father of Lorenzo il Magnifico.

Exit the piazza on Via di S. Caterina da Siena to walk along the side of the church. Continue past Via del Gesù (where the 16th-century

**Palazzo Frangipane-Capocci** is located mid-block with a portal decorated with herms) when the name changes to Via del Piè di Marmo ('Street of the Marble Foot'), named for the colossal **Marble Foot** at the corner of Via di S. Stefano del Cacco. It was moved from its medieval location on the Via del Piè di Marmo at the entrance to Piazza del Collegio Romano to this side street in 1878 for the funeral of King Vittorio Emanuele II in the Pantheon. The foot seems to come from a cult statue from the ancient **Iseum Campense** (Temple of Isis) in the Campus Martius that was located near the **Serapeum** in the area now occupied by the Collegio Romano.

Continue into Piazza del Collegio Romano that is named for **Palazzo del Collegio Romano** that was likely built by Giuseppe Valeriano for Pope Gregory XIII Boncompagni in 1582–1583 to house the Society of Jesus School founded by St Ignatius of Loyola in 1551 to educate Counter-Reformation priests. It is across the piazza from **Palazzo Doria Pamphilj** (Tour 7). The clock on the facade was once used to set the time of all public clocks in Rome. At the top of the facade are a bell tower, sundial and astronomical observatory. The complex of buildings includes the church of S. Ignazio directly behind the collegio that was initially built as the school's chapel. The school also taught mathematical and scientific subjects including astronomy and it is here that the Jesuit Christopher Clavius developed the Gregorian Calendar named for Pope Gregory XIII. In 1870, the collegio property was confiscated by the Italian state and the school relocated to Palazzo Gabrielli-Borromeo on Via del Seminario, but moved again to its current location in Piazza della Pilotta at the foot of the Quirinal Hill as the Gregorian University (Pontificia Universitas Gregoriana) that opened in 1930. The Collegio Romano was rededicated as a high school, the Liceo Ennio Quirino Visconti.

Exit the piazza onto Via di Sant'Ignazio. To your left at No. 52 is the **Biblioteca Casanatense**, a library founded by Cardinal Casanate for the Dominican Convent of S. Maria Sopra Minerva (1701) that was also open to the public according to the cardinal's instructions. It was confiscated by the Italian state in 1873 and is currently operated by the Ministry of Culture. Walk through the arch along the side of S. Ignazio until you reach the charming **Piazza di Sant'Ignazio**. The late-Baroque Rococo facades of the five buildings designed by Filippo Raguzzini for Pope Benedict XIII (1727–1735) evoke a theatre set design and exude a sense of lightness that contrasts with the heaviness of the older buildings in the nearby dark narrow streets.

The church of **Sant'Ignazio di Loyola in Campo Marzio** is dedicated to St Ignatius of Loyola who was canonised by Pope Gregory XV Ludovisi in 1622 as the church of the Collegio Romano founded by Pope Gregory XIII Boncompagni. The church was begun in 1626 by Orazio Grassi to a design by Carlo Maderno. It was built on the site of S. Maria Annunziata that had been funded by Vittoria Frangipane whose family lived nearby and which gave Via di Sant'Ignazio its former name of Via Annunziata. The facade shows the influence of the Gesù, the principal Jesuit church in Rome (Tour 7), as does the sumptuous interior. A dome was planned for the church but it was never completed. Andrea Pozzo painted the ceiling fresco *The Glory of St Ignatius* and a trompe l'oeil dome whose perspective begins to fail midway up the nave beyond the disc in the pavement that provides the best perspective vantage point. The apse frescoes from the life of St Ignatius are by Andrea Pozzo. To the right of the apse is the Boncompagni Ludovisi Chapel with the Tomb of Pope Gregory XV Ludovisi and his nephew Cardinal Ludovico Ludovisi designed by Pierre Legros with *Cardinal Virtues* by Camillo Rusconi (1686) and *Angels* by Pierre-Étienne Monnot (1697).

The south transept altar design is by Andrea Pozzo, with the *Glory of St Aloysius Gonzaga* by Pierre Legros (1697–1699). The saint's relics are in the lapis lazuli urn below the altar. His head was transferred to the Basilica of S. Luigi Gonzaga in his birthplace of Castiglione delle Stiviere. The third chapel (south side) contains the Tomb of S. Roberto Bellarmino (St Robert Bellarmine, 1542–1621) whose relics are displayed in the glass sarcophagus. The north transept altar design is by Andrea Pozzo with *Annunciation* by Filippo della Valle and allegorical figures *Chastity* and *Humility* and *Angels* by Pietro Bracci. The lapis lazuli urn contains the relics of St John Berchmans (d. 1621). The inscription on the west wall commemorating the consecration of the church (1650) has allegorical figures of *Religion* and *Magnificence* by Alessandro Algardi, who also sculpted the friezes above the triumphal arch entrances of the chapels.

Exit the piazza by Via de' Burrò and continue on the street as it winds past the building shaped like a desk (burrò) that gives the street its name. The street exits into Piazza di Pietra. The **Temple of the Deified**

**Hadrian (Hadrianeum)** is to your left and was dedicated in 145 CE by his adopted son the Emperor Antoninus Pius. The temple was enclosed by a portico and faced east towards Via del Corso. The marble pedestal panels with allegorical reliefs of the Provinces and Trophies now in the Courtyard of Palazzo dei Conservatori, Capitoline Museums (Tour 5), and in the National Archaeological Museum, Naples, were found here. The north side of the temple was incorporated into **Palazzo della Borsa** in 1695 by Carlo and Francesco Fontana when the building served as the Customs Office (Dogana di Terra) for goods arriving by land and for visitors to receive a permit after leaving travel documents at the city gate. In 1879 it housed the Stock Exchange that is now based in Milan and now serves as the Chamber of Commerce. In the western corner of the narrow piazza is the 17th-century **Palazzo Ferrini**.

Exit the piazza by Via di Pietra (to your left facing the Temple of Hadrian) and continue to Via del Corso. Cross to the other side of the street to Via delle Muratte and proceed into Piazza di Trevi. Look to your right as you cross Via di S. Maria in Via for a view of the **Galleria Sciarra** with Art Nouveau frescoes in the courtyard that depict personifications of feminine virtues. To your left at No. 78 is a plaque that commemorates where composer Gaetano Donizetti lived.

The world famous **Trevi Fountain** (Fontana di Trevi) is named after Piazza di Trevi that receives its name because of its location at the intersection of three streets (*tre vie*) that also gives the Rione Trevi its name. The fountain is the terminus point of the Acqua Vergine (the ancient Aqua Virgo) established by Marcus Agrippa in 19 BCE and restored by Pope Nicholas V in 1453. The theatrical and dynamic design of the fountain calls attention away from the low water flow, but the sunken design also contributes to the illusion of a dramatic water flow. It is the most recent of Rome's monumental fountains but also the most famous and visited by tourists who toss a coin over their shoulder into the fountain for a return trip to Rome. Anita Ekberg splashing in the fountain in Federico Fellini's *La Dolce Vita* (1960) is one of cinema's most iconic scenes.

The fountain was built against the wall of **Palazzo Poli** by Nicola Salvi who did not win the competition for its design (he came in second) organised by Pope Clement XII Corsini in 1730 to replace a 15th-century fountain by Leon Battista Alberti, but he was selected after an outcry accompanied the selection of the winner Alessandro Galilei because he was from Florence instead of Rome. Galilei was a member of the same family as Galileo Galilei and designed the facades of S. Giovanni in Laterano (Tour 13) and S. Giovanni Battista dei Fiorentini (Tour 3). Salvi began work in 1732 but the fountain was completed after his death by Giuseppe Panini (also Pannini) in 1762. The Neoclassical triumphal arch design forms the backdrop and the source of spectacle (*mostra*) entertainment. Earlier designs for the fountain were made by Bernini, Pietro da Cortona and Ferdinando Fuga. The absence of a formal approach to the fountain enhances its theatrical engagement with spectators who chance upon it.

The decoration on the arch, whose Corinthian columns continue the pilasters of the palace's facade, commemorates the founding of the fountain and the aqueduct. The far right pilaster is broken to symbolise the synthesis of nature and civilisation. Below the crest with the Corsini family emblem that is flanked by allegorical figures of *Fama* (Fame), are the *Four Seasons* (1735). The two reliefs by Giovanni Battista Grossi depict *Marcus Agrippa surveying plans* and *Trivia pointing out the source of the Aqua Virgo to Roman soldiers* above the niches with the allegorical figures of *Abundance* (left) and *Health* (right) by Filippo della Valle. Pietro Bracci carved the figure of Oceanus in the central niche (1759–1762) who presides over Hippocamps (marine horses) representing the calm and agitated nature of the sea being led by Tritons in the basin on top of an immense artificial rock from which water pours into the monumental basin. The obelisk now at the top of the Spanish Steps in Piazza della Trinità dei Monti was considered for the basin.

In Piazza di Trevi, the building across from the fountain at No. 93 has a medieval portico with spoliated ancient columns. The **church of Ss. Vincenzo ed Anastasio** by Martino Longhi the Younger (1640–1646) contains a collection of praecordia (hearts and lungs) of popes from Sixtus V (d. 1590) to Pope Leo XIII (d. 1903). On the right side of the church is the Vicolo de' Modelli where boys sollicited artists and others for patronage.

On the right hand side of the fountain is Via della Stamperia. The **Calcografia Nazionale** at No. 6 is a Neoclassical palazzetto designed by Giuseppe Valadier (1837) and contains the most extensive collection of copper plate engravings in the world, many of which were printed in **Palazzo della Stamperia** after which the street is named. Opposite, at No. 77 Piazza dell'Accademia di S. Luca, is the 16th-/17th-century

9. Trevi Fountain

**Palazzo Carpegna** enlarged by Borromini. It is the home of the **Accademia Nazionale di S. Luca.** The academy of painters whose patron saint was St Luke, and which comprised Italians and artists visiting and working in Rome, was founded in 1577 in a building that was adjacent to the church of Ss. Luca e Martina (Tour 5) and which contains works of art donated by its members displayed in the **Galleria**

**dell'Accademia Nazionale di S. Luca**. The 'skull' of Raphael was displayed here until 1833 when Raphael's tomb in the Pantheon was opened and his body was found to be intact.

Exit Piazza di Trevi to the left side of the fountain on Via Poli and turn left onto Via de' Crociferi. The little church at the corner, **S. Maria in Trivio**, with a facade begun by Giacomo della Porta but completed by Carlo Rainaldi (1670), contains a beautiful nave fresco cycle *Life of the Virgin* by Antonio Gherardi (1669–1670). Continue straight on when the name changes to Via dei Sabini and then Via del Corso. Cross to the other side of the street and turn right into Piazza Colonna to begin Tour 9.

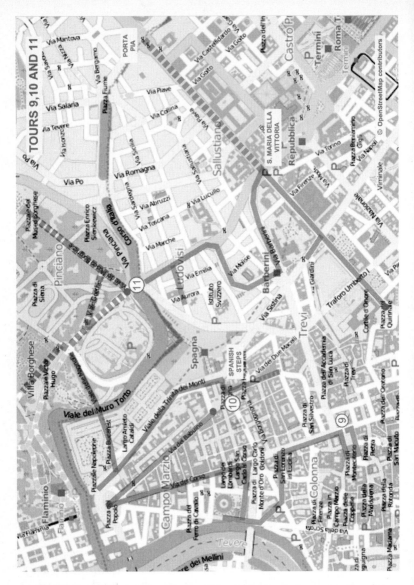

Sites: Piazza Colonna; Column of Marcus Aurelius; Palazzo di Montecitorio; S. Lorenzo in Lucina; Palazzo Borghese; S. Girolamo degli Schiavoni; S. Rocco; Piazza Augusto Imperatore: Mausoleum of Augustus; Ara Pacis Museum; Ss. Ambrogio e Carlo al Corso; Via del Corso; Piazza del Popolo; S. Maria del Popolo; Via del Babuino; Via Margutta; *il Babuino* (Option: from tram on Via Flaminia: Museo Nazionale Etrusco di Villa Giulia; MAXXI; Foro Italico).

Distance: 2.5km.

# VIA DEL CORSO AND PIAZZA DEL POPOLO

The northern end of Via del Corso is a popular destination for strolling and people-watching as crowds make their way to Piazza del Popolo with the must-see church of S. Maria del Poppolo or to Via Condotti and the Spanish Steps. The monuments and churches from different historic periods offer interesting contrasts in a part of the city noted for Neoclassicism and Fascist reworking of Rome's Imperial past. The Piazza del Popolo is a Neoclassical showpiece by Giuseppe Valadier that was once the main entry point to the city that welcomed Queen Christina of Sweden and visitors on the Grand Tour. There are several options to tour museums and the Foro Italico beyond the piazza along Via Flaminia.

The **Column of Marcus Aurelius** stands in the centre of Piazza Colonna in the area once controlled by the Colonna family whose name is reflected in the family emblem of a single column and the name of the Rione Colonna. It was built between 180 and *c.*193 CE as a funerary monument and modelled after the Column of Trajan (Tour 6). The original bronze statue of Marcus Aurelius (emperor from 161 to 180) and his wife Faustina (daughter of Antoninus Pius) that was placed on top was melted and replaced with a statue of St Paul designed by Domenico Fontana in 1589 for Pope Sixtus V to correspond to the statue of St Peter on top of the Column of Trajan. The running frieze reliefs commemorate campaigns against the Germans (172–173) on the lower half and Sarmatians (174–175) higher up the column. The original inscriptions and decorations on the base were removed and replaced with inscriptions on all four sides commemorating Pope

Sixtus V's restoration of the column with blocks of marble from the Septizodium (Tour 13) that were also used in the creation of the **fountain** by Giacomo della Porta (1576–1577). The dolphins and shells were added by Achille Stocchi in 1830.

In the piazza, bordering Via del Corso is **Palazzo Chigi** that was begun in 1562 by Giacomo della Porta for the Aldobrandini but completed by Carlo Maderno in 1580. In 1659 it was acquired and remodelled by the Chigi family. Today it serves as the official residence of the Prime Minister of Italy. **Palazzo Wedekind** (1838) that faces Via del Corso was built on the site of a palazzo owned by the Boncompagni Ludovisi who also owned a palace adjacent to Palazzo Chigi that is now part of Palazzo di Montecitorio. It has a ground level portico comprised of 12 ancient Ionic columns that came from a temple in Veii. The newspaper *Il Tempo* currently occupies the building. The church of **Ss. Bartolomeo e Alessandro dei Bergamaschi** was given a charming Baroque facade by Carlo De Domenicis (1728–1731). Next to it and facing the column is **Palazzo Ferrajoli** (*c.*1600), formerly owned by the del Bufalo (the family of Pope Innocent X Pamphilj's mother). On the other side of Via del Corso is the **Galleria Alberto Sordi** (formerly called Galleria Colonna) by Dario Carbone (1922) and named for the famous Italian actor. The Galleria replaced **Palazzo Piombino al Corso** that was designed by Giacomo della Porta (1594) for Cosimo Giustini that passed to the Spada family and was last owned by the Boncompagni Ludovisi and renamed after their Principate of Piombino. Despite its history and prominent location in Piazza Colonna, it was demolished in 1889 to regularise Via del Corso, ending the centuries-long association of the family with the piazza.

Exit the piazza by Via della Colonna Antonina on the left side of Palazzo Wedekind and proceed into Piazza di Montecitorio that derives its name from its Medieval Latin name of Mons Acceptorius. The Egyptian **Obelisk** (22m high), originally erected by Psamtik II (595–589 BCE) in Heliopolis, was brought to Rome by the Emperor Augustus to serve as the gnomon of his Horologium (sundial) that was originally placed in the area of Piazza del Parliamento (a plaque on No. 3 commemorates its discovery in five pieces). The inscription on the base dates to 10 BCE and commemorates the 20th anniversary of his conquest of Egypt at the naval Battle of Actium in 31 BCE, in which Augustus' forces under Marcus Agrippa defeated the forces of Mark

Antony and Cleopatra. It was erected here by Pope Pius VI (1792) who added holes in the globe and a meridian in the pavement to return the obelisk to its use as a gnomon. The Emperor Antoninus Pius (138–161) was cremated on a tiered pyre in the area of the piazza and his apotheosis was commemorated with a sacred precinct. The **Column of Antoninus Pius**, whose base is now in the Cortile della Pinacoteca of the Vatican Museums, was erected in the current area of the obelisk that was repaired with granite from the column. His adopted son and successor, Marcus Aurelius, was cremated in the area of Piazza Colonna.

Facing the piazza is **Palazzo di Montecitorio** that is the current seat of the Italian Parliament. Pope Innocent X Pamphilj commissioned Bernini to design the palace for the Ludovisi family (1653) on the site of the earlier Palazzo Gaddi. Bernini gave the facade a convex curve with angular segments. Carlo Fontana added the bell tower to the facade and remodelled the palazzo to serve as the State Tribunal (Curia Innocenziana) for Pope Innocent XII (1694). Ernesto Basile enlarged the palazzo to accommodate Parliament (1903–1927) and gave it a new facade on the north side that faces Piazza del Parlamento (1918).

Walk through the piazza towards the facade of Palazzo di Montecitorio to see the meridian in the pavement and turn right to return to Piazza Colonna. Turn left at **Via del Corso** to walk north in the direction of Piazza del Popolo whose obelisk is visible at the end of the street. Via del Tritone to your right connects the Corso to Piazza Barberini (Tour 11). Just beyond Palazzo Chigi to your left at No. 374 is **Palazzo Verospi** (now a bank). A plaque above the ground floor windows commemorates that this is where Percy Bysshe Shelley lived in 1819 and composed *Prometheus Unbound* and *The Cenci*. The Keats-Shelley house at the base of the Spanish Steps (Tour 10) is a museum devoted to their sojourn in Rome. At the corner of Via della Vite is **Palazzo Fiano** (after Marco Ottoboni, the Duke of Fiano) to your left, formerly called Palazzo Peretti but now known as Palazzo Fiano-Almagià. Fragments of the Ara Pacis of Augustus were excavated beneath the palace in the 16th century and incorporated into the Villa Medici (Tour 10). The palazzo also faces Piazza S. Lorenzo in Lucina adjacent to the church of S. Lorenzo in Lucina. The Arch of Hadrian, known as the **Arco di Portogallo**, once spanned the street at the corner of Via della Vite that was named after one of the titular Cardinals of S. Lorenzo in Lucina, the Portuguese Cardinal Jorge da

Costa who occupied the post from 1488 to 1508 and lived in the church-owned palazzo that was sold to the Peretti in 1624. Over time, the property included two palazzi on either side of the Via del Corso that were spanned by a passageway above the arch. Pope Alexander VII Chigi demolished the arch in 1662 to improve the circulation of the street. The relief panels depicting Hadrian were installed in Palazzo dei Conservatori (Capitoline Museums, Tour 5). A plaque high up on the palazzo across the street at the corner of Via della Vite commemorates the original location of the arch.

At the end of the block turn left to enter Piazza di S. Lorenzo in Lucina. The church is to your left beyond Palazzo Fiano-Almagià. Across from the church is the immense **Palazzo Ruspoli** (formerly owned by the Ruccellai and Caetani families) that was started by Bartolomeo Ammannati before 1560 but completed around 1586 by Bartolomeo Breccioli and takes up the entire block facing the Via del Corso.

The church of **S. Lorenzo in Lucina** dates to at least the reign of Pope Sixtus III (432–440) on the site of a titular church owned by Lucina that was built over a Roman house from the reign of Hadrian, later apartment buildings and part of a temple. Pope Paschal II rebuilt the church in the 12th century on the foundations of the earlier church that was damaged by Robert Guiscard during the Norman sack of Rome. It was rebuilt again in 1650 and earlier elements were retained such as campanile, portico and main entrance. The renovations of Andrea Busiri Vici (1856–1858) for Pope Pius IX removed a great part of the Baroque decoration. The atrium contains two 12th-century lions and fragments of funerary monuments. To the far right of the entrance is the Neoclassical funerary monument to Clelia Severini by Pietro Tenerani (1825). A plaque to the right of the entrance indicates the level of the flood of 28 December 1870.

Over the high altar designed by Carlo Rainaldi (1669) is the *Crucifixion* by Guido Reni. In the apse is the 12th-century marble cathedra of Pope Paschal II. On the south side, the first chapel reliquary contains part of the gridiron used in St Lawrence's marytyrdom. The tomb of important French artist Nicolas Poussin, who died in Rome (1665), is in the second chapel by Carlo Rainaldi with painting by Jan Miel. The funerary monument to him on the pilaster outside by the Romantic writer François-René de Chateaubriand (1829–1830) includes a relief by Louis Desprez of his painting *Et in Arcadia Ego*, now in the Louvre Museum in Paris. The fourth chapel was designed by Bernini for Gabriele Fonseca (Pope Innocent X Pamphilj's doctor) whose portrait to the left of the altar is also by Bernini (1668). On the north side, the fifth chapel was designed by Simon Vouet with his frescoes from the *Life of St Francis* (1624) on the side walls. In the second chapel, the altarpiece *S. Carlo Borromeo* is by Carlo Saraceni. The baptistery was designed by Giuseppe Sardi (1721). Excavations below the church in 1568 revealed fragments from the Ara Pacis that are now in the Ara Pacis Museum. A fragment of the meridian from the Horologium Augusti was also excavated here in 1463.

Exit the piazza on the right side past **Casa Castellani** at No. 29 designed by Giuseppe Valadier (1823–25). Continue onto Via del Leone then stroll through Largo della Fontanella di Borghese (look behind you for a view of the Spanish Steps on the other side of Via del Corso at the end of Via Condotti) to Piazza Borghese in Rione Campo Marzio to your right. Antique book and print dealers set up their carts in the piazza. The piazza is named after the huge **Palazzo Borghese**, nicknamed the Harpsichord (*il Cembalo*) because of its shape, that is now mainly occupied by the Spanish Embassy. The palazzo was built for Cardinal Camillo Borghese (the future Pope Paul V) by Flaminio Ponzio (1605–1614) and completed after his death by Carlo Maderno and Giovanni Vasanzio (Jan van Santen), though an earlier design phase is attributed to Vignola. The famous Borghese art collection was on display here until transferred to the Villa Borghese (Tour 10). In the courtyard are ancient statues including *Muses* from the Theatre of Pompey (Tour 7) and a monumental Baroque nymphaeum called the *Bath of Venus*. Opposite the palazzo is **Palazzo della Famiglia Borghese** that was built by the pope's nephew, Cardinal Scipione Borghese, to house servants and the stables.

Walk through Piazza Borghese with the palazzo to your right (Via Borghese). At the end, turn right on Via di Ripetta (formerly called Via Leonina after Pope Leo X de' Medici) into Piazza di Ripetta. This side of the palazzo at the corner of Via di Ripetta and Via Tomacelli with two balconies was nicknamed the Keyboard of the Harpsichord (*la Tastiera del Cembalo*), now the **Galleria del Cembalo**. It was designed by Flamio Ponzio with a loggia by Carlo Rainaldi (1671–76) to face the Tiber and the Borghese port (Nuovo Porto) built for Pope Paul V Borghese by Carlo Maderno (1614) and later replaced by the Porto di Ripetta.

The **Porto di Ripetta** was a sweeping Baroque staircase that was built by Alessandro Specchi (1703–1705) for Pope Clement XI. It cascaded around a semicircular overlook of the port in front of the church of S. Girolamo and served as the landing point for passengers and small boats or barges carrying merchandise and wood downriver from Tuscany and Umbria. The Porto di Ripetta was demolished during the construction of the Tiber Embankment that isolated the river from the cultural life of the city. The area was succeeded by a temporary iron bridge and now the Ponte Cavour. Specchi later lost the competition for the design of the Spanish Steps (Tour 10) that give a sense of the Baroque elegance that once greeted visitors on the Grand Tour alighting here.

Cross to the other side of Via Tomacelli whose realignment in 1873 to connect with the Ponte Cavour required the demolition of buildings between Palazzo Borghese and the National Croatian church of **S. Girolamo dei Croati a Ripetta** to your right. Formerly called S. Girolamo degli Illirici and S. Girolamo degli Schiavoni after the Serbian congregation that settled in the area following the Battle of Kosovo in 1389, it was rebuilt in 1587 by Martino Longhi the Elder using marble from the Septizodium (Tour 13). The area around the church was reconstructed after the demolition of the area for the construction of Piazza Augusto Imperatore.

Just beyond to your right is the church of **S. Rocco all'Augusteo**, named for its proximity to the Mausoleum of Augustus, with a Neoclassical facade designed by Giuseppe Valadier (1834) that replaced a Baroque facade by Giovanni Antonio de Rossi (1645–1654). An embedded column (*Idrometro di Ripetta*) along the right side of the facade (1821) measured the flood levels of the Tiber. The church was originally built in 1499 by the Confraternity of S. Rocco that was comprised of innkeepers and the boat operators of the Porto di Ripetta. The demolition of the campanile and adjacent hospital of S. Rocco for the isolation of the Mausoleum of Augustus required the reconstruction of the north-facing wall. Over the high altar is *S. Rocco* by Giacinto Brandi (1674), a *Nativity* by Baldassarre Peruzzi (north side, second chapel), and *Madonna and Saints Rocco and Anthony* (*c.*1660) altarpiece by Baciccia in the sacristy.

Continue into **Piazza Augusto Imperatore** with the **Ara Pacis Museum** to your left. In the centre of the piazza is the neglected ruin of the **Mausoleum of Augustus**. A vast area around the mausoleum was cleared of medieval to 19th-century era buildings and redesigned by Vittorio Ballio Morpurgo (1937–1940) to create a piazza as a focal point for Fascist ideology for Mussolini with the help of archaeologist and architect Antonio Muñoz, who also excavated the mausoleum down to its concrete and tufa core.

Augustus returned to Rome in 29 BCE as sole ruler following his victory at the Battle of Actium. He began construction of his mausoleum as a traditional Italic tumulus tomb on a monumental scale as a dynastic statement in the Egyptian and Hellenistic tradition, which was completed in 28 BCE. Following Augustus' death, bronze copies of his *Res Gestae Divi Augusti* (*The Accomplishments of the Deified Augustus*) were added to each side of the entrance. A copy of the text is incorporated into the facade of the Ara Pacis Museum. At a later date, the entrance was also flanked by two obelisks that are now in Piazza del Quirinale (Tour 11) and Piazza dell'Esquilino (Tour 12).

The tomb was part of Augustus' funerary site including his cremation whose location was later consecrated. His wife Livia remained at the site with the leading aristocratic women until the embers cooled to collect his ashes and bones. The mausoleum was the burial place of many Julio Claudians beginning in 23 BCE with Marcellus, the son of the emperor's sister Octavia whom he considered for his heir. Notable exceptions included Augustus' daughter Julia, who was exiled for immorality, Gaius Caligula and Nero. The base on which the cinerary urn of Agrippina the Elder, the granddaughter of Augustus and the wife of Germanicus, stood is now in the Capitoline Museums (Tour 5). The tomb was also used by members of the subsequent Flavian dynasty and the Emperor Nerva.

In 410, Alaric and the Visigoths plundered the mausoleum and its contents. Later it was converted into a fortress by the Colonna who controlled the area from Montecitorio to Ss. Apostoli. The fortress was damaged when the Colonna were expelled from Rome in 1167 and destroyed in 1241. Other uses for the mausoleum included formal gardens in the 16th century for the Soderini family and an arena for bullfights and animal baiting in the 18th and 19th centuries. Goethe attended an animal baiting spectacle here on 16 July 1787 and described the experience as 'less than edifying'. The latest incarnation at the time of its excavation was as a theatre called the Augusteo.

Facing the mausoleum on the bank of the Tiber is the **Ara Pacis Museum**, designed by Richard Meier (2006) for Augustus' monumental altar, the Ara Pacis Augustae (Altar of the Augustan Peace), that was dedicated on 30 January 9 BCE to commemorate Augustus' return from Gaul and Spain in 13 BCE. Fragments of the altar were discovered under S. Lorenzo in Lucina in 1568 and under Palazzo Fiano on Via del Corso (then known as Palazzo Peretti) in 1859 and were displayed in various collections until reassembled. It was moved to Piazza Imperatore Augusto by Mussolini in 1938 and displayed in Morpurgo's original pavilion that was replaced by Meier's building.

The altar is approached by steps within a marble enclosure decorated with bas-reliefs of a procession with Augustus and members of the Imperial family along one side and public officials and their attendants on the other with reliefs of the Lupercal (Romulus, Remus and the She-Wolf) and Trojan Aeneas, the mythological son of Venus and ancestor of the Julian clan through his son Ascanius (also known as Iulus) to either side of the entrance wall. On the opposite side that originally faced Via del Corso (then Via Flaminia) are Roma and another seated figure identified as Tellus (Mother Earth), who recalls Venus in her persona of Venus Genetrix (Venus the Ancestor of the Julian Clan), but she may also be Pax (Peace) whose benefits led to the flourishing of empire. Along the bottom half of the enclosure walls are scrolls of acanthus plants and ivy. Italian fashion designer Valentino held his retrospective show, 'Valentino in Rome: 45 Years of Style', here in 2007. The centrepiece was a dress called 'Peace' that he designed during the First Gulf War.

The Fascist-era buildings that surround the Mausoleum of Augustus act as propaganda through proximity to the mausoleum but also through art. Reliefs depict civic virtues and the restoration of rustic values. On the facade of the building to the north of the mausoleum (Istituto Nazionale della Previdenza Sociale B) on Via Ara Pacis are the mosaic mural reliefs of the *Birth of Rome* by Ferruccio Ferrazzi with the Tiber holding the twins Romulus and Remus in the centre. Below is a relief of two flying victories holding fasces on either side of a Latin inscription that commemorates Mussolini's creation of the piazza in language that evokes Augustus' *Res Gestae*: 'This place, where the spirit of Augustus flies through the breezes, after the Mausoleum of the emperor was lifted from the shadows of the ages and the scattered pieces of the Ara Pacis were reassembled, Mussolini il Duce ordered, after the demolition of ancient narrow spaces, to be restored with grander streets, buildings and shrines more suited to the customs of humanity in the year 1940 in the 18th year of the Fascist era.' On the facade of the building to the east of the mausoleum (Istituto Nazionale della Previdenza Sociale A) an inscription in Italian commemorates the Italian people.

Behind the church of **Ss. Ambrogio e Carlo al Corso** are monumental statues of S. Carlo by Attilio Selva and S. Ambrogio by Arturo Dazzi. To enter the church and continue on the tour, exit the piazza to the right of the church on Vicolo del Grottino and turn left onto Via del Corso. The church was designed by Onorio Longhi (begun in 1612) and completed by his son Martino Longhi the Younger (1668–1669) with a cupola, tribune and interior stucco decoration by Pietro da Cortona (1668). The monumental facade was designed by Cardinal Luigi Alessandro Omodei. The late Baroque interior is richly decorated. The high altar with *The Madonna presenting Saints Ambrosius and Charles Borromeo to Christ* is by Carlo Maratta. Behind the altar is a reliquary that contains the heart of S. Carlo Borromeo.

Walk up Via del Corso towards Piazza del Popolo. Via del Corso becomes a popular pedestrian mall at this point but taxis and small buses still have access. During the Christmas season, lights are hung for the entire length of the corso and vendors of *caldarroste* (roasted chestnuts) set up braziers. At No. 63 is the **Casa Lezzani** by Giuseppe Valadier (1830). Just before Piazza del Popolo, to your right is the **Casa di Goethe** at No. 18 where Johann Wolfgang von Goethe lived from 1786 to 1788 (look for the commemorative plaque to the right of the entrance) and recorded the details of his visit for his *Italian Journey*. On display in the museum is the plaster cast of the *Juno Ludovisi* in the Museo Nazionale Romano Palazzo Altemps (Tour 8) and Andy Warhol's portrait of him (1982).

Opposite is the 18th-century **Palazzo Rondinini** (also Rondanini) at Nos 518–519, now a bank that incorporates the early 17th-century palazzetto of Cavalier d'Arpino designed by Flaminio Ponzio. The palace, which has a courtyard with ancient funerary sculpture and a six-hour clock, gives its name to Michelangelo's *Rondanini Pietà* (1564), now in the Castello Sforzesco Castle, Milan, that was once displayed here. The 'Arco Temporaneo' (1850s) once spanned the corso between the two churches of S. Maria dei Miracoli and S. Maria in Montesanto.

**Piazza del Popolo** is one of the most beautiful and important examples of urban design in Rome (with St Peter's Square) at the point where the Via del Corso forms a trident with Via di Ripetta and Via del Babuino. The Neoclassical design of the piazza evolved over centuries. The piazza was first created by Pope Paul III Farnese (1538) but the original Neoclassical design for it was by Domenico Fontana for Pope Sixtus V (who considered extending Via Sistina here as the terminal focal point with Trinità dei Monti and S. Maria Maggiore) that was realised only later with designs by Giuseppe Valadier (1816–1820) for Pope Pius VII including the two hemicycles with fountains by Giovanni Ceccarini (1824), one with Neptune holding his trident (alluding to the trident shape created by the three access streets) and two Tritons and the other with Roma between the Tiber and Anio rivers along terraces that lead up to the Passeggiata del Pincio (Tour 10). This second fountain is the termination point of the Acqua Vergine Nuova aqueduct. Later, designs increased in scope to include the Pincian Hill (1834). The vast piazza is the backdrop for popular entertainment such as New Year's Eve celebrations with concert and fireworks (Festa di S. Silvestro) followed by New Year's Day events.

The **Obelisk** was moved from the Circus Maximus and erected here in 1589 by Fontana for Pope Sixtus V, who also considered moving it to S. Croce in Gerusalemme. Augustus brought it back to Rome from Heliopolis at the same time as the obelisk used for his Horologium (now in front of Palazzo di Montecitorio), following the Battle of Actium in 31 BCE, and dedicated it to the Sun, like the other obelisk, in the Circus Maximus. It is 24m high with hieroglyphics that commemorate the reigns of Ramesses II and Merenpath (13th and 12th century BCE). Thirty-three blocks of stone from the Septizodium (Tour 13) that had already been quarried by Sixtus V for the base of the Column of Marcus Aurelius were used in the construction of the fountain's base. The obelisk originally stood next to an octagonal basin fountain by Giacomo della Porta for Pope Gregory XIII Boncompagni (1574), but it was removed and lions were added by Valadier (1823) at the corners of the base for Pope Leo XII (1825). Della Porta's fountain was moved to Piazza Nicosia that lies between Palazzo Borghese and the Tiber.

Ironically, a Roman Republican-era pyramid tomb, known simply as *la Meta*, that would have suited Valadier's Neoclassical reworking of the piazza, was demolished to build **S. Maria dei Miracoli** (on the right side looking down Via del Corso – the other matching church is **S. Maria in Montesanto**). The matching facades were designed by Carlo Rainaldi but later modified by Bernini and Carlo Fontana (1671–1678) with the travertine of the facades coming from Bernini's campanile for St Peter's Basilica that was torn down after the foundation sank. The symmetry frames Via del Corso behind the obelisk when entering the piazza from the Porta del Popolo. Valadier altered the dome of the Cybo Chapel in S. Maria del Popolo and constructed a matching dome on the opposite side of the gate and installed two ancient sarcophagi fountains to give a symmetrical background view of the obelisk when approaching from Via del Corso.

The Porta del Popolo is the ancient gate (Porta Flaminia) with later additions. In 1655, Pope Alexander VII Chigi commissioned Bernini to decorate the inner side of the gate for Queen Christina of Sweden's entry into Rome. The Chigi emblems of mounds and sun decorate the facade. Two square towers were removed for the addition of the two side gates in 1878. On the Piazzale Flaminio side of the gate is Nanni di Baccio Bigio's triumphal arch design for Pope Pius IV de' Medici (1561–1562). Statues of St Peter and St Paul flank the entrance above which bears the Medici coat of arms. The gate was the main entry point prior to the construction of Termini train station. Outside the Viterbo-line train station in Piazzale Flaminio is a sign with Luigi's Pirandello's Italian translation of Goethe's 'Roman Elegy VII'.

The church of **S. Maria del Popolo** next to the Porta del Popolo is a must-see church with works by Bramante, Pinturicchio, Raphael, Caravaggio, Bernini and Annibale Carracci. According to medieval legend, the ghost of the Emperor Nero haunted the area of the Tomb of the Domitii, the clan of his father. At the expense of the Roman people (retained in the name of the church), Pope Paschal II (1099) demolished the tomb and built a chapel that was enlarged by Pope Gregory IX (1227). Pope Sixtus IV della Rovere rebuilt the church (1475–1477), but the name of the architect is unknown. Andrea Bregno may have designed the simple facade that was later modified by Bernini who added the Chigi family emblem of Pope Alexander

VII. When Martin Luther was summoned to Rome (1510–1511), he stayed in the Augustinian convent that adjoined S. Maria del Popolo and which was demolished (1811–1813) as part of Valadier's reworking of Piazza del Popolo.

The beautiful Renaissance interior was renovated by Bernini for Pope Alexander VII Chigi (1655–1659). The nave commemorates female saints grouped in pairs over the side arches with the crest of Alexander VII Chigi and two angels over the spanning arch. The two angels on the triumphal arch of the sanctuary are by Ercole Ferrata. The church is filled with pavement tombs and distinctive funerary monuments. Bramante designed the apse and choir in the shape of a shell for Pope Julius II della Rovere (*c.*1500), while Pinturicchio painted the vault frescoes (1508–1509). The high altar (1627) incorporates the 13th/14th-century icon of *Madonna del Popolo* and replaces the former high altar by Andrea Bregno (signed 1473). The latter is now in the corridor off the south transept that leads to the sacristy where other sculptures from the church and demolished convent are stored. On the left wall is the Tomb of Cardinal Ascanio Sforza (1505) and on the right wall is the Tomb of Girolamo Basso della Rovere (1507), a nephew of Pope Sixtus IV, that is signed by Andrea Sansovino. The stained glass windows designed by Guillaume de Marcillat for Pope Julius II della Rovere were the first in Rome (1509). Bernini designed both transept altars. The *Angel* on the right side of the north transept altar is by Antonio Raggi. On the south transept altar, the *Angel* to the right is by Ercole Ferrata. The sculpture decoration below the organ is by Antonio Raggi to designs of Bernini for Pope Alexander VII Chigi.

To the left of the sanctuary is the **Cerasi Chapel** that was designed by Carlo Maderno for Monsignor Tiberio Cerasi. An endless stream of visitors makes its way to this chapel to see Caravaggio's *Crucifixion of St Peter* and *Conversion of St Paul* (1600–1601). Cerasi rejected the original versions of both paintings. The first version of the *Conversion of St Paul* is in the Odescalchi Balbi Collection in Palazzo Odescalchi in Piazza dei Ss. Apostoli. The original version of the *Crucifixion of St Peter* has disappeared. Above the altar is Annibale Carracci's *Assumption* (1601) that was also commissioned by Tiberio Cerasi whose tomb is on the left wall. Carracci's idealised depiction of the Virgin contrasts with Caravaggio's realistic portrayal of Saints Peter and Paul.

On the north side, the baptistery sculpture is by Andrea Bregno and tombs by his followers. On the pier is the funerary monument to Maria Flaminia Chigi Odescalchi (d. 1771), designed by Paolo Posi. The **Chigi Chapel** (second) was designed by Raphael (1513–1516) for Agostino Chigi as an octagonal temple that includes two pyramid funerary monuments. A third pyramid was planned to be visible below the floor where now is the pavement medallion with the Chigi emblem and figure of death by Bernini. The chapel was dedicated to the Madonna di Loreto and the Neoclassical elements are contextualised within the Christian symbolism of the Corinthian order associated with St Mary. Pope Paul V Borghese's Column of the Virgin in Piazza S. Maria Maggiore (Tour 12) gives ultimate architectural expression to the association. The chapel was unfinished at the time of Raphael's death in 1520 but the funerary monuments were completed to his designs by Lorenzetto and later reworked by Bernini (1652–1656) for Pope Alexander VII Chigi. Bernini added the portrait medallions of Agostino Chigi and his brother Sigismondo Chigi. *Elijah* was designed by Raphael but sculpted by Lorenzetto with the assistance of Raffaello da Montelupo. Lorenzetto also sculpted the figure of *Jonah* to designs by Raphael. Bernini sculpted the statues of *Habakkuk* and *Daniel with the lion*. The dome mosaics were completed to Raphael's designs. Over the altar is the *Nativity of the Virgin* by Sebastiano del Piombo (1530–1534). Lorenzetto's bronze bas-relief of *Christ with the Woman from Samaria* below the altar was relocated here by Bernini from the base of Agostino Chigi's tomb. The lunette frescoes are by Raffaele Vanni (1653). In the Mellini Chapel (third), the Tomb of Cardinal Giovanni Garcia Mellini on the left wall is by Alessandro Algardi (*c*.1630) and the Tomb of Savo Mellini on the right wall is by Pierre-Étienne Monnot.

On the south side, in the Della Rovere Chapel (first), are frescoes by Pinturicchio including the *Nativity* over the altar (*c*.1490). Pinturicchio's student Tiberio d'Assisi assisted in painting *Scenes from the Life of St Jerome* and the lunettes. The Tombs of Cardinals Cristoforo (d. 1478) and Domenico della Rovere on the left side are by Andrea Bregno with a *Madonna* by Mino da Fiesole. The balustrade is by Andrea Bregno and assistants. The Cybo Chapel (second) is on a Greek cross plan with a remarkable collection of marbles designed by Carlo Fontana for Cardinal Lorenzo Cybo (d. 1683). The altarpiece *Immaculate Conception and Saints* is by Carlo Maratta (1682–1687).

In the third chapel is a Pinturicchio altarpiece, *Madonna and Saints*, with monochrome frescoes below (1503) by a follower. In the Costa Chapel (fourth) is the bronze effigy of Cardinal Pietro Foscari (*c.*1485) by Giovanni di Stefano (formerly attributed to Vecchietta).

To continue on the tour, exit the piazza onto Via del Babuino (formerly called Via Paolina after Pope Paul III Farnese) and proceed to the Spanish Steps in Piazza di Spagna. Directions for optional itineraries along the Via Flaminia are given below. Parallel to Via del Babuino to your left between Via Margutta to Via Alibert is the fashionable **Via Margutta**, with art galleries and restaurants, that was home to famous actors like Federico Fellini and numerous artists including Pablo Picasso and Giorgio de Chirico. Claude Lorrain lived on Via Margutta before moving to Via del Babuino, where he lived until his death in 1682. The annual art fair, 'Cento Pittori a Via Margutta', is held here. The **Fontana delle Arti** by Pietro Lombardi (1927) commemorates the street's ongoing contributions to Rome's art scene.

To your left on Via del Babuino at No. 92 is the **Palazzetto Raffaeli** designed by Giuseppe Valadier (1826) for the Counsellor to the Vatican of the Tsar of Russia. At the corner of Via dei Greci beyond **All Saints' Anglican Church** with a distinctive bell tower that was designed by architect George Edmund Street (who also designed S. Paolo entro le Mura on Via Nazionale, Tour 12) is the **Museum-Atelier Canova-Tadolini** at No. 150 A/B, once the Rome studio of Neoclassical sculptor Antonio Canova. In front is the famous *il Babuino,* or the Fontana del Sileno, one of the talking statues set up here in 1957, replacing the earlier fountain of 1571. The figure of a reclining Silenus was given the name *il Babuino* ('the Baboon') to refer to someone behaving like a fool. The composer Richard Wagner lived at No. 79 to your left (look up to see the plaque). Giuseppe Valadier lived just ahead in the **Palazzetto Valadier** at No. 89 (look up above the main entrance to see the plaque). Valadier lived here while working on the redesign of Piazza del Popolo and the Pincian Hill. He died here in 1839. Continue into Piazza di Spagna to begin Tour 10.

For optional itineraries along Via Flaminia to museums with Etruscan or modern art or to the Foro Italico before proceeding to Tour 10, then exit the church of S. Maria del Popolo and turn right to walk through the Porta del Popolo into Piazzale Flaminio. Cross the street to Via Flaminia: take tram No. 2 to Piazzale delle Belle Arti for Museo

Nazionale Etrusco di Villa Giulia (also accessible on foot through the Villa Borghese, Tour 10) or further up Via Flaminia to the Piazza Apollodoro stop for the Maxxi and Foro Italico.

To visit the **Museo Nazionale Etrusco di Villa Giulia**, exit the tram at Piazzale delle Belle Arti (second stop) and walk in the direction of Piazzale Flaminio to Viale delle Belle Arti then turn left. The Villa Giulia is straight ahead in Piazzale di Villa Giulia. The villa was built for Pope Julius III Chiocchi Del Monte from 1551 to 1555 by Giorgio Vasari, Bartolomeo Ammannati and Vignola. The beautiful grounds include a nymphaeum once filled with ancient sculpture. There is an extensive collection of Etruscan art and Greek pottery including the *Sarcophagus of the Married Couple* from Cerveteri (*c.*530 BCE), terra cotta statues from the Apollo and Hercules group from the Portonaccio Sanctuary in Veii, the *Euphronios Krater* (*c.*510 BCE) and Etruscan tombs with frescoes.

Retrace your steps back to Piazzale delle Belle Arti. To return to Piazzale Flaminio, take the tram on the Via Flamina side of the piazzale. To visit the MAXXI from the Villa Giulia, get back onto the tram at the stop that you used to arrive at the piazzale and continue north a few stops to Piazza Apollodoro (passing the Stadio Flaminio to your right).

To visit the **MAXXI**, the National Museum of the 21st Century Arts (Museo Nazionale delle Arti del XXI Secolo), from Piazza Apollodoro, cross Viale Tiziano to your left to walk through Piazza Apollodoro and cross to the other side of Via Flaminia. Immediately cross to the other side of Via Guido Reni and turn left to arrive at the MAXXI, which is the white modern building to your right. The museum displays contemporary art (MAXXI Art) and architecture (MAXXI Architecture) in an innovative building designed by Zaha Hadid that opened in 2010. To return to Piazzale Flaminio, retrace your steps to Via Flaminia and take the tram No. 2 at the corner of Via Flaminia and Via Guido Reni to Piazzale Flaminio.

To visit the **Foro Italico**, the Fascist-era sports complex, from the MAXXI, continue past the MAXXI on Via Guido Reni (with the museum to your right). At the end of the street (Piazza Gentile da Fabriano), turn right onto Via G. P. Pannini and cross Viale Pinturicchio to continue on Via Romano Antoniazzo. Turn right on Lungotevere Flaminio and cross to the other side of the street to walk across the Ponte Duca d'Aosta into Piazza de Bosis. The Foro Italico (1928–1938) was formerly called Foro Mussolini and was designed by Enrico del Debbio and later, Luigi Moretti. The **Stadio Olimpico** (1932), which hosted the opening and closing ceremonies of the 1960 Olympics and the track and field events, is behind Palazzo Acca del Foro Italico to your right, so walk around the right-hand side of the building for access. The **Stadio dei Marmi** (1928) with marble statues of athletes is to your right. To return to Piazzale Flaminio, retrace your steps and cross the bridge and continue through the park on Via Filippo Brunelleschi to Piazza Antonio Mancini to the No. 2 tram stop to your left.

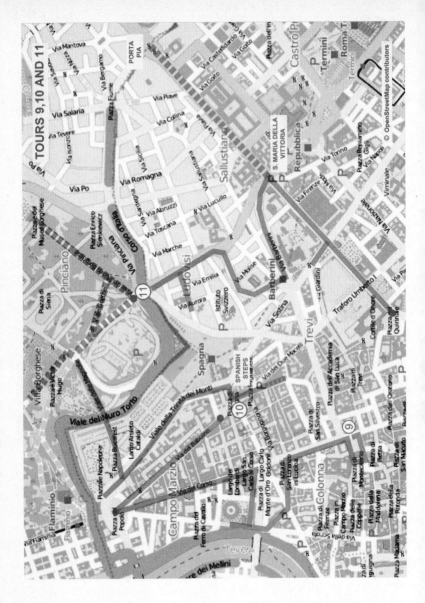

Sites: Spanish Steps; Keats-Shelley Memorial House; Colonna dell'Immacolata; Collegio di Propaganda Fide; Sant'Andrea delle Fratte; SS. Trinità dei Monti; Villa Medici; Pincian Hill Park; Villa Borghese (Options: Bioparco Zoo; Galleria Nazionale d'Arte Moderna; Museo Carlo Bilotti (Aranceria di Villa Borghese); Museo e Galleria Borghese).
Distance: 2.5km.

# SPANISH STEPS, PINCIAN HILL AND VILLA BORGHESE

The elegant Spanish Steps in a fashionable quarter of the city with luxury hotels and smart shops have long attracted visitors to Rome. At the top of the steps are the church of SS. Trinità dei Monti and the Villa Medici with distinct twin towers. Nearby is Borromini's masterpiece facade for the Collegio di Propaganda Fide. The Pincian Hill Park and the Villa Borghese provide perfect settings to stroll under Italian umbrella pine trees, rent a bicycle or a row boat, or let children play in the amusement areas. In the grounds of the villa are several options to visit the Bioparco Zoo and art galleries including the Museo e Galleria Borghese with famous works by Raphael, Caravaggio and Bernini.

The world famous **Spanish Steps** (Scalinata della Trinità dei Monti) in Piazza di Spagna were designed by Francesco de Sanctis (1723–1726) for Pope Innocent XIII. The dramatic Baroque staircase is a beautiful focal point (especially in spring when covered with potted azaleas) that mediates the change in elevation between Piazza di Spagna and the Pincian Hill, but they also divide the former Spanish territory from the former French territory at the top of the steps in Piazza della Trinità dei Monti. The axis of the steps is not perpendicular to the facade of SS. Trinità dei Monti. The decorative motifs of the columns and globes include the eagle family symbol of Pope Innocent XIII and the fleur-de-lys of King Louis XV of France. The flight of 137 steps on terraces evoke a series of rippling waterfalls that descend into the piazza and end at the charming **Fontana della Barcaccia** (1627–1629) that may be the work of Gian Lorenzo Bernini and not of his father Pietro as once thought. The fountain design of a leaking boat playfully takes into account

10. The Spanish Steps and church of SS. Trinità dei Monti

the low water pressure from the Acqua Vergine Nuova aqueduct. On the ship are the family emblems of Pope Urban VIII Barberini who commissioned the fountain.

On the right-hand side looking up the steps is the **Keats-Shelley Memorial House**. The Casina Rossa was the residence of John Keats for the last three months of his life until his death on 23 February 1821 at the age of 25. There is a commemorative plaque on the wall facing the steps. He lived with his friend, the artist Joseph Severn who erected their tombs in the Protestant Cemetery (Tour 14). Percy Bysshe Shelly lived with his wife Mary on Via del Corso near Piazza Colonna (Tour 9) but the Keats-Shelley Memorial House was opened as a museum and library in 1909 (purchased by the Keats-Shelley Memorial Association in 1906). The library contains over 7,000 volumes and personal correspondence of Keats, Shelley, Byron and Leigh Hunt. The museum displays the reliquary of Pope Pius V once owned by Hunt that was used to store the hair of John Milton and Elizabeth Barrett Browning. To the right of the museum at No. 31 in the 16th-century Palazzetto del Borgognoni is the **Casa Museo di Giorgio de Chirico** where the artist lived and worked from 1947 until his death in 1978. He is buried in S. Francesco a Ripa (Tour 4).

English visitors on the Grand Tour formed a colony in the area by the Spanish Steps and Trinità dei Monti. Once established, aristocrats sought out the famous portraitists Pompeo Batoni and Angelica Kauffmann to commemorate their sojourn in Rome. The art collectors Gavin Hamilton and Thomas Jenkins supplied visitors with antiquities for the decoration of townhouses and country estates. Later visitors included Charles Dickens, Thomas Hardy, Nathaniel Hawthorne, Henry James and Edith Wharton. An historic reminder of the Grand Tour is **Babington's English Tea Rooms** on the left side of the Spanish Steps that were opened in 1893 by two English women. Earlier, **Caffè Greco** at No. 86 Via Condotti that attracted Grand Tour visitors since opening in 1760 is now an Italian national monument (since 1953). A plaque at No. 80 commemorates the house of Giacomo Leopardi (1798–1837), the Italian Romantic poet. James Joyce lived at No. 50 Via Frattina in 1906.

Before climbing the steps, continue on Via del Babuino towards Piazza Mignanelli with the **Colonna dell'Immacolata** in the centre that commemorates Pope Pius IX's proclamation of the Dogma of the Immaculate Conception (1854). The column evokes Pope Paul V Borghese's Column of the Virgin in front of S. Maria Maggiore (Tour 12) and was inaugurated in 1857 with a statue of the Virgin by Giuseppe Obici. On the Feast Day of the Immaculate Conception (8 December), the pope leads a procession to lay a wreath at the column. Opposite the column to your right is **Palazzo di Spagna** that houses the Spanish Embassy to the Holy See (since 1622), after which the piazza is named. Continue past the Colonna dell'Immacolata and veer right onto Via di Propaganda.

Facing the column and taking up the entire block is **Palazzo di Propaganda Fide** (Palace of the Propagation of the Faith) that is the seat of the Congregazione di Propaganda Fide (Congregation for the Evangelisation of Peoples) founded by Pope Gregory XV Ludovisi (1622). The Latin name *Collegium Urbanum De Propaganda Fide* appears on the facade. Bernini worked on the main facade facing Piazza di Spagna (1644) for Pope Urban VIII Barberini whose emblem of the bee appears on architectural elements. The dramatic and influential facade with the concave and convex curves facing Via di Propaganda is by Borromini (1646). Rival designs extend to the **Cappella dei Re Magi** inside the palazzo. Bernini's oval chapel for Pope Urban VIII Barberini (1634) was demolished by Borromini (1660–1666) who took over the project following the accession of Pope Innocent X Pamphilj and substituted a rectangular-shaped chapel. The palazzo was completed under Pope Alexander VII Chigi whose emblems are found on the Via di Capo le Case side of the building.

Continue to the end of the block to the church of Sant'Andrea delle Fratte at Via della Mercede. The building at the corner to your right is **Palazzo Bernini** at No. 12A Via della Mercede. After living with his father Pietro across from S. Maria Maggiore (where he is buried), Bernini moved to this area that was under the patronage of Pope Urban VIII Barberini whose palazzo overlooks the nearby Piazza Barberini (Tour 11). A plaque with a portrait bust commemorates Bernini's residence here since 1641 but he also owned the building next to it that served as his studio and living quarters. According to legend, when Queen Christina of Sweden visited him here, he received her wearing his work clothes. Bernini died here in 1680. His descendants later moved to Via del Corso (the building is also known as Palazzo Bernini) across the street from Palazzo Ruspoli.

The church of **Sant'Andrea delle Fratte** is named after the woods (*fratte*) and orchards (it was also known as S. Andrea de hortis) of this once uninhabited area of the city. It occupies the site of the Scottish Hospice and is a reminder of Scotland's historical ties to Rome (Scottish hero William Wallace sought a meeting with Pope Boniface VIII in 1300 through envoys but it is not clear whether he intended to visit Rome). It was the church of the Scots in Rome until 1585 when Pope

Sixtus V gave the church to the Minim Order of S. Francesco di Paolo whose convent is next to SS. Trinità dei Monti at the top of the Spanish Steps. The church was rebuilt by Gaspare Guerra (1604–1612) funded by the del Bufalo family whose 16th-century palazzo with lioness emblem and motto *Cum Feris Ferus* ('Merciless with the merciless') is nearby at the end of Via S. Andrea della Fratte opposite the Collegio Nazzareno. The apse, dome and campanile are by Borromini (from 1653 to 1667) and were completed by Mattia de Rossi (1691). The late-Renaissance style of the facade was completed by Pasquale Belli (1826). Pope Clement VIII established the **Scots College** (1600) on Via del Tritone opposite S. Maria di Constantinopoli but the college later moved to Via delle Quattro Fontane opposite Palazzo Barberini (1604–1962). Today, the Pontifical Scots College is located on Via Cassia on the outskirts of the city.

Inside are the two angels that Bernini made for Ponte Sant'Angelo, holding the titulus of the crucifixion and the crown of thorns (Tour 3) that were given to the church by his nephew Prospero. Giuseppe Valadier and Luigi Vanvitelli designed the north transept altar. The epitaph of Angelica Kauffmann is to the left of the north-side entrance. The funerary monument to Cardinal Leopoldo Calcagnini by Pietro Bracci (1746–1749) on the west wall shows the influence of Raphael and Bernini. Bracci also carved the monument to Cardinal Pierluigi Carafa on the south side (third chapel). The cloister by Guerra (1604) is a tranquil oasis with ancient cypress trees. Retrace your steps to the Spanish Steps.

At the top of the Spanish Steps is **Piazza della Trinità dei Monti** that was formerly known as Piazza di Francia (Piazza of France). The **Obelisk** in the centre of the piazza is much travelled: it was brought to Rome from Egypt and decorated here with the same hieroglyphics of the obelisk of Ramesses II that was brought to Rome by Augustus for the Circus Maximus and is now in Piazza del Popolo. It was originally erected in the Gardens of Sallust and discovered in Piazza Sallustio (Tour 11). It was considered for the basin of the Trevi Fountain (Tour 8) but was erected here by Pope Pius VI in 1788 and capped with the fleur-de-lys of France.

The **Gardens of Lucullus** (Horti Luculliani) begun after 63 BCE following L. Licinius Lucullus' triumph over Mithridates occupied the site of the church and convent with terraces and a monumental flight of stairs that roughly corresponds to the location of the Spanish Steps. The luxurious villa later passed into the Imperial estate through Messalina, the wife of the Emperor Claudius, after she forced the suicide of a subsequent owner, Valerius Asiaticus. The emperor would later execute his wife for marrying her lover. The historian Tacitus places Messalina's assassination here as poetic justice for her greed and claims her body was heaped on top of a cart used for garden refuse. Felice della Rovere, the daughter of Pope Julius II della Rovere, owned the property in the 16th century.

The construction of the church of **SS. Trinità dei Monti** and the Convent of the Minim Order of S. Francesco di Paolo was begun in 1493 by King Louis XII of France. The facade was started in 1519 and probably completed by Giacomo della Porta towards the end of the century with twin campanile towers that evoke French cathedrals. The double staircase by Domenico Fontana (1587) evokes the staircase in front of Palazzo Senatorio in Piazza del Campidoglio.

The interior with dome frescoes by Perino del Vaga has beautifully decorated chapels. On the north side, in the Aldobrandini-Bonfil Chapel (second) is Daniele da Volterra's *Descent from the Cross* (after 1546), whose design is often attributed to Michelangelo, his mentor. It originally hung in the Orsini Chapel (third) but was lost during the French occupation. It was found in the 19th century and placed in this chapel. It was once a must-see painting that influenced artists such as Rubens. Da Voltera also painted the *Assumption of the Virgin* (1548–1550) and *Presentation of the Virgin* in the Della Rovere Chapel on the south side (third). The last figure to the right is a portrait of Michelangelo. The vault of the Massimo Chapel on the north side (fifth) collapsed in the 19th century destroying the frescoes of Giulio Romano, Giovan Francesco Penni and Perino del Vago (1537) that were finished by Taddeo and Federico Zuccari (1563–1589). The Pucci Chapel (seventh) contains the frescoes *Scenes from the Old and New Testament* by Perino del Vaga (1524).

**Palazzo Zuccari** (1592) is in the triangle formed by Via Sistina and Via Gregoriana to your right as you face the church. Queen Maria Casimira of Poland added the porch and balcony (1700–1714). The palazzo was the home of English painter Sir Joshua Reynolds (1752–1753) and art historian Johann Joachim Winckelmann (1755–1768). Occupying the palazzo and the adjacent **Palazzo Stroganoff** is the **Biblioteca Hertziana** (named after Enrichetta Hertziana who left her library and the palazzo to the German government in 1900) that houses one of the most important art history book collections in Italy. Via

Sistina descends to Piazza Barberini (Tour 11) and continues as Via delle Quattro Fontane and then Via A. Depretis to S. Maria Maggiore. It was formerly called Strada Felice after Pope Sixtus V. The engraver and architect Giovanni Battista Piranesi, the Neoclassical sculptor Bertel Thorvaldsen and the archaeologist and architect Luigi Canina lived in succession at No. 48. Hans Christian Andersen lived at No. 104, and Nikolai Gogol lived at No. 126.

As you stroll up Viale della Trinità dei Monti to the Pincian Hill Overlook, the **Villa Medici** with the imposing facade and twin towers is to your right. The villa was built by Nanni di Baccio Bigio and Annibale Lippi for Cardinal Ricci da Montepulciano between 1564 and 1574 and replaced an earlier casina owned by Cardinal Marcello Crescenzi. Cardinal Ferdinando de' Medici bought the villa in 1576 (he later became Grand Duke of Tuscany and married Christina of Lorraine in 1589). He hired Bartolomeo Ammannati who enlarged the villa, added a loggia and incorporated ancient reliefs into walls including from the Arcus Novus of Diocletian that once spanned the Via del Corso. The reliefs with garlands are from the Ara Pacis of Augustus (Tour 9). The villa was decorated with the ancient art collection bought from Cardinal Andrea della Valle in 1584 that was formerly housed in Palazzo Valle on Corso Vittorio Emanuele II (Tour 7). The vestibule contains painted scenes of the villa in various periods. Cardinal Alessandro de' Medici lived here until becoming Pope Leo XI (1–27 April 1605). Napoleon bought the villa in 1801 and transferred the French Academy in Rome here in 1803 that had been founded by King Louis XIV in 1666. The *Prix de Rome* is awarded to students at the École des Beaux Arts in Paris for residency at the villa paid for by the French government. Famous past recipients include Ingres, Berlioz, Debussy and Balthus. Both Ingres and Balthus later returned as directors.

The restored 16th-century garden has fountains supplied with water brought in by the Acqua Felice whose terminus point is the Moses Fountain (Tour 11). An ancient sculpture group of *Niobe* and her children was found in Rome in 1583 near S. Giovanni in Laterano (Tour 13) and placed in the garden. A copy of the Niobe group replaced the original that was installed in the Uffizi Gallery, Florence, by Leopold I, Grand Duke of Tuscany. At this time, other important ancient sculptures such as the *Medici Venus* and the *Wrestlers* were moved to the Uffizi in Florence or installed in the Boboli Gardens, including the obelisk discovered on the Pincian. The *Medici Lions* were moved to the Loggia dei Lanzi in Florence in 1789. The copies on display are by Augustin Pajou. The other statues placed throughout the garden are copies of the ancient originals except for the seated female figure that was given to Cardinal de' Medici by Pope Gregory XIII Boncompagni and reworked to resemble *Dea Roma*. Giambologna's statue of *Mercury*, now in the Museo Nazionale del Bargello in Florence, was commissioned for the site but is now replaced by a copy. The obelisk was made by Balthus. Archaeological excavations on the property have uncovered mosaic pavements of a Roman house and the ruins of 5th-century CE structures.

The fountain in front of the Villa on Viale della Trinità dei Monti was designed by Annibale Lippi in 1589. It incorporates an ancient Roman porphyry basin with a cannon ball that legend claims was shot from a cannon from Castel Sant'Angelo by Queen Christina of Sweden. The monument to the Cairoli brothers Enrico and Giovanni by Ercole Rosa (1883) commemorates their deaths fighting on behalf of Garibaldi in 1867.

Continue past the Villa Medici and take the ramp (Viale Mickiewicz) to your right that leads to the Pincian Hill Park (Parco del Pincio) with a view of St Peter's Basilica at the top. The Neoclassical **Casina Valadier**, by Giuseppe Valadier (1813–1817) remodelled into a café, is to your right. Continue straight to reach the **Passeggiata del Pincio** on the terrace above Piazza del Popolo in Piazzale Napoleone with sweeping views of the city. The park, laid out by Giuseppe Valadier (1809–1814), was completed in 1834 and includes portrait busts of famous Italians. The Pincian was a popular destination in the 19th century for a *passeggiata* or evening stroll along the tree-lined avenues and paths of the adjoining Villa Borghese. Umbrella pines, magnolias and other mature trees provide shaded walks that lead to Neoclassical fountains and temples and commemorative monuments. Retrace your steps towards Viale Mickiewicz and turn left onto Viale dell'Obelisco. The **Obelisk of Antinous** was erected here in Piazza Bucarest by Giuseppe Marini for Pope Pius VII in 1822. It was originally dedicated to Antinous by the Emperor Hadrian in 130 CE and possibly brought to Rome by the Emperor Elagabulus in the 3rd century. It was found in 1570 outside the Porta Maggiore and moved to Piazza Barberini but never erected, lying in pieces in the area in front of Bernini's Triton fountain. In 1773, the Barberini family donated it to Pope Clement

XIV who installed it for a short while in the Cortile della Pigna of the Vatican Museums, but it was transferred here in 1822. This section of the park has a playground area for children that includes bicycle and go-cart rentals.

Continue on Viale dell'Obelisco to enter the Villa Borghese beyond Piazza dei Martiri on Viale delle Magnolie and follow to Piazzale delle Canestre. The **Villa Borghese** is an immense garden villa estate outside the Aurelianic Walls that was begun in the 17th century by Pope Paul V Borghese's nephew, Cardinal Scipione Borghese. The villa later passed to Camillo Borghese (who married Pauline Bonaparte) through his father Prince Marcantonio IV Borghese who, in the 18th century, hired the Scottish architect Jacob Moore to design the landscape. The villa was enlarged in the 19th century with the acquisition of the Giustiniani Gardens and became a public park after the Italian state acquired it in 1902 and gave it to the Comune of Rome.

On the monumental entrances from Piazzale Flaminio (by Luigi Canina) and Porta Pinciana (Antonio and Mario Asprucci), the Borghese family symbols of the dragon and eagle are prominently displayed. Neoclassical and Egyptianising statues and monuments and faux temple ruins (such at the Tempio di Annia Faustina e Cerere) are found throughout the villa but there are also commemorative statues that honour the Italian Royal family and heroes of the Risorgimento as well as famous artists, authors (the monument to Goethe was a gift of Emperor Wilhem II in 1902 and was followed by the French gift of the monument to Victor Hugo) and foreign political figures like George Washington whose name was given to the Viale G. Washington that provides access to the villa from Piazzale Flaminio.

Once you reach Piazzale delle Canestre, there are several options. To exit the villa by the most direct route, from Piazzale delle Canestre turn right on Viale S. Paolo del Brasile to exit by the Porta Pinciana. Cross to the other side of the Via di Porta Pinciana and Viale del Muro Torto intersection and walk through the arch in the Porta Pinciana that dates to the reign of Emperor Honorius to the start of Via Veneto to begin Tour 11.

If visiting sites in the villa, from Piazzale delle Canestre continue straight through the gates onto Viale Pietro Canonica. The **Museo Carlo Bilotti** is to your left. Turn left at Viale del' Aranciera for the serene **Giardino del Lago** (Garden of the Lake) area with the Neoclassical

11. Temple of Aesculapius, Villa Borghese

**Temple of Aesculapius** situated on an island. Rental boats are available. From the temple, signs indicate directions to the **Galleria Nazionale D'Arte Moderna** (in Palazzo delle Belle Arti that houses 18th- and 19th-century Italian art including works by Canova and Neoclassical sculpture from the Torlonia collection), the **Museo Nazionale Etrusco di Villa Giulia** and the **Bioparco Zoo** (Giardino Zoologico). The **British School at Rome** (61 Via Antonio Gramsci) occupies the British Pavilion of the 1911 International Exhibition of Fine Arts in Rome that commemorated the 50th anniversary of Italian unification. It was designed by Sir Edwin Lutyens, known for his architecture in New Delhi and the Cenotaph in Whitehall in London. Continue on Viale Pietro Canonica and follow signs to visit the **Museo Canonica**, **Piazza di Siena**, the **Temple of Diana** and the **Casina di Raffaelo**. The villa that Raphael designed for Pope Clement VII de' Medici was destroyed in the Sack of Rome of 1527. To continue onto Tour 11 from any of these sites, retrace your steps to Piazzale delle Canestre, turn left on Viale S. Paolo del Brasile and follow directions (above) to Via Veneto.

If visiting the **Museo e Galleria Borghese**, from Piazzale Canestre turn right onto Viale S. Paolo del Brasile. You may cross to the other side of the street at the Goethe monument and take Viale Goethe to Viale del Museo Borghese and turn left to reach the museum or stay on Viale S. Paolo del Brasile and turn left onto Viale del Museo Borghese near the Porta Pinciana. Turn left and follow straight through to the museum.

The **Casino Borghese** was begun by Flaminio Ponzio (1608) for Cardinal Scipione Borghese. After his death (1613), Giovanni Vasanzio continued his work and then under Prince Marcantonio IV Borghese the work was continued by Antonio and Mario Asprucci and Christopher Unterberger (1775–1790). Cardinal Scipione Borghese collected contemporary and ancient art: he was one of Bernini's earliest patrons and commissioned some of his finest sculptures that are still on display. He also commissioned 12 paintings from Caravaggio, six of which are still on display here. Ancient sculpture and 4th-century floor mosaics were altered and integrated into the casino's decoration according to contemporary tastes so it is difficult at times to distinguish the ancient pieces from the collection of 16th- to 18th/19th-century Neoclassical art. Like his father Prince Marcantonio IV Borghese, Camillo Borghese continued to acquire art and commissioned the reclining portrait of his wife Pauline from Antonio Canova, but he also sold much of the ancient sculpture to his brother-in-law Napoleon in 1807 that is now on display in the Louvre.

The **Museo e Galleria Borghese** is a must-see museum that requires reservations in advance. The entrance is under the portico. Depending on the number of visitors, the museum may begin your visit on either the Ground (Museo) or Upper floor (Galleria).

On the **Ground floor** (Museo), the eight rooms and portico are arranged around the central salone. Decoration of the rooms is by Giovanni Battista Marchetti and frescoes by Tommaso Conca, Paul Bril and others. The entrance from the circular staircase is into **Room IV** which displays Gian Lorenzo Bernini's *Rape of Persephone/Proserpina* (1622) for Cardinal Scipione Borghese, depicting her attempt to free herself from Hades/Pluto as he passes Cerberus to re-enter the Underworld. Upon receipt of the statue, Cardinal Scipione Borghese gave it to Cardinal Ludovico Ludovisi who displayed it with his famous collection of ancient sculpture at the Villa Ludovisi (Tour 11). It remained in the Boncompagni Ludovisi collection until 1901 when it was bought by the Italian state and displayed here. On the tables is the bronze *bozzetto* of *Neptune* by Bernini of the *Neptune and Triton* group (1622–1623) in the Victoria and Albert Museum, London, and Antonio Sussini's *Farnese Bull* copy. The busts of Roman emperors in porphyry and alabaster are from the 17th century.

The relief of Curtius throwing himself into the lake in the **Salone** dates to the 2nd century CE but was hung on an angle by Pietro Bernini, the father of Gian Lorenzo. The busts of Roman emperors are by Giovanni Battista della Porta. Off the salone is the **Portico** with ancient sculpture. In the corridor leading to Room I is Jean-Antoine Houdon's *Il Battista* (1768), the gesso model for his colossal statue of St John the Baptist for S. Maria degli Angeli (Tour 12) that fell from its niche and does not survive. Houdon's famous *Écorché* anatomical study was completed at the same time with the same pose. Antonio Canova's half-nude portrait of Pauline Borghese as *Venus Victrix* (1805–1808) in **Room I** was hidden from view by her husband Camillo Borghese.

Bernini's dynamic *David* (1623–1624) in **Room II** for Cardinal Scipione Borghese is a self-portrait made when he was only 25 years old as the biblical hero in the act of releasing the stone from his slingshot. In **Room III** is Bernini's *Apollo and Daphne* (1622–1625). The myth of Daphne's transformation into the laurel tree to prevent her rape by Apollo is related in Ovid's *Metamorphoses*. The figure of Apollo is modelled after the *Apollo Belvedere* in the Vatican Museums. The *Hermaphrodite* (*c.*150 CE) in **Room V** is after an original by Polyclitus. *Agrippina the Elder* is the granddaughter of Augustus and wife of Germanicus (*c.*37 CE). In **Room VI** are Bernini's earliest and one of his later works: the *Aeneas and Anchises* (1613) was carved when he was only 15 years old with the assistance of his father Pietro, and his *Truth* (1645) was intended for a group *Truth unveiled by Time*. The ancient *Leda and the Swan* is by Timotheus. On the walls are slabs from Diocletian's *Arcus Novus* from the Via del Corso. In the Egyptian Room (**Room VII**) with paintings by Tommaso Conca, the *Sphinx* to the left is ancient but the one on the right is by Luigi Canina (1828).

There are six Caravaggio paintings in **Room VIII**: *Sick Bacchus* (*c.*1594), a self-portrait of the artist; *Boy with a Basket of Fruit* (*c.*1594); *Madonna of the Palafrenieri* (1605), with St Anne and the Madonna teaching the Christ child how to crush a snake; *St Jerome* (1605); *David with the Head of Goliath* (1609/10), which includes Caravaggio's self-portrait as Goliath; and *Young St John the Baptist* (*c.*1609/10), the last known work that was sent to Cardinal Scipione Borghese with two other paintings to obtain a pardon for murder and permission to return to Rome. The *Capture of Christ* and the *Rape of Europa* are by Cavalier d'Arpino, Caravaggio's mentor. The *Dancing Satyr* is a 2nd-century copy of an original by Lyssipus (restored by Thorvaldsen).

On the **Upper floor** (Galleria), important Renaissance paintings in **Room IX** include Raphael's *Entombment* (1507), showing the influence of Michelangelo. Cardinal Scipione Borghese removed it from the church of S. Francesco al Prato, Perugia, to add to his painting collection that included Raphael's *Lady with a Unicorn* (c.1506) and *Portrait of a Man* (1502). The *Portrait of Pope Julius II* may be a copy of an original by him. The *Fornarina* is a copy by Raffaellino del Colle. The original is in Palazzo Barberini (Tour 11). **Room X** includes Correggio's *Danaë* (1530–1531); Ridolfo del Ghirlandaio's *Leda* (c.1565); Lucas Cranach the Elder's *Venus and Cupid with a Honeycomb* (c.1531); and Dosso Dossi's *David with the head of Goliath*. In the centre of the room is Nicolas Cordier's *La Zingarella* from a reworked ancient fragment. In **Room XII** are Baldassarre Peruzzi's *Venus*; Sodoma's *Holy Family* and *Pietà*; Giulio Romano's *Madonna and Child with St John*; and a copy of Leonardo da Vinci's *Leda and the Swan*. Examples of Bernini's earliest and later works are in **Room XV**: *Amalthea with Zeus* (1615), two marble portrait busts of Cardinal Scipione Borghese (c.1632), a portrait bust of Pope Paul V Borghese (c.1618), and a terra cotta model for a monumental equestrian statue of King Louis XIV (c.1670). The two self-portraits are from 1623 and around 1633. The ceiling fresco *Council of the Gods* is by Giovanni Lanfranco (1624–1625). In **Room XVIII** is Rubens' *Deposition*. Domenichino's *Diana* (1616–1617) is in **Room XIX** with Annibale Carracci's *Head of a Youth Laughing* (1583–1585). In **Room XX** is Titian's early masterpiece, *Sacred and Profane Love* (1514), and later works. Also here is Antonello da Messina *Portrait of a Young Man* (c.1475).

The exit is into the garden with the monumental fountain and **Teatro** that imitates an ancient Roman stage facade. To continue to Tour 11, retrace your steps on Viale del Museo Borghese to exit the villa at the Porta Pinciana. Cross to the other side of the Via di Porta Pinciana and Viale del Muro Torto intersection and walk through the arch in the Porta Pinciana to the start of Via Veneto.

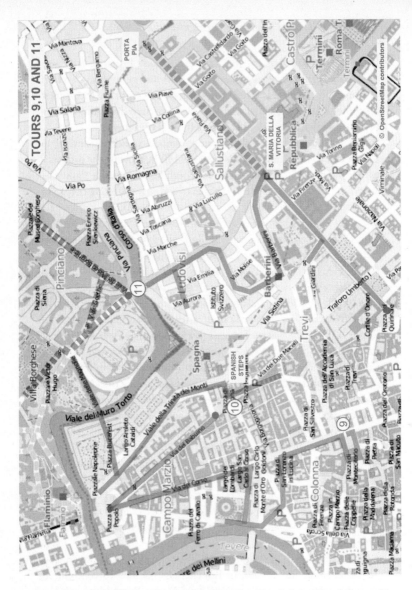

Sites: Via Vittorio Veneto; Villa Aurora; S. Maria della Concezione; Piazza Barberini; Largo S. Susanna; Moses Fountain; S. Maria della Vittoria; S. Susanna; S. Bernardo alle Terme (Options: Piazza Sallustio; Porta Pia; Porta Salaria; Praetorian Camp; Via Nomentana: Villa Torlonia; Sant'Agnese fuori le Mura; S. Costanza; S. Lorenzo fuori le Mura; Campo Verano Cemetery); Piazza delle Quattro Fontane; Palazzo Barberini; San Carlo alle Quattro Fontane; Sant'Andrea al Quirinale; Piazza del Quirinale; Quirinal Palace.
Distance: 2.5km.

# Tour 11

# QUIRINAL HILL
## AND THE BAROQUE

Stroll along the fashionable Via Veneto, made famous by Federico Fellini's film *La Dolce Vita*, in the area of the Pincian, formerly part of the vast Villa Ludovisi. The Quirinal Hill was once home to the legendary Sabines of ancient Rome who worshipped the god Quirinus here, giving the hill its name. The area was abandoned after the fall of Rome but it attracted new residents following Sixtus V's opening of the Acqua Felice aqueduct in 1587. Construction of Counter-Reformation churches filled the area with must-see Baroque masterpieces by Maderno, Bernini and Borromini. The tour contains options from Porta Pia to visit ancient churches associated with Constantine outside the city centre on Via Nomentana.

From the Porta Pinciana stroll along Via Vittorio Veneto, known popularly as **Via Veneto**, the fashionable street in the Rione Ludovisi that winds its way down to Piazza Barberini with many luxury hotels built in the late 19th century and sidewalk cafés. The area was formerly occupied by the ancient Gardens of Sallust and the vast **Villa Ludovisi** owned by the Boncompagni Ludovisi. The villa was the largest private residence within the walls of Rome (almost 90 acres on both sides of Via Veneto and stretching to Porta Salaria), acquired by Cardinal Ludovico Ludovisi, the nephew of Pope Gregory XV Ludovisi, in 1621 from Cardinal Francesco Maria Del Monte. The Boncompagni and Ludovisi families were united in 1681 when Olimpia Ippolita Ludovisi, Princess of Piombino, married Gregorio Boncompagni, Duke of Sora and grandnephew of Pope Gregory XIII Boncompagni.

The **Villa Aurora** to your right at the end of Via Lombardia at No. 44 (visits by appointment only) survives from the dissolution of the larger estate (1886) of famous gardens and collection of ancient sculpture. John Evelyn visited the villa (1644) that later became an essential site on the Grand Tour, including visits by Goethe (1787), Stendhal (1828), Nikolai Gogol (1838–1842), Nathaniel Hawthorne (1858) and Henry James (1883). The Villa Aurora was home to the American Academy in Rome (1895–1907) that is now located on the Janiculum Hill (Tour 3). The villa is still occupied by the Boncompagni Ludovisi family. From the entrance gate, elements from the 16th-century garden are visible including a section of ancient entablature from Hadrian's Villa at Tivoli that was carved into a trough in the medieval era.

The **Casino dell'Aurora** (1570) with 19th-century additions is named after the masterpiece fresco *Aurora* in the **Great Hall** by Guercino (1621), which depicts Aurora guiding her chariot above a dramatic illusionistic perspective. Guercino also painted *Allegory of the Day* and *Allegory of the Night* in the lunettes with architectural decoration by Agostino Tassi. When Cardinal Francesco Maria Del Monte acquired the villa in 1595 he commissioned Caravaggio to paint *Jupiter, Neptune, and Pluto* (1597) on the ceiling of his Alchemy Study, now known as the **Caravaggio Room**. This is the only ceiling fresco (oil on plaster) painted by Caravaggio, who depicted the gods with his own self-portrait. The fresco was discovered in 1978 when a later layer of paint was removed.

In the **Room of the Landscapes**, Guercino, Domenichino, Paul Bril and Giovanni Battista Viola each painted landscapes on the ceiling around a *Wreath of Putti* by Pomarancio (Antonio Circignani) to compete for the commission to paint the Great Hall that Guercino won. Guercino also painted another ceiling fresco, *La Fama* (Fame with a Phoenix Rising from the Ashes), with Agostino Tassi who painted the lunettes and medallions with mythological scenes. In the **Valesio Room**, the illusionistic ceiling fresco *Putti with the Ludovisi Crest* by Giovanni Luigi Valesio (1621) anticipates Pietro da Cortona's depiction of Pope Urban VIII's crest in his *Triumph of Divine Providence* (1633–1639) in Palazzo Barberini. Sculpture in the **Gardens** of the villa includes a *Satyr* attributed to Michelangelo, two *Dacians* from a Trajanic monument, a colossal head of *Aesculapius* and ancient funerary stele. Retrace your steps to Via Veneto and continue to your right.

At the intersection of Via Veneto and Via Ludovisi (a plaque at the corner commemorates Federico Fellini), cross to the other side of Via Veneto to **Palazzo Margherita** where the name of Via Ludovisi changes to Via Boncompagni. The palazzo, formerly called Palazzo Boncompagni or Palazzo Piombino, was built for Prince Rodolfo Boncompagni Ludovisi, Principe di Piombino VIII, to a design by Gaetano Koch (1886–1890) to serve as the family residence following the demoliton of Palazzo Piombino al Corso opposite Piazza Colonna (Tour 9). The palazzo modified the earlier **Palazzo Grande di Villa Ludovisi** built by Cardinal Ludovico Ludovisi to designs by Domenichino. The **Casino delle Statue** (now a parking garage) was built to house the famous collection of ancient sculpture that was acquired by the Italian state (1901) and now displayed in Palazzo Altemps (Tour 8).

The palazzo was the residence of Queen Margherita of Savoy following the assassination of her husband King Umberto I. In 1931 the palazzo became the property of the Italian state and now houses the United States Embassy. A plaque commemorates Brigadier General Robert F. Frederick, Commander of the United States–Canadian 1st Special Service Force, who established headquarters here in World War II. One block behind the palazzo is the **Museo Boncompagni Ludovisi** at No. 18 Via Boncompagni that is devoted to 19th- and 20th-century decorative arts, costume and fashion.

Ahead to your left is the church of **S. Maria della Concezione**, also called Chiesa dell'Immacolata Concezione Della Beata Virgine Maria, that contains the famous **Crypt of the Capuchins** (Cappuccini) after whose cloak and hood (*cappuccio*) the coffee drink is named. The Franciscan church of the Order of Friars Minor Capuchin was designed by Antonio Casoni (1626–1630) for Cardinal Antonio Marcello Barberini, the brother of Pope Urban VIII. On the south side, Guido Reni's *St Michael the Archangel* (*c.*1635) in the first chapel is reproduced in mosaic in St Peter's Basilica. The face of the devil is a portrait of Pope Innocent X Pamphilj. The *Nativity* (second chapel) is by Giovanni Lanfranco (*c.*1632). In the third chapel is Domenichino's *Ecstasy of St Francis* and *Death of St Francis*. In front of the high altar is the pavement Tomb of Cardinal Antonio Barberini (d. 1646) with the

Latin epitaph, *hic iacet pulvis, cinis et nihil* ('Here lies dust, ashes, and nothing'). On the north side (first chapel) is *Ananias restoring the sight of St Paul* (*c.*1631) by Pietro da Cortona.

The entrance to the **Museum and Crypt** is on the right side of the church's double staircase. The museum with *St Francis in Meditation* (*c.*1603) attributed to Caravaggio leads to the crypt decorated with the skeletons and bones of about 4,000 Capuchin friars that was once visited by the Marquis de Sade (1775).

Continue down Via Veneto past **Palazzo Boscolo** with Latin inscriptions to your left at No. 7 by Gino Coppedè (1925–1927) into **Piazza Barberini** in the Rione Trevi. At this corner of the piazza is Bernini's **Fontana delle Api** (Bee Fountain) of 1644 with the family emblem of the Barberini that was originally attached to a building on the other side of Via Sistina but relocated here in 1917. Palazzo Barberini rises on the other side of the piazza and is accessed by Via delle Quattro Fontane. In the centre of the piazza is Bernini's **Fontana del Tritone** (Triton Fountain) of 1642–1643 for Pope Urban VIII Barberini. Opposite the fountain at No. 12 between Via della Purificazione and Via Sistina is **Palazzo Ferri Orsini** (16th century). The obelisk of Antinous now on the Pincian Hill was formerly displayed in the piazza as a fallen ruin. During Hanukkah, the Jewish community lights the candles of a large Menorah in the piazza. Via del Tritone, named for the fountain, was regularised from 1911 to 1925 to connect the piazza with Via del Corso.

Exit the piazza by Via Barberini that was laid out from 1926 to 1932 (and originally named Via Regina Elena). Construction of the street caused the demolition of an entry gate to Palazzo Barberini from the piazza that was designed by Pietro da Cortona (1630–1635). In the courtyards of the buildings to your right as you leave the piazza, look for square Roman bricks in a diagonal pattern (*opus reticulatum*) from a massive retaining wall that supported the Republican Walls. The street winds its way uphill and intersects Via Leonida Bissolati that was laid out in 1933 (originally called Via XXIII Marzo) to provide a route to Termini train station from the historic centre of the city. In the traffic island to your left is a section of the Republican Walls discovered during the demolition of **Palazzo Amici** between S. Maria della Vittoria and S. Susanna. Longer segments are visible at the intersections of Via Carducci and Via Salandra.

The **Largo di S. Susanna** was reworked as a traffic hub in 1870 for the government offices and various ministry buildings that line **Via XX Settembre** (called the Alta Semita in antiquity). Pope Pius IV de' Medici renamed the street that extends from his Porta Pia to Piazza delle Quattro Fontane, the Strada Pia (1560). Straight ahead beyond the St Regis Grand Hotel (the first hotel in Rome to have electricity) is the Naiad Fountain at the head of Via Nazionale in Piazza della Repubblica (Tour 12), occupying the area of the exedra terrace of the Baths of Diocletian (305–306 CE). Cult objects in a votive deposit from the late 8th/early 7th century BCE were discovered in front of S. Maria della Vittoria to the left of the Moses Fountain. Porta Pia is to your far left at the end of Via XX Settembre and to your right is the church of S. Susanna with Piazza del Quirinale in the distance. The Largo di S. Susanna adjoins **Piazza di S. Bernardo**. It was formerly called the Borgo Felice di S. Bernardo after Pope Sixtus V (Felice Peretti di Montalto). The name recalls his plans to turn the previously unpopulated area into a commercial centre in his planned reorientation of the city's spiritual focus to the Basilica of S. Maria Maggiore (Tour 12). His Villa Peretti was nearby in Piazza dei Cinquecento (Tour 12).

The **Moses Fountain** (Fontana dell'Acqua Felice) started as a private venture by citizens of the area, but the project was appropriated by Pope Sixtus V who commissioned Domenico Fontana to design it (1587) as the terminal point of the Acqua Felice aqueduct (1585) named after him. The popular name of the fountain refers to the statue of Moses in the centre of the Roman triumphal arch design that advertises the triumph of Christianity over paganism. The figure of Moses was sculpted by Prospero Bresciano with Leonardo Sormani (1588). Legend claims that the artist committed suicide after the statue was mocked as grotesque at the unveiling ceremony. The bas-relief panels depict *Aaron guiding the Israelites* by Giovanni Battista della Porta (left side) and *Joshua leading the Israelites across the Jordan River* by Flaminio Vacca (right side). The lions are copies of the original ancient Egyptian lions moved to the Egyptian Museum of the Vatican Museums by Pope Gregory XVI.

Walk across Via Barberini to **S. Maria della Vittoria**, a must-see Baroque gem with an interior designed by Carlo Maderno. The facade was designed by Giovanni Battista Soria (1626) and inspired by Maderno's facade of S. Susanna. The church was formerly named S. Paolo for the Carmelites but was rebuilt (from 1608 to 1620) for Cardinal Scipione Borghese and renamed S. Maria della Vittoria following the victory of the Catholic army over the Protestants at the Battle of White Mountain near Prague during the Thirty Years War on 8 November 1620. The nave ceiling *The triumph of the Madonna over heresy* and *Fall of the rebel angels* are by Giovanni Domenico Cerrini (1675) who also painted the cupola *Ascension in Glory*.

The **Cornaro Chapel** (north transept) displays Bernini's masterpiece *Ecstasy of St Teresa* (1647–1652) composition for Cardinal Federigo Cornaro of Venice. The spectators who witness the Angel's sensual piercing of Saint Teresa of Avila's heart with an arrow are portraits by Bernini's students of Cardinal Cornaro and his family comprising cardinals and Doge Giovanni, the father of Cardinal Federigo Cornaro, who is the last figure of the left-side group whose portrait appears to be based on Bernini's. The focus is on the ecstasy but the theatricality of the composition extends to the spectators in their theatre boxes who are viewed as part of the unfolding drama. The chapel is filled with natural light from a hidden window.

Opposite in the south transept is Pierre-Étienne Monnot's *Nativity* and *Flight into Egypt* to either side of Domenico Guidi's *Dream of St Joseph* with a simulacrum and relics of St Victoria beneath. On the south side (second chapel) is Domenichino's *Madonna and St Francis* in the centre with his *Stigmatisation of St Francis* and *St Francis in Ecstasy* on the side walls (1630). In the third chapel on the north side is the *Holy Trinity* by Guercino (*c.*1642).

Recross Via Barberini to visit the church of **S. Susanna**, the American Catholic church in Rome that was founded by the Cistercian Order on the site where the martyr Susanna was beheaded (*c.*295). It has been used for Christian worship since the 4th century on an earlier site. The facade by Carlo Maderno (1603) for Cardinal Girolamo Rusticucci is among his most successful designs. The interior, remodelled in the 8th and 15th centuries, was again remodelled in the 16th century with decoration by Baldassarre Croce, Cesare Nebbia and Paris Nogari. Over the high altar the *Death of St Susanna* is by Tommaso Laureti. The crypt provides access to the ruins of a 2nd-century CE building and other structures connected to the apse. Inquire at the sacristy.

Across the largo from S. Susanna is the round-shaped church of **S. Bernardo alle Terme** dedicated to St Bernard of Clairvaux and founded by the Cistercian Order. The church was built by Caterina de' Nobili Sforza di Santa Fiora, the niece of Pope Julius III, into one of two pavilions from the Baths of Diocletian that gives it its distinctive round shape (1598). The other pavilion flanked the other side of the exedra terrace of the baths (Piazza della Repubblica) near Palazzo Massimo alle Terme (Tour 12). The round interior preserves the original ancient octagonal-shaped coffered ceiling that is similar to the ceiling of the Pantheon. Plaster statues of saints by Camillo Mariani (*c.*1600–1605) occupy eight encircling niches.

To continue on the tour, walk down Via XX Settembre in the direction of Piazza del Quirinale. In the area just beyond S. Susanna was the **Temple of the Gens Flavia** (Templum Gentis Flaviae) that was a funerary monument to the Flavian dynasty built by Domitian at the site of his uncle Flavius Sabinus's house in which he was born. Midway to Piazza del Quirinale, passing the church of **St Andrew's Church of Scotland** to your right and various ministry buildings, is the busy intersection at Via delle Quattro Fontane (**Piazza delle Quattro Fontane**) where the tour resumes following the description of optional tours to Porta Pia and beyond.

To take the optional stroll to Porta Pia (a 1.32km round trip by foot from Largo S. Susanna) and points beyond by bus before continuing on the tour, from S. Bernardo alle Terme retrace your steps past S. Maria della Vittoria in the direction of Porta Pia. The area beyond Largo S. Susanna is dominated by the massive Ministry of Finance building.

Turn left on Via Servio Tullio to **Piazza Sallustio**. The surviving ancient structures from the **Gardens of Sallust** (Horti Sallustiani) and the modern Villa Ludovisi are now in a pentagon-shaped piazza well below current ground level. The gardens of the suburban villa were owned by Julius Caesar but after his assassination they were bought by the historian Sallust (Gaius Sallustius Crispus), after whom they were named. The villa was later acquired by Tiberius and so entered Imperial possession. The gardens were lavishly decorated with statuary including the *Dying Gaul* in the Capitoline Museums (Tour 5) and the *Suicidal Gaul* in Palazzo Altemps (Tour 8) that were discovered in the grounds of the Villa Ludovisi. Also discovered here was the obelisk now in Piazza della Trinità dei Monti. The surviving structures include a pavilion with a circular hall and summer banquet room that date to the reign of Hadrian, with some later additions by the Emperor Aurelian. The relocation of soil for the construction of the Ministry of Finance building on Via XX Settembre raised the ground level in the area but the pavilion once had commanding views at the point where the Pincian and Quirinal Hills meet. The villa was heavily damaged by Alaric and the Visigoths who entered the city by the Porta Salaria on 24 August 410 CE.

Retrace your steps to Via XX Settembre and continue towards Porta Pia. At Via Piave, where the Porta Collina stood in the Republican Walls, Piazza Fiume is visible to your left where the Roman funerary **Monument to Q. Sulpicius Maximus** (died at the age of 11) was uncovered when the Porta Salaria was demolished in 1871. It was replaced with a copy of the original that is now in the Capitoline Museums. Beyond on Via Salaria is the **Villa Albani-Torlonia** built by architect Carlo Marchionni for Cardinal Alessandro Albani (1774–1767) with a collection of ancient sculpture from Palazzo Torlonia alla Lungara (Tour 3), viewed by appointment only. Opposite the villa is the tumulus **Tomb of M. Lucilius Paetus** and his sister **Lucilia Polla** that is contemporaneous with the Mausoleum of Augustus (Tour 9).

Just before Porta Pia, the **British Embassy** is to your right, whose modern design of a building on pillars above a pool was designed by Sir Basil Spence (inaugurated in 1968) as a replacement for the original building that was damaged by terrorists in 1946. Opposite is the **Villa Paolina Bonaparte** in which Napoleon's sister Pauline lived from 1816 to 1824. It is currently the French Embassy to the Holy See. The ancient Tomb of the Licinii and Calpurnii was discovered (1884–1885) on property once part of the villa near the Porta Salaria.

The **Porta Pia** is the last architectural work designed by Michelangelo (1561–1564) for Pope Pius IV de' Medici and served as an entry point into the city on Strada Pia. It was named for the pope who also commissioned Porta del Popolo (Tour 9) whose design shares similarities. The facade decoration is by Virginio Vespignani (1868) for Pope Pius IX, whose crest was added to complement the crest of Pope Pius IV de' Medici that is flanked with *Angels* by Nardo de' Rossi (1564). The **Museo Storico dei Bersaglieri** commemorates the troops (Bersaglieri) that breached the Aurelianic Walls on 20 September 1870 (hence the XX Settembre of the street's name) under General Raffaele Cadorna. On the other side of the gate is the **Monument to the Bersaglieri** at the start of Via Nomentana, the ancient consular road that was once lined with tombs, including the tomb of the Roman historian Tacitus. To your left the portion of the wall that was breached is now commemorated with a **column** on Corso d'Italia that was opened in 1885.

From the Via Nomentana side of Porta Pia, there are several optional itineraries by bus: Villa Torlonia and churches associated with Constantine on Via Nomentana (Sant'Agnese fuori le Mura and S. Costanza, about 2km beyond Porta Pia), the Praetorian Camp then further afield to Via Tiburtina to the early Christian Basilica of S. Lorenzo fuori le Mura and Campo Verano Cemetery.

For sites on Via Nomentana, walk to the bus stop just ahead to your right on Via Nomentana and take either the No. 36 or the No. 84. The **Villa Torlonia**, a landscaped villa and museum with Neoclassical architecture and garden decoration that is now a public park owned by the Comune di Roma, is just a few bus stops away opposite **Quartiere Coppedè** with Art Nouveau architecture. Exit at the stop in front of the villa that is to your right. The villa was begun by Giuseppe Valadier in 1802 for Giovanni Torlonia and completed for his son Alessandro Torlonia by Giovanni Battista Caretti (1832–1842). Caretti also designed the **Casino Nobile** (also called Palazzo Nobiliare) that is now a museum. The **Jewish Catacombs** from the 3rd to 4th century CE were excavated in the grounds in 1918 but are not open to the public. Mussolini resided at the villa from 1925 to 1943 that was then occupied by the Allied High Command from 1944 until 1947.

If visiting Sant'Agnese fuori le Mura and S. Costanza, remain on the bus beyond Villa Torlonia and look for the bus stop at Via di Sant'Agnese with the 19th-century **Acqua Marcia Fountain** to your right (just beyond Via di S. Costanza). Exit the bus and cross to the other side of Via Nomentana to the main entrance to Sant'Agnese that leads to a cortile with the basilica to your right and S. Costanza to your left. Exiting by the rear entrance of the basilica takes you into a garden with a grotto and ex-voto plaques. If the main doors to Sant'Agnese are closed, walk to Via di Sant'Agnese and down the hill to the side entrance that contains a monumental marble staircase (1590) with funerary inscriptions and sculpture fragments that come from the catacombs below the church. Santa Costanza is straight ahead at the end of the lane.

**Sant'Agnese fuori le Mura** (The Basilica of St Agnes Outside the Walls) was founded by Constantia (S. Costanza/St Constance), the daughter of Constantine, in 342 CE at the catacomb site of St Agnes' tomb where, according to legend, Constantia prayed to the saint to cure her of leprosy. Spoliated columns divide the interior with a women's gallery (matronea) above the aisles and west end. The 19th-century triumphal arch fresco *Martyrdom of St Agnes* is by Pietro Gagliardi. On the ceiling of the apse the 7th-century mosaic of *St Agnes with Pope Honorius I who holds a model of the church and Pope Symmachus* dates to the reign of Pope Honorius I (625–638) who built the current basilica over the Tomb of St Agnes next to the original cemetery basilica founded by Constantia. The marble paneling with porphyry detail along the walls of the apse is also from the 7th century, but the cathedra (throne) and the marble candelabrum are earlier (2nd century CE). The statue of St Agnes on the altar is by Nicolas Cordier (1605) who added marble and bronze elements to an ancient alabaster torso. The relics of St Agnes are beneath the ciborium with those of S. Emerenziana, her foster-sister, but her skull is in the church of Sant'Agnese in Agone in Piazza Navona (Tour 8), the site of her martyrdom. The entry to the **Catacombs** (discovered in 1865–1866) is by the north side. They cover an area of 6km and were active from the 3rd to 4th centuries.

The church of **S. Costanza** was founded in 1254 in the round mausoleum of Constantia (built between 337 and 357 CE). Constantia lived in the area between 337 and 351. The entrance porch of the tomb was originally attached to the outer wall of the cemetery basilica that she founded. Ruins from the basilica are visible in the field to the right of the entrance. The beautiful interior contains 12 pairs of granite columns that support arcades. The monumental sarcophagus in the niche opposite the entrance is a copy of the porphyry original that is now in the Vatican Museums. In the ambulatory are beautiful 4th-century mosaics on the vault that include panels that repeat the theme of the grape harvest on the sarcophagus. The mosaics that once decorated the dome do not survive but they depicted a Paradise scene. Square and semicircular niches alternate along the wall with 5th- or 7th-century mosaics of Christ with St Peter and St Paul in the large semicircular niches at the sides.

Retrace your steps to Via Nomentana. The bus stop for either the No. 36 or No. 84 to return to Porta Pia is at the corner of Via di S.

Agnese in the traffic island. From Porta Pia, retrace your steps to Largo S. Susanna and continue in the direction of Piazza del Quirinale to Via delle Quattro Fontane.

If visiting S. Lorenzo fuori le Mura and the Campo Verano Cemetery, begin with the Roman **Praetorian Camp** (Castro Pretorio). From Porta Pia (facing Via Nomentana), take Viale del Policlinico to your right and walk along a stretch of the **Aurelianic Walls** with the remnants of a circular tower of the **Porta Nomentana** next to the bus stop to your right just beyond the two square towers. The walls were built by Aurelian (271–275) and encircle the city (*c.*19km) to see the walls of the Praetorian Camp that was built by the Emperor Tiberius (21–23 CE) and restored by Maxentius who also raised the height of the Aurelianic Walls (*c.*306 CE).

To visit S. Lorenzo fuori le Mura and the Campo Verano Cemetery, return to the bus stop just to the right of Porta Pia (when facing Via Nomentana) on Viale del Policlinico and take either bus No. 490 or No. 495. Exit the bus at the Valerio Massimo stop on Via Tiburtina, the ancient consular road to Tivoli (ancient Tibur). Walk in the opposite direction to that of the bus along the walls of the **Campo Verano Cemetery** (to your left) into Piazzale del Verano with a column erected by Pope Pius IX in front of the Basilica of S. Lorenzo fuori le Mura (also called the Basilica di S. Lorenzo al Verano).

**San Lorenzo fuori le Mura** (St Lawrence Outside the Walls) commemorates the location of St Lawrence's martyrdom in the persecutions of the Emperor Valerian (258 CE) and his burial in the ancient necropolis (Catacomb of Cyriaca) at the location of the current Campo Verano cemetery. Like other early cemetery basilicas founded by Constantine the Great and his daughter, it is on an Imperial estate property outside of the city walls at the site of a martyr saint's burial.

The site is comprised of a complex once known as Laurentiopolis with several structures spanning the 4th to the 13th centuries. The original cemetery basilica founded by Constantine was circus-shaped and was followed by two later basilicas. The first was built over the Tomb of St Lawrence by Pope Pelagius II (579 CE) adjacent to the original Constantinian basilica with its apse also on the west end. Pope Honorius III (1216) added a second basilica to the apse end (west) of the 6th-century basilica (the area in front of baldacchino) to form one long basilica with a new entrance at the opposite end that is still the main entrance facing Piazzale del Verano. The basilica was renovated by Virginio Vespignani (1864–1870) for Pope Pius IX who is buried here. Much of the 19th-century additions were removed and the church was restored to its 13th-century appearance during reconstruction work after a stray Allied bomb in a raid (19 July 1943) had killed 2,000–3,000 civilians and accidentally damaged the facade wall that required restoration of the frescoes in the portico that depict the *Lives of St Lawrence and St Stephen*. The portico with spoliated columns includes a cosmatesque frieze that is likely by the Vassalletto family (*c.*1220). Inside are three Roman sarcophagi including the sarcophagus of Pope Damasus III with grape vine decoration.

The interior is comprised of 22 spoliated ancient Ionic columns and 13th-century cosmatesque pavement. The funerary monument of Cardinal Guglielmo Fieschi (d. 1256), with a 3rd-century pagan sarcophagus that depicts a marriage scene, is on the west wall. It was reconstructed after the damage sustained by the facade wall. Each ambo in the nave is cosmatesque (13th century) as is the Paschal candelabrum attached to the one on the south side of the nave. From the Chapel of S. Tarcisius there is access to the sacristy that contains historic photographs of the damage caused by the bomb and the cloister and entrance to the **Catacomb of Cyriaca**. At the end of the north side is the entrance to the Chapel of St Cyriaca.

Stairs ascend to the area (chancel) around the sanctuary with 13th-century cosmatesque pavement and cathedra (throne) and two long marble benches with lion statues. The baldacchino with four ancient porphyry columns is signed by Giovanni, Pietro, Angelo and Sasso, the sons of Paolo (1148). Beneath it are the relics of St Lawrence and those of two of his companions. From this raised height, the mosaic on the side of the triumphal arch that originally faced the 6th-century church nave is visible, with Christ seated on a globe with saints including Pope Pelagius II holding a model of the 6th-century church that he founded. Bethlehem and Jerusalem are represented beneath the windows. The two 4th-century capitals of the columns closest to the triumphal arch have trophy decoration including winged victories. The columns with composite capitals support an arcade on beautiful spoliated entablatures (4th century) on which are smaller columns and windows in the area formerly occupied by the women's gallery (matronea). In the former narthex of the 6th-century church is the mausoleum Tomb of Pope

Pius IX by Raffaele Cattaneo (1882–1895). The marble slab on which St Lawrence was placed following his martydom is displayed here but the gridiron on which he was tortured is displayed in S. Lorenzo in Panisperna.

The **Campo Verano Cemetery** (Cimitero Monumentale del Verano) adjacent to the basilica is operated by the Comune di Roma. The municipal cemetery for Catholic and Jewish burials with a monument to the victims in World War I was originally designed by Giuseppe Valadier (1807–1812) during the French occupation of Rome following Napoleon's Edict of St Cloud (1804, that was applied to Italy in 1806) that forbade intramural burials. The name Verano derives from the Emperor Lucius Verus whose estate occupied the site. The monumental entrance gate with 19th-century allegorical statues and the tomb-lined avenue that leads to the area of the Quadriporticus (1880) was designed by Virginio Vespignani for Pope Pius IX. The Jewish cemetery that was formerly in the Roseto Comunale on the Aventine Hill facing the Circus Maximus (Tour 4) was relocated here. The cemetery is an open-air museum of Neoclassical, Victorian and 20th-century funerary monuments and mausolea.

To return to Porta Pia, walk to the other side of the piazzale to Via Cesare de Lollis to the No. 492 bus stop (just ahead to your right). Exit at the stop on Via Palestro next to the British Embassy on Via XX Settembre to return to Porta Pia or stay on the bus for one more stop to exit on Via XX Settembre in front of the Ministry of Finance building for a short walk back to Largo S. Susanna. Continue walking down Via XX Settembre in the direction of Piazza del Quirinale to Via delle Quattro Fontane.

The name **Piazza delle Quattro Fontane** (Piazza of the Four Fountains) is misleading since this is the busy intersection of Via XX Settembre and Via delle Quattro Fontane with four fountains (1588–1593) that frame the intersection: two male figures – *Tiber River with the She-Wolf* and the *Arno* or the *Aniene* (ancient Anio) river (attached to Palazzo Albani del Drago whose design was begun by Domenico Fontana) – and two female figures – *Strength* or *Juno* and *Fidelity* or *Diana*, reclining next to her dog. Like Bernini's Fontana dei Quattro Fiumi in Piazza Navona (Tour 8), the four fountain allegories may allude to the nymphs/rivers from the four parts of the world. From here are views of three obelisks in Piazza del Quirinale (ahead), Piazza

dell'Esquilino (Tour 12) to your left, and Piazza della Trinità dei Monti
(Tour 10) to your right. In ancient Rome, this was the highest point
of the Quirinal Hill that was a sheer cliff, but in-fill over the centuries
raised the street level in the direction of S. Maria Maggiore. The Porta
Quirinalis in the Republican Walls was nearby.

At the intersection, turn right on Via delle Quattro Fontane.
**Palazzo Barberini** is just to your right behind the 18th-century
monumental gate with iron grille and Atlas figures (by Francesco
Azzurri). The palazzo is now the **Galleria Nazionale d'Arte Antica**
whose collection is also displayed in Palazzo Corsini in Trastevere
(Tour 3). The area was once the site of the ancient **Temple of
Quirinus** that commemorated the defied Romulus. A **Mithraeum**
was discovered in the area of the garden under the Villa Savorgnan di
Brazzà opposite the ramp. In the 16th century, the property was the
villa of Cardinal Rodolfo Pio da Carpi, with a garden famous for its
ancient sculpture collection. The villa then passed to the Sforza family
until Cardinal Alessandro Sforza sold it to Pope Urban VIII Barberini
in 1625. He commissioned Carlo Maderno (1625) to modify the
earlier Palazzo Sforza into a Roman villa. After his death, the work
was continued by Bernini (on the central block), Borromini (windows
on the first floor, staircases, and decorative architectural details) and
Pietro da Cortona. From the entrance door to the **Istituto Italiano
di Numismatica** is a view of **Borromini's Staircase** that is heliocoidal
with pairs of columns.

Rooms 1–9 on the **ground floor** of the **Galleria Nazionale d'Arte
Antica** are devoted to icons, early Italian altarpieces and art from the
early Renaissance arranged by regions in Italy and northern Europe,
including paintings by Fra' Filippo Lippi, Perugino and Antoniazzo
Romano. The staircase designed by Bernini leads to the **first floor** with
his portrait busts of *Pope Urban VIII* (1632) and *Cardinal Antonio
Barberini* (1632) at the top of the stairs. Sixteenth- and seventeenth-
century art is displayed in 24 rooms including paintings by Piero di
Cosimo, Andrea del Sarto, Raphael (*La Fornarina*), Giulio Romano,
Baldassarre Peruzzi and Sodoma (Rooms 10–13). Rooms 14–17
include Titian's *Venus and Adonis*, Hans Holbein's *Portrait of Henry VIII*
(1540), Quentin Massys' *Erasmus of Rotterdam* and Bronzino's *Portrait
of Stefano IV Colonna* (1546). The Chapel of Pietro da Cortona with
his *Crucifixion* was inaugurated on 18 September 1632 for the baptism

of a child of Taddeo Barberini, the nephew of Pope Urban VIII and Anna Colonna. The ceiling in Room 17 is from the original Sforza part of the palazzo with a fresco by Pomarancio (Cristoforo Roncalli) and Baldassarre Croce.

Rooms 18–24 include paintings by El Greco, Pietro da Cortona (*View of the Villa Sacchetti at Castelfusano*) (Room 19), Guercino (*Et Ego in Arcadia*, 1618–1622), Nicolas Poussin, Paul Bril, Caravaggio (*Narcissus*, 1597–1598, *Judith and Holofernes*, 1598–1599, and *St Francis in Meditation*), Guido Reni (*Portrait of Beatrice Cenci*), Guercino (*Flagellation of Christ, St Matthew and the Angel, St Luke, St Jerome*) and Annibale Carracci.

From the **Oval Room** designed by Bernini with ancient statues in the niches there is access to the **Salone Pietro da Cortona**, named for the artist's masterpiece ceiling fresco *Triumph of Divine Providence* (1633–1639). The fresco depicts Divine Providence crowning the Barberini family crest of three bees with a laurel wreath, the symbol of Apollo, as a Christian allegory for Pope Urban VIII's victory of moderation over excessive vice represented by the Dionysiac pagan scenes of lust and consuming ambition represented by the Rebel Giants who fall from the sky. Off the salone is the **Hall of Marbles** with ancient sculpture with later pieces.

On the **second floor**, 17th/18th-century art displayed in Rooms 25–34 includes paintngs by Jusepe de Ribera, Pietro da Cortona, Giovanni Lanfranco, Baciccia (*Portrait of Gian Lorenzo Bernini, c.*1666), Angelica Kauffmann, Pompeo Batoni, Antonio Canaletto and Giovanni Battista Tiepolo. The **Sala Corvi** reception room was painted by Domenico Corvi and Nicolò Ricciolini with architectural elements and statues of historic and legendary figures for Cornelia Costanza Barberini who also decorated the **Apartment** rooms in the Rococo style (1750–1770) in which members of Barberini family lived until 1960.

Retrace your steps back to the intersection of the Quattro Fontane to **S. Carlo alle Quattro Fontane** that is also called S. Carlino ('Little S. Carlo') to distinguish it from S. Carlo ai Catinari (Tour 7). Francesco Borromini was commissioned to build the church and convent by the Spanish Trinitarian Order in 1638 in honour of Cardinal Carlo Borromeo (canonised in 1620). This was his first major commission. The small size of the church is famously described as being able to fit into one of the piers of St Peter's dome. The bold facade (much later in date than the interior) is emblematic of Borromini's architectural style of blending concave and convex lines and using angels as architectural elements. The statue of S. Carlo Borromeo above the entrance is by Antonio Raggi. The interior is designed around the shape of an oval that is repeated in the shape of the cupola and stucco decoration that also include the shape of the Trinitarian cross. The **crypt** repeats the complex interplay of shapes of the upper church. The octagonal shape of the adjacent convent **cloister**, also by Borromini (1635–1636), complements the shape of the church and is equally creative in the use of convex and concave shapes.

Continue walking in the direction of Piazza del Quirinale. The street changes name from Via XX Settembre to Via del Quirinale beyond Via delle Quattro Fontane. To your right is the immense Palazzo del Quirinale whose entry is in Piazza del Quirinale. At No. 27 to your left is the **Giardino di San Andrea al Quirinale** that was designed in 1888 and is now a public park owned by the Comune di Roma.

**Sant'Andrea al Quirinale** is ahead to your left. The church was commissioned by Pope Alexander VII Chigi for the Jesuit Order and designed by Bernini but completed by his assistants including Mattia de' Rossi (between 1658 and 1670). It replaced an earlier church on the site called Sant'Andrea a Montecavallo. The facade is a semicircular aedicule with alternating concave and convex elements to create a half-elliptical forecourt that anticipates the elliptical shape inside. The chapels (first chapel on south side by Baciccia and second chapel on north side by Carlo Maratta) are on radial lines that focus attention on the altar. The three various manifestations of St Andrew on the altar, architrave and cupola create a sense of theatricality: the crucified St Andrew on the high altarpiece (by Borgognone) looks up at the stucco version of himself depicted in his former life as a fisherman (by Antonio Raggi) who in turn looks up to the Holy Spirit who brings his soul to Heaven enveloped by cherubims (by Antonio Raggi). The figures along the architrave are also by Antonio Raggi. In the sacristy (entry by permission only) is a fresco ceiling designed by Bernini and a lavabo perhaps also by him. The adjacent convent contains the rooms of St Stanislaus Kostka in which he died (1568) with a statue of the saint by Pierre Legros.

Continue on Via del Quirinale in the direction of Piazza del Quirinale. To your left is the **Giardino del Quirinale**, a public park built for the 1888 visit of the German Emperor Wilhelm II on the former site of the churches of S. Chiara and S. Maria Maddalena that were demolished for its construction. In the centre is a monumental **Equestrian Statue of King Carlo Alberto Amadeo** (1798–1849), the King of Piedmont-Sardinia (1831–1849) and father of King Vittorio Emanuele II, by Raffaele Romanelli (1900). The garden was originally named the Giardino Carlo Alberto.

At the end of **Piazza del Quirinale** is the **Fontana di Monte Cavallo** with 5th-century statues of Castor and Pollux (known collectively as the Dioscuri) and their horses that are copies of Greek originals (the names of the Greek sculptors Phidias and Praxiteles are on the bases). The statues were found in the area of the nearby **Baths of Constantine** and erected here by Domenico Fontana for Pope Sixtus V in 1589. The horses are the source of the name Monte Cavallo of the piazza. The obelisk in the centre is one of two that originally flanked the entrance to Augustus' Mausoleum (the other one is behind S. Maria Maggiore) and was erected here in 1786 by Pope Pius VI. The basin that was formerly used as a cattle trough in the Campo Vaccino was added by Pope Pius VII (1818).

The Dioscuri statues originally faced **Palazzo della Consulta** on Via XX Settembre whose facade was designed by Ferdinando Fuga (1732–1734). Over the main entrance are the allegorical figures of *Justice* and *Religion* and the crest of Pope Clement XII Corsini for whose nephew Fuga rebuilt Palazzo Corsini in Trastevere (Tour 3). The trophy decoration over the secondary entrance is by Filippo delle Valle (1735). Formerly the Tribune Court of the Papal States, it is now the location of the Italian Constitutional Court.

To the right of Palazzo della Consulta on Via XXIV Maggio is **Palazzo Pallavicini-Rospigliosi** that was originally built for Cardinal Scipione Borghese, the nephew of Pope Paul V Borghese, by Flaminio Ponzio (1605) and completed by Giovanni Vasanzio and Carlo Maderno (1616) on the site of the Baths of Constantine. The palazzo passed to Cardinal Jules Mazarin (born Julio Mazzarino, who succeeded Cardinal Richelieu at the French Court) and ultimately to the Pallavicini-Rospigliosi (1704). In the **Casino dell'Aurora Pallavicini** is the beautiful ceiling fresco of *Aurora Scattering Flowers before the Chariot of the Sun* by Guido Reni (1613–1614). Admission to the **Galleria Pallavicini**, that includes works by Rubens, Guercino and Annibale Carracci, is by special permission.

Opposite Palazzo del Quirinale are the **Scuderie del Quirinale** that were formerly the papal stables (Scuderie Pontificie), built from 1721 to 1730 by Alessandro Specchi and Ferdinando Fuga. The stables were subsequently converted into special exhibition space. In the area behind the scuderie is the **Villa Colonna** (1618) that is connected to Palazzo Colonna (Tour 7). The colossal **Serapeum** (Temple of Serapis), built in the 2nd/3rd century CE with phases of construction variously attributed to Hadrian, Septimius Severus and Caracalla, was located here. The ruins are visible from the scuderie. From the overlook at the open side of the piazza is a view of the dome of St Peter's Basilica.

**Palazzo del Quirinale** was originally the site of Cardinal Oliviero Carafa's villa that passed to Cardinal Ippolito d'Este who added formal gardens and fountains as he did for the Villa d'Este in Tivoli. The villa was converted into a papal summer palace by Ottaviano Mascherino for Pope Gregory XIII Boncompagni in 1574. Other architects continued work for subsequent popes. Domenico Fontana designed the main facade for Pope Sixtus V (1589). For Pope Paul V Borghese, Flaminio Ponzio designed a wing of the garden courtyard, the **Scalone d'Onore** (Staircase of Honour), where Melozzo da Forlì's *Christ in Glory with Angels* (1480), originally painted for the apse of Ss. Apostoli (Tour 7), is displayed, but the Angels from the fresco are now in the Pinacoteca Vaticana (Tour 2). Ponzio also designed the **Salone delle Feste** and the **Cappella dell'Annunziata** that was completed by Carlo Maderno (1610) and painted by Guido Reni (1609–1612), Lanfranco, Francesco Albani and Antonio Carracci. Carlo Maderno also designed the **Cappella Paolina** (1617), the Sala Regia, now called the **Salone dei Corazzieri**, and the main entrance (1615), but Bernini designed the **Loggia of the Benediction** (1638), the circular tower (1626) and the **Manica Lunga** (long wing) on Via del Quirinale for Pope Urban VIII Barberini with later additions by Ferdinando Fuga for Pope Clement XII Corsini (1730–1740). Pietro da Cortona painted frescoes in the **Sala del Balcone** for Pope Alexander VII Chigi. Pope Pius IX was the last pope to live in the palazzo. Following the defeat of his forces in 1870, it became the residence of King Vittorio Emanuele II, who died here on 9 January 1878, and of subsequent kings of Italy. Since 1948 it has been the residence of the President of the Italian Republic.

To continue to Tour 12 from Piazza del Quirinale, walk across Via del Quirinale to the start of Via della Consulta (to the left of Palazzo della

12. The *Aurora* by Guercino in the Casino dell'Aurora, Villa Aurora

Consulta when facing it) and walk one block to Via Nazionale. From Via della Consulta, the **Teatro Eliseo** (first built in 1901 as an arena but rebuilt as a theatre from 1906 to 1910 and again from 1936 to 1938) is to your right and across the street is the Neo-Renaissance **Palazzo della Banca d'Italia** by Gaetano Koch (1887–1902). Turn left on Via Nazionale to begin Tour 12. To explore the area around Piazza Venezia (Tour 7) instead, turn right on Via Nazionale and continue beyond Largo Magnanapoli to the staircase by the Markets of Trajan (Tour 6) that descend to the area of the Forum of Trajan and Piazza Venezia.

Sites: Via Nazionale; Palazzo delle Esposizione; S. Vitale; S. Paolo entro le Mura; Piazza della Repubblica; Baths of Diocletian; S. Maria degli Angeli e dei Martiri; Museo Nazionale Romano delle Terme di Diocleziano; Piazza dei Cinquecento; Stazione Termini; Palazzo Massimo alle Terme (Museo Nazionale Romano); Teatro dell'Opera; Piazza del Viminale; S. Pudenziana; Piazza dell'Esquilino; S. Maria Maggiore; S. Prassede; Arch of Gallienus; S. Martino ai Monti; S. Pietro in Vincoli.

Distance: 3.0km.

# Tour 12

# STAZIONE TERMINI AREA
# AND THE ESQUILINE HILL

The tour of the vast Rione Monti starts on Via Nazionale with sites associated with Italian unification and Renaissance Rome. In the area of the Baths of Diocletian are the church of S. Maria degli Angeli e dei Martiri designed by Michelangelo and important collections of ancient art in the Terme museums. The tour continues to quiet areas of the Viminal and Esquiline Hills. Explore beautiful late Roman and Byzantine mosaics in the Basilica of S. Maria Maggiore, important to Pope Sixtus V and Pope Paul V Borghese, and the churches of S. Pudenziana and S. Prassede. The tour ends with Michelangelo's statue of Moses in S. Pietro in Vincoli.

**Via Nazionale** was the first road constructed in the modern city and follows the ancient Vicus Longus that connected the Baths of Diocletian to the Forum of Augustus (Tour 6). It was built in a series of construction phases beginning with the start of the street at Piazza della Repubblica (1864–1866) that was intended to connect to Piazza Venezia but it was only extended to Largo Magnanapoli (1875–1876), destroying the ruins of the Baths of Constantine.

**Palazzo delle Esposizione** was designed by Pio Piacentini (1880–1883) with a monumental entrance that evokes an ancient Roman triumphal arch. Above a dedicatory inscription to King Umberto I, *Art* stands between *Peace* and *Study*. On the reliefs, Pope Julius II della Rovere and Michelangelo display the *Laocoön* sculpture (left) and the celebration of early Renaissance artist Cimabue's painting *Virgin and Christ Child* (right). Across the facade are 12 statues commemorating famous artists.

Just beyond, a flight of stairs leads to the church of **S. Vitale**, below the current street level, also known as the Basilica of Ss. Vitale, Valeria, Gervasio e Protasio, the wife and sons of St Vitalis who were also martyred in Ravenna by being buried alive in a pit (which gives an alternate name for the church of S. Vitale e Compagni Martiri in Fovea). It was built in 400 on the site of a titular church (*titulus Vestinae*) and consecrated by Pope Innocent I. The medieval exterior with a 5th-century portico of spoliated columns was restored in 1937–1938. The interior was altered by Pope Sixtus IV delle Rovere (1475) and later given to the Jesuits with Sant'Andrea al Quirinale (Tour 11), located behind the church, by Pope Clement VIII (1595). Isabella della Rovere, a patron of the Jesuits, paid for church renovations. The *Capitoline Venus*, now in the Capitoline Museums (Tour 5), was found in the area of the church.

Continue your stroll towards Piazza della Repubblica. As you cross Via delle Quattro Fontane and Via A. Depretis, look left for the obelisk in Piazza della Trinità dei Monti and right for the obelisk behind S. Maria Maggiore in Piazza dell'Esquilino. Cross to the other side of Via Nazionale and continue walking towards Piazza della Repubblica.

At the corner of Via Napoli is the church of **S. Paolo entro le Mura** (St Paul's Within the Walls), the American Episcopal church in Rome, designed in the Romanesque style by George Edmund Street (1872–1876). The opening of a Protestant church on Via Nazionale is emblematic of the changes in the new Italian constitution that included freedom of religion. The 'Arts and Crafts' interior contains mosaics by the Pre-Raphaelite artist Edward Burne-Jones with portraits in the choir including those of J. P. Morgan who contributed to the construction of the church, General Grant who was then president of the USA, Garibaldi and Abraham Lincoln. The maiolica tiles on the walls of the nave were designed by William Morris and the mosaics on the west wall by George Breck (1909).

Continue up Via Nazionale into **Piazza della Repubblica** on the summit of the Viminal Hill. Follow the right side of the curve to walk across Via delle Terme di Diocleziano to Viale Einaudi and the area in front of S. Maria degli Angeli e dei Martiri. The piazza commemorates Italian unification against the backdrop of the Baths of Diocletian. It was formerly called Piazza delle Terme and later Piazza dell'Esedra after the semicircular exedra terrace of the Baths of Diocletian. Sixtus

V demolished surviving parts of the baths that obstructed the view of the church and wanted to erect the Piazza Sallustio obelisk here that was eventually erected in Piazza della Trinità dei Monti (Tour 10). In planning the location of the King Vittorio Emanuele II monument, several designs that were submitted in the 1882 contest proposed demolishing the Baths of Diocletian.

The piazza is flanked by two palazzi with porticoes that were designed by Gaetano Koch (1887–1898). In the centre is the **Fontana delle Naiadi** (Fountain of the Naiads) by Mario Rutelli (1901) at the terminal point of the Aqua Marcia aqueduct. It replaced the Acqua Pia Fountain that was nearby and inaugurated by Pope Pius IX only a short time before the forces of the Papal States were defeated at the Porta Pia (Tour 11). The frolicking female figures represent nymphs of water sources with their animal attributes: lakes (swan), rivers (water snake), oceans (horse) and streams (lizard). When the fountain was unveiled, public reaction to the nymphs was mixed but supporters were successful in blocking efforts to remove it. The Glaucus group in the centre (1911–1912) replaced an earlier model made by Rutelli (moved to Piazza Vittorio Emanuele II) with three human figures and a dolphin tangled together that critics called *fritti* (fried fish).

The **Baths of Diocletian** (Thermae Diocletiani), Terme di Diocleziano in Italian, were dedicated between 1 May 305 CE and 25 July 306 CE. It was designed on the model of the Baths of Trajan (Tour 6) and the Baths of Caracalla (Tour 13). The rectangular bath complex area (244m x 144m) was within an enclosed area with gardens, shrines, alcoves, fountains and pavilions along the perimeter including the exedra that had panoramic views of Rome over the valley now occupied by Via Nazionale. Within the bath complex area were the various baths that progressed in sequence from the entrance that faced the modern Via Volturno: an outdoor cool water pool (*natatio*); an indoor cool water pool (*frigidarium*); a warm water pool (*tepidarium*) and a hot water pool (*caldarium*) with several side rooms flanking the pools for undressing, plunge baths and other purposes. To either side of the pools were two courtyards for outdoor physical activities (*palaestrae*).

**Santa Maria degli Angeli e dei Martiri** was designed by Michelangelo for Pope Pius IV de' Medici (1561) into the ruins of the Baths of Diocletian with an entrance facing Strada Pia built by the same pope, though his design was extensively reworked by Luigi Vanvitelli (1749) for the Carthusian Order. Earlier designs for the conversion of the baths into the church were made by Giuliano da Sangallo and by Baldassarre Peruzzi (*c.*1515). The church was used for official ceremonies of the new Italian state following the completion of Piazza della Repubblica and Via Nazionale.

The facade is built into the ruins of an apsidal wall of the *caldarium*. Vanvitelli changed the orientation of the church with a new entrance and axis that turned the nave into a transept. The circular vestibule by Vanvitelli is set into the *tepidarium*. In one of the niches is Jean-Antoine Houdon's colossal *St Bruno* (1766–1768), the founder of the Carthusian Order. The other held his *St John the Baptist* (il Battista) which fell from the niche in 1894. A plaster model is on display in the Galleria Borghese (Tour 10). It was replaced by Giuseppe Ducrot's *St John the Baptist*. The columns are brick and plaster with a faux granite finish to match the ancient columns in the nave. Funerary monuments pay tribute to the painters Carlo Maratta (d. 1713) to the right and the influential landscape painter Salvator Rosa (d. 1673) to the left.

Michelangelo converted the *frigidarium* into the nave (*c.*90m x 28m x 22m high) of the church. The eight colossal pink Egyptian granite monolithic columns (*c.*14m) are original to the 4th century CE. The column bases are not original since Michelangelo covered the originals when he raised the floor. Vanvitelli designed the apse and choir from the area of the *natatio*. The Tomb of Pope Pius IV de' Medici (d. 1565) is under the altar. The Chapel of St Bruno at the north end is by Carlo Maratta at the former entrance to the church. On the west wall is *The Fall of Simon Magus* by Pompeo Batoni (1755). An indication of the vast size of the interior is the relocation here of monumental paintings that once hung in St Peter's Basilica when replaced with mosaic copies including Domenichino's *Martyrdom of St Sebastian* (1629) and the *Baptism of Christ* by Carlo Maratta (*c.*1697). The meridian (*Linea Clementina*) in the pavement is by Francesco Bianchini for Pope Clement XI Albani (1702). Tombs nearby commemorate major World War I figures in Italy. The sacristy occupies the area of a plunge pool off the *frigidarium*, now a display area documenting the history of the church. The courtyard beyond is built into the *natatio*.

Exit the church to your right for the **Aule Ottogone** (Octagonal Hall), the former Planetarium (1928) that is part of the Museo

Nazionale Romano. Retrace your steps to the church and continue walking along Viale Einaudi in the direction of Termini train station. To your right is the **Dogali Monument** with an **obelisk** dedicated '*Agli Eroi di Dogali*' that was found near Sant'Ignazio (originally erected in Heliopolis by Ramesses II). It formerly stood in front of the old Termini train station but was moved here in 1924. Today it commemorates the 500 Italian soldiers who fell in Dogali (now Eritrea) in January 1887. The **Piazza dei Cinquecento** in front of Termini train station is named after them.

Turn left at the end of the block on Viale Enrico de Nicola for the entrance to the **Museo Nazionale Romano delle Terme di Diocleziano** that faces Piazza dei Cinquecento. The entrance courtyard ('Garden of the Cinquecento') is filled with funerary monuments and sculpture from the Rome environs with an ancient Roman cantharus urn fountain in the centre. The **Epigraphic Museum** contains about 10,000 Latin inscriptions that document facets of Roman life on votive, political, dedicatory, social and funerary objects, including the inscription of the historian Tacitus that was discovered near Porta Pia (Tour 11), Christian epitaphs from catacombs and Jewish epitaphs from the Via Portuense Necropolis (Tour 4). The **Museum of Protohistory** traces the development of the Latin peoples. Archaeological evidence for the development of Latin communities from the environs of Rome focuses mostly on funerary objects. Ancient sculpture from the Imperial period is displayed in the **Great Cloister** (Chiostro Grande), attributed to Michelangelo (1565), that was part of the Carthusian Monastery.

Off the entrance courtyard is the vast **Aula Decima** (Hall X) that includes the Tomb of the Platorini (1st century CE) from the area of Porta Settimiana in Trastevere (Tour 3), with cinerary urns in the niches and funerary portraits. The two columbaria tombs (2nd century CE), the Painted Tomb and the Stuccoed Tomb, are from the Via Portuense Necropolis (Tour 4). The ruins of the Porta Romana necropolis in Ostia Antica (Tour 15) give a sense of the impact of entering and exiting an ancient Roman city through necropolis sites located just outside the gates. Also in the room is an Imperial period statue of *Venus and Mars* identified as portraits of Commodus and Crispina. In the adjoining Hall XI are mosaic pavements including a skeleton that reclines over the Apolline injunction written in Greek: 'Know thyself'.

Retrace your steps to the corner of Viale Einaudi. Cross to the other side of Viale Enrico de Nicola to the statue of Pope St John Paul II in Piazza dei Cinquecento that was reworked by the artist Oliviero Rainaldi after an outcry followed the unveiling (2011) that the facial features did not resemble those of the pope.

**Stazione Termini** (Termini train station) or Roma Termini takes its name from the Baths of Diocletian. It is a busy transportation hub that provides train services for over 150 million passengers each year, as well as Metro access and city and regional bus and tram services; the station also acts as a tour bus and taxi stand. The original temporary station (1863), on the site of the former **Villa Peretti Montalto** built by Pope Sixtus V Peretti di Montalto in conjunction with other projects in the area and later purchased by Cardinal Francesco Negroni (1696), was opened by Pope Pius IX, but work began on a permanent station soon after in 1868. Construction continued after the fall of the Papal States and establishment of the new Italian state and the station was opened in 1874. It was associated with Italian unification and was decorated in mourning for the death of King Umberto I. The modern Via Cavour (1890) connects the station to the Imperial Fora. A modern station with more train lines was begun in 1937 by Angiolo Mazzoni in anticipation of the 1942 World's Fair. World War II interrupted construction, but was resumed in 1947 with the addition of the distinctive cantilevered roof and station to Mazzoni's earlier design and inaugurated in 1950.

A segment of the ancient Republican Walls is preserved to the left of the main entrance. Roman villas were discovered under the current Piazza dei Cinquecento. The station occupies part of the area of the ancient Lamian Gardens that extended to the modern Piazza Vittorio Emanuele II, which the ghost of the infamous Emperor Gaius Caligula was believed to haunt since his corpse had only been partially cremated in the gardens.

Cross to the other side of Viale Einaudi with Termini train station to your left to the **Museo Nazionale Romano Palazzo Massimo alle Terme**. Part of Palazzo Massimo alle Terme occupies the original site of the Villa Peretti Montalto. Bernini's *Neptune and Triton* sculpture (1622–1623) was displayed in the villa's pond until sold to the English painter Joshua Reynolds in 1786 by the art collector Thomas Jenkins. It was resold to Charles Pelham (1792) and displayed in the gardens of

Walpole House until 1906. In 1950, the family sold it to the Victoria and Albert Museum in London. The palazzo was built by Camillo Pistrucci (1883–1887) for the Massimo family and later became the seat of the Jesuit Collegio Massimo until 1960 when it was purchased by the Italian state to serve as the museum that opened to the public in 1998 with a collection of ancient sculpture, frescoes, metalwork and mosaics, most of which was discovered when the city underwent rapid and extensive expansion following its selection as the capital city of Italy.

The museum collection is displayed on three levels. On the **basement level** is the numismatic and treasury collection of jewellery and grave goods and the recently discovered Imperial symbols of the Emperor Maxentius. On the **ground floor** are Republican portraits from the time of Sulla to the principate of Augustus (including the *Via Labicana Augustus*) that trace the arrival of Hellenism in Rome to early Imperial portraits and sculpture. A room is devoted to the famous bronze sculptures *Boxer Resting* signed by Apollonius (1st century BCE) and the so-called *Prince* or *Hellenistic Ruler* (early 2nd century BCE) that were found in the Baths of Constantine during the construction of Via Nazionale. The *Dying Niobid* is from the Gardens of Sallust.

On the **first floor** are Imperial-era portraits and sculptures representing the main dynasties of Roman emperors. Garden sculpture from the Villa of Nero in Antium (Anzio) and Subiaco and from the Villa of Hadrian at Tivoli are displayed alongside Roman copies of Myron's 5th century BCE *Discobolus* (Discus Thrower). The *Discobolus ex Lancellotti* (2nd century CE) was found in the Lamian Gardens, now part of the site of the Stazione Termini and owned by the Massimo family and later the Lancellotti family. It was taken from Rome by Hitler in 1938 and returned in 1948. The other copy dates to the early 1st century CE and was discovered on an Imperial estate in Castel Porziano (1906) with its head missing. Pagan and Christian sarcophagi include the monumental *Portonaccio Sarcophagus* (180–190 CE) that was found near Via Tiburtina. A room is devoted to the decorative bronze from the Emperor Caligula's ships from Lake Nemi that were destroyed when the museum that housed them was burned by retreating German soldiers on 31 May 1944. On the **second floor** are beautiful wall and pavement mosaics and wall paintings including frescoes of garden scenes from the Villa of Livia at Primaporta, where the famous statue of *Augustus of*

*Primaporta* was found, and wall paintings from the Villa Farnesina in Trastevere (Tour 3).

Continue past the museum on Via Viminale. To your right is a surviving pavilion tower from the Baths of Diocletian that flanked the exedra and corrésponds to the tower that is now the church of S. Bernardo alle Terme (Tour 11). The **Teatro dell'Opera** is to your right on the other side of Via Torino with a view of the obelisk in Piazza dell'Esquilino to your left. The theatre was built from 1878 to 1880 but the original facade was replaced by Marcello Piacentini (1926–1928). The interior retains its 19th-century appearance. Continue to **Piazza del Viminale** on the other side of Via A. Depretis with the massive **Palazzo del Viminale** by Manfredo Manfredi (1912–1921), the seat of the Ministry of the Interior of the Italian Republic. The palazzo served as the residence of the prime minister until 1961 when it moved to the current residence of Palazzo Chigi (Tour 9). At an angle to the piazza on Via A. Depretis is the deconsecrated church of **S. Paolo Primo Eremita** ('St Paul the First Hermit') by Clemente Orlandi (1767–1775), considered one of the last Baroque churches in Rome.

Take Via A. Depretis towards Piazza dell'Esquilino behind the Basilica of S. Maria Maggiore (with Piazza del Viminale behind you). Turn right on Via Urbana for the 4th-century church of **S. Pudenziana** just to your right below the modern level of the street. The church with a medieval porch and other 12th-century additions is considered the oldest place of Christian worship in Rome. According to tradition, S. Pudenziana (St Pudentiana) and her sister S. Prassede (St Praxedes) are associated with the arrival of St Peter in Rome at the site of the church that was the home of their father Pudens. The two sisters were martyred for collecting the bones and blood of martyrs. The identity of the family is problematic since the Latin for the house of Pudens (*Domus Pudentiana*) may account for the attribution of a daughter at this location.

The interior was drastically restored in 1589 and the apse mosaic of *Christ Enthroned* (*c.*390) was damaged during the process when two of the Apostles were removed. A bearded Christ sits on a throne with an Imperial aura. Saint Peter and Saint Paul are crowned by female figures identified as Saint Pudentiana and Saint Praxedes. The depiction of the Gospel writers by their iconographic images is the earliest in Christian art. To the left of the apse is the **Chapel of St Peter** with a portion of the table used by Peter to celebrate the Eucharist in the home of Pudens. The rest of the table is incorporated into the high altar of S. Giovanni in Laterano (Tour 13). Today it is the national church of the Philippines. Retrace your steps to Via A. Depretis and proceed to **Piazza dell'Esquilino** straight ahead.

The **Obelisk** in **Piazza dell'Esquilino** was erected in 1587 and is one of two obelisks from the Mausoleum of Augustus. The other one is in Piazza del Quirinale (Tour 11). The staircase behind the apse by Flaminio Ponzio and Domenico Fontana was completed by Carlo Rainaldi (around 1673). It adds Pope Paul's presence to the piazza that formed an important part of Pope Sixtus V's programme and legacy, contrasting with the later programme of Pope Paul V Borghese that dominates the front of the basilica. The basilica was part of Pope Sixtus V's urban design, the so-called stellar plan in which streets would radiate out from S. Maria Maggiore with the obelisk serving as a pilgrim guide to connect the major Constantinian churches in Rome. The Cappella Sistina inside the basilica was also part of the axis of the stellar plan that connected Pope Sixtus V's tomb with the most important Marian church in Rome.

Walk to the front of the basilica in **Piazza di S. Maria Maggiore** where Pope Paul V Borghese commissioned Carlo Maderno to erect the **Column of the Virgin** (1613–1614). Maderno also designed the capital, base (with the Borghese emblems of the eagle and dragon) and the fountain. The column stands 38m high including the 4m-high statue of the Virgin standing on a crescent moon and holding the Christ Child designed by Guillaume Berthelot but cast in bronze and gilded by Domenico Ferreri after Pope Paul V Borghese ordered the melting of the bronze dolphins and other elements of Pope Symmachus' *Fountain of Paradise* (6th century) that was in the atrium of the Old St Peter's.

The column was the last remaining intact column in the Basilica of Maxentius (Tour 6) that was then incorrectly identified as Vespasian's Temple of Peace and influenced the design and theology of the new St Peter's. The column's connection to the Temple of Peace denoted both the Christian triumph over paganism and Christ as the Prince of Peace and St Mary as the Protector of Peace in its new location in front of S. Maria Maggiore. Sixtus V planned to move the column in front of S. Maria degli Angeli in the current Piazza della Repubblica as part of his urban plan of the Quirinal Hill but the project was never realised. It took six months to move the column the 1.5km from the Forum to S. Maria Maggiore. The Corinthian order of the column had previous associations with St Mary. Almost a century earlier, Raphael had designed the Chigi Chapel in S. Maria del Popolo (Tour 9) in the Corinthian order based on her associations with the order made earlier with the rededication of the Pantheon as S. Maria ad Martyres. St Mary's association with the column is older and appears in the Old Testament, hymns and prayers and it was on a column that she appeared to St James as he was preaching in Saragossa, Spain.

The Column of the Virgin elevates Mary above the city like Sixtus V's statues of St Peter and St Paul on top of the Columns of Trajan (Tour 6) and Marcus Aurelius (Tour 9) – another statement of Christianity's triumph over paganism. Pope Paul V Borghese straightened out the Via Gregoriana (now Via Merulana) that provides a direct route between S. Giovanni in Laterano and S. Maria Maggiore so that the column would serve as a pilgrim guide and focal point. The column marks the location of Pope Paul V's burial in the Cappella Paolina just as earlier the obelisk had marked the location of Pope Sixtus V's tomb in the Cappella Sistina. The column was copied for the Column of Mary in Marienplatz, Munich (1638), and Pope Pius IX's Column of the Virgin near Piazza di Spagna (1857) that celebrates the Dogma of the Immaculate Conception.

The Basilica of **S. Maria Maggiore** (St Mary Major) is the most important Marian church in Rome. The Festa della Madonna della Neve 5 August commemorates the miracle of the snowfall on 5 August 358 CE that was a sign foretold by St Mary in an apparition to Pope Liberius (352–366) and to John, a patrician of Rome, of the location of the future church on the Cispius summit of the Esquiline Hill that was initially called S. Maria ad Nives. Pope Liberius traced the outline of the future basilica in the snow. The history of Laberius' basilica is obscure but it was the site of a battle between the forces of the antipope Ursinus and Pope Damasus I (366–384) in which the pope's forces used roof tiles against their rivals. The present basilica dates to the reign of Pope Sixtus III (432–444) who began construction after the Council of Ephesus (431) had declared St Mary the Mother of God (*Theotokos*). The evolving cult and depiction of St Mary as the *Salus Populi Romani* ('Salvation of the Roman People') is traced in the **Museum** that also adjoins the **Archaeological site** beneath the church with the foundations of the 5th-century basilica founded by Pope Sixtus III that are built upon the ruins of a Roman house (occupied from the 1st to the 4th century CE) with a surviving fresco of a calendar.

The facade by Ferdinando Fuga (1743) was built over the original 12th-century facade of the church, including the **Loggia of the Benediction** with two mosaic cycles completed under Pope Nicholas IV (1288–1292). The upper cycle by Filippo Rusuti depicts 'Christ Pantocrator' with saints and angels. The figure of St Mary is damaged by the support of Fuga's facade as are the two saints on the far sides. The lower cycle is later in date and was likely made by Rusuti's assistants. It depicts Pope Laberius and the *Miracle of the Snow*. Fuga's facade obscured the mosaics but it harmonised all the diverse architectural elements at the front of the church, including the palazzo built by Pope Paul V Borghese to the right of the entrance that is accessed by a helical staircase by Bernini through the Hall of the Popes. The campanile that dates to the reign of Pope Gregory XI (1377) is the tallest in Rome. In the portico, the bronze statue of Philip IV of Spain is by Bernini and Girolamo Lucenti (1665). The four angels by Pietro Bracci were originally over the high altar.

The vast interior (86m long) retains the original 5th-century mosaics (from the reign of Pope Sixtus III) along the nave with biblical scenes and on the triumphal arch with scenes from the childhood of Christ that show the influence of the Classical tradition with naturalistic portraiture before the transition to iconic Byzantine art. Fuga (1746–1750) systematised the 40 ancient monolithic columns that were altered by the addition of the Cappella Sistina and Cappella Paolina. The cosmatesque pavement dates to around 1150. The **baptistery** is by Flaminio Ponzio, and the relief of the *Assumption* is by Pietro Bernini (father of Gian Lorenzo). The entry to the **Museum** is through the adjoining **Cappella S. Michele** that is a souvenir shop. Outside the museum entrance is a column that commemorates the conversion of King Francis IV of France. The **Cappella delle Reliquie** was rebuilt by Fuga. Outside the chapel is an altar with an *Annunciation* by Pompeo Batoni (*c.*1750).

The **Cappella Sistina** on the south side is by Domenico Fontana (1584–1587) on a Greek cross plan with a cupola for Pope Sixtus V whose tomb, also designed by Fontana (1588–1590), is on the right wall. Some of the marble was taken from Septizodium on the slope of the Palatine Hill (Tour 13). The *tempietto*-shaped ciborium by Ludovico del Duca (1590) with four gilt angels by Sebastiano Torrigiani covers the original Chapel of the Relics by Arnolfo di Cambio (13th century) that contains pieces of the crib or manger of Christ. The presepio that comprised the 'Oratory of the Nativity' alludes to the early name of the church as S. Maria ad Praesepe and is now displayed in the museum. The Tomb of Pope Pius V to a design by Fontana (1586–1588) is to the left. The decoration of the chapel was directed by Cesare Nebbia and Giovanni Guerra (1587–1589).

A baldacchino of four porphyry columns by Ferdinando Fuga decorated with gilded bronze ornament by Giuseppe Valadier (1823) covers the **high altar** that is comprised of a porphyry sarcophagus with the relics of St Matthew and other martyrs. Beneath the altar is the **Crypt of the Reliquary** with the silver and crystal Reliquary of the Holy Crib by Giuseppe Valadier that is preceded by the **confessio** by Virginio Vespignani (1862–1864) with a colossal statue of Pius IX in prayer by Ignazio Jacometti (1883). Pope Nicholas IV (1288–1292) added the transepts and apse with mosaics that date to this time signed by Jacopo Torriti. The *Coronation of the Virgin* shares similarities with the earlier apse mosaic in S. Maria in Trastevere (Tour 4). Below are scenes from the *Life of the Virgin*, also by Torriti, that are contemporaneous with Pietro Cavallini's mosaic cycle of the same theme in S. Maria in Trastevere. The apse was rebuilt by Pope Clement X.

The pavement **Tomb of Bernini** and family members is on the steps to the right of the sanctuary. Gian Lorenzo Bernini lived with his father in the area across from the basilica. Through the patronage of Pope Urban VIII, he acquired a palazzo on Via della Mercede (Tour 10). The chapel to the right of the sanctuary (and of the south aisle) contains the **Tomb of Cardinal Consalvo Rodriguez** (d. 1299) with a recumbent effigy and two angels beneath a canopy and beautiful mosaic work signed by Giovanni di Cosma (one of the Cosmati). To the left side of the sanctuary is the **Sacristy** by Flaminio Ponzio with painted decoration by Passignano.

The **Cappella Paolina** for Pope Paul V Borghese (d. 1621) by Flaminio Ponzio (1605–1611) on the north side is richly decorated with a cupola that balances the Cappella Sistina. Among the semi-precious stones that adorn the chapel is marble from the Temple of Minerva that stood in the Forum of Nerva (Tour 6). The altar (1613) that incorporates the icon of the *Salus Populi Romani*, traditionally venerated for the prevention of plague in the city, and the lunette fresco that continues up to the cupola with the Virgin standing on a column (both by Cavalier d'Arpino) allude to the Column of the Virgin in front of the basilica. The **Tomb of Pope Paul V Borghese** to the left is by Ponzio but the portrait of the pope kneeling bare-headed is by Giacomo Silla Longhi. The **Tomb of Pope Clement VIII Aldobrandini** by Ponzio is to the right, while a portrait of the pope also by Longhi includes a bas-relief by Pietro Bernini. The pope sentenced Giordano Bruno (Tour 7) and Beatrice Cenci (Tour 3) to their deaths but is better known for blessing coffee for Catholic consumption. Pauline Bonaparte (Napoleon's sister), who married Camillo Borghese, is buried here. Painted decoration is by Guido Reni and Giovanni Baglione.

The **Sforza Chapel** to the left of the Cappella Paolina was designed by Michelangelo in 1562 for Cardinal Guido Ascanio, the grandson of Pope Paul III Farnese, but built by Tiberio Calcagni and Giacomo della Porta (1564–1573). The *Assumption* is by Sermoneta (1565) and the frescoes are by Cesare Nebbia. The tombs of Cardinal Guido and his brother Alessio are by Giacomo della Porta. In the **Cesi Chapel** (*c.*1550), the *Beheading of St Catherine* is by Sermoneta who also painted the frescoes. The tombs of Cesi family members are by Guglielmo della Porta (1565). At the end of the nave opposite the Monument to Pope Clement IX is the **Tomb of Nicholas IV**, designed by Domenico Fontana (1574) three centuries after the pope's death. To the left above the Porta Santa is the **Tomb of Cardinals Philippe and Eustache de Levis** (1489).

Exit the basilica and make a hard right to cross to the other side of Via Liberiana. Turn left and cross Via dell'Olmata to Via di S. Prassede. The side entrance to the church of S. Prassede is just ahead to your right. The church of **S. Prassede** (St Praxedes, the sister of St Pudentiana) is a must-see, with its beautiful 9th-century Byzantine mosaics. The basilica was built in the early 9th century by Pope St Paschal I on the site of an earlier church (5th century) that replaced an even earlier titular church (*c.*112 CE). It was restored by Antonio Muñoz in 1914. The main entrance is on Via di S. Martino ai Monti with a medieval porch that leads up a flight of stairs to a courtyard with columns from the earlier 5th-century church. The church is the setting for Robert Browning's 'The Bishop orders his Tomb at Saint Praxed's Church, Rome 15–'.

An architrave of spoliated ancient entablature and 16th-century trompe l'oeil frescoes line the nave with a porphyry disc that covers the well that St Praxedes used to hide the bones of the martyrs. The baldacchino with four porphyry columns by Francesco Ferrari (1730) with angels by Giuseppe Rusconi is above the **crypt**. Martyr relics from the catacombs were translated here by Pope St Paschal I in imitation of St Praxedes whose relics with those of St Pudentiana are here in a sarcophagus. On the **triumphal arch**, the 9th-century mosaics depict Christ surrounded by angels and Elijah and Moses. To either side are the Apostles and the New Jerusalem with St Peter and St Paul receiving the elect into Heaven. On the inner side, Christ is depicted with saints. On the **apse arch** (9th century), the Lamb of God is flanked by seven candlesticks, symbols of the Evangelists and 24 Elders with hands raising garlands. The **apse** mosaic (9th century) is of Christ with groups of saints – St Peter, St Pudentiana, St Zeno, St Paul, St Praxedes and Pope St Paschal I – holding a model of the church. The blue square nimbus around his head signifies that he was depicted during his lifetime. He is similarly depicted in S. Maria in Domnica (Tour 13) and S. Cecilia in Trastevere (Tour 4).

Adjoining the Cesi chapel on the south side, with a fragment of the **Column of Christ's flagellation** that was brought to Rome from Jerusalem in the Sixth Crusade (1228), is the magnificent funerary **Chapel of S. Zeno** (817–824) dedicated to St Paschal I's mother, Theodora. The entrance with an ancient marble vase and spoliated elements is decorated with a mosaic frieze with two rows of portrait medallions of Christ and saints. Inside, the chapel is cross-shaped with spoliated columns and capitals. In the altar niche, the Virgin is enthroned with the Christ Child between St Praxedes and St Pudenziana. Over the entrance door, St Peter and St Paul uphold the throne of God. In one of the lunettes, St Paschal I's mother, Theodora, depicted with a blue square nimbus around her head, stands next to the Virgin and two saints. Christ as Saviour looks down from the ceiling inside a medallion held up by four angels. Opposite on the third pilaster the **funerary monument to Giovanni Battista Santoni** (d. 1592) is one of Bernini's earliest works (*c*.1614).

If the main entrance is open, exit left onto Via di S. Martino ai Monti. If closed, exit right from the side entrance of the church onto Via di S. Prassede. Turn left at the end of the block onto Via di S. Martino ai Monti. Walk across Via Merulana. Continue straight on Via di S. Vito to the **Arch of Gallienus** that commemorates the Emperor Galienus and his consort Salonina (262 CE). The arch is the central archway that survives of the triple gate of the Porta Esquilina in the Republican Walls that had been rebuilt during the reign of the Emperor Augustus. The church of **Ss. Vito e Modesto** was built into the arch by Sixtus IV della Rovere (1477) when he relocated it here from the area of Piazza Vittorio Emanuele II, so it was also known as the Arch of S. Vito. Near the arch is the **fountain** commemorating the Rione Monti by Pietro Lombardi (1926).

Retrace your steps to Via di S. Martino ai Monti on the other side of Via Merulana and walk past the front entrance of the church of S. Prassede. Continue until you reach Piazza di S. Martino ai Monti. Cross Via Giovanni Lanza to Via Equizia to walk up to the front of the church of **S. Martino ai Monti** (formally called the Basilica Ss. Silvestro e Martino ai Monti) that currently belongs to the Carmelite Order. The church has occupied this site since the 3rd century: it was built in the 9th century on the site of an earlier church by Pope St Symmachus that replaced the original 4th-century CE church founded by Pope Sylvester on the site of the 3rd-century titular church of Equitius. Filippo Gagliardi extensively remodelled the church (1650) and painted interior views of St Peter's Basilica and S. Giovanni in Laterano on the north side of the nave prior to their reconstruction.

Turn right onto Viale del Monte Oppio and veer to the right when the road splits to take the winding Via delle Sette Sale with the Parco di Traiano to your left. You will walk along the side wall of S. Pietro in Vincoli just before entering into Piazza di San Pietro in Vincoli. The staircase beneath the arch (Via S. Francesco di Paola) descends to Via Cavour that legend connects to the Via Scelerata ('Street of Crime') that the Roman historian Livy claims was the street in which Tullia ran over the body of her father, the legendary King Servius Tullius, following the coup that put her husband, King Tarquin the Proud, the last of the kings of Rome, on the throne (535 BCE). The loggia above the arch was once part of the palazzo where the mistress of Pope Alexander VI Borgia lived, Vannozza dei Cattanei, the mother of Lucrezia and Cesare Borgia.

The **Basilica of S. Pietro in Vincoli** was built by Meo del Caprina (Amadeo de Francesco di Settignano) for Pope Sixtus IV della Rovere. He also designed the Turin Cathedral. The church was an important medieval pilgrim site, also known as the Basilica Eudossiana after the earliest church on the site (S. Petri ad vincula consecrated by Pope Sixtus III) built by Eudoxia, the wife of the Emperor Valentinian III. She presented the **Chains of St Peter** to Sixtus III's successor, Pope Leo the Great, which had been given to her by her mother Eudoxia. When the pope compared them to the chains from the Mamertine Prison where St Peter was imprisoned (Tour 5), the chains miraculously joined. They are displayed in the glass reliquary beneath the baldacchino by Virginio Vespignani (1876). In the **crypt** accessed from the confessio is an urn associated with the relics of the seven Jewish Maccabee brothers.

To the right of the high altar is Michelangelo's unfinished **Tomb of Pope Julius II della Rovere** that includes the figures of Moses (begun in 1514) and Leah and Rachel in the niches, assisted by Raffaello da Montelupo (1542–1545) who also sculpted the Prophet and Sibyl. The recumbent effigy of the pope is by Tommaso Boscoli, and the Madonna and Child is by Alessandro Scherano da Settignano. There were multiple versions over 40 years (1505–1545) but the original design called for a free-standing monument in the new St Peter's over the Tomb of St Peter where Bernini's baldacchino is today. The monument was moved here because of the della Rovere connections to the church (their family crest is above the entrance). As cardinal, Pope Julius II succeeded his uncle, Pope Sixtus IV (then Cardinal Francesco della Rovere), as Cardinal Titular of the church. Other figures intended for the monument are in the Galleria dell'Accademia and Palazzo Vecchio in Florence and the Musée du Louvre, Paris. Both Julius II and his uncle, Pope Sixtus IV, are buried in St Peter's Basilica.

The nave ceiling fresco, *Miracle of the Chains*, is by Giovanni Battista Parodi (1706). On the south side (first altar) is *St Augustine* by Guercino. Over the second altar hangs a copy of Domenichino's *Liberation of St Peter* (1604), the original of which is outside the sacristy. In the chapel to the right of the high altar is Guercino's *St Margaret*. On the north side (first altar) is *Deposition* by Pomarancio (Cristoforo Roncalli). To the left is Andrea Bregno's **Monument to Cardinal Nicholas of Cusa (Kues)** (d. 1464). Over the second altar, a 7th-century mosaic of St Sebastian depicts him as bearded instead of as the youth of later iconography. On the west wall is the **Tomb of Antonio del Pollaiuolo** and his brother Piero with portrait busts attributed to Luigi Capponi. Pollaiuolo designed the Tomb of Sixtus IV della Rovere now in the Treasury Museum of St Peter's Basilica and added the figures of Romulus and Remus to the *Capitoline She-Wolf* (Tour 5). Above is a fresco of a procession seeking divine protection from the plague of 1476.

Tour 13 begins at the **Basilica of S. Clemente** (.50km from here). Exit the church and turn left on Via Eudossiana then turn right on Via delle Polveriera (the name preserves the stone-crushers who worked in the area). The Colosseum will come into view. Take the footbridge and then turn left to walk down the steps to Via dei Fori Imperiali. Turn left with the Colosseum to your right to reach the start of Via Labicana. The entrance to the Golden House of Nero (Tour 6) is straight ahead through the gates that bear his portrait. Cross to the other side of Via Labicana with the Ludus Magnus (gladiatorial training school with half of the amphitheatre arena visible) to your left (Tour 6). Turn left onto Via di S. Giovanni in Laterano. The obelisk in Piazza di S. Giovanni in Laterano is visible straight ahead. The entrance to the Basilica of S. Clemente is just beyond the second block to your left.

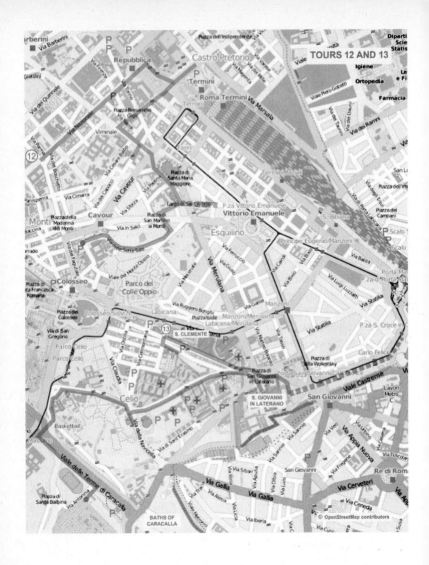

Sites: S. Clemente; Ss. Quarto Coronati; San Giovanni in Laterano (Option: Santa Croce in Gerusalemme; Museo degli Strumenti Musicali; Porta Maggiore); S. Stefano Rotondo; S. Maria in Domnica; Villa Celimontana; Ss. Giovanni e Paolo; S. Gregorio Magno; Piazza di Porta Capena; Circus Maximus; Baths of Caracalla. Distance: 2.5km + optional 2km.

# The Lateran and Caelian Hill

## Popes and Emperors

Explore the areas around the Lateran and Caelian Hill destroyed by the Normans under Robert Guiscard in 1084 but rebuilt with churches filled with beautiful mosaics and frescoes. Go under the Basilica of S. Clemente and Ss. Giovanni e Paolo through successive layers to the 1st-century CE level of the city to document Rome's transition layer upon layer from a pagan to a Christian city. Sites associated with powerful popes and emperors include S. Giovanni in Laterano that was the first Christian basilica in Rome founded by Constantine and the residence of popes in the Lateran Palace until the Great Schism. The church of S. Gregorio Magno al Celio, founded by Pope St Gregory the Great on his family estate, was where the Apostolic mission of St Augustine started.

The **Basilica of S. Clemente** is important for the buildings from successive eras superimposed on each other at the site. The upper basilica (12th century) is over the original larger 4th-century basilica (partially destroyed by Robert Guiscard in 1084 during the Norman sack of Rome) that was built over a 1st-century CE private home and adjacent Roman buildings that replaced buildings destroyed in the Great Fire of 64 CE. The excavations beneath the upper basilica were carried out by Father Mullooly (1861) and the Irish Dominicans who have occupied the adjacent monastery of Collegio S. Clemente since 1667. Pope Paschal II, who was elected pope in the lower basilica (1099), began construction of the upper basilica in 1108 with elements preserved and reused from the lower basilica. The main entrance to the upper basilica has a medieval porch with spoliated columns and architrave fragments that leads to an atrium with spoliated columns. The basilica including the facade was renovated by Carlo Stefano Fontana (1713–1719) for Pope Clement XI Albani.

In the central nave of the **upper basilica**, the schola cantorum and other marble elements such as the ambones, candelabrum and desk come from the lower basilica. The choir screen dates to the reign of Pope John II (533–535). The columns are ancient but the capitals were added in the 18th century. The ceiling fresco, *The Glory of St Clement*, is by Giuseppe Chiari (1714–1719). The baldacchino and cathedra are both from the 12th century. On the triumphal arch (12th century), below Christ and the symbols of the Evangelists are, to the left, St Paul with St Lawrence, the prophet Isaiah and Bethlehem; and to the right, St Peter with St Clement, the prophet Jeremiah and Jerusalem. Saint Clement, the fourth pope, was most likely a freedman (formerly identified with the Flavian family) who was martyred during the reign of Domitian (81–96). Later tradition placed his martyrdom under the Emperor Trajan by being tied to an anchor in the Black Sea for performing a miracle during his banishment to a stone quarry in Chersonesus. His relics were translated here in the 8th century.

The apse mosaics (12th century) depict the *Triumph of the Cross* with Christ on the crucifix with 12 doves to represent the Apostles, the Virgin and St John. Above, the Hand of God appears in the Dome of Heaven. The Tree of Life produces tendrils and the rivers of Paradise flow along the bottom to quench the thirst of the faithful represented by stags and peacocks, the symbols of immortality. On the apse wall are frescoes (14th century) of Christ, the Virgin and the Apostles.

The Chapel of St Catherine next to the side entrance is decorated with frescoes including an 'Anunciation' over the entrance arch, *Crucifixion* and *Scenes from the Life of St Catherine of Alexandria* by Masolino da Panicale for Cardinal Branda Castiglioni, perhaps with the assistance of the Florentine artist Masaccio who was also in Rome at this time (1428). Outside the chapel, *St Christopher* is painted on the left pier. Next to the church entrance are two sinopie for Masolino's *Crucifixion* and the *Beheading of St Catherine*.

From the sacristy, stairs descend to the narthex of the **lower basilica**. To the right of the central nave entrance is the fresco *Miracle of St*

*Clement* (11th century), part of the fresco cycle in the lower basilica on the *Life of St Clement* for patrons Beno de Rapiza and his wife Maria Macellaria. The lower basilica was mentioned by St Jerome (392) and was the site of councils presided over by Pope Zosimus (417) and Pope Symmachus (499). It was restored in the 8th and 9th centuries. The 9th- and 11th-century frescoes survived the damage caused by the Norman sack of Rome and the construction of the upper basilica when the upper portion of the wall was removed. The apse was rebuilt by Father Mullooly but not according to the original dimensions. The Byzantine fresco of the *Madonna and Child* (5th/6th century, but perhaps 8th/9th century) on the south side resembles portraits of the Empress Theodora. Frescoes on the north side include an *Ascension* (9th century), a *Crucifixion* that depicts Christ as alive, and the *Legend of Sisinius* with early Italian writing (11th century). On display is a copy of the Mithraeum altar. At the end of the north aisle is the **Tomb of St Cyril** with a modern mosaic.

Stairs (4th century) next to the chapel descend to the 1st-century CE **Roman level** that served as the foundation of the lower basilica. To your left is a Roman house from the 1st century that was transformed into a **Mithraeum** (late 2nd/early 3rd century) with dining couches and cult altar beneath the roof that imitates a cavern. Opposite is the pronaos of the **Temple**. The **Mithraic School** where the cult was taught is at the end of the corridor to your right. Beyond the Mithraeum through a narrow passageway is a two-storey public building (late 1st century) that may be the Imperial mint. A series of rooms that once faced a courtyard leads to a room with running water through a tunnel that was opened in 1937–1939. The public building has also been identified as the house of Flavius Clemens, the cousin and co-consul of the Emperor Domitian, for whom St Clement likely worked as a freedman. The stairs to return to the lower basilica go past a small catacomb (*c.*5th century).

Exit by the side entrance to the church and turn left on Via di S. Giovanni in Laterano. Turn right at the end of the block on Via dei Querceti then a quick left onto Via dei Ss. Quattro Coronati. Walk up the north side of the Caelian Hill a short distance to the small flight of stairs to your right that leads to the Basilica of Ss. Quattro Coronati. The entrance to the basilica is through the arch in the Carolingian tower into a courtyard that leads into a second courtyard.

The Augustinian Monastery of **Ss. Quattro Coronati** (converted in the 16th century to an orphanage for girls until the late 19th century) is dedicated to the four crowned (coronati) martyrs: Castorius, Claudius, Nicostratus and Symphorian. All four were sculptors in Pannonia and were martyred under Domitian for refusing to make a statue of the pagan god of medicine Aesculapius. The saints were venerated in the 16th century by the Confraternity of the Marmorari (marble makers). The oldest part of the complex is the basilica nave and apse (6th century) that were built over a Roman villa that had been converted into a titular church in the 4th century. In the 9th century, Pope Leo IV added the side aisles and chapels. This basilica was severely damaged in the Norman sack of Rome under Robert Guiscard (1084) and was rebuilt by Pope Paschal II for the Benedictine Order but to only half of its original size, as indicated by the now oversized apse. He also added the semicircular crypt below the sanctuary for the saints' relics that are stored in ancient sarcophagi. The basilica was renovated by Antonio Muñoz (1914) who uncovered the fresco fragments (13th/14th century). The dark interior is hauntingly beautiful with spoliated elements from its various reconstructions and an upper gallery (matronea). The cosmatesque **Cloister** (13th century) is accessed from the north side. Twin spoliated columns support the arches around the courtyard with a 14th-century fountain and sculpture fragments from the earlier basilicas displayed in the galleries. The **Chapel of St Barbara** with damaged frescoes of Madonna and Child and saints (9th to 13th century) was originally one of the side chapels of the 9th-century basilica.

The **Oratory of St Sylvester** (Oratorio di S. Silvestro) consecrated in 1247 as part of the palace constructed by Cardinal Stefano Conti, the nephew of Pope Innocent III, is a rarely visited gem. The entrance is from the second courtyard to the right of the portico. Ring the bell for access. Until recently, donations were left in the rota and visitors would receive the key from an unseen nun. Lining the walls is a 13th-century fresco cycle of Constantine the Great and Pope St Sylvester that includes panels depicting the *Curing of Constantine of leprosy*, the *Baptism of Constantine* and the *Donation of Constantine*, in which he gives the papal tiara and Imperial parasol to the pope. Over the entrance door is a fresco of *Christ Enthroned with the Virgin, St John the Baptist, the Apostles and angels*. The frescoes in the altar area are attributed to Raffaellino da Reggio (16th century).

Retrace your steps to Via di S. Giovanni in Laterano. Turn right in the direction of S. Giovanni (the obelisk is visible straight ahead) and continue through to **Piazza di S. Giovanni in Laterano**. The obelisk is at the side the basilica facing the Lateran Palace (to your left) and the Scala Santa beyond it, with the Lateran Baptistery to your right. This complex comprises the **Lateran** in the Rione Monti that was recognised as extraterritorial Vatican property according to the pacts of the Lateran Treaty of 1929 that was signed in the Lateran Palace.

The **obelisk** was brought to Rome by Constantius II (357) and erected in the Circus Maximus. Constantine had intended to erect it in Constantinople in 350 but it remained in the port at Alexandria. It is the oldest and tallest obelisk in Rome (31m; 47m with base), originally erected by the Pharaoh Thothmes IV in front of the Temple of Ammon in Thebes in the 15th century BCE. After its discovery in the Circus Maximus in 1587, Pope Sixtus V commissioned Domenico Fontana to erect it here to guide pilgrims to the basilica. The **Loggia of the Benediction** on the north facade of S. Giovanni facing the obelisk is also by Domenico Fontana (1586) for Pope Sixtus V, with marble from the ancient Septizodium. The twin campanili are from the 14th century. The bronze statue of King Henri IV of France is by Nicolas Cordier (1608).

The **Lateran Palace** (Palazzo Lateranense) was built by Domenico Fontana for Pope Sixtus V (1586–1589) and serves as the seat of the Rome Vicariate and the Offices of the Rome Diocese. Fontana also designed the facade of Palazzo Quirinale (1589) for Pope Sixtus V to serve as the summer papal residence (Tour 11). This new palace replaced the old Lateran Palace (Lateran Patriarchium) that had been the residence of popes since the reign of Pope Zacharias (741–752) until the papacy moved to Avignon in 1309. When the papacy returned to Rome in 1377 the residence of the pope was moved to the Vatican. The current **Museo Storico Vaticano** features the decorated interiors of the Papal Apartments and rooms devoted to the history of the papacy from the 16th century to the present.

Continue left to walk around the Lateran Palace to the **Scala Santa**, the original steps from the old Lateran Palace that were believed to be those of Pontius Pilate's house in Jerusalem that Christ descended following his condemnation and that were brought to Rome by St Helena. Domenico Fontana moved the steps here in the building he designed (1589) for Pope Sixtus V. At the top of the steps is the **Sancta Sanctorum**, the Chapel of St Lawrence that is the private chapel of the pope, with 13th-century frescoes and the venerated relic painting of Christ (5th century) known as *acheiropoeiton* (Greek for 'not made by hand') to signify divine origins. The **Tribune** to the east of the Scala Santa facing Piazza di Porta di S. Giovanni by Ferdinando Fuga for Pope Benedict XIV (1743) contains copies of the mosaics that once lined the banquet hall of the Old Lateran Palace, the *Triclinium of Pope Leo III*, built for the arrival of Charlemagne in Rome (800) and demolished in 1733. The **Piazza di Porta di S. Giovanni** is the biggest piazza in Rome where the festival of St John the Baptist (23–24 June) is held. The **Porta di S. Giovanni** was built by Giacomo del Duca for Pope Gregory XIII Boncompagni (1574) next to the ancient **Porta Asinaria** that is visible to the right of the Porta di S. Giovanni between the two towers built by the Emperor Honorius. The Porta di S. Giovanni was important in the liberation of Rome from Nazi occupation. The American Fifth Army entered Rome on 4 June 1944 from the gates in these south-eastern quarters including the Porta di S. Giovanni. One of the first stops upon entering the gate was No. 145 Via Tasso, the headquarters of the SS and the Gestapo (to the left of the Scala Santa when facing it), to liberate prisoners. It is now the **Museo Storico della Lotta di Liberazione di Roma** (Historical Museum of the Liberation of Rome). Beyond the Porta di S. Giovanni is **Piazzale Appio**, a shopping and transportation hub that leads to popular residential areas beyond including the Quartiere Tuscolano and the Quartiere Appio Latino.

**San Giovanni in Laterano**, the Papal Archbasilica of St John Lateran (SS. Salvatore e dei Ss. Giovanni Battista e Giovanni Evangelista), is the domicile of Rome's bishop, the pope, and ranks as the highest of Rome's four major basilicas with cathedral status. It was the first basilica founded by Constantine (*c.*313–318) and was originally dedicated to Christ the Saviour soon after the 313 Edict of Milan decriminalising Christianity. It was constructed over the ruins of the new camp of the Imperial Cavalry Bodyguard that he destroyed (*castra nova equitum singularium*). Pope Sergius III (904–911) added the dedication to St John the Baptist, and Pope Lucius II (1144–1145) added the dedication to St John the Evangelist. The name Lateran derives from the property of the Plautii Laterani family that Nero confiscated following the

Pisonian conspiracy in 65 CE that remained part of the Imperial estates. It eventually passed to Constantine's second wife Fausta, the sister of his rival Maxentius whose father was the Emperor Maximian, as part of her dowry. In 326, for reasons unknown, Constantine (with the apparent support of his mother, St Helena) ordered her death by suffocation in a bath, yet their sons Constantine II, Constantius II and Constans would succeed him on the throne.

As the first Christian basilica, its design and orientation were influential and were adopted for St Peter's Basilica, including the placing of the altar to face west towards the apse (rather than east in the later liturgical tradition). The orientation of the entrance away from the city was awkward for later urban planning. The north entrance and obelisk in Piazza di S. Giovanni Laterano provided a visual solution to this problem as pilgrims walked from basilica to basilica from one end of the city to the other. It was a journey shared by popes who were crowned here until 1870, after which the coronation procession travelled from S. Giovanni in Laterano to St Peter's Basilica along the Via Papalis, the current Corso Vittorio Emanuele II (Tour 7).

The original basilica with a nave, four aisles and an apse had been repaired (especially after the earthquake of 896) and decorated over centuries. It was visited by Dante but destroyed by fire in 1308. It was rebuilt with frescoes by Giotto but was again destroyed by fire in 1360. Pope Gregory XI (1370–1378) rebuilt the basilica when the papacy returned to Rome from Avignon and Pope Martin V Colonna (1417–1431) continued its reconstruction after the Great Schism. The basilica contains six extant papal tombs. The Equestrian statue of Marcus Aurelius was displayed in front of the basilica since the 8th century until moved to Piazza del Campidoglio by Pope Paul III Farnese (1538). The *Capitoline She-Wolf* and the *Spinario*, now in the Capitoline Museums (Tour 5), were also displayed here.

The current appearance of the basilica complex started to take shape in the 16th century when Pope Sixtus V commissioned Domenico Fontana to design the north entrance and the buildings in Piazza di S. Giovanni. Interior designs were carried out under Pope Innocent X Pamphilj and Clement XI Albani. The main West entrance facade with statues of Christ, the Apostles and saints and the portico are by Alessandro Galilei for Pope Clement XII Corsini (1735). The dedicatory inscription on the Neoclassical facade reads: 'Clement XII, in his 5th year as Pontifex Maximus to Christ the Saviour and the Saints John the Baptist and John the Evangelist.' The ancient bronze doors in the **portico** are from the Curia in the Roman Forum, moved here by Pope Alexander VII Chigi who also added his family emblem of the stars (1660). The statue of Constantine was found in his baths on the Quirinal Hill in the current area of Largo Magnanapoli (Tour 12). The high relief of the *Life of St John the Baptist* is by Pietro Bracci, Filippo della Valle, Bernardino Ludovisi and Giovanni Battista Maini.

The niches with ancient green columns along the **nave** (130m long) were added by Borromini (1646–1649) for Pope Innocent X Pamphilj. The statues of the Apostles were commissioned by Pope Clement XI Albani (1718) including St Peter and St Paul by Pierre Étienne Monnot; St Thomas and St Bartholomew by Pierre Legros; and St Matthew, St John, St Andrew and St James the Greater by Camillo Rusconi. The stucco reliefs with scenes from the Old and New Testament are by Alessandro Algardi and Antonio Raggi. Above are oval paintings of the prophets. The ceiling (1567) with ornament by Daniele da Volterra was commissioned by Pope Pius V. The cosmatesque pavement bears the family emblem (column) of Pope Martin V Colonna. Pope Clement VIII Aldobrandini (1592–1605) ordered the demolition of the Arch of Claudius on the Via Flaminia to supply 136 cartloads of marble that was cut into slabs for the pavement of the transept designed by Giacomo della Porta.

The **baldacchino** is by Giovanni di Stefano for Pope Urban V (1367) with 14th-century frescoes by Barna da Siena (1367–1368), but was repainted by Antoniazzo Romano. According to tradition, the reliquaries contain the heads of St Peter and St Paul. The papal altar incorporates part of the table St Peter used to celebrate the Eucharist at the house of Pudens. The other portion of the table is in the church of S. Pudenziana (Tour 12). The **Confessio** contains the **Tomb of Pope Martin V** (d. 1431) by Simone Ghini. The original mosaics in the **apse** by Jacopo Torriti and Jacopo da Camerino (1288–94) for Pope Nicholas IV, the first Franciscan pope who added the figures of St Francis of Assisi and St Anthony of Padua, were destroyed when the apse was rebuilt by Virginio and Francesco Vespignani (1885). In the frieze below are kneeling portraits of the artists. To the right of the sanctuary is the **Tomb of Pope Innocent III** by Giuseppe Lucchetti (1861) and to the far right is the **Chapel of the Crucifix**. To the left of the sanctuary is the **Tomb of Pope Leo XIII** by Giulio Tadolini (1907). Beyond in the corridor are the **Tomb of Cavalier d'Arpino** (1640) and the **Tomb of Andrea Sacchi** (1661) and Deodato di Cosma's statues of St Peter and St Paul (closed to the public). To the far left is the **Colonna Chapel of the Choir** by Girolamo Rainaldi (*c.*1625).

The 13th-century cosmatesque **Cloister** entered from the north side aisle was built by Jacopo and Pietro Vassalletto (*c.*1222–1232) with spoliated and Solomonic columns supporting the arcade and a cosmatesque frieze. In the centre is a 9th-century wellhead. Displayed around the courtyard are ancient and medieval funerary monuments including the **Tomb of Riccardo Annibaldi** (d.1289) by Arnolfo di Cambio, and altar fragments from the earlier basilica. The *Mensura Christi* is a porphyry slab on which, according to tradition, Roman soldiers tossed dice for the prize of Christ's robe. The adjoining **Museum** contains altarpieces and vestments, including the cope of Pope Boniface VIII.

The north transept **Altar of the Blessed Sacrament** is by Pietro Paolo Olivieri (*c.*1600). On the fifth pier is the **Tomb of Elena Savelli** by Jacopo del Duca (1570) and opposite is the **Tomb of Cardinal Casanate** (d. 1700) by Pierre Legros. On the north side, the **Corsini Chapel** (first) was built for Pope Clement XII Corsini by Alessandro Galilei (1732–1735) with the **Tomb of Pope Clement XII** (d. 1740) whose porphyry sarcophagus came from the Pantheon.

On the fist pier of the nave on the south side is a fresco fragment by Giotto that depicts Boniface VIII announcing the Holy Year 1300 from the loggia on the west front. On the second pier is the **Cenotaph of Pope Sylvester II** (d. 1003). Opposite in front of the **Massimo Chapel** by Giacomo della Porta is a **Statuette of St James** from the De Pereriis Altar attributed to Andrea Bregno. On the third pier is the **Tomb of Pope Alexander III** (d. 1181) and on the fourth pier is the **Tomb of Pope Sergius IV** (d. 1012). The **Tomb of Cardinal Ranuccio Farnese** (d. 1565), the nephew of Pope Paul III Farnese, by Vignola is on the fifth pier, opposite the **Tomb of Cardinal Antonio Martino de Chaves** (d. 1447) by Isaia di Pisa. From the south transept with **Organ** by Luca Blasi (1598) and ancient antico giallo columns is the entrance from the north facade facing Piazza di S. Giovanni in Laterano.

To continue on the tour, exit the basilica from the south transept into Piazza di S. Giovanni in Laterano then veer left to enter the Lateran

Baptistery that is described following the optional tour directions and site descriptions. To take the optional 2km return stroll in the area of the Esquiline Hill to Santa Croce in Gerusalemme, the Museo degli Strumenti Musicali and the Porta Maggiore before continuing with the tour at the Lateran Baptistery, exit by the main entrance to the basilica into Piazza di Porta di S. Giovanni. Walk straight ahead on Viale Carlo Felice along the Aurelianic Walls and the Severan-era **Amphitheatrum Castrense** (not open to the public) that was incorporated into the wall to your right until you reach **Piazza di S. Croce in Gerusalemme**.

The Basilica of **S. Croce in Gerusalemme** occupies the site of a great hall of the Sessorium, the Imperial palace (late 2nd century/early 3rd century) later owned by St Helena that gave its name to the early basilica that she founded, the Basilica Sessoria (also called the Basilica Eleniana). The basilica is named for the relics of the True Cross that St Helena discovered on Mount Calvary (Golgotha) in Jerusalem. The basilica was rebuilt by Pope Lucius II (1144) and given to the Cistercian Order in 1561. The Rococo facade by Domenico Gregorini and Pietro Passalacqua (1743–1744) was added for Pope Benedict XIV whose elegant elliptical-shaped atrium with dome continues the theatricality of the facade. Statues on top depict St Helena, Constantine the Great and the Evangelists. The campanile dates to Pope Lucius' reconstruction of the basilica.

The ceiling fresco of *St Helena in Glory* and the *Apparition of the Cross* is by Corrado Giaquinto (1744). The 12 spoliated granite columns and cosmatesque pavement are preserved from the earlier church. Beneath the baldacchino, also by Gregorini and Passalacqua, are the relics of St Anastasius and St Caesarius. The apse fresco *Invention of the Cross* is attributed to Antoniazzo Romano. The **Tomb of Cardinal Francisco Quiñones** (d. 1540) is by Jacopo Sansovino. The cardinal negotiated the release of Pope Clement VII de' Medici from imprisonment following Emperor Charles V's Sack of Rome in 1527. At the end of the north aisle is the entrance to the **Chapel of the Relics** designed by Florestano di Fausto (1930). The reliquary by Giuseppe Valadier holds the relics of the True Cross and the Titulus. Other reliquaries hold the Holy Nail and Thorns. A copy of the Shroud of Turin is in an adjacent chapel. At the end of the south aisle is the entrance to the **Chapel of St Helen** at the level of the Sessorium. The vault mosaic design of *Christ, the Evangelists, St Peter,*

*St Paul, St Sylvester and Cardinal Carvajal* with *Scenes from the History of the Cross* is attributed to Melozzo da Forlì (*c.*1484) or Baldassarre Peruzzi (*c.*1510). On the west wall is the **Epitaph of Pope Benedict VII** (d. 983).

The **Museo degli Strumenti Musicali** is just beyond the basilica to your right through an ornamental gate. The museum is housed in the former barracks (Caserma dei Granatieri) next to the ruins of the so-called **Temple of Venus and Cupid**, an early 4th-century hall with apse by Maxentius or Constantine. The collection of instruments from antiquity to the 19th century, including the 'Barberini Harp' (early 17th century), was assembled by the Italian tenor Evan Gorga (Evangelista Gennaro Gorga) (1865–1957) who originated the role of Rodolfo in the original production of Puccini's *La Bohème* (1896). Behind the museum is the area of the **Circus Varianus** built by the Emperor Elagabulus and where he relocated the obelisk of Antinous now on the Pincian (Tour 10).

To visit the **Porta Maggiore**, continue on Viale Carlo Felice to Via Eleniana through to **Piazza di Porta Maggiore**. The Porta Maggiore was built by the Emperor Claudius (52 CE) from the arches supporting the aqueduct channels above from the Aqua Claudia and the Anio Novus. The inscription above the gates reveals the emperor's interest in antiquarian studies and language. Look up Via Giovanni Giolitti for the ruins of the so-called **Temple of Minerva Medica** (4th century), a monumental hemispherical structure with semicircular niches. It was formerly identified as a nymphaeum but may have been a dining pavilion in the Gardens of the Licinii (Horti Liciniani), the family of the Emperor Gallienus (253–268).

The gate was restored by the Emperor Honorius (405 CE) at which time the **Tomb of Eurysaces** on the **Piazzale Labicano** side was enclosed in a defence tower. The monumental tomb (*c.*30 BCE) belongs to the freedman Marcus Vergilius Eurysaces, the owner of a bakery, and his wife Atistia, and was uncovered during the restorations of Pope Gregory XVI (1838). It is in the shape of an oven and the frieze depicts scenes associated with breadmaking for commercial production.

Beyond Piazzale Labicano is the Quartiere Prenestino-Labicano that includes the popular residential area of Pigneto. On Via Prenestina (the ancient consular road Via Praenestina) just beyond Piazzale Prenestino (*c.*1.3km from Porta Maggiore) are the ruins of a 1st-century BCE circular tomb (42m diameter) known as the **Torrione**. Beyond on Via Prenestina, but too far to walk (*c.*3.3km from Porta Maggiore) is the 3rd-century CE **Villa of the Gordiani** with tombs lining the road including another circular mausoleum known as **Tor de' Schiavi** next to a circus-shaped basilica.

The **Lateran Baptistery**, contemporaneous with the original Constantinian basilica, was built over baths (2nd century CE) on the site of a 1st-century CE house. The baths are associated with the *Domus Faustae*, the house of Constantine's second wife, Fausta, where Pope Melchiades (313) convoked a synod and performed baptisms. Contrary to legend, Constantine was not baptised here, but rather on his deathbed in Constantinople. The current entrance by Pope Sixtus V replaced the original **atrium** entrance of Sixtus III on the opposite side. The interior of the baptistery was remodelled by Pope Sixtus III (432) who added the eight porphyry columns that support an architrave with eight smaller white marble columns. Pope Urban VIII Barberini added the ancient green basalt font with further restorations made by Borromini for Pope Alexander VII Chigi (1657) including the exterior frieze. To the right side of the entrance is the **Chapel of St John the Baptist** with a statue of St John the Baptist by Luigi Valadier and dedicated by Pope St Hilarius (461–468). The **Chapel of Ss. Rufina and Seconda** (also dedicated to **Ss. Cyprian and Justina**) by Pope Anastasius IV (1154) is in the original atrium entrance with an apse mosaic (5th century) of acanthus scrolls. Over the door is a *Crucifixion* relief by Andrea Bregno (1492). The **Chapel of St Venantius** was built by Pope John IV (640) with apse mosaics commissioned by Pope Theodore I (642–649) that depict Christ between two angels with the Virgin and saints. The **Chapel of St John the Evangelist** with a ceiling mosaic of the Lamb of God and flowers was dedicated by Pope St Hilarius (461–468).

Cross the piazza to the start of Via di S. Giovanni in Laterano. Retrace your steps towards the Colosseum for a very short distance when Via di S. Stefano Rotondo veers to your left along the route of the ancient Via Caelimontana. Proceed to the church of S. Stefano Rotondo on the Caelian Hill. The Caelian Hill (Celio in Italian) had the ancient name of Mons Querquetulanus (Oak Mountain) that tradition later associated with the Etruscan general Caele Vibenna from Vulci (6th century BCE). It was a residential area in antiquity with aristocratic villas mixed with multi-storey apartment buildings. The house of Domitia Lucilla Minor in the vicinity was where where she gave birth to the Emperor Marcus Aurelius. The area was sacked by Alaric in 410 and was rebuilt as a largely residential area that was destroyed again under the Normans. From the 4th to the 7th centuries, the hill was the site of the powerful titular churches of Ss. Giovanni e Paolo and the S. Gregorio Magno.

On the way to the church you pass several hospitals: the Ospedale Militare and the Ospedale Addolorata to your left on the site of the 4th-century house of the aristocratic Valerii family. To your right and later on the left are the ruins of the **Aqueduct of Nero** that was constructed after the Great Fire of 64 as an extension of the Aqua Claudia from the Porta Maggiore that extended to the Palatine Hill. Behind and to your right is the Ospedale Militare del Celio.

**Santo Stefano Rotondo** is a round 5th-century church built by Pope St Simplicius (468–483) to the protomartyr St Stephen over the site of a Mithraeum (2nd/3rd century) and part of the Castra Peregrina, the barracks for soldiers from the provinces. The original plan of three rings was altered in the 12th century and again in the 15th century by Pope Nicholas V who removed the third outer ring (1450) and commissioned the early Renaissance architect Bernardo Rossellino to make further alterations. The apse mosaic (7th century) depicts Christ on a jewelled cross but not crucified. In the Chapel of St Primus and Felicianus are early mosaics of the saints whose relics were translated here in the 7th century from a necropolis on the Via Nomentana. Pope Gregory XIII Boncompagni commissioned Pomarancio (Niccolò Circignani) and Antonio Tempesta to paint the frescoes with gruesome scenes of martyrdom.

Continue on Via di S. Stefano Rotondo. Cross Via della Navicella (look right to see the Colosseum) through Largo della Sanità Militare to reach S. Maria in Domnica just to your left in Piazza della Navicella. The fountain of the marble ship (*navicella*) was commissioned by Pope Leo X de' Medici (1513) in imitation of an ancient version that was on the site.

**Santa Maria in Domnica** (also called S. Maria della Navicella) was built into the ruins of the barracks of the V Cohort of the fire and police brigade (*Vigiles*) by Pope St Paschal I (817–824). It was later the titular church of Cardinal Giovanni de' Medici (the future Pope Leo X de' Medici) who commissioned Andrea Sansovino to redesign the facade and portico. The ceiling (1566) is decorated with symbols of the

*Litany of the Blessed Virgin Mary.* At the end of the nave with an arcade of spoliated columns is the triumphal arch with 9th-century mosaics of Christ between two angels and the Apostles with the prophets Moses and Elijah below. The 9th-century apse mosaic depicts the Virgin enthroned with the Christ Child with angels to either side in a field of flowers. Pope St Paschal I, kneeling, holds the right foot of the Virgin. The blue square nimbus around his head signifies that he was alive at the time of the mosaic's creation. The frieze frescoes are by Perino del Vaga to designs by Giulio Romano.

Adjacent to the church (to the left of the facade) is the monumental gate entrance (1615) to the **Villa Celimontana** that was formerly the Villa Mattei (1553), with gardens built by Cardinal Ciriaco Mattei (1582) and an ancient sculpture collection, many pieces of which are now in Palazzo Altemps (Tour 8). To your left on Viale Cardinale Francesco Spellman is an ancient **obelisk** from the Iseum in the Campus Martius that was given to Cardinal Mattei by the Senate (1582). It forms a pair with the obelisk now in the Fontana di Piazza della Rotonda in front of the Pantheon that dates to the reign of Ramesses II. The villa casino was designed by Jacopo del Duca (1581–1586) and since 1926 has been the home to the Società Geografica Italiana, with an extensive library and map collection, that was founded in Florence in 1867.

Retrace your steps and walk past the front of S. Maria in Domnica. On the other side of Via di S. Stefano Rotondo (the name changes to Via Claudia that descends to the Colosseum past the Parco del Celio), pass through the **Caelian Gate** (built in 10 CE), also known as the **Arch of Dolabella**, to your left and past the church of S. Tommaso in Formis at the start of Via di S. Paolo della Croce. Follow Via di S. Paolo della Croce into Piazza di Ss. Giovanni e Paolo. The church is straight ahead.

The Basilica of **Ss. Giovanni e Paolo** commemorates two officials in the court of Constantine who were martyred in 362 under the Emperor Julian. The site of the church with its successive layers of buildings that date back to the 1st century CE preserves archaeological evidence for the founding of an early Christian basilica and the importance of the Caelian Hill in the emergence of powerful titular churches. The 4th-century titular church (*Titulus Pammachii*) was built by St Pammachius on top of the house of his father, the Senator Byzantius, whose name also appears as a titular name of the church (*Titulus Byzantis*). The church was damaged by Alaric (410), destroyed by the Normans

(1084) and rebuilt by Pope Paschal II (1099–1118) who also rebuilt the adjoining convent over the site of the Temple of Deified Claudius, some of whose travertine blocks are visible at the base of his campanile. The portico (12th century) with spoliated columns and architrave support a closed gallery. Two lions flank the cosmatesque entrance. The interior, restored by Antonio Canevari (1715–1718) for Cardinal Paolucci, is lit by numerous chandeliers that give the church its familiar name of the Church of the Chandeliers (Chiesa dei Lampadari). In the cosmatesque pavement in the nave is the slab **Tomb of the Saints**. The busts of Cardinal Paolucci and Pope Innocent XII at the start of the nave are by Pietro Bracci (1725) who also made the stucco angels. The apse fresco of *Christ in Glory* (1588) is by Pomarancio (Cristoforo Roncalli). In the chapel at the end of the south aisle is the Tomb of St Paul of the Cross (1694–1775), the founder of the Passionists.

Follow Clivo di Scauro, the ancient Clivus Scauri (1st century BCE), to descend the hill along the wall of the church. The entrance to the **Roman Houses** and **Antiquarium** is between the arches. The site preserves successive levels of ancient Roman habitation and important fresco decoration. Excavations in 1887 revealed buildings (from the 1st to 4th century) associated with a 3rd-century *domus* that had incorporated a two-storey 2nd-century house with a private bath and an adjoining two-storey early 3rd-century apartment building (*insula*) with a portico and tabernae along Clivo di Scauro. Its outer wall was incorporated into the facade on this side of the church. This highly decorated *domus* passed to the ownership of Byzantius in the 4th century. He transformed it into the *domus ecclesiae* over which his son Pammachius built the titular church. The room of Pammachius and the Tomb of the Saints in the confessio were preserved in the foundations of the 12th-century church. The **Antiquarium** preserves sculpture fragments from the archaeological excavations with a collection of ancient glass and ceramics.

Continue on Clivo di Scauro past the ruins of the apse of the **Bibliotheca Agapeti**, the Ecclesiastic library of Greek and Latin texts built by Pope St Agapetus I on the grounds of his family villa (his father Gordianus was a priest at Ss. Paolo e Giovanni) that is connected to the adjacent villa of Pope St Gregory the Great. The ruins of 2nd- and 3rd-century apartment blocks (*insulae*) are in the area between the library and the church of S. Gregorio Magno. The Palatine Hill is visible straight ahead. Turn left on Salita di S. Gregorio to enter the church by the flight of stairs. If you would like to visit the ruins of the **Temple of the Deified Claudius** that extended from the area of the church of Ss. Giovanni e Paolo (built by his widow and niece Agrippina in 54 CE and converted by his heir Nero into a nymphaeum) or the former **Caelian Antiquarium** (Ex Antiquarium Comunale del Celio) in the Casino Salvi (1835), restored by Antonio Muñoz, turn right on Viale del Parco del Celio at the end of Clivo di Scauro then retrace your steps.

The church of **S. Gregorio Magno al Celio** (for entry, ring the monastery bell) is built on the site of Pope St Gregory the Great's (590–604) ancestral estate (gens Anicii Petronii), where he had constructed a monastery dedicated to St Andrew. The selection of the site indicates the collective importance of the Basilica of Ss. Giovanni e Paolo (that was on the pilgrim route of liturgical processions that he organised), the Bibliotheca Agapeti and his own monastery to the emergence of a papal centre on the Caelian Hill in the 7th century before the construction of the old Lateran Palace (the Lateran Patriarchium) as a permanent residence of popes in the 8th century. The Apostolic mission of St Augustine in Canterbury started here from the house of St Gregory in 596 before he began serving as the Archbishop of Canterbury in 597. In 1573 the monastery passed from the Benedictines to the Camaldolese Order which still resides here.

Cardinal Scipione Borghese, whose name appears over the main entrance to the portico with his family emblems of eagles and dragons, commissioned Giovanni Battista Soria (1629–1633) to remodel the exterior of the medieval church including the steps, facade and atrium. The funerary monuments were relocated in the **atrium** when the interior of the church was remodelled by Francesco Ferrari (1725–1734). The Renaissance **Monument to Lelio Guidiccione** (d. 1643) originally belonged to the famous courtesan Imperia. She was the mistress of the banker Agostino Chigi, Giacomo Sadoleto, the Secretary to Pope Leo X de' Medici, Filippo Beroaldo, the Prefect of the Vatican Library, and others including Angelo del Bufalo. She committed suicide at the age of 26 (1512) and was granted burial here by Pope Julius II della Rovere. The **Monument to Sir Edward Carne** (d. 1561) commemorates the Catholic ambassador of Queen Mary I of England who remained in Rome on the accession of Queen Elizabeth I. The **Monument to the Bonsi Brothers** is by Luigi Capponi (end of 15th/early 16th century).

The interior retains medieval elements of spoliated columns and the cosmatesque pavement (restored in 1745). The nave ceiling fresco is by Placido Costanzi (1727). Over the high altar is Antonio Balestra's *Madonna with St Andrew and St Gregory* (1734). To the right of the sanctuary in the **Chapel of St Gregory** are the *Altar of St Gregory* with three reliefs by Luigi Capponi and the *Throne of St Gregory* (1st century BCE). On the north side (second chapel), the *Madonna Enthroned with Christ Child and Saints* is by Pompeo Batoni (1739). The **Salviati Chapel** was completed by Carlo Maderno to designs by Francesco da Volterra (1600). The marble tabernacle is by Andrea Bregno and workshop. Tradition relates that the ancient fresco (repainted in the 14th/15th century) of the *Madonna and Child* spoke to St Gregory.

The **Oratories** are accessed to the left of the front steps through a gated garden (the former Benedictine cemetery) with ancient cypress trees. A gate that connects S. Gregorio Magno to the Bibliotheca Agapeti is closed to the public. In the centre is the **Chapel of Sant'Andrea** with a portico of spoliated columns by Flaminio Ponzio for Cardinal Borghese (1607–1608). The altarpiece *Madonna with St Andrew and St Gregory* (1602–1603) is by Pomarancio (Cristoforo Roncalli). On the right wall is the *Flagellation of St Andrew* by Domenichino (1608); on the left wall, *St Andrew being led to his martyrdom* by Guido Reni (1608); and on the west wall, *St Sylvia and St Gregory* by Giovanni Lanfranco (1608). To the left is the **Chapel of S. Barbara** (also called the Chapel of the Triclinium) with a statue of St Gregory by Nicolas Cordier (1602) and frescoes by Antonio Viviani (1602). According to tradition, St Gregory served the poor on the 3rd-century table. To the right is the **Chapel of S. Silvia**, the mother of St Gregory, with an apse fresco *Concert of Angels* by Guido Reni and Sisto Badalocchio (1602–1606) with a statue of St Silvia by Nicolas Cordier (1603–1604). The frescoes on the side walls of *David* and *Isaiah* are by Sisto Badalocchio Rosa (1608–1609).

Follow Salita di S. Gregorio along Via di S. Gregorio Magno. The Circus Maximus is to your right as you descend to Piazza di Porta Capena. The line of cypress trees to your right at the foot of the Palatine Hill marks the location of the **Septizodium** built by the Emperor Septimius Severus (193–211) as a monumental facade located at the important entry point of the Via Appia Antica through the Porta Capena. Pope Sixtus V used the surviving marble elements for many of his projects.

At the bottom of the salita is the **Vignola**, a Renaissance casino (16th century) that was relocated here from the area of S. Balbina in 1911. In the wooded valley behind it and S. Gregorio Magno is the **Grove of the Camenae** (water goddesses associated with springs), where the Vestal Virgins drew water daily. The grove was sacred to the nymph Egeria whom legend connected romantically with King Numa Pompilius. In the 1st century CE, the satirist Juvenal claims the area was home to a Jewish community. The grove was active until the late 4th century.

The **Piazza di Porta Capena** was the site of the ancient Porta Capena (now destroyed) in the Republican Walls at the start of the Via Appia Antica, the most important of the consular roads named for the censor Appius Claudius Caecus (312 BCE). The road led south through Campania to southern Italy and from there to North Africa. It also led to the Adriatic port city of Brindisi (ancient Brundisium) and from there to Greece and the eastern Mediterranean. For official business outside the pomerium of the city, the Senate met outside the gate in the Senaculum. Its prime location also made it a site where aristocrats and later emperors vied for the attention of passers-by with temples, altars, memorials and tombs such as the Tomb of the Scipios and later Imperial monuments that became enclosed within the city by the later Aurelianic Walls. Beyond the walls, the Via Appia Antica was crowded with tombs and catacombs for miles, and it is here that tradition places the meeting between Christ and St Peter (Tour 14). The twin columns in the centre of the piazza that are evocative of the World Trade Center Towers commemorate the victims of 9/11.

Walk across Via di S. Gregorio then across Via dei Cerchi to reach the **Circus Maximus** (Circo Massimo) in the valley (the ancient Vallis Murcia) between the Palatine (later connected with an Imperial viewing box) and Aventine Hills. The original circus at this location dates back to the period of the kings under Tarquinius Priscus (616–579 BCE). The grassy depression makes it difficult to imagine a monumental venue (600m x 200m) for chariot races and other spectacle entertainment (including executions) that could accommodate around 250,000 spectators in the 1st century CE. The original 12 starting gates (*carceres*) at the northern end were made of wood (329 BCE) but were later replaced with stone (174 BCE). The Ara Maxima of Hercules stood outside that end (Tour 4). A *spina* (long narrow island) in the centre was used originally for the counting of laps, originally with seven eggs but later also with seven dolphins added by Marcus Agrippa (33 BCE). A cone-shaped turning post (*meta*) was placed at the ends of the spina. The obelisk now in Piazza del Popolo was erected in the spina by the Emperor Augustus (10 BCE) and the obelisk now in Piazza di S. Giovanni in Laterano was erected here by Constantius II.

At the curved end facing Piazza di Porta Capena stood the Porta Triumphalis from which winning chariots and triumphing generals left the circus. It was later rebuilt and dedicated to the Deified Titus (81 CE) to commemorate his (and his father Vespasian's) victory in the Jewish War (70–71 CE), thus linking it and the Arch of Titus (Tour 6) with triumphing generals along the triumphal route. Sections of the arch's columns, stairs and seating (dating from the reign of Trajan) are visible near the medieval **Torre di Moletta** (12th century). The circus was active into the 5th century CE. The last known official races were organised by Totila, the King of the Ostrogoths, in 549 CE. It was systematically mined for building materials throughout the Middle Ages and remained empty until it became an industrial site in the 19th century. The area was cleared in the Fascist era and excavations begun in 1930s are still ongoing. The Circus of Maxentius on the Via Appia Antica (Tour 14) is better preserved, making it easier to reconstruct the various elements that are no longer visible here.

On the other side of the piazza from which you entered, cross the Viale Aventino onto Via Terme di Caracalla and continue past the UN Food and Agriculture Organisation (FAO) to your right. In front of the Stadio delle Terme di Caracalla, the street breaks, so cross the street and veer left to continue walking on Via Terme di Caracalla. The entrance to the Baths of Caracalla is to your right.

The **Baths of Caracalla** (Thermae Antoninianae) were built from 212 to 216 CE as part of the Severan monumental redesign of the area. The ruins still give a sense of their immense size and grandeur. They were the second largest bath complex in Rome after the Baths of Trajan (Tour 6). Water was supplied from a branch (the Aqua Antoniniana) of the Aqua Marcia. The ramp into the site gives a sense of the height of the platform on which the baths stand. Within the walls were two facing exedrae, two libraries and a stadium that formed three sides around ornamental gardens behind the bathing complex. In the centre of the bathing complex arranged from the main entrance facing Via Terme di Caracalla (in antiquity the Via Nova that was built parallel to the Via Appia) was the sequence of pools – *natatio* (open air pool), *frigidarium* (covered cool water pool), *tepidarium* (warm water) and circular *caldarium* (hot water) – that looked onto the gardens. Entry into the *frigidarium* from the flanking *palaestrae* was through an exedra and vestibule (off which were other rooms including changing rooms) that were symmetrically arranged to either side.

The baths remained active until the 6th century. A cemetery from the adjacent church of Ss. Nereus and Achilleus (founded in 595) occupied the eastern corner. Like the other sites of ancient Rome in the Middle Ages, it was systematically stripped of building materials, marbles, mosaic pavements and decoration including column capitals that were used in S. Maria in Trastevere (Tour 4) in the 12th century. In 1560, Cosimo I de' Medici requested a surviving granite column from his distant kinsman Pope Pius IV de' Medici for his Column of Justice in Piazza S. Trínita in Florence (1565–1581). Many famous statues in the Farnese collection were found here including the *Farnese Bull* and the *Farnese Hercules* that was found in several pieces and first displayed in Palazzo Farnese (Tour 3). The two granite basins that were in the vestibules that flanked the *frigidarium* are now in Piazza Farnese (Tour 3). The ruins of the baths provide a spectacular backdrop as the venue for the summer opera.

From the Baths of Caracalla, retrace your steps to Piazza di Porta Capena. From here you may walk or take the Metro to Piazzale Ostiense to continue to Tour 14. To walk, turn left at Viale Aventino to Piazzale Ostiense (.90km), walk along Viale Aventino through Piazza Albania in the area known as the Piccolo Aventino (in the centre is the **Equestrian statue of George Kastrioti Skanderbeg** and on the other side of the piazza are remnants of the **Republican Walls** that once enclosed the Porta Raudusculana) where the name changes to Viale di Piramide Cestia. Beyond the piazza to your right is the **Parco della Resistenza dell'8 Settembre** that was designed in 1939 and integrates the **Post Office** (1933–1935) in the Italian Rationalist architectural style. When you arrive at the end of Viale di Piramide Cestia into Piazza di Porta S. Paolo, cross to the other side of the street and walk past the gate of the Porta S. Paolo to your right into Piazzale Ostiense. Walk to the front of the Pyramid of Cestius to your right.

To take the Metro to Piazzale Ostiense, from Piazza di Porta Capena, turn left on Viale Aventino for the Circo Massimo entrance of the Metro line B and take the Metro one stop to Piramide. Exit the station and turn left, making your way to the Pyramid of Cestius by crossing to the other side of Viale Ostiense and then crossing Viale del Campo Boario.

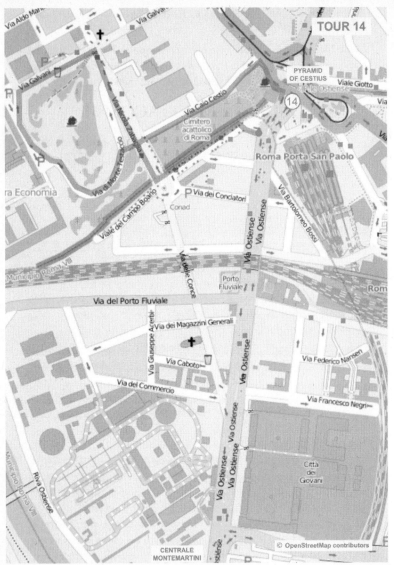

Sites: Piazzale Ostiense; Porta S. Paolo; Pyramid of Cestius; Protestant Cemetery; Rome British Military Cemetery; Testaccio; Macro Testaccio Museo d'Arte Contemporanea Roma (formerly Mattatoio di Testaccio). Options: Musei Capitolini Centrale Montemartini; Basilica S. Paolo fuori le Mura; EUR; Via Appia Antica: Domine, Quo Vadis?; Catacombs of S. Callisto; Basilica S. Sebastiano ad Catacumbas; Catacombs of Sebastiano; Villa of Maxentius; Tomb of Caecilia Metella; Tour of Tombs.

Distance: 1.25km + options: Museo Centrale Montemartini; Basilica S. Paolo fuori le Mura; EUR; and Via Appia Antica.

Tour 14

# TOMBS AND CATACOMBS

## Pyramid of Cestius and Via Appia Antica

The area of Testaccio features the ancient Pyramid of Cestius next to the beautifully landscaped Protestant Cemetery with Neoclassical and modern graves, including those of the English Romantic poets John Keats and Percy Bysshe Shelley. Nearby are Monte Testaccio, a relic of the ancient commercial port, and the Musei Capitolini Centrale Montemartini that is a satellite location of the Capitoline Museums. From Piazzale Ostiense there are several options to explore sites along Via Ostiense and points south, from antiquity to the Fascist era, accessible by bus or Metro line B, including the Basilica of S. Paolo fuori le Mura, EUR (Esposizione Universale di Roma) or the Via Appia Antica lined with catacombs and restored tombs.

**Piazzale Ostiense** outside the Aurelianic Walls is at the start of Via Ostiense which connected the ancient port city of Ostia to Rome as the main thoroughfare for commercial goods. The piazza is a commuting hub with bus stops, the **Piramide Metro line B station** (named after the Pyramid of Cestius) and the adjacent Porta S. Paolo rail station of the **Stazione Ferrovia Roma-Lido**. The latter was designed by Marcello Piacentini (1924) and built in conjunction with Piazza Venezia and Via del Teatro di Marcello (Tour 7) to connect the city to the Lido di Ostia (Tour 15). Along the side of the Piramide Metro station at the end of Viale Cave Ardeatine is the **Stazione Roma Ostiense** in **Piazzale dei Partigiani**, a Fascist-era train station designed by Roberto Narducci (1938) for the arrival of Hitler. The relief of *Bellerophon and Pegasus* on the facade is by Francesco Nagni (1940).

The now isolated **Porta S. Paolo** is the ancient Porta Ostiense with medieval additions, including a chapel, to the round towers to either side of the gate built by the Emperor Honorius (401–403). The Aurelianic Walls were built into the pyramid at the time of the Porta Ostiense's construction. A plaque commemorates the location of the Resistance of 10 September 1943 when the wall was breached between the gate and the pyramid. Nearby memorials commemorate the Liberation of Rome on 4 June 1944 by the 'Devil's Brigade', the American and Canadian 1st Special Service Force. The wider breach on the other side of the gate was opened earlier in 1920 to accommodate increased traffic. Inside the gate is the **Museo della Via Ostiense** devoted to the Via Ostiense between the gate and Ostia Antica (Tour 15).

The **Pyramid of Cestius** was built between 18 and 12 BCE with blocks of white Luna marble over a cement core (36.4m high x 30m base) as the Tomb of Gaius Cestius whose public offices are recorded in identical inscriptions on both the east and west sides. The barrel-vaulted burial chamber (*c.*6m x 4m) was decorated with wall paintings. The opening on the west side dates to the excavations under Pope Alexander VII Chigi who restored the monument in 1663. The two columns at the western corners of the pyramid were found at this time and re-erected at their original location. The Ptolemaic pyramid form reflects the Egyptomania following Augustus' defeat of Mark Antony and Cleopatra at the Battle of Actium in 31 BCE and the annexation of Egypt as a province. In the Middle Ages, it was known as the *Meta Remi* (Tomb of Remus) in conjunction with another pyramid tomb, the *Meta Romuli* (Tomb of Romulus), near the Vatican (Tour 2). For English Grand Tour visitors to Rome, including Charles Dickens and Thomas Hardy, the pyramid marked the location of the tombs of Keats and Shelley in the Protestant Cemetery.

Walk around the right side of the pyramid then follow the curve of the road along the wall of the cemetery along Via Raffaele Persichetti then Via Caio Cestio. Look for a window in the wall when you first turn the corner onto Via Caio Cestio to see the Tomb of Keats. A second window a short distance beyond gives a view of the Old Cemetery. The entrance to the cemetery is to your left at No. 6.

The **Protestant Cemetery** (officially the Cimitero Acattolico di Roma that is also known as the Cimitero Acattolico per gli Stranieri al Testaccio) is the historic cemetery for non-Catholic burials in the city

13. Protestant Cemetery with a view of the Pyramid of Cestius

(some 4,000 burials). Pope Clement XI Albani allowed burials of non-Catholics next to the pyramid but services could only be held at night and no expression of salvation could appear in epitaphs. Among the earliest Protestant burials were Jacobites associated with the Stuart court and travellers including the Anglican Thomas Pakington (d. 1720), the son of Sir John Pakington, who contracted fever in Rome while on the Grand Tour, and Oxford student George Langton, who was laid to rest next to the pyramid (1738). It is a beautiful place to stroll amidst the unique memorials including the tombs of Percy Bysshe Shelley (1792–1822) and John Keats (1796–1821) who is next to his friend Joseph Severn (1793–1879), the painter and later British Consul in Rome who paid for the matching tombstones. Keats died at the Keats-Shelley Memorial House next to the Spanish Steps (Tour 10). Keats wrote his own epitaph: 'Here lies one whose name was writ in water.' In the preface to *Adonais: An Elegy on the Death of John Keats* (1821), Shelley described the setting of Keats' tomb: 'It might make one in love with death, to think that one should be buried in so sweet a place.'

To the far right of the entrance is the **Tomb of Antonio Gramsci** (1891–1937), the influential Marxist and one of the founders of communism in Italy who was imprisoned by the Fascists from 1926 until his death. The grave was immortalised in Pier Paolo Pasolini's poem 'Le ceneri di Gramsci' (1957). In this section are also Greek Orthodox and Jewish burials.

Continue along the cemetery wall on Via Caio Cestio to the end of the block. The **Rome British Military Cemetery**, also known as the Rome Commonwealth Military Cemetery, is across the street to your left on Via Nicola Zabaglia at No. 50. The cemetery contains 426 Commonwealth burials of World War II.

Facing the cemetery, turn right to walk along Via Nicola Zabaglia. The hill that rises behind the row of bars and restaurants is **Monte Testaccio** (*c.*30m above the current street level) that the tour circles before returning to Piazzale Ostiense. At the end of the street are the ruins of the ancient warehouse, the **Porticus Aemilia** (193 BCE and rebuilt in 174 BCE), that was associated with the nearby harbour complex. Turn left on Via Galvani for a better view of the hill (*c.*1.0km in circumference) that takes its name from the pile of ancient Roman potsherds that was terraced using broken storage vessels (*amphorae*) used for the transport of wine, olive oil, fish sauce and other products. The Amphora Fountain (Fontana delle Anfore) in **Piazzale dell'Emporio**, where Via Marmorata meets the Tiber, commemorates the ancient harbour and warehouses that led to the creation of Monte Testaccio.

Continue on Via Galvani to the end of the block to Piazza Orazio Giustiniani to the former slaughterhouse (**ex Mattatoio di Testaccio**) designed by Gioacchino Ersoch (1888–91) with a distinctive cow statue over the facade. It is now the **Macro Testataccio Museo D'Arte Contemporanea Roma** with exhibitions of contemporary art and events.

Turn left to walk along the curved Via di Monte Testaccio. The shops of ironworkers line the street but at night it is famous for bars and dance clubs. The street ends at the staircase next to the **Fontana del Boccale** ('Fountain of the Jug') by Raffaele de Vico (1931) next to the Rome British Military Cemetery. Cross to the other side of Via Nicola Zabaglia and turn right to walk along the outer wall of the Protestant Cemetery. Go through the arch and turn left to walk along the Aurelianic Walls on Via del Campo Boario. The Pyramid of Cestius is straight ahead. Cross to the other side of Via del Campo Boario when you reach Piazzale Ostiense at the start of Via Ostiense.

14. Via Appia Antica

From this point, there are several options to continue the tour by bus from Piazzale Ostiense or by Metro line B Stazione Piramide: Musei Capitolini Centrale Montemartini, the Basilica of S. Paolo fuori le Mura, EUR, or to visit the catacombs and walk along the Via Appia Antica. You may also take the Roma–Lido train from the Porta S. Paolo train station to visit Ostia Antica or the Lido di Ostia (Tour 15) or take the Roma–Lido train from the Basilica S. Paolo station after visiting the basilica. An ATAC ticket is valid for all transportation options.

The **Musei Capitolini Centrale Montemartini** is a satellite of the Capitoline Museums opened in 1997 in the former location of Rome's first power plant, the Giovanni Montemartini Thermoelectric Centre (1912). To walk, the Museum is .80km away (walk up Via Ostiense with Piazzale Ostiense behind you). To take the bus, cross Via Ostiense to the island in the middle of the street. Take bus No. 23 or No. 769 at the stop to your right that goes up Via Ostiense. The Museum is only three stops away on the right side of the street with a banner hanging outside at No. 106.

Relics from the ancient city were unearthed as construction of the modern city progressed and displayed here juxtaposed with industrial machinery. On the **ground floor**, beyond the displays in the **atrium** on the history of the building and its conversion into the museum, is the **Hall of the Columns** with displays of funerary and domestic goods and Late Republican portraiture including portraits of Julius Caesar and Augustus (27–20 BCE) and the famous *Barberini Togatus* of a man who carries the portrait busts of his ancestors in evocation of an aristocratic Roman funeral procession. On the **first floor** in the **Hall of the Machines**, the former engine room, are Roman copies of Greek sculpture (faithful reproductions and variations). These include statues from the pediment of the Temple of Apollo Medicus near the Theatre of Marcellus (Tour 4) that are Greek originals depicting a battle between Greeks and Amazons and from the Area Sacra of Largo di Torre Argentina (Tour 7) with the colossal acrolith statue of *Fortuna Huiusce Diei* from Temple B. In the **Boiler Room** are sculptures from ancient gardens (*horti*) and villas, including the Gardens of Sallust (Tour 11) with Greek original statues and sculpture from the reign of Augustus. Return to Piazzale Ostiense to continue with the other tour options.

To visit the Basilica S. Paolo fuori le Mura, from the Piramide Metro line B station take the train two stops in the direction of Laurentina to the Basilica S. Paolo stop (that is also a station for the Roma–Ostia train). Exit Via Ostiense and turn right. The basilica is ahead to your left but you need to walk around the apse and north side to reach the front entrance. The distance from the Metro stop is about .40km.

The **Basilica of S. Paolo fuori le Mura** ('St Paul Outside the Walls') is one of four extraterritorial basilicas and the second in size after St Peter's. According to the Book of Acts, St Paul arrived in Rome in 60 CE to visit with the Christian community. Paul spent two years under house arrest, which Church tradition places in the Mamertine Prison (Tour 5), before his transfer to the place of his martyrdom farther south on the Via Ostiense at the site of **Abbazia delle Tre Fontane**. The Chiesa di San Paolo alle Tre Fontane (also known as the Chiesa del Martirio di San Paolo) commemorates the location of his martyrdom. The Feast day of Saints Peter and Paul (29 June) is celebrated with a street fair on Via Ostiense. The basilica marks the site where St Paul was buried by a matron named Lucina in the **Necropoli Ostiense**, the extant ruins of which are visible in the archaeological area that is covered by a roof just north of the basilica on Via Ostiense. In 324, Pope Sylvester I consecrated the small basilica founded by Constantine the Great on the site of an earlier memorial chapel (*tropaeum*). Constantine's basilica was replaced by a larger basilica by the Emperors Valentinian II and Theodosius I that was further enlarged by Emperor Honorius in 395 and Pope Leo III (795–816). The basilica, Benedictine monastery and surrounding village areas were fortified by Pope John VIII (872–882) after an attack by the Saracens and named after him 'Giovannopolis'. The renovations by Onorio Longhi and Carlo Maderno for Pope Sixtus V destroyed 13th-century artwork by Pietro Vassalletto, Pietro Cavallini (nave frescoes) and Arnolfo di Cambio and 15th-century artwork by Benozzo Gozzoli and Antoniazzo Romano.

A devastating fire on 15 and 16 July 1823 destroyed most of the church except for areas around the sanctuary and transept. It was rebuilt by Pope Leo XII who copied the exterior facade and Neoclassical interior of the church. Pope Gregory XVI consecrated the rebuilt transept (1840) and the entire church was consecrated soon after by Pope Pius IX (1854). The stain glass windows were destroyed by a nearby explosion (1891) and replaced with alabaster. The **campanile** with its lighthouse shape and facade are by Luigi Poletti (1833–1869), while the **quadriporticus** by Virginio Vespignani (1890–1892) was remodelled by Guglielmo Calderini (1892–1928). The statue of St Paul is by Giuseppe Obici. The main door is by Antonio Maraini (1929–1931). The **Porta Santa** (far right of the entrance) is only opened in

Holy years and just inside are the Byzantine bronze doors from the Old Church by Stavrakios (1070).

The vast interior (132m x 65m with a height of 30m) in the shape of an Egyptian cross (Tau) has five aisles with 80 columns that date to the 19th-century reconstruction. The six alabaster columns at the west end were a gift from Mohammed Ali of Egypt who also gave the four alabaster columns by the ciborium. The walls are lined with 19th-century frescoes on the *Life of St Paul* with mosaics of the popes below. The mosaics on the **triumphal arch** survived the fire and were restored. Facing the nave, Christ blessing in the Greek manner is flanked by angels, symbols of the Evangelists, Church Elders and Saints Peter and Paul. On the side facing the apse are mosaics by Pietro Cavallini. The **ciborium** over the high altar with four porphyry columns is by Arnolfo di Cambio (1285). The Paschal Candelabrum is signed by Nicolò di Angelo and Pietro Vassalletto (12th century). The **Tomb of St Paul** is in the **confessio** with his relics (except for his head that, according to tradition, is in S. Giovanni in Laterano) in a 4th-century marble sarcophagus inscribed in Latin 'To Paul the Apostle and Martyr'. Holes in the front indicate that pipes once allowed libations to be poured from above ground in the ancient Roman custom.

The **apse mosaic** (*c*.1220) is a Venetian work that depicts Christ blessing in the Greek manner flanked by St Peter and St Luke (to his right) and St Paul and St Andrew (to his left). At Christ's foot is Pope Honorius III who commissioned the mosaic from the Doge Pietro Ziani who sent the artists. To the left of the sanctuary is the **Chapel of the Crucifix** (Cappella del SS. Sacramento) by Carlo Maderno, with the **Tomb of Pietro Cavallini,** that survived the fire. The 14th-century Crucifix was formerly attributed to him. Saint Ignatius of Loyola and his companions made their first public vows before the chapel with the Byzantine icon of the *Madonna and Child* (12th/13th century) on 22 August 1541. To the far left is the **Chapel of St Stephen** the Protomartyr. Over the north transept altar is the *Conversion of St Paul* by Vincenzo Camuccini. The malachite and lapis lazuli for both transept altars were gifts of Tsar Nicholas I of Russia. From the north transept there is access to the north portico with 12 Hymettian marble columns that were salvaged from the old church (one has a 4th-century inscription of Pope Siricius).

To the right of the sanctuary is the **Chapel of the Choir** (also known as the **Chapel of St Lawrence**) by Carlo Maderno (1629). The 15th-century marble triptych is attributed to the school of Andrea Bregno. To the far right is the **Chapel of St Benedict**. In the south transept over the altar is a copy of Giulio Romano's *Coronation of the Virgin*. To the right of the altar, through the Oratory of St Julian (S. Giuliano), there is access to the **baptistery** (1930) and the **cloister** whose more successful north wall was designed by the Vassalletti family (*c.*1228). The other walls, also in the cosmatesque style (from 1208) with double columns supporting the arcades, are similar to those in the cloister at S. Giovanni in Laterano. Sculpture fragments and inscriptions line the walls. In the adjacent **Pinacoteca** and **Chapel of the Reliquaries** (Cappella delle Reliquie) is a collection of liturgical items including silver and vestments. Paintings include the *Madonna and Child with Four Saints* by Antoniazzo Romano.

Retrace your steps to the Metro line B Basilica S. Paolo station. From here there are several options: take Metro line B (in the direction of Rebibbia) to return to Piramide station and Piazzale Ostiense; take Metro line B (in the direction of Laurentina) to visit EUR (exit at the EUR Fermi station); or take the Roma–Lido train to Ostia Antica or the Lido di Ostia (Tour 15).

To visit **EUR** (**Esposizione Universale di Roma**), from Metro line B (in the direction of Laurentina) exit the EUR Fermi station onto Viale America. Walk straight ahead one block to Largo G. Pella at Via Cristoforo Colombo, the main road that cuts through the centre of EUR. The initial design of EUR was by Marcello Piacentini (1938) for the 1942 World's Fair as a showplace for the achievements of Fascism, but the event was cancelled because of World War II. Construction resumed in 1952 with the addition of various government offices. To your left beyond the lake is **Palazzo dello Sport** (now called PalaLottomatica) designed by Pier Luigi Nervi and Marcello Piacentini (1958–1960) for the 1960 Olympic Games. The cupola is 100m in diameter. To your right, Via Cristoforo Colombo leads to the main sites and museums.

Turn right on Via Cristoforo Colombo to walk towards Piazza Guglielmo Marconi. At Viale Europa, to your left is the **Museo Storico delle Poste e delle Telecommunicazioni**. To your far left is the monumental church of **Ss. Pietro e Paolo a Via Ostiense** that was begun by Arnaldo Foschini (1938) but completed in 1955. The dome is

72m high with a diameter of 28m. To your right is the Ministero delle Finanze and to your far right is Piazzale dei Archivi.

The **Piazza Marconi** is named for the radio and telegraph pioneer Guglielmo Marconi (1874–1937). In the centre is the **Stele a Guglielmo Marconi** (45m high), also called the Obelisco dell'EUR, that commemorates his achievements by Arturo Dazzi (1938–1959). Upon entering the piazza, to your right is the **Museo Nazionale Preistorico ed Etnografico Luigi Pigorini**. The prehistoric collection focuses on the various regions of Italy in the Stone, Bronze and Iron Ages. The ethnogrpahic collection features objects from Africa, the Americas and Oceania. Opposite the stele to your left is the skyscraper **Grattacielo Italia** by Luigi Mattioni (1959–1960).

To the right of the stele is Viale della Civiltà Romana. The **Museo Nazionale dell'Alto Medioevo** is to your right with a collection of late antique to the 10th-century objects including jewellery, pottery and mosaics (*opus sectile*) from a reconsructed room from Ostia Antica (Tour 15). Beyond it at the end of the street is the **Museo della Civiltà Romana** that is housed in two buildings (1939–1952) connected by a double colonnade. The collection of plaster casts of monuments and statues surveys various historical periods of Roman civilisation (rooms to the right of the museum entrance) and daily life of the ancient Romans (rooms to the left of the museum entrance). In the exhibition space beneath the colonnade are plaster casts of the reliefs from the Column of Trajan (Tour 6) made by Napoleon III (1860). In the far wing are rooms devoted to Roman achievements in the arts and sciences and a **plastic model of Rome** (scale 1:250) in the time of Constantine, first displayed in 1937 at an exhibition called 'Augustea della Romanità' held in the Baths of Diocletian (Tour 12).

Return to Piazza Marconi and continue walking up Via Cristoforo Colombo. Upon leaving the piazza, to your right is the entrance to the **Museo Nazionale delle Arti e delle Tradizione Popolari**. The collection focuses on Italian daily life up to World War II with displays of arts and crafts, furniture, costumes, toys and transportation. Continue walking up Via Cristoforo Colombo to Viale della Civiltà del Lavoro. Beyond, is **Piazzale delle Nazioni Unite** that is flanked by the hemicycles of facing palazzi. To your right is **Palazzo dei Ricevimenti dei Congressi**, or simply, **Palazzo dei Congressi**, designed by Adalberto Libera (1938–1954) with atrium paintings by Gino Severini. To your left is the monumental **Palazzo della Civiltà del Lavoro** (1938–1943), now called **Palazzo della Civiltà Italiana** but it is also known as the **Quadrato della Concordia** or simply, the **Colosseo Quadrato**. It was designed by Giovanni Guerrini, Ernesto Bruno La Padula and Mario Romano. The distinctive design of a cube consisting of six levels of tiered arches is synonymous with EUR. At the corners are statues of the *Dioscuri* (Castor and Pollux) by Publio Morbiducci and Alberto Felci with statues on the lower level representing the arts and sciences. The inscription reads 'A people of poets, artists, heroes, saints, thinkers, scientists, navigators, transmigrants'. Walk down the steps behind the palazzo and cross Viale Romolo Murri and turn right on Viale Val Fiorita to Piazzale di Val Fiorita to the Magliana station of Metro line B. To return to Piazzale Ostiense or other points in the historic centre of Rome, take Metro line B in the direction of Rebibbia. To visit Ostia Antica or the Lido di Ostia (Tour 15), take the Roma–Lido train from the Magiana station in the direction of Cristoforo Colombo.

From Piazzale Ostiense, take bus No. 118 (the stop is in the centre island) to the Catacombs of S. Sebastiano on the **Via Appia Antica**. There are many tombs of historic significance such as the Tomb of the Scipios, between Porta Capena and Porta S. Sebastiano. The bus exits the Aurelianic Walls at Porta S. Sebastiano. The column imbedded in the wall just past the gates is a copy of the first milestone that is now displayed in Piazza del Campidoglio. The Via Appia Antica forks into Via Ardeatina at the church of Domine, Quo Vadis? When the Tomb of Caecilia Metella becomes visible after a few stops, ring the bell. The bus stops in front of the Basilica of S. Sebastiano (description follows tour options).

To visit the church of Domine, Quo Vadis? and the Catacombs of S. Callisto, exit the bus earlier. The stop is just beyond the church at the entrance to the Catacombs of S. Callisto in the island formed by the fork in the road between Via Appia Antica and Via Ardeatina.

The church of **Domine, Quo Vadis?** (also known as S. Maria in Palmis) marks the location where, according to tradition (based on the Apocryphal Acts of Peter), St Peter fleeing persecution encountered the Risen Christ and asked, '*Domine, quo vadis?*' ('Lord, where are you going?'). Christ replied, '*Romam vado iterum crucifigi*' ('I am going to Rome to be crucified again'). This exchange shamed Peter to return to the city for his own crucifixion. There is a plaster copy of the stone that tradition preserves as bearing the imprint of Christ's footprints embedded in the nave (the original is in the Basilica of S. Sebastiano). St Paul also entered the city by the ancient Via Appia.

Opposite the church is the cylinder tomb identified as the **Tomb of Priscilla**, wife of T. Flavius Abascantus, the freedman of the Emperor Domitian. The information office of the **Parco Regionale dell'Appia Antica** is at No. 60 (in the direction of Rome) where bicycle rentals are available.

Cross the street to enter the Catacombs of S. Callisto or continue on Via Appia Antica (in the opposite direction of Rome) for the main entrance. Traffic in the narrow roadway makes walking this stretch difficult. The Via della Caffarella to your left leads to the **Parco della Caffarella**, a 400-hectare public park with grazing sheep that preserves an area of the historic Campagna Romana including the **Tomb of Annia Regilla** (the wife of Herodes Atticus), the **Nymphaeum of Egeria**, the church of **Sant'Urbano** and the **Catacombs of Praetextatus**.

A short distance from the church on the Via Appia Antica at the second Roman mile mark are the ruins of the **Columbarium of the Freedmen of Augustus** (No. 87). The **Columbarium of the Freedmen of Livia** was discovered (1725) nearby but is now destroyed. Its inscriptions now line the Galleria of Palazzo Nuovo, Capitoline Museums (Tour 5). At No. 119a are the **Jewish Catacombs** (no public entry).

The **Catacombs of S. Callisto** are named for St Callixtus who was appointed caretaker of them by Pope Zepherinus (199–217), whom he succeeded as pope. Over multiple levels, niches (*loculi*) for inhumation burial line the tunnels, with taller rounded niches (*arcosolia*) for sarcophagus burials in approximately 20km of tunnels. Larger spaces (*cubicula*) were carved out of the tufa rock for multiple burials. The catacombs contain the burials of 16 popes (3rd to 4th century) in the **Papal Chapel**, 50 martyrs and the **Cubiculum of S. Cecilia** that was visited by pilgrims at an early date and where there is a copy of Stefano Maderno's statue in S. Cecilia in Trastevere (Tour 4) portraying how her body was discovered.

From the grounds of the site, there is access to Via Ardeatine. Exit and walk away from Rome just beyond Via delle Sette Chiese. The **Mausoleo delle Fosse Ardeatine** is ahead to your right at No. 174. The memorial and museum commemorate the former quarry site where on 24 March 1944 Nazis killed 335 civilians and prisoners of the Italian

Resistance (including Jews) in retaliation for the death of 33 Germans on Via Rasella. The statues over the mass grave are by Francesco Coccia (1950). The **Catacombs of Domitilla** are on Via delle Sette Chiese at No. 282, in the direction of Rome.

The **Basilica S. Sebastiano ad Catacumbas** (also called S. Sebastiano fuori le Mura) was originally built by Constantine the Great as a circus-shaped basilica over the necropolis site (active from the 2nd to the 5th century), the name of which is the origin of the word catacombs. It is one of the seven pilgrim churches of Rome. After St Sebastian was martyred on the Palatine Hill in the so-called Stadium of Domitian (Tour 6), his body was thrown into the Cloaca Maxima and later buried in the necropolis here. Pope Honorius III Savelli (1216–1227) returned the relics of St Sebastian here after they were relocated to St Peter's Basilica during the 9th-century Saracen invasion of Italy. The church was rebuilt (1608–1613) by Flaminio Ponzio and Giovanni Vasanzio for Cardinal Scipione Borghese, the nephew of Pope Paul V Borghese. The facade arcade incorporates columns from the original church.

The ceiling decoration is by Giovanni Vasanzio (17th century). In the sanctuary, the high altar aedicula with ancient columns is by Flaminio Ponzio (1610–1612). The altar is made from an ancient Christian sarcophagus. The **Chapel of St Sebastian** on the north side is directly above his grave in the Catacombs. The statue is by Antonio Giorgetti (1671–1672) to a design by Bernini. On the south side, the **Chapel of the Relics** (1625) contains the stone relic of Christ's footprints from the church of Domine, Quo Vadis? The bust of Christ, *Salvator Mundi*, is among Bernini's last works (1678–1679). The **Albani Chapel** was built for Pope Clement XI Albani by Carlo Fontana, Alessandro Specchi and Filippo Barigioni to a design by Carlo Maratta (1706–1712).

The **Catacombs of S. Sebastiano** necropolis site were active from the end of the 1st/beginning of the 2nd century to the 5th century CE. The excavations by Giovanni Battista de Rossi (1850) made the underground world of early Christianity more accessible to pilgrims and travellers. A large display of early Christian sarcophagi and inscriptions (*tituli*) precedes the descent into the catacombs. Many of the niches remain unexplored but those along the tour are empty. Beyond a series of *cubicula* including the **Cubiculum of Jonah** (4th century), named after the fresco decoration, is the **Crypt of St Sebastian** with a 4th-century staircase that led to the tomb from the original basilica. At a lower level is the area called the **Piazzuola** with three pagan so-called House tombs (2nd century CE) with stucco and painting decoration, including the **Tomb of M. Clodius Hermes** that has a fresco of a funeral banquet and another of a Gorgon. The middle tomb seems to have added Christian burials. Fresco decorations include a peacock, acanthus and lotus leaves. The third is decorated with a grapevine motif. Returning to a higher level, funerary feasts were celebrated in the communal area called the **Triclia** (perhaps related to *triglia*, the fish eaten here) that was once open-air but covered over at a later date.

To return to Piazzale Ostiense, exit the basilica piazza left in the direction of the city. Look for the busy Via Appia Pignatelli to your right. Carefully cross the street and turn right to walk on the far side to the No. 118 bus stop just ahead to your left. There is another bus stop on Via Appia Antica opposite the entrance gate in the wall to the Catacombs of S. Callisto. To continue with the tour, exit the basilica piazza right. Opposite is the **Column of Pope Pius IX** that commemorates the restoration of the tombs along Via Appia Antica by archaeologist and architect Luigi Canina (1851–1853) from the basilica to the town of Bovillae.

The **Via Appia Antica**, preserved as an archaeological park called the Parco Regionale dell'Appia Antica with ancient cypress and pine trees that were planted in the late 19th century, is closed to vehicle traffic beyond the Tomb of Caecilia Metella where bicycle rentals are currently available. The picturesque road that inspired composer Ottorino Respighi's *Pini di Roma* ('The Pines of Rome') preserves the longest stretch of straight road in Europe (62km). The tour distance is 4.71km from the Catacombs of S. Sebastiano to Via Erode Attico, just before the ancient Roman fifth mile mark (1 Roman mile = 1.48km) with an option to continue strolling to just before the Roman sixth mile mark at Casal Rotondo. There are few places to purchase food or beverages, so plan an *al fresco* lunch.

The ancient Via Appia was built by the censor Appius Claudius Caecus (312 BCE) during the Samnite Wars. The 'Appian Way' was the most important consular road, referred to by the poet Statius as the 'Queen of Roads'. It connected the city of Rome through Campania to southern Italy and from there to Africa but also to the port city of Brindisi (ancient Brundisium) to sail to Greece and the eastern Mediterranean. It entered Rome at Porta Capena (Tour 13). The road was much travelled by the Roman army, governors setting out for their provinces with their retinue, aristocrats studying in Athens and local Romans visiting the tombs. On portions of the road, wheel ruts are still visible but gone are traces of the crucifixions that lined the road – after Spartacus' revolt was quelled in 71 BCE, 6,000 men were crucified along the road from Rome to Capua, a distance of 200km.

After burial, sites were visited on special feast days to offer sacrifices, pour libations and eat funerary meals. Later, Christians shared meals at the catacombs that they visited as martyr shrines. A wide variety of tombs and memorials lined the consular roads. After the catacombs were abandoned in the 5th century, intramural burials in Rome clustered around churches, pilgrim sites and the ruins of ancient monuments including the Colosseum. In the Middle Ages deteriorating tombs would provide visitors with their first glimpse of the city whose ancient monuments were also decaying and being absorbed into medieval buildings. The foundations of roadside tombs survive in Ostia Antica (Tour 15).

A visit to the Via Appia and surrounding countryside (Campagna Romana) was an essential part of the Grand Tour and the reaction of Charles Dickens (*Pictures from Italy*, 1844) to its evocative and instructive power is typical: 'Here was Rome at last; and such a Rome as no one can imagine in its full and awful grandeur! We wandered out upon the Appian Way, and then went on, through miles of ruined tombs and broken walls [...] A desert of decay, sombre and desolate beyond all expression; and with a history in every stone that strews the ground.' Today, private villas built after World War II line the road behind high walls and hedges but a view through the occasional gate gives an impression of the vast area unspoiled by urban sprawl.

In the distance to your left are the arcades of the **Aqua Claudia** in the **Parco degli Acquedotti** with the Acqua Felice in a low covered vault and the traditional farm house known as the Casale di Roma Vecchia that are best accessed from Metro line A. Exit the Giulio Agricola station and follow Via Giulio Agricola to the park entrance next to the church of S. Policarpo on Via Lemonia at No. 256.

The ruins of the **Villa of Maxentius (Villa di Massenzio)**, Constantine's co-emperor and rival, are to your left at No. 153. The villa complex (309 CE) includes the well-preserved **Circus of Maxentius** (*c.*513m x 90m) that was not for the public but for the emperor's use, and the circular **Mausoleum of Romulus**, the emperor's son (d. 307), visible from the road behind the farmhouse. Its design resembles the Pantheon (surrounded by a quadriporticus) and it may have been built as a dynastic complex to include his father Maximian (d. 310) and other family members. Continue walking along the Via Appia Antica. At the third Roman milestone to your left at No. 161 is the famous monumental circular **Tomb of Caecilia Metella** (**Sepolcro di Cecilia Metella**). The inscription identies Caecilia as the daughter of Quintus Creticus and the wife of Crassus. Quintus Metellus Creticus was consul in 69 BCE and her husband M. Licinius Crassus was the elder son of the triumvir (with Pompey and Julius Caesar) who lost the Roman standards to the Parthians at the Battle of Carrhae (53 BCE). Their son was M. Licinius Crassus, the consul of 30 BCE, who was denied the spoils of a general whom he killed in battle (*spolia opima*) by the Emperor Augustus, who nonetheless granted him a triumph, the last celebrated by a non-member of the Imperial family.

In the Middle Ages, the tomb was known as Torre di Capo di Bove because of the bucrania (ox head skulls) decoration of the frieze and was incorporated into the fortress of the Caetani (given to them by their relative Pope Boniface VIII, allowing them to control access to the city) when the crenellated top was added to the tower. The fortress passed in turn to the powerful Savelli (in 1302), Colonna and Orsini families until it was demolished by Pope Sixtus V. The entrance to the fortress was bricked off in the 19th century and now contains a display of sculpture fragments. The small museum of grave markers, memorials and cinerary urns in the courtyard was arranged by Antonio Muñoz. The interior of the tower (*c*.30m in diameter) is now empty. Across the street are the ruins of the church of **S. Nicola di Bari** (also called S. Nicola a Capo di Bove) that was built by the Caetani and once enclosed in the fortress complex.

Currently at No. 175, at the corner of Via dei Metelli, the Bar Appia Antica Caffè offers bicycle rentals every day except Mondays. After you pass several modern villas, you come to the round tomb to your left called **Capo di Bove** at No. 222. Across the street to your right are archaeological ruins of a Roman bath complex (2nd century CE) that was active until the 4th century. The adjacent **Capo di Bove Museum** is dedicated to the Via Appia Antica and contains didactic texts and the archive of Antonio Cederna.

To return to Piazzale Ostiense, retrace your steps to the Basilica of S. Sebastiano and follow directions (given above) to the No. 118 bus stop. To continue, stroll past more modern villas until the archaeological zone comes into view for a **Tour of Tombs**.

The **Tomb of the Heroic Nude** to your right is a copy of the life-size statue of a nude male that is Hellenistic in its sculptural style. On the other side of the fence in the Appio Fortress (1870) to your right is the brick core of a circular tower monument. The **Tomb of M. Servilius Quartus** to your left was restored by Antonio Canova (1808) and was the first monument restored on the Via Appia Antica. The so-called **Tomb of Seneca** to your left, just beyond the fourth Roman milestone, incorporates fragments of a lion's head and other decoration. It was also restored by Antonio Canova. This is the vicinity of the villa that he owned in which he was forced to commit suicide by the Emperor Nero. The **Circular Mausoleum** to your left still has fragments of decoration attached to the stone core. The vaulted interior contained four niches with sarcophagi. The **Casale** at No. 199B to your left incorporates various ancient fragments in the exterior walls. The **Monument to the Children of Sextus Pompeius Iustus** to your left at Via dei Lugari was restored by Antonio Canova.

The **Tomb of Licinia** to your right (her name is on the marble slab) preserves part of the lower brick exterior and a stone core. Next to it is the **Tomb of the Doric Frieze** comprised of blocks made from tufa (peperino) and decorated with a Doric frieze. The tomb dates to the Sullan period and is an early surviving example of this decoration type. The tomb was restored by Luigi Canina (1851–1853).

The **Monument to Hilarus Fuscus** to your right contains a freedmen's relief of five figures (*c.*30 BCE). This is a copy of the original now in the Museo delle Terme di Diocleziano (Tour 12) and other marble fragments. Freedmen reliefs depict portrait busts of former slaves situated within a framed area of a funerary monument. The monument was restored by Luigi Canina (1851–1853). The **Monument to the Freedmen of T. Claudius Secundus** is to your right. Funerary altars were placed on top in the restoration by Luigi Canina (1851–1853). The **Monument to Q. Apuleius Pamphilus** to your right is comprised of various architectural decorative fragments including floral decoration. The reconstruction does not include the original inscription that identified the deceased. The **Temple-style Tomb** just beyond Via degli

Eugenii to your right dates to the 2nd century CE and is constructed of bricks (opus latericium pattern). Below the temple-style shrine on a high podium and frontal staircase is a cella with niches for sarcophagi. Around the sides are beautiful pilasters and cornice decoration.

The **Tomb of the Rabirii** is to your right and is one of the most famous reconstructed funerary monuments on the Via Appia Antica, restored by Luigi Canina (1851–1853). The freedmen relief on the altar depicts three individuals. This a copy of the original now in Palazzo Massimo (Tour 12). The first two (C. Rabirius Hermodorus and Rabiria Demaris) appear to be the freedmen of C. Rabirius Postumus, famously defended by Cicero. The third figure, Usia Prima, is identified as a priestess of Isis (cult instruments are carved around her) and seems to be a later recarving of an original male figure. The **Tomb of the Festoons** is to your right next to a pile of + fragments with inscriptions. Like the Tomb of the Doric Frieze, the tomb dates to the Sullan period and includes similar blocks of tufa (peperino). The frieze of the funerary altar consists of garlands (hence the traditional name of the tomb) held up by cupids. The stone core of the tomb behind the altar gives an indication of how heavily restored the monument is. The **Tomb of the Frontispiece** is right next to the Tomb of the Festoons and derives its name from the freedmen relief of four figures (a copy) situated below a rosette in the pediment. A married couple in the centre clasp right hands to evoke their exchange of marriage vows. The stone core of the high tower shape of the tomb survives behind the pediment. The monument was restored by Luigi Canina (1851–1853).

The next stretch of the Via Appia Antica continues on the other side of Via Erode Attico/Via Tor Carbone beyond the fifth Roman mile mark past several tumuli tombs associated with the legendary Republican figures of the Horatii and Curiatii in the area of the Villa of the Quintilii and ends at Casal Rotondo at Via di Torricola. To return to Piazzale Ostiense, turn left on Via Erode Attico at the intersection with Via di Tor Carbone and follow the curve left to Via Appia Pignatelli. Turn left for the No. 118 bus stop that is ahead to your right.

The **Tomb of Herodes Atticus** is to your left beyond the intersection but it is not visible from the Via Appia Antica. The **Tomb of a Togate Woman** at No. 247 is to your left after you pass the fragments of several tombs and marble slabs with partial inscriptions. The **Tomb of Jewish Freedmen** is to your right at the entrance to the Villa Appia Antica at

No. 288A. A marble slab in front of a tower tomb core identifies the deceased (Baricha, Zabda and Achiba) as the freedmen of L. Valerius. The name of **Tomb Laterizio I** (to your left refers to the brickwork (*opus latericium*) of the tomb (2nd century CE). It was restored by Luigi Canina (1851–1853). The brick facade of the cella incorporates marble fragments. Walk around to the sides to see the pilasters on the upper level and windows that reveal that, like Tomb Laterizio II, the tomb had later served as a house. Across the street is a freedmen relief with two figures. The **Tomb Laterizio II** is next to Tomb Laterizio I and was also restored by Luigi Canina (1851–1853). The **Circular Mausoleum** across the street to your right was also reused in the Middle Ages.

The Via Appia Antica curves at this point (fifth Roman mile mark). Pomponius Atticus, the friend and correspondent of the orator Marcus Cicero, was buried in the tomb of his uncle Q. Caecilius Metellus at the fifth milestone in 32 BCE. The area has traditionally been associated with the *Fossae Cluiliae* that formed the boundary between the territories of Rome and Alba Longa. The area is marked by several tumuli tombs that legend associates with the Republican figures of the Horatii and Curiatii. The so-called **Tomb of the Curiatii** is to your right with the ruins of a round medieval tower on top. The **Villa of the Quintilii** begins to your left. This immense villa with elements that date back to the reign of Hadrian belonged to the brothers S. Quintilius Condianus Maximus and S. Quintilius Valerianus Maximus who were accused of conspiracy by the Emperor Commodus and executed in 182 CE, at which point their property passed into the Imperial estate. A large number of statues were found on the estate whose ruins include baths and the so-called **Maritime Theatre** that evokes the building of the same name at the Villa of Hadrian in Tivoli. The **Pyramid Tomb** core on a base that was parallelepiped to your left may be connected with the Quintilii.

The so-called **Tomb of the Horatii** – the circular mausolea to your right – have been identified as the Tombs of the Horatii and the Curiatii but the identification has now been rejected. The tombs date to the late Republic/early Empire. The historian Livy states that their tombs were at the fifth milestone but his reference may be to a later reconstruction of unrelated tombs by the Emperor Augustus to propagate the legends of early Republican history as analogues to his own reign. The **Nymphaeum of the Villa of the Quintilii** is to your left. Once a monumental fountain, the ruins that include those of a medieval castle are now host to cultural events. Beyond to your right is an **Octagonal Tomb** with a winding staircase inside and alternating bands of multi-coloured brick that was restored in 2006.

Along the next stretch of the Via Appia Antica, the fragments of marble slabs with epitaphs and togate figures line both sides of the road that also contains the cores of tombs. **Casal Rotondo** is to your left and is located just before the sixth Roman milestone. The tomb is the largest on the Via Appia Antica and measures 35m on each side of its base. Luigi Canina restored the tomb in 1851–1853 and placed the decorative marble fragments on the adjacent wall that he associated with the tomb but they probably belong to another one.

At Via di Torricola, turn around and look to your left for a view of the dome of St Peter's Basilica. The tombs beyond this point are sparse and include the tower known as **Torre de Selce**. To return to Piazzale Ostiense, retrace your steps towards the city and turn right on Via Erode Attico at the intersection with Via di Tor Carbone and follow the curve to Via Appia Pignatelli. Turn left and the No. 118 bus stop is ahead to your right.

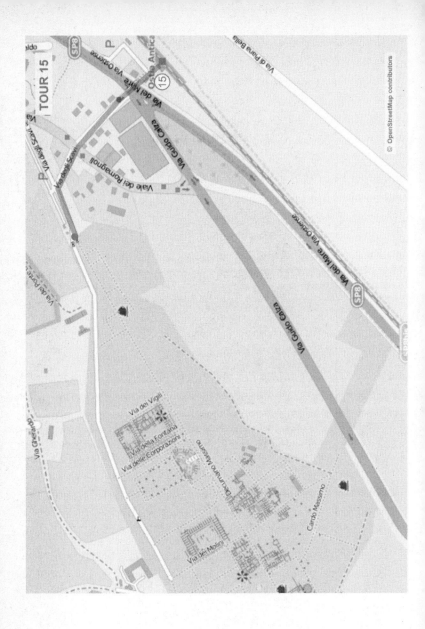

Sites: Ostia Antica; Museo Ostiense; Lido di Ostia (Ostia Lido).
Distance: 2.5km.

Tour 15

# Ostia Antica
# and Lido di Ostia

Explore daily life in the ancient Roman town of Ostia Antica, now an archaeological site. Stroll amidst the ruins of bath complexes, theatre, market, forum, apartment buildings, houses, taverns and sites important to early Jewish, Christian and pagan worship. The tour departs from Piazzale Ostiense (Tour 14) with options to end the tour with a stroll through the nearby medieval Borgo of modern-day Ostia Antica or visit the beach of Lido di Ostia (Ostia Lido).

Depart Rome from Stazione Porta S. Paolo of the Roma–Lido train line that is adjacent to the Metro line B Piramide station. Take the train to the Ostia Antica stop. All of the trains follow the same route and leave about every 15 minutes. The regular integtrated ATAC bus ticket/pass is valid for travel and there is a ticket booth at the entrance to the station.

Once you arrive at the Ostia Antica station, take the passageway underneath the tracks to exit on the other side. From the small station, walk straight ahead to the pedestrian overpass bridge and continue straight ahead. To your right is the **Castle of Pope Julius II della Rovere** by Baccio Pontelli (1483–1486) that he built while he was still a cardinal. At the end of the block, cross Viale dei Romagnoli. Enter the archaeological area (scavi) of Ostia Antica straight ahead on Via degli Scavi di Ostia Antica. Site maps are available. The short walk from the station to the archaeological area should take about ten minutes.

To go directly to the beach, **Lido di Ostia** (Ostia Lido), from Stazione Porta S. Paolo, remain on the train beyond Ostia Antica and exit at any of the stops that have access to the beach or stay on the train to the final stop (Cristoforo Colombo) where there are beach clubs that charge a fee for entrance and beach services. At the station exit is the ATAC bus stop for local buses (during the summer beach season that begins at the end of May) that go along the coast for several miles where there are more beaches with public access. Return to Rome by retracing the route.

**Ostia** was the earliest colony of Rome, founded in the 4th century BCE to secure the supply of salt and grain. It was developed as Rome's harbour, linked to the city by the Tiber river and the Via Ostiense that entered Rome at the Porta Ostiense. The word Ostia derives from the Latin word for mouth or entrance (*ostium*) to describe its location at the mouth of the Tiber. The Emperor Augustus planned a new port for the city, Portus, but it was not constructed until the reign of Claudius who also ensured a steady supply of grain at Rome by appointing a public official (*procurator annonae*) in the city. This new port silted soon after its construction and it was later enlarged by Trajan.

The layout of the city reflects its original function as a military camp (*castrum*) and the main roads follow typical Roman city planning: the main road (Decumanus Maximus) is actually Via Ostiense inside the Republican Walls that is 9m wide and runs straight through the town and is intersected by another main road (Cardo Maximus). A forum was normally placed at the intersection of these two axis roads. In Ostia, this intersection is at the heart of the original military camp where the capitolium faces the forum. With the success of Portus as Rome's port city, Ostia became a residential area, in time outgrowing its original boundaries and expanding towards the west. Emperors lavished the city with public monuments, especially under Augustus, Domitian, Hadrian and the Antonines when the city reached its maximum population of around 50,000. Ostia was not a luxury resort town like Pompeii so the architecture mostly reflects the working population.

As a port city, Ostia attracted a wide variety of cultures with varying forms of religious worship. Pagan worship included traditional Roman and foreign Eastern cults. The city also had early Jewish and Christian communities with one of the first synagogues in Europe and early basilicas preserved here. The city sided with Maxentius, but after his victory, Constantine founded a basilica here dedicated to Saints Peter, Paul and John the Baptist that is not extant. Saint Monica died here on her return trip to Africa with her son St Augustine. She is buried in the church of Sant'Agostino (Tour 8). The change in the course of the Tiber and threat of malaria from mosquitoes led to the abandonment of the town. In 830, Pope Gregory IV founded the adjacent village to the east as Gregoriopolis. The site of Ostia Antica was systematically plundered for building materials for Rome and other cities in Italy. The ruins of the city began to be excavated in the 19th century and later Italian archaeologist Guido Calza (1888–1946) was tasked with excavating large areas of the city for the planned 1942 World's Fair. Excavation and conservation work is ongoing.

From the archaeological site entry point, the Via Ostiense enters the city by the **Porta Romana**. The necropolis is outside the city walls. The **Street of Tombs** (Via delle Tombe) that runs parallel to the **Decumanus Maximus** to your left is lined with ancient roadside tombs that are missing their upper portions. Some tombs still contain niches for cinerary urns. Sarcophagi and fragments of funerary monuments line the road.

Follow the Decumanus Maximus into Piazzale della Vittoria, named for the winged figure to your left identified as **Minerva or a Winged Victory** (a copy of the original that dates to the reign of Domitian in the museum) that formed part of the Porta Romana. There is a Roman mosaic in front of the statue. Beyond is a nymphaeum to your left and Republican-era **Warehouses** to your right and the **Baths of the Charioteers** (*Cisiarii*), who drove a cabriolet-type wagon, are beyond them to the right, best seen from the road as you leave the site. The column to your right marks the location of **Porticoes** that lined the street to the end of the block.

A portico also lined the next block. Opposite the **Well** in the middle of the Decumanus Maximus are the 2nd-century CE **Baths of Neptune** that were begun under Hadrian but completed by Antoninus Pius. Climb up the steps to the terrace to see the black and white mosaic pavement of *Neptune with mythological maritime figures* in the entrance hall. Partially visible in the adjacent room is the mosaic of *Amphitrite*, the wife of Neptune. The baths complex also includes a gymnasium and other areas visible from the terrace.

Across the street from the baths is Via del Sabazeo at the end of which stood the 4th-century **Basilica of Constantine** dedicated to Saints Peter, Paul and John the Baptist. The basilica was systematically stripped of building materials in the 8th/9th centuries.

Continue on the Decumanus Maximus just beyond the baths to the **Tavern of Fortunatus** (Caupona di Fortunato) at the corner of Via della Fontana to your right. The floor mosaic contains a chalice and the Latin quote: *Dicit Fortunatus vinum cratera quod sitis bibe* ('Fortunatus says drink wine from the bowl because you are thirsty'). The identification of the building as a tavern is problematic since no serving counter was discovered and letters missing from the quote before Fortunatus' name, make its context unclear. Similarity to the wording of John 7.37–38, in which Jesus calls the thirsty to him to drink, may point to some connection with the nearby Christian oratory.

Walk through the tavern to stroll along Via della Fontana that is lined with apartment blocks (*insulae*), with shops on the ground floor and apartments above them. Midway down the block is the covered fountain for which the street is named. Beyond to your right is the **Caserma dei Vigili** (Firemen's Barracks). The entrance is by the street to your right. In the courtyard of the two-storey barracks is a **Caesareum** (also known as an Augusteum) with dedication altars to emperors and a mosaic of a sacrifice scene.

Retrace your steps to the Decumanus Maximus. At the corner of Via delle Corporazioni next to the theatre are a **Nymphaeum** and **Christian Oratory** where Christian martyrs were venerated. On display here is a Christian sarcophagus.

Turn right on Via delle Corporazioni at the corner to enter into **Piazzale delle Corporazioni** that is to your left behind the theatre. In the centre is the **Temple of Ceres** with a high podium and approached by a flight of steps. Her cult reflects the importance of the grain supply to Rome. Lining the piazzale are the offices of guilds, such as ship owners, and merchants from all over the empire. The floor mosaics with trademarks and inscriptions in the black and white tiles indicate their various professions, commercial specialties and nationalities. Look for the elephant dealer whose trademark is an elephant. Guido Calza planted pine trees to evoke a porticus around the piazzale. A copy of the **Altar of Romulus and Remus**, now in Palazzo Massimo alle Terme in Rome (Tour 12), is in front of an area with the foundations of Republican temples and shrines.

From the piazzale, enter the **Roman Theatre**, built by Marcus Agrippa, Augustus' naval general and son-in-law who sponsored public works, that was restored in the 2nd century under Commodus and Septimius Severus. The brick restoration of the porticus (1927) includes a display of dedicatory inscriptions and architectural fragments. The stage backdrop (*scaenae frons*) is missing but theatre masks that were part of the decoration are displayed along the back of the long narrow stage. The orchestra area reflects Roman modifications of Greek theatres that had circular orchestras for choral spectacle. Of the original three tiers of seating in the curved seating area (*cavea*) that could accommodate from 2,500 to 3,000 spectators, only two tiers survive divided by aisles.

Return to the Decumanus Maximus from the right side of the theatre (facing the seats), continue right, past the **House of the Augustales** to your left (and behind it a **Fullonica** for dying clothes and the **Mithraeum of Felicissimus** with pavement mosaics outlining the stages of initiation) and the large grain **Warehouses** (*horrea*) to your right. Turn right on Via dei Molini to the **Mill of Silvanus** (Molino del Silvano) just beyond Via della Casa di Diana. The mills were turned by mules and the storage jar (*dolium*) containers buried in the floor to economise space and keep contents cool.

Retrace your steps a short distance on Via dei Molini then turn right on Via della Casa di Diana that is lined with apartment blocks (*insulae*) of multiple storeys with projecting balconies and shops on the ground level including the **Casa di Diana** to your right. Shops occupied the ground floor with living areas on the first and second storeys. Fresco fragments are preserved in a room on the ground floor (2nd century CE). In the courtyard with a fountain there is a terra cotta relief of Diana.

Just beyond and to your left is the **Thermopolium** with food counter and display shelving inside with a fresco of fruit and vegetables. The interior included eating areas and at the rear is a courtyard and fountain. Across the street from the thermopolium to your right is a doorway with stairs of the 2nd-century CE **House of the Wall Paintings** (Casa dei Dipinti) that is named for the fresco decoration that included a scene with Jupiter and Ganymede. Climb up the stairs to access the upper levels and a terrace at the top of the building for a view of the Forum area and the site of Ostia Antica. The ground floor areas are accessed from Via dei Dipinti (around corner to right) where 4th-century mosaics of the 'Months' are displayed.

At the end of Via della Casa di Diana, turn left to enter the **Forum** area (turning right leads to the Museum area). The **Capitolium** with the high podium and steps to your right was built on the **Cardo Maximus** facing the Decumanus Maximus. Its construction with the Forum on the Cardo Maximus indicates that there was no need for a forum area when the colony was founded and one had to be worked into the existing layout. The capitolium is dedicated to the Capitoline Triad of Jupiter, Juno and Minerva and dates to Hadrian's reign. A portico flanked the temple that is set on a very high podium with a frontal staircase. Six columns were across the front with marble slabs covering the brick walls. In front is the round **Shrine of the Lares of Augustus** (Sacellum dei Lares Augusti) that was part of the Imperial cult.

Across the street from the capitolium is the **Forum** that was also built into the Cardo Maximus. The Emperor Hadrian revised the forum that was built by Tiberius who also built the **Temple of Roma and Augustus** at the far end. Fragments from the rear pediment of the temple are displayed at the entrance to the Forum Baths, including a statue of *Roma as an Amazon*. Beyond the temple on the Cardo Maximus is the **House of the Fish** with a Christian mosaic of a chalice and fish that is accessed from a side street. At some distance at the **Porta Laurentina** is the **Campo della Magna Mater**, an Augustan-era sanctuary devoted to Cybele the Great Mother and to Attis.

Walk halfway down the Forum on Via dei Fori to Via della Casa dei Triclinii to your left. Walk up the short flight of steps to the end of the block to the public **latrines** (*forica*) lined with 22 seats. Retrace your steps to Via dei Fori and turn left to enter the **Forum Baths** that were built in the 2nd century by M. Gavius Maximus during the reign of Antoninus Pius and restored in the 4th century when one of the original entrances facing the latrines was changed to the entrance facing the Forum. This is the largest bath complex in Ostia. From the vestibule or *palaestra* (exercise area), a series of changing rooms flank the central cold water pool (*frigidarium*) that is decorated with cipollino columns. To your diagonal right as you enter the baths is a progression of pools from a cold plunge pool to a steam room, several warm water pools (*tepidarium*) that were heated by steam and then the hot water pool (*caldarium*). Along the sides of the square pillars in this last room are holes where the window frame was fastened. The square terra cotta pipes that brought steam from the furnaces operated by slaves below are still visible along the walls.

Retrace your steps to the front of the baths. Turn right to continue to the basilica next to the forum on the Decumanus Maximus or turn left for a detour to the House of Fortuna Annonaria: walk up the short flight of steps then take another left to walk around the back of the bath complex for a view of the substructures where slaves maintained the fires that heated the rooms and pools above. Follow the path around the outside of the bath complex as it winds to the street behind it called Semita dei Cippi. Veer to your right for the start of Via della Fortuna Annonaria. The entrance to the **House of Fortuna Annonaria** is just to your right, dating from the 4th century CE with earlier 1st-century BCE and 2nd-century CE elements. The house is named for the statue of Fortuna Annonaria in the peristyle garden courtyard and is unique in having a private latrine that is to the right of the entrance in the area beyond the pillars, behind the wall in the far left corner.

Retrace your steps to the start of Via Fortuna Annonaria then turn right on Semita dei Cippi and proceed to the Decumanus Maximus. Turn left to return to the forum area. To your left is the 4th-century CE **Foro della Statua Eroica**, named after the heroic nude statue discovered there. Next to it to your left is the **Casegiatto dei Triclini** (House of the Dining rooms), the headquarters of the carpenters guild (*fabri tignuarii*) that was built during the reign of Hadrian. Continue to the basilica.

The **Basilica**, next to the forum, is approached by a short flight of steps. The early 2nd-century CE basilica served as a covered gathering place where court cases were commonly heard. Colonnades surrounded it on all four sides with entrances facing the Decumanus Maximus and the forum. The podium where the judges presided over cases is on the south end. The basilica is across the street from the **Curia** that was built at the same time and where members of the city council held meetings. It is possible that the building was the meeting hall of the Priests of Augustus (*Augustales*).

Next to the basilica is the **Tempio Rotondo**, a 3rd-century CE circular temple on a high podium that is preceded by a forecourt. The temple was devoted to the Imperial cult and the interior contains niches for the portraits of emperors. Opposite is the early 2nd-century CE **House of the Lararium** (Caseggiato del Larario), named for the wall shrine dedicated to the *Lares*, the household gods, in the courtyard of the building that was occupied by shops on the ground floor and apartments on the upper floors.

The Decumanus Maximus forks at **Bivio di Castrum** beyond the boundary of the original camp where the town was extended outside the Porta Occidentale. The street to your sharp right (Via Horrea Epagathiana) leads to warehouses owned by freedmen, the **Horrea Epaghathiana** and **Horrea Epaphroditiana**. Behind it is a storage area for archaeological finds and inscriptions in the **Piccolo Mercato**. Veer left at the fork in the road to continue on the Decumanus Maximus. To your left are the **Tabernae of the Fish Sellers** with a marble table, fountain and mosaic floor pavement. Behind it is a **Macellum**, the butcher shop, and a market area.

Ahead to your right is the **Christian Basilica**, a home that was modified in the 4th century into a house for Christian worship (*domus ecclesiae*) or possibly a guesthouse for Christian pilgrims making their way to Rome. There is a double nave that ends in apses. If a Christian house of worship, it offers a sense of the foundations of some of the earliest titular churches in Rome.

Beyond this point, you may continue with an optional stroll down the Decumanus Maximus to the area beyond the Porta Marina. To your left before the **Porta Marina** is the **Caupona of Alexander Helix** with a mosaic of boxers. To your right is the **Domus of the Nymphaeum** and behind it, more apartment blocks and homes with gardens. The Decumanus Maximus was extended beyond the gate during the reign of Augustus and was formerly the site of a Republican-era necropolis. The **Forum of the Porta Marina** was added in the reign of Hadrian. At Via di Cartilio Poplicola, named after the Republican-era **Tomb of C. Cartilius Poplicola** whose status as a leading citizen ensured that his tomb survived the redevelopment of the area (the frieze depicts a trireme and a goddess), turn left to explore the area around the **Baths of the Porta Marina** that dates to the reign of Trajan. The black and white mosaic pavements include athletic scenes. The Scottish painter and antiquarian Gavin Hamilton visited the ruins of the baths in 1775 looking for sculpture for the Grand Tour trade.

From the rear of the baths, follow the road through the fields to your left to visit the **Synagogue** that once faced the sea. It is one of the earliest synagogues in Europe (active from the 1st to the 5th century CE) with earlier Jewish worship in the Trastevere area of Rome since the 1st century BCE (Tour 4). Surviving architectural elements include Ionic columns and mosaics. Other elements including a relief of a Menorah were moved to the area in front of the museum.

Retrace your steps on the Decumanus Maximus and return to the fork in the road and turn left on Via della Foce. To your right is the Sacred Area of the Republican era (Area Sacra Repubblicana) with a **Temple of Hercules** in the centre that dates to the end of the 2nd to the mid-1st century BCE. The idealised statue is of C. Cartilius Poplicola whose tomb is outside the Porta Marina (the original is in the museum). At the corner of Via del Tempio di Ercole is the **Tempio dell'Ara Rotonda** that was modified in the 1st century CE. The Temple of the Round Altar is named after a round altar decorated with cupids that was found in its sanctuary area and is now in the museum. Extant marble decoration is displayed on the adjacent wall.

Turn right on Via del Tempio di Ercole, a footpath, and proceed to the first street to your right to the **House of Cupid and Psyche** (late 3rd century CE) on your left. At the entrance is a monumental nymphaeum fountain with marble columns. The corridor to the right of the fountain leads to a private latrine. In a room to the left of the atrium is a copy of a statue of Cupid and Psyche after which the house is named (the original is in the museum). There is a beautiful marble pavement (*opus sectile*) in the large room at the end of the atrium.

Exit the house and walk through the ruins of the **Baths of Buticosus** across the street to reach the footpath that leads to the front of the Temple of Hercules. From here, retrace your steps to Via delle Foce and turn right. Take the next right onto Via delle Terme del Mitra to the 2nd-century CE **Baths of Mithras** (Terme del Mitra). The area is often overgrown so use caution. When you see a break in the wall that leads to the single standing column, enter the bath complex. Walk to the other side of the complex and once outside turn right to the corner of the baths. Walk down the steps to enter the late 2nd-/early 3rd-century CE **Mithraeum**. At the end of the corridor lined with dining couches for ritual meals is a copy of the statue of Mithras slaying the bull that was found here (the original is in the museum).

Retrace your steps to Via delle Foce and turn right to enter the **House of Serapis** with a **Serapeum** just to your left. From here continue into the adjoining **Baths of the Seven Sages** (Terme di Sette Sapienti), named after a satirical fresco of the Seven Greek Sages. Explore the complex that contains a round frigidarium, mosaics and frescoes including *Venus rising from the sea*. At the far end of the complex is entry into the neighbouring apartment block known as the **Insula of the Charioteer** after the frescoes of charioteers in the alley between the apartments and the baths. Climb up the stairs to the terrace for a panoramic view of this section of the town. With the capitolium to your left, look out to your diagonal right to see the synagogue in the distance in the open field.

Exit and turn right to retrace your steps on Via delle Foce to the Decumanus Maximus. Turn left to walk through the forum area and then turn left on the Cardo Maximus (alongside the capitolium). Turn right on Via della Casa di Diana and then another quick left on Via dei Depinti and proceed to the end of the street to the museum. At the end of the street to your right is a display that features architectural elements that contain a relief of a menorah from the synagogue. There is also a display area of sunken storage jars. In the piazza in front of the museum are sarcophagi that are also displayed along the administrative building next to the cafe.

The **Museum** (Museo Ostiense) contains an excellent sculpture collection of Imperial portraits, Greek originals, Roman copies of Greek art, Imperial and Eastern cult statues and Roman sarcophagi that were discovered in Ostia Antica. The original statue of *Mithras slaying the bull* from the Baths of Mithras is signed by the Athenian sculptor Kriton and shows signs of deliberate destruction, most likely at the hands of early Christians. The cult statues of emperors and empresses include Augustus and the Emperor Maxentius, Constantine's co-emperor and rival who was defeated at the Battle of the Milvian Bridge in 312 CE. An excellent collection of sarcophagi from the city's necropolis sites includes examples with mythological scenes and portraits of the deceased.

Exit the museum and turn left to follow the road to the exit past sculpture fragments to your left and a view of more ruins of the town to your right. If you wish to explore the modern town of Ostia Antica and the **medieval Borgo**, turn left from the exit of the archeological area and continue a short distance into the main piazza Umberto I. There are a number of restaurants in the area with outdoor seating when weather permits.

To return to Rome by train or to proceed to Lido di Ostia (Ostia Lido), turn right from the exit of the archaeological site and walk past the Castle of Pope Julius II della Rovere and retrace your steps to the pedestrian bridge and the Ostia Antica train station. If you are returning to Stazione S. Paolo/Piramide in Rome, stay on the platform on the side that you clear the turnstile.

To visit the beach Lido di Ostia (Ostia Lido) from the Ostia Antica train station, take the passageway below the tracks and exit at any of the beach stops or take the train to the last stop, Cristoforo Colombo, where there are beach clubs (an entrance fee is payable) and ATAC buses that travel several miles along the coast (during the beach season that begins at the end of May) where there are many public beaches.

# Opening Hours of Monuments and Museums

The opening and closing times of churches vary and some are only open on Sunday and for evening rosary. Most monuments and museums operated by the Italian state and the City of Rome are closed on Mondays, 25 December, 1 January and 1 May. Ticket offices close a half-hour to one hour before closing time (D= daily, cl. = closed, Ss.= multiple Saints, SS.= Most Holy).

Ara Pacis Museum: Tues.–Sun. 9–7.

Baths of Caracalla: Tues.–Sun. 9–6.30; Mon. 9–2.

Baths of Diocletian: Tues.–Sun. 9–7.45.

Botanical Gardens: Nov. to Feb., Mon.–Sat. 9–5.30; Mar. to Oct., Mon.–Sat. 9–6.30.

Capitoline Museums: Tues.–Sun. 9–8.

Capitoline Museums Centrale Montemartini: Tues.–Sun. 9–7.

Capo di Bove Museum: Mon.–Sat. 10–4; Sun. 10–6.

Casino dell'Aurora Pallavicini: 1st day of every month, except 1 Jan., 10–12; 3–5.

Castel Sant'Angelo: Tues.–Sun. 9–7.30.

Catacombs of S. Callisto: 8.30–12; 2.30–5.30. cl. Wed. and month of Feb.

Catacombs of S. Sebastiano: Mon.–Sat. 10–4.30. cl. Sun. and 26 Nov. to 25 Dec.

Chiesa Nuova (S. Maria in Vallicella): D. 7.30–12; 4.30–7; Rooms of S. Filippo Neri 26 May or Tues., Thurs. and Sat. 10–12 by appointment.

Chiostro del Bramante: D. 10–8.

Colosseum: D. 8.30 to dusk.

Crypta Balbi: Tues.–Sun. 9–7.45.

Domine, Quo Vadis?: D. 8–2; 2.30–6.

EUR Museo della Civiltà Romana: Tues.–Sun. 9–2; cl. Mon.; Museo Nazionale dell'Alto Medioevo: Tues.–Sat. 9–2; cl. Mon.; Museo Nazionale delle Arti e delle Tradizione Popolari: Tues.–Fri. 9–6; Sat.–Sun. 9–8; cl. Mon.; Museo Nazionale Preistorico ed Etnografico Luigi Pigorini: Tues.–Sun. 10–6; Museo Storico delle Poste e delle Telecommunicazioni: Mon.–Fri. 9–1 by appointment.

Galleria Colonna: Sat. 9.00–1.15.

Galleria dell'Accademia di S. Luca: Mon., Wed., Fri. and last Sun. of the month 10–1.

Galleria Doria Pamphilj: D. 10–5.

The Gesù: D. 6–12; 4–7.30; Rooms of S. Ignatius Mon.–Sat. 4–6; Holidays 10–12.

Great Synagogue of Rome: Mon.–Fri. 7.45; Sabbath and Holidays 8.30.

Keats-Shelley Memorial House: Mon.–Fri. 10–1; 2–6; Sat. 11–2; 3–6.

Macro Testataccio Museo D'Arte Contemporanea Roma: Tues.–Sun. 4–10.

Mausoleo delle Fosse Ardeatine: Mon.–Fri. 8.15–3; Sat.–Sun. 8.15–4.30.

MAXXI: Tues.–Sun. 11–2.

Museo Boncompagni Ludovisi: Tues.–Sun. 8.30–5.30.

Museo dei Fori Imperiali in Trajan's Markets: Tues.–Sun. 9–7.

Museo e Galleria Borghese: Tues.–Sun. 8.30–5.30, advance purchase necessary.

Museo Mario Praz: Tues.–Sun. 9–6.30.

Museo Napoleonico: Tues.–Sun. 10–6.

Museo di Roma (Palazzo Braschi): Tues.–Sun. 9–7.

Museo di Scultura Antica Giovanni Barracco: Oct. to May, Tues.–Sun. 10–4; June to Sept., Tues.–Sun. 1–7.

Museo Storico della Lotta di Liberazione di Roma: Tues.–Sun. 9.30–12.30; Tues., Thurs. and Fri. 3.30–7.30.

Museo degli Strumenti Musicali: Tues.–Sun. 8.30–7.30.

Museo della Via Ostiense: Tues. 9–4.30; Wed. 9–1.30; Thurs. 9–4.30; Fri. and Sat. 9–1.30; 1st and 3rd Sunday 9–1.30.

National Monument to Vittorio Emanuele II: Mon.–Fri. 9.30–5.30; cl. Sat., Sun.

Ostia Antica: Apr.–Oct., cl. Mon., Tues.–Sun. 8.30–6; Nov.–Feb. 8.30–4; Mar. 8.30–5.

Palazzo Altemps: Tues.–Sun. 9–7.45.

Palazzo Barberini: Tues.–Sun. 8.30–7.

Palazzo Corsini: Tues.–Sun. 8.30–7.30.

Palazzo Massimo alle Terme: Tues.–Sun. 9–7.45.

Palazzo del Quirinale: Sun. 8.30–12; cl. July/Aug. Gardens 2 June.

Palazzo Spada: Tues.–Sun. 8.30–7.30.

Palazzo di Venezia: Tues.–Sun. 8.30–7.

Pantheon (S. Maria ad Martyres): Mon.–Sat. 8.30–7.30; Sun. 9–6.

Parco Regionale dell'Appia Antica: D. 9.30–1; 2–5.30.

Protestant Cemetery: Mon.–Sat. 9–5; Sun. and Holidays 9–1.

Pyramid of Cestius: 2nd/4th Sat. 11.00, by appointment.

Roman Forum: D. 8.30–7.

Roseto Comunale: D. May and June 8–7.30.

Sant'Agnese in Agone: D. 9.30–12.30; Tues.–Sun. 4–7.

Sant'Agnese fuori le Mura: D. 7.30–12; 4–7.30; Catacombs D. 9–12; 4–6.

Sant'Agostino: D. 7.45–12; 4.30–7.30.

Sant'Alessio all'Aventino: D. 8.30–12.30; 3.30–6.30.

Ss. Ambrogio e Carlo al Corso: D. 9.30–12; 4 or 5–7.

Sant'Andrea delle Fratte: D. 6.30–12.30; 4–7.

Sant'Andrea al Quirinale: Wed.–Sun. 8–12; 4–7; cl. Tues.

Sant'Andrea della Valle: D. 7.30–12; 4.30–7.30.

Ss. Apostoli: D. 7–12; 4–7.

S. Bartolomeo All'Isola: D. 9.30–2; 3.30–7; Sun. 9–1.

S. Carlo ai Catinari: D. 7.30–12; 4.30–7.

S. Carlo alle Quattro Fontane: Mon.–Fri. 10–1; 3–6; Sat. 10–1; Sun. 12–1.

S. Cecilia in Trastevere: D. 9.30–1; 4–7.15; Choir of the Benedictine Convent Mon.–Sat. 10.15–12.15; Sun. 11.15–12.15.

S. Clemente: Mon.–Sat. 9–12.30; 3–6; Sun. and Holidays 12–6.

Ss. Cosma e Damiano: D. 9–1; 3–7.

S. Costanza: Tues.–Sun. 9–12; 4–6; Mon. 9–12.

S. Crisogono: D. 7.30–1.30; 4–6.30.

S. Croce in Gerusalemme: D. 7–12.45; 3.30–7.30.

Sant'Eustachio: D. 8.30–12.30.

S. Francesco a Ripa: D. 7–12; 4–7.30.

S. Giorgio in Velabro: D. 10–12.30; 4–6.30.

S. Giovanni in Laterano: D. 7–6.30; Cloister: D. 9–6; Scala Santa: D. 6.15 –12.15; 3–6.30; Lateran Palace: Mon.–Sat. with guided tours of the Vatican History Museum at 9, 10, 11 and 12; Lateran Baptistery: D. 7–12.30; 4–7.30.

S. Giovanni Battista dei Fiorentini: D. 7.25–12; 5–7.

Ss. Giovanni e Paolo: D. 8.30–12; 3.30–6; Roman Houses 10–1; 3–6; cl. Tues./Wed.

S. Girolamo della Carità: Sun. 10.30.

S. Giuseppe dei Falegnami: D. 9–12; 2.30–5.

S. Gregorio Magno al Celio: D. 9–1; 3.30–7; Oratories Tues., Thurs., Sat. and Sun. 9.30–12.30.

Sant'Ignazio di Loyola in Campo Marzio: Mon.–Fri. 7.30–7; Sat.–Sun. 9–7.

Sant'Ivo alla Sapienza: Sun. 9–12.

S. Lorenzo fuori le Mura: D. 8–12; 4–6.30.

S. Lorenzo in Damaso: D. 7.30–12; 4.30–8.

S. Lorenzo in Lucina: D. 8–8. The archeological excavations are shown by tour (in Italian only) currently on the 1st Sat. of the month at 5.

S. Lorenzo in Miranda: Thurs. 10–12.

Ss. Luca e Martina: Sat. 9–6; by chance weekday mornings.

S. Luigi dei Francesi: D. 10–12.30; 4–7 (3–7 during high tourist season).

S. Marco: Tues.–Sun. 9.30–12; 4–6.30.

S. Maria degli Angeli e dei Martiri: D. 7.30–12.30; 4–6.30.

S. Maria dell'Anima: D. 9–12.45; 3–7.

S. Maria in Aracoeli al Campidoglio: May–Sept., D. 9–6.30; Oct.–Apr., 9.30–12.30; 2.30–5.30.

S. Maria della Concezione: D. 9–12; 3–6; Museum and Crypt D. 9–7.

S. Maria in Cosmedin: D. 9.30–4.50; Summer to 5.40.

S. Maria in Domnica (S. Maria della Navicella): D. 9–12.30; 4.30–7.30.

S. Maria Maddalena: D. 7.30–11.45; 5–7.45.

S. Maria Maggiore: D. 7–7; Museum: D. 9.30–6.30; Loggia of the Benediction: 9.30; 1.

S. Maria sopra Minerva: D. 7–7.

S. Maria di Monserrato degli Spagnoli: Sun. 10–1.

S. Maria della Pace: Mon., Wed., Sat. 9–12.

S. Maria del Popolo: D. 7–12; 4–7; Holidays 8–1.30; 4.30–7.30.

S. Maria in Portico in Campitelli: D. 7–12.30; 3.30–7.

S. Maria in Trastevere: D. 7.30–12.30; 3.30–9.

S. Maria della Vittoria: D. 7–12; 3.30–7.

S. Martino ai Monti: D. 7.30–12; 4–7.

S. Nicola in Carcere: D. 7.30–12; 4.30–7.

S. Paolo entro le Mura: D. 9.30–4.30.

S. Paolo fuori le Mura: D. 7–6.30; Cloister D. 8–6.15.

St Peter's Basilica: Apr.–Sept., D. 7–6.30; Oct.–Mar., D. 7–6.

S. Pietro in Montorio: D. 8.30–12; Mon.–Fri. 3–4.

S. Pietro in Vincoli: D. 8–12.30; 3–6.

S. Prassede: D. 7–12; 4–6.30.

S. Pudenziana: D. 9–12; 3–6.

Ss. Quattro Coronati: D. 6.15–12.45; 3.15–8; Cloister: D. 10–11.45;
    4–5.45; Oratory of St Sylvester: D. 10–11.45; 4–5.45.

S. Rocco all'Augusteo: D. 7.30–9; 4.30–8.

S. Sabina all'Aventino: D. 8.15–12.30; 3.30–6.

S. Sebastiano ad Catacumbas: D. 8–1; 2–5.30.

S. Stefano Rotondo: Tues.–Sun. 9.30–12.30; 2–5.

S. Susanna: D. 9–12; 4–7. Archaeological area 9.30–11.30; 4–5.45.

S. Teodoro al Palatino: D. 9–12.30; 3.30–6; Archaeological area 1st/3rd
    Sun. 11.30.

SS. Trinità dei Monti: 10–1; 4–6.30.

Stadium of Domitian: Mon.–Sun. 10–7; Sat. 10–8.

Tomb of Caecilia Metella: Summer, Tues.–Sun. 9–7.15; Winter, Tues.–
    Sun. 9–4.30.

Vatican Museums: Mon.–Sat. 9–6; cl. Holidays and Sun. except for the
    last Sun. of the month when it is open 9–2 and the entrance fee is
    waived.

Vatican Necropolis: 9–5; cl. Sun. and Holidays, by appointment only.

Villa Albani-Torlonia: by appointment only.

Villa Aurora and Casino dell'Aurora: by appointment only.

Villa Farnesina: Mon.–Sat. 9–2; 2nd Sun. of the month 9–5.

Villa Giulia: Tues.–Sun. 8.30–7.30.

Villa of Maxentius: Tues.–Sun. 10–4; cl. Mon.

Villa of the Quintilii: Summer, Tues.–Sun. 9–7.15; Winter, Tues.–Sun.
    9–4.30.

# GLOSSARY

| | |
|---|---|
| ambo (pl. ambones) | pulpit in a basilica |
| apse | semicircular area at the end of a sanctuary or chapel that is usually vaulted |
| arcade | a covered gallery supported by arches |
| *baldacchino* | canopy over an altar |
| *cella* | interior room of a temple |
| *cippus* (pl. cippi) | burial marker |
| colonnade | a row of columns that supports an arcade, entablature, or roof |
| columbarium | funerary monument with niches for cremation urns |
| *confessio* | crypt beneath the high altar where saint relics are kept |
| *cosmatesque* | refers to the inlaid marble work of the Cosmati |
| cryptoporticus | covered corridor, usually subterranean |
| entablature | elements of a temple above the columns: architrave, cornice and frieze |
| forum (pl. fora) | open space in the centre of an ancient town for business and assemblies, often with commemorative monuments |
| *gens* | clan or family group in ancient Rome |
| hypogeum | subterranean burial chamber |
| *loggia* | covered balcony |
| meta | turning post in the circus; a marker of any sort including an obelisk or pyramid |
| peripteral | temple with a single row of columns on all sides |
| pomerium | sacred boundary |

| portico | the porch, atrium or narthex (if a church), entrance of a building usually defined by a colonnade |
| quadriporticus | a squared courtyard lined with colonnaded porticoes |
| sinopia (pl. sinopie) | fresco sketch on a wall in a red pigment |
| spina | narrow centre island in a circus |
| spoliation | reuse of architectural or sculptural materials from a monument |
| titulus | inscription that defines a property or burial location, also used to describe board placed on Christ's cross with INRI inscribed on it |
| tribune | raised platform that normally defines the sanctuary of a church or gallery |
| tufa | travertine (a type of limestone) quarried near Tivoli |

# INDEX